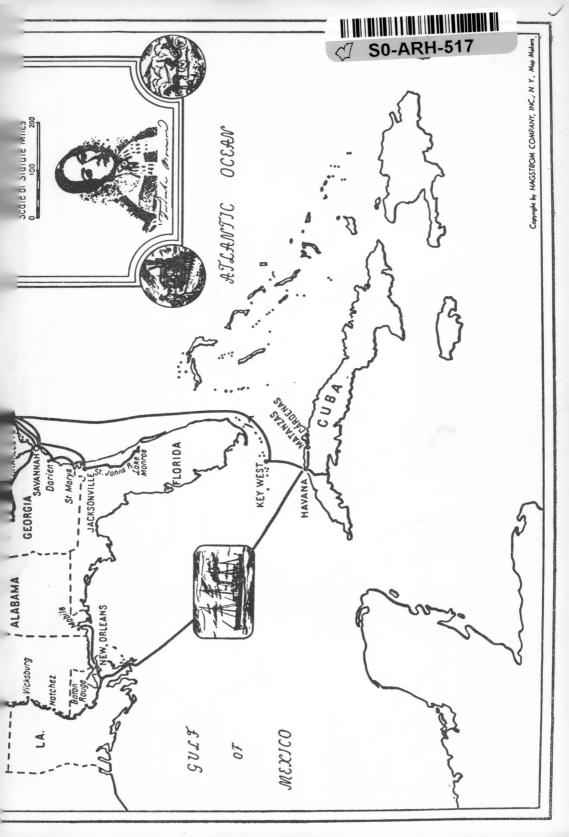

ATLANTIC OCEAN

GEORGIA

ALABAMA

LA.

Vicksburg
Natchez
Baton Rouge
Mobile
NEW ORLEANS

SAVANNAH
Darien
St. Marys
JACKSONVILLE
St. Johns
Lake Monroe
FLORIDA

KEY WEST

HAVANA
MATANZAS
CARDENAS

CUBA

GULF OF MEXICO

Copyright by HAGSTROM COMPANY, INC., N.Y., Map Makers

Scale of Statute Miles
0   100   200

Seeress of the Northland

Fredrika Bremer's American Journey

1849 - 1851

This is the revised version of a dissertation originally submitted to the Faculty of the Division of the Humanities, University of Chicago, in candidacy for the degree of Doctor of Philosophy.

June 12, 1953

The frontispiece has graciously been made available by Frederick Hill Meserve, New York, from his collection of Brady photographs.

ii

Fredrika Bremer

SIGNE ALICE ROOTH

Seeress of the Northland

Fredrika Bremer's American Journey

1849 - 1851

AMERICAN SWEDISH HISTORICAL FOUNDATION

Philadelphia, Pennsylvania

THE CHANCELLOR PRESS
Bridgeport, Pa.

Printed in the United States of America

TO MY DEAR PARENTS

Table of Contents

List of Illustrations

PREFACE *

FREDRIKA BREMER came to the United States in 1849 and remained for two years, during which she traveled about extensively. Her interest in America was strong; it had been awakened long before her visit and continued to the end of her life. This volume proposes to shed some new light on the literary and social contacts the Swedish writer had with Americans. While journeying in twenty-seven states she wrote letters to her sister in Sweden. They later appeared in her book *Hemmen i den nya verlden* (1853-1854), which was translated into English as *Homes of the New World* (1853). Miss Bremer also contributed a number of articles, stories, and poems to *Sartain's Union Magazine,* a Philadelphia literary periodical. Her social impressions of America had a profound effect upon her later writings. For example, the novel *Hertha* (1856), whose theme is women's rights, was largely inspired by her observations on the status of women in the United States.

The American phase of Fredrika Bremer's life and letters has not been sufficiently explored, although many articles have touched upon her visit,[1] and Swedish biographies include chapters describing her sojourn.[2] Dr. Adolph B. Benson edited selections from *Homes of the New World* with the title *America of the Fifties* (1924). Two Swedish authors, Dr. Hanna Rydh and Gunhild Tegen, in 1939 and 1941 wrote articles in the magazine *Hertha* about their respective experiences while retracing part of Fredrika Bremer's American itinerary. Another Swedish author, Tora Nordström-Bonnier, later visited many of the same places as Miss Bremer, and she wrote *Resa kring en resa* (*Journey About a Journey;* 1950).

During a visit to Sweden in 1949 I became greatly interested in the career of Fredrika Bremer, and I learned that material existed in America concerning her and the prominent people she had known here. After some preliminary research at Stockholm, Uppsala, and Lund I continued the investigation in the United

---

The notes to the Preface are to be found on page 299.

xiii

States, and this proved even more rewarding. For instance, I located unpublished, candid letters from Miss Bremer to American friends,[3] which are especially important because they complement *Homes of the New World*. Various libraries and historical societies — in Boston, Chicago, New York, Philadelphia, St. Paul, San Marino, and elsewhere — yielded material; in the Library of Congress in Washington I read through numerous old newspapers from cities I had not visited. The most important and pertinent letters of the more than one hundred I found are printed in this volume, including the collection at the Henry E. Huntington Library in California; only two of its thirty-six Bremer letters have previously been published. The letters were written by Miss Bremer during the years 1849-1865 to her close friends Marcus and Rebecca Spring. The original spelling, punctuation, and grammar are retained; occasionally a bracketed insertion is added to clarify the meaning. An introduction accompanies seventy-five transcriptions in the Appendix. Translated quotations in the text from Miss Bremer's works or correspondence are marked (Tr.).

I wish to express my appreciation to a number of people. Dr. Gunnar Axberger of Stockholm University first suggested the subject to me in January, 1949. The members of my dissertation committee at the University of Chicago — Dr. Gösta Franzen, chairman; Dr. Helena M. Gamer; and Mr. Rolf Nettum — gave me valuable guidance. Dr. Adolph B. Benson, Dr. Amandus Johnson, and Dr. Karl A. Olsson offered constructive suggestions. I am grateful to the American Daughters of Sweden in Chicago for their 1950 fellowship award, enabling me to begin graduate work at the University of Chicago. I have received full cooperation from *Fredrika-Bremer-Förbundet,* Stockholm, and the American Swedish Historical Museum, Philadelphia. The libraries and historical societies I consulted have kindly granted permission to publish their documents. Mr. Andrew Hagstrom of New York City produced the excellent map of Miss Bremer's travels. I also wish to thank Dr. Nils G. Sahlin, director of the American Swedish Historical Foundation, for his expert help in preparing the volume for publication.

S. A. R.

Washington, D. C., July, 1955.

Seeress of the Northland

Fredrika Bremer's American Journey
1849 - 1851

CHAPTER I

The New World*

Background to Fredrika Bremer's Journey

AMERICA WAS in the middle of the nineteenth century a young, dynamic, and fast-growing country. In a favorable environment of human liberty and successful democracy, ambition stirred the hearts of men; an awakened hope for a better life furnished an incentive for great achievements. Improved transportation provided by canals, steamboats, and railroads furthered the nation's development, and communications made rapid strides after the first telegraphic message was sent in 1844. The era was productive of new inventions, such as the McCormick reaper, which modernized agriculture, and Howe's sewing machine, which was soon to play an important part in the American industrial revolution; the perfection of earlier inventions, such as Whitney's cotton gin, also influenced progress.

The frontier was pushed steadily westward, and vast sections of virgin territory were opened up as the wilderness yielded to man. The discovery of gold in California gave added impetus to America's expansion and settlement. Zachary Taylor, victorious general of the Mexican War, was president at the time. Thirty states comprised the Union by 1849, and the following year the population numbered over 23,000,000. In the East, especially in New England, New York, and Pennsylvania, a world of industry and finance was rising. The North Atlantic states began to produce more than they consumed, though the South provided the nation's principal export — cotton.

This bright land of promise attracted to its beckoning shores Fredrika Bremer, the eminent Swedish novelist. Her reasons for wanting to come were different from those of the thousands of

---

*The notes to Chapter I begin on page 299.

European immigrants who sought the greater freedom and opportunity offered by the United States. In October, 1846, three years before her arrival in America, Miss Bremer affirmed:

... It has long been a wish of my heart to visit America and to see with my own eyes that new, rising world. Indeed there is no foreign land in the world that I wish to know out[side] of North America and that especially for the peculiar turn of Mind of its people and its management of life in public as in private life, in the state, the home, in society and in Nature. In many of these sferes Methoug[h]t I see the Idea — the sun of intellectual life — clearing up, making its way to earthly reality, and transforming chaos into harmony and beauty.[1]

She was one of many Europeans aware of the vibrant currents emanating from the New World, and she felt the challenge of its pioneering spirit. Fredrika Bremer was interested in social welfare, education, the women's movement, and experiments in communal living, such as the cooperative-socialistic settlements. As early as August 30, 1843, she stated in a letter: "It is remarkable to see, especially in America, how through rapid and general distribution everything is for everybody, how each thought can immediately become the property of all, just as it with reason is considered to be everyone's right."[2] (Tr.)

Reports had reached Sweden of the growing success of the American form of government. Miss Bremer was familiar with Alexis de Tocqueville's important work *De la Démocratie en Amérique* (1835) and she had read the earlier account by de Tocqueville and Beaumont on the penitentiary system in the United States. The book on American democracy aroused her keen interest and she made copious notes in French. Miss Bremer later wrote to a good friend that *De la Démocratie en Amérique* was an epoch-making book in her life.[3] Besides reading de Tocqueville's works and Harriet Martineau's *Society in America* (1837), she no doubt also knew of the criticisms Mrs. Frances Trollope and Charles Dickens had leveled against America in the 1830's and 1840's. She later referred to some of their unfavorable remarks in her book *Homes of the New World*.

Miss Bremer's works had become known to Americans in translations by Mary Howitt, an English author who had introduced the novels to the British public. In 1840, when the Howitts were visiting Heidelberg, Mrs. Howitt happened to read one of the Bremer novels

in German. Fascinated by *Die Nachbarn,* she thought the English
people would also enjoy it. She translated and in 1842 published
The Neighbors at her own expense. Longfellow read this edition and
correctly surmised that Mary Howitt had worked from the German
version rather than the Swedish original. In a letter to the poet
Ferdinand Freiligrath in 1843 Longfellow wrote:

... Mrs. Howitt's translation from the Swedish (or did she translate
from a German version? I suspect she did; for she uses such expressions as "Fetch me the devil," which is very different from "Devil
take me!") — this translation, *The Neighbors,* has been republished
here, and is very much liked. It is printed as an extra number of
The New World, a newspaper, and sold for four groschen! In this
form it will be scattered far and wide over the whole country. A
handsomer and dearer edition is also in press.[4]

Mrs. Howitt later learned Swedish in order to translate most of
Fredrika Bremer's works, sometimes assisted by her author-husband.
She felt it would profit England to learn about Sweden through the
Bremer novels, so she helped to publicize them. In the Preface to
A Diary (1844) Mrs. Howitt stated:

... No one could have opened up more successfully the intellectual
intercourse [between England and Sweden] than Miss Bremer; and
I regard it as one of the happiest and most honourable events of my
life ... that I have introduced her beautiful and ennobling writings,
not only to these islands, but to the whole vast English family. I
have sent them expressly to Australia; and in America, in India, at
the Cape, as well as in Australasia, *Miss Bremer* is now a household
word — nay, more — a household possession and blessing.[5]

By 1845 Fredrika Bremer was definitely contemplating a visit
to America; in fact, the Cleveland *Herald* of December 31, 1845,
announced somewhat prematurely: "Miss Bremer, the celebrated
Swedish authoress, will not visit America till next summer, when
she may be confidently expected."[6] Earlier that year she had made
a notation that she wanted to see what effect the American democratic institutions had upon the individual and his life.[7] To a
close friend she wrote that she intended to choose Boston as her
place of observation and that she would live there a while. She
continued: "There is the soil of the Pilgrims, there the agitated, restless American life has settled itself, according to what I have been
told, and produces noble fruits in politics and literature."[8] (Tr.)

Miss Bremer received "fan mail" from Americans who had read
her novels and was highly pleased to learn of their genuine interest

in Swedish literature. She felt that she was performing a useful service for her beloved Sweden through her books. A poet of the time, Anne Lynch, sent a poem she had dedicated to her. (See p. 37.) As a result of the ensuing correspondence, the "muse of America" — as Fredrika Bremer called her — extended an invitation to visit her in New York. A letter of 1846 shows the mounting interest in the United States:

. . . It will greatly interest me to see a truthful and unbiased picture of private life in that part of America where you reside, its influence on the morals and happiness of individual man and particularly of woman. It will be to me a precious introduction to the chapter I myself wish to study, if I once can come to your shores.[9]

Another literary woman, Lydia Maria Child, was also in touch with Miss Bremer about this time. In fact, Mrs. Child sent her a copy of *Letters from New York* (1843) with the following inscription: "To Fredrika Bremer. With the author's best respects, and warm thanks, from a far land, for minds strengthened, and hearts refreshed, by her pen."[10] Later Mrs. Child sent her the second series of *Letters from New York* (1846). Through reading these and other books about America Miss Bremer felt closer to that "far land" across the ocean; she wanted to meet in person both Anne Lynch and Lydia Maria Child, and America began to play a larger role in her thoughts. One of the objectives of her journey is expressed in this message to a Mr. S. Arnold: "Give my kind regards to your Mother and tell her how much I long to see the homes of America and the women which in the New World have inspired the men with a spirit of noble chivalry which the Old World must admire."[11]

Miss Bremer also exchanged letters with the New York horticulturist and author Andrew Jackson Downing, who in the summer of 1846 sent her a copy of one of his works. With it he enclosed a friendly letter, urging her to visit the United States and inviting her to his home. Two years later a letter from her to Downing[12] dealt with plans he had already suggested; she promised to follow with entire confidence his advice on her American pilgrimage. Instead of a picture of herself, which Downing and his wife had requested, she mailed a copy of her recently published book, *The Midnight Sun*.

By the end of 1848 Miss Bremer's literary works included eight novels, three volumes of *Sketches of Every-day Life*, one religious essay, a short play, and a number of poems. Her fame had reached a peak and she moved in the best literary circles. When, for example, she spent about eight months in Denmark (1848-1849), she associated with such authors as Hans Christian Andersen, B. S. Ingemann, and Adam Oehlenschläger. She also became friendly with Dowager Queen Caroline Amalie in Copenhagen and promised to write to her if she journeyed to America. The Swedish novelist met the intellectuals N. F. S. Grundtvig, H. L. Martensen, and H. C. Örsted, but the physicist Örsted was the only one who understood her ambition to visit America. He thought that country would be of the highest interest to observe at first hand.

When Miss Bremer's novel *Syskonlif* (1848) proved successful and its English translation, *Brothers and Sisters*, sold well, she received good royalties; she herself had the means to visit the distant land which so greatly attracted her. In September, 1849, the way cleared for her to realize the cherished ambition and she overruled family objections. Her mother and sisters were worried about her traveling alone, even though Miss Bremer was then forty-eight years old. Not even the tears of Agathe could alter her determination to go, but as partial consolation she promised to write most of her letters from America to her younger sister. This was an important promise, for it led eventually to the publication of *Homes of the New World*. Charlotte Bremer Quiding subsequently confessed:

. . . I do not deny that it appeared to me really awful, that Fredrika, this delicate little creature, should start quite alone on such a voyage, and I did not understand how she could have the courage to do it; but she never wanted courage; and I remembered her wish, when she was a child, to enter the army and join the Swedish troops in Germany.[13]

So it was with great emotion that Fredrika Bremer said goodbye to her family; she traveled from Marstrand on the west coast of Sweden to Copenhagen and left Denmark on September 11, 1849, for England. The author was imbued with the Viking spirit of adventure:

My soul longs to tussle with big things and thoughts. Only they deliver one from the small. And I hate the small. Now I want to travel and see the human being of the New World; but I do not go merely to see him but also in order that the new human being in me, in thoughts, in will, may develop its wings more freely, come to a consciousness which it cannot win under the old conditions at home.[14] (Tr.)

Arriving in London, Miss Bremer found that a cholera epidemic was raging and that many of the inhabitants had fled the stricken city. Her stay in the British capital was short, for her ship was sailing soon, but she planned to remain longer on her return. She was a guest in the home of her translator, Mrs. Howitt, who wrote that she had won their affection by her "warm-heartedness and freedom from ostentation."[15]

In some degree the visit to England served to introduce Fredrika Bremer to the English-speaking peoples. Said she: "I did not wish to be too much overcome by New York, therefore I would know something of the mother before I made acquaintance with the daughter, in order to have a point and rule of comparison, that I might correctly understand the type."[16] After the train ride to Liverpool she boarded the *Canada* on September 22, 1849; it was the beginning of a journey that proved to be a crested wave in her experience.

Cunard Steam-Ship Co. Ltd.

S.S. CANADA

Résumé of Miss Bremer's Life and Career, 1801-1849

When Fredrika Bremer sailed for America, she had behind her a long and successful career. She was born August 17, 1801, in Finland, then part of Sweden. Her parents, Carl Fredric and Birgitta Bremer, moved from Åbo (Turku) to Stockholm in 1804. There were four children in the family, Fredrika being the second oldest, and three more were born in Sweden. She spent most of her childhood at their Årsta estate, some eighteen miles southeast of Stockholm. Despite the comfortable surroundings and economic advantages provided by her father, a wealthy ironmaster, she was not happy. Years later she confided to an American friend about her childhood: "I lived in material affluence but my heart and mind starved."[17] Fredrika was not her father's favorite child; toward the sensitive and at the time somewhat introvert girl, he lacked warmth and understanding. It has been said that she both loved and hated her father. His domineering temperament caused a strained atmosphere in the home and in later years he often had morose moods.

Birgitta Bremer, a beautiful and socially accomplished woman, worried about daughter Fredrika's awkwardness and rather large nose. The girl had fine eyes, however, and a quick, alert mind. Her mother placed emphasis on learning languages — French, English, and German, besides Swedish — and sometimes the children had foreign tutors. Mrs. Bremer believed that her daughters should learn as much as possible, but be kept in ignorance of evil. She also thought they should eat a minimum of food in order to remain slender. Their private lessons included art and music; Fredrika became skilled in both. As a young girl she showed a lively imagination; she wrote poems and playlets for reading and presentation at family birthdays. During adolescent years the talented Fredrika read widely, including French and English novels, poetry, and history.

In the summer of 1821 the father, mother, and six children traveled to the Continent in two coaches of their own. The inconveniences of the journey from Sweden through Germany to Lake Geneva upset the father, who became irritable whenever his prearranged plan had to be changed. After the visit in Switzerland they rode on to Paris to spend the winter. The cultural environment of the French capital was stimulating for all the Bremers and they made the most of their stay. Fredrika took music and drawing lessons; she went often to the art galleries and the theater. She and her family saw François Joseph Talma, the tragedian, and Mademoiselle Mars, the popular actress, both of whom Fredrika admired. The extended sojourn — nearly a year — was marked by delightful episodes, but on the whole her memories were not lastingly happy.

Upon returning to Årsta the family resumed its strict routine. However, Fredrika had greater opportunities to pursue her studies because she had more time to herself. By aiding poor and suffering people in the community she found an outlet for her strong desire to be useful; she painted and sold miniature portraits to earn money for her charitable work. At last she felt she was leading a purposeful life — helping others less fortunate than herself had good psychological effects. She thought of becoming a nurse but was dissuaded by her family. For two winters Fredrika took care of her sister Agathe, who had a back ailment. They stayed at Årsta while the rest of the family was in Stockholm, and this period of freedom from parental supervision was a blessing. The aspiring novelist found time to write and in 1828 published anonymously her first book, *Teckningar utur hvardagslifvet* (*Sketches of Every-day Life*). It was well received by the public; the stories were admired for their sprightly dialogue and vividness of detail. The author was encouraged to write a second volume of *Sketches,* which included part of a novelette, *Famillen H.* (*The H— Family*). The first mention of America in one of her works is to be found here — the unhappy heroine, Elisabeth, dreams of America as the land of deliverance and freedom. This volume received good press reviews, and the young writer, now twenty-nine, disclosed her authorship to her mother. The father, who died in 1830, never learned of his daughter's literary success. Fredrika revealed her secret to a prominent author and good friend of the family, Bishop Frans Michael Franzén. He praised the books and became an influential ally in gaining recognition for her; he informed the Swedish Academy, of which he was a member, that Fredrika Bremer had written the *Sketches*. The third volume appeared in 1831, and that year the Academy awarded her its smaller gold medal as a token of respect and approval.

Fredrika excelled in the realistic portrayal of Swedish family life, which she knew well. The lively descriptions of upper middle class life, customs, and festivities were an innovation in the literature of Sweden. This style has been termed "poetic realism," with under-currents of social ideas or *Tendenz*. The first three decades of the nineteenth century had been characterized by romanticism, among whose leading Swedish exponents were Per Atterbom and Esaias Tegnér, both of whom Fredrika knew. When the romantic movement began to wane, a transition to realism set in; during this time literary works bore some realistic details presaging the new style, in addition to the romantic characteristics. Fredrika's novels belong in this dual category. She was one of the early modern Swedish novelists; at first she wrote only to entertain her readers, but gradually, as she developed, a more serious note entered her works.

In 1831 Fredrika met Frances Lewin, a young Englishwoman then visiting Stockholm. Miss Lewin was a devotee of Jeremy Bentham's utilitarian philosophy and for a while she influenced Fredrika in the same direction. The doctrine "what is useful is good" appealed to the Swedish author; she believed that she herself could be useful to others through the medium of her writing. She subscribed to Bentham's idea of "the greatest happiness of the greatest number"; as a democratic ideal it sounded almost perfect. However, the utilitarian tenet that the ethical value of conduct is determined by the usefulness of its results proved a serious obstacle to her acceptance of this doctrine as a whole, for it conflicted with her deeply religious nature. The utilitarian system was not, after all, the answer she was seeking; she rejected it, stating that its morality was not based upon eternal justice.

In September of 1831 Fredrika left Stockholm to visit her married sister, Charlotte Quiding, in Kristianstad, a city in southern Sweden. Her brother-in-law, Assessor Per Quiding, invited to his home Per Johan Böklin (1796-1867), a learned teacher and later clergyman. He had studied at the University of Lund and was especially interested in philosophy. This meeting between Böklin and Fredrika coincided with a period of intense truth-seeking on her part, for she was speculating on such eternal questions as the nature of good and evil, immortality, free will and determinism. Böklin set about guiding Fredrika's studies, answering her questions in his own way, strengthening her belief in God, and helping her to acquire mental serenity. She was an eager pupil and under his tutelage she read Plato for eight months, followed by the works of other philosophers. At last she had found a kindred spirit to whom she could confide her innermost thoughts and even doubts, someone who understood her thirst for knowledge and truth. Fredrika was happy as she explored the world of ideas with Böklin; she felt stimulated and enlightened as they discussed religion, ethics, politics, and philosophy.

After her return to Stockholm Fredrika corresponded in the same vein with her friend. For example, she asked him whether there can be a merciful God when so much suffering exists in the world. She also wanted him to discuss pre-existence of the soul, and to tell her "what death is." She felt Böklin was qualified to answer her metaphysical inquiries, and it has been said that she received from him the equivalent of a university course in philosophy. Fredrika was also grateful for the helpful advice he gave her about her books. The friendship deepened gradually and even before she returned to Kristianstad in 1832 a warmer, more personal tone entered their correspondence. A letter to Böklin dated October 11 of that year, however, reveals her ambition:

... I know all too well how little a truly capable and good housewife and a meditating and pondering author can be combined. One of them must give in, and the latter has already taken too firm a footing in me to be accommodating.

In another way than the usual one I want to try to fulfill my womanly calling: that of being an alleviating and animating power in life. I want to go in my Saviour's footsteps and seek the sick and the distressed with words of consolation.[18] (Tr.)

An offer of marriage from Böklin precipitated an emotional crisis and she found it extremely difficult to make up her mind. The question of why Fredrika, who was then over thirty, chose not to marry is a complex one. Professor Gunnar Axberger's valuable study, *Jaget och skuggorna* (*The Ego and the Shadows*), brings to light certain psychological aspects of her emotional background to explain why she did not accept Böklin's proposal.[19] She had some fear of marriage, apparently, but she was no doubt also influenced by her sense of mission — a feeling that she had a larger purpose to fulfill.

For almost three years she vacillated and Böklin's hopes were raised time and again by her numerous letters. Finally, in 1835, he felt that her trip to Norway was a definite rejection of his proposal. That same year in the autumn he married a young governess named Carolina Nilsson, with whom he settled in a Kristianstad parish. It was several months before Fredrika learned of her friend's marriage, but then she sought to ease the strained feelings. The Böklins named their first girl after Fredrika and she was the child's godmother. The Böklin-Bremer correspondence went on for the rest of her life. However, she did not have an opportunity to visit the Böklins until 1848, when she stayed with them for about two months.

Fredrika had begun to write *Presidentens döttrar* (*The President's Daughters*) in 1834, at Årsta. This novel shows traces of Böklin's influence; for instance, the heroine Edla longs to improve her mind, so she studies Plato instead of learning to keep house. At that time Swedish women, like those in other European countries, did not have the same educational opportunities as men. Furthermore, if a woman did not marry, she remained subject to the authority of her father or a male guardian for the rest of her life. Fredrika had already become concerned about equality and social justice for women, an interest which played a significant role in her writing.

On Countess Stina Sommerhielm's country estate, near the Oslo fjord, Fredrika found the solitude she needed to resume writing. The sequel to *The President's Daughters,* entitled *Nina* (1835), had been criticized for its sentimentality, lengthy reflective passages, and lack of a convincing plot. The persevering author resolved to avoid these flaws in her next story. During two years in Norway she wrote *Grannarne* (*The Neighbors;* 1837), which proved to be her most successful novel. It tells of three neighbor families who live in the province of Småland; outstanding among the characters is "Ma chère mère," an autocratic but colorful personality. This epistolary novel delighted both foreign and Swedish readers.

Fredrika returned to Stockholm in the summer of 1837 to be with her sister Hedda, who was very ill. Hedda died late in September, and Fredrika remained with the other members of her family. She had few social contacts then but enjoyed her meetings with Erik Gustaf Geijer, for she was a warm admirer of this eminent historian and poet. In Stockholm Fredrika also met the Swedish author C. J. L. Almquist, who later spent fifteen years in America, arriving in New York two months before she left the country.

Included in Fredrika's reading that year was the controversial *Age of Reason* by Thomas Paine. She differed vehemently with his religious views and copied passages in her notebook,[20] adding comments in Swedish which affirmed her belief in the Bible. Occasionally she referred to the deist Paine in her correspondence; some years later she expressed the opinion to Lars Johan Hierta, the publisher, that men like Thomas Paine and David F. Strauss must exist in the world. They serve God in their way, she said, because they force those who do believe to assert and defend their faith more strongly.[21] She was a devout churchgoer and a Christian in thought and deed. It has been said that her panacea was love.

Fredrika left Stockholm in the autumn of 1838 and returned to Norway, where the estate of Countess Sommerhielm again offered a quiet retreat. There she wrote her fifth novel, *Hemmet* (*The Home;* 1839), which glorifies the joys of family life. One of the main characters, Petrea, is in many respects a counterpart of the author, and the somewhat autobiographical story is realistic with deftly humorous touches. Before leaving Norway in 1840 Fredrika nearly finished *Strid och frid* (*Strife and Peace*), a book in which the Swedish heroine and the Norwegian hero marry and, despite friendly bickering, find happiness together. Another work, *En dagbok* (*A Diary*), appeared in 1843.

Fredrika Bremer developed her own theory of the novel, which she elucidated in an essay, "The Novel and the Novels."[22] She had been an avid reader of fiction in her youth, particularly of stories intended solely for entertainment. When she became an author, however, she stated: "Novels certainly must have a sensible, good aim; must have the right of citizenship in the world."[23] According to her, it is not enough to amuse, to awaken sympathy, or to excite the imagination; man's inner development and the vicissitudes of human life should also be portrayed. The ideal novel should teach a lesson and have a beneficial influence upon youthful minds. Her reputation as a leading novelist in Sweden was firmly established by this time. Her works were also known through translations in America, Denmark, England, France, Germany, Holland, and other countries. In 1844 the Swedish Academy awarded her its large gold medal, which carries the inscription: *Snille och Smak* (*Genius and Taste*). When presenting the medal, Geijer paid tribute to her patriotic service in furthering the fame of Swedish literature abroad.

Mary Howitt had called her "the Jane Austen of Sweden"; much later G. Barnett Smith drew a comparison between the two women:

Fredrika Bremer has been compared with Jane Austen; but the Swedish writer was the intellectual superior of the English. Though not so great as a novelist, her culture was wider, and her thought deeper; she had also a more vigorous imagination, and a greater command both of the springs of humour and of pathos. She had the delicacy of perception and love of quiet home life which distinguished Jane Austen; but she could not rival the style of the English novelist; a style that is inimitable, but one likewise as difficult to define as it is easy to appreciate; nor could she lay claim to Jane Austen's marvellous insight into character, with its thousand little shades and divergences. But Fredrika Bremer was an authoress of whom any country or people might be proud.[24]

Fredrika was fond of traveling as well as writing. Her journeys in Sweden, to Dalecarlia and Norrland, inspired her to write *I Dalarne* (*Life in Dalecarlia;* 1845) and *Midsommarresan* (*The Midnight Sun;* 1848). She also visited the Rhineland in 1846 and wrote a series of articles, published two years later as *Ett par blad från Rhenstranden* ("Leaves from the Banks of the Rhine"). In 1848 she finished *Syskonlif* (*Brothers and Sisters*), which portrayed family life in relation to the outer world. It is interesting to note that two of the characters, Gerda Dahlberg and her brother Ivar, make a trip to America and later help to found a communal society in Sweden, said to be patterned somewhat on Lowell, Massachusetts.

Fredrika Bremer's Renown in America Prior to Her Visit

Miss Bremer's books were published in the United States during her lifetime by such firms as Harper & Brothers and G. P. Putnam & Company in New York, T. B. Peterson Brothers and J. M. Campbell in Philadelphia, Redding & Company and J. Munroe & Company in Boston. De luxe editions of her works were printed and also many paper-bound "extras" of the *New World*, which sold for twenty-five cents or less. These cheaper copies ensured a large sale and may be compared with the pocket editions of today, although their format was larger. No international copyright laws existed then and most American publishers simply pirated the Howitt translations.

The Bremer novels were popular indeed, as a Swedish gentleman learned while traveling in America in the mid-forties. While on a train he was startled by newsboys who came through calling out: "Miss Bremer's latest!"[25] *The Neighbors,* along with Balzac's *Père Goriot* and William Cullen Bryant's *Poetical Works,* became a "better seller" in 1843.[26] Her books also had to compete for public favor with William H. Prescott's *Conquest of Mexico* (1843) and, in 1844, with Charles Dickens's *Martin Chuzzlewit* and *A Christmas Carol*, which sold more than 175,000 copies each and were considered "best sellers." Mrs. Howitt said of Fredrika Bremer's works: "Cheap editions ran like wildfire through the United States, and the boys who hawked them in the streets might be seen deep in *The Neighbours, The Home,* and *The H— Family*."[27] A number of factors contributed to the popularity of these novels: their entertainment value, the universal appeal of their characters and situations, their suitability for the entire family, and the fact that foreign authors were in vogue. Each new Bremer novel was pleasurably anticipated and was reviewed by the press when it appeared. It may be mentioned that Miss Bremer's style probably influenced contemporary American women writers; they, more than the men writers, would be inclined to imitate portrayals of domesticity and everyday life.

In 1843 several critiques of her novels appeared; for example, *The Pioneer* of Boston, edited by James Russell Lowell and Robert Carter, in March reviewed *The Neighbors*. The page-long notice, probably written by Lowell, was most complimentary in tone. It called attention to the spirit of charity which permeates the book and to Fredrika Bremer's power of condensation — nothing "wearisome" is to be found in the work. The reviewer said it was difficult to avoid identifying the author with the heroine, Franziska, also of quick perception and ardent temperament. He added:

The chief characteristic of the book seems to us to be its acute sensibility. Sensibility to all forms of beauty, to all nobleness, to music, to flowers, to all that lends life its charm, and this combined with great ardor, enthusiasm and with a poetical organization, make it one of the rarest novels of the day.[28]

Publication of *The Pioneer* was discontinued after the March issue; despite contributions by Hawthorne, Lowell, and Poe it had not been a financial success. In April *The Dial*, edited by Ralph Waldo Emerson, also reported on *The Neighbors*:

No work of fiction that has appeared of late has met with so kindly a reception, on all hands, as this. In part this may be ascribed to our pleasure at getting a peep into the domestic life of a country hitherto little known to us, except in the broader, colder outline of history, but far more to the intrinsic merit of the work, its lively nature, wisdom, and gentle affectionate morality. The representation of character, if not deeply "motived" is faithful, and, though best in the range of such persons as Bear and his charming little wife, yet the bolder attempts in the sketches of Ma chère mère, Bruno, and

Serena do not fail, if they do not entirely succeed. These persons are painted, not indeed as by one of their own rank, but as they may be seen from Fanny's point of view. The playfulness of the book seldom rises to wit, but is very light and pretty; the dew is on the grass, the insect on the wing, round the happy country home. The common sense is truly "the wisdom of nations," not the cold prudence of skepticism, but the net result of observations taken by healthy hearts and heads, educated in that golden mean which most harmoniously, if not most rapidly, unfolds the affections, the intellect, and the energies for active life.[29]

The Dial was the organ of the transcendentalists, and Margaret Fuller had been its first editor. In a letter from New York dated February 12, 1843, Emerson asked her for notices of new books, among them The Neighbors.[30] Whether Miss Fuller or Emerson wrote the preceding review has not been established.[31] Three months later The Dial mentioned the Bremer novels again.[32]

A notice in the April North American Review described some of the main characters in The Neighbors, but the writer deemed it unnecessary to review the plot because of the book's wide circulation. Its truth, simplicity, and naturalness were commended. In July the same periodical devoted twenty-one pages to "Miss Bremer's Novels."[33] The author of the article had an excellent opinion of Fredrika Bremer's works; he praised their emphasis on the power of love and their ability to teach a lesson with tenderness and delicacy. The reviewer also discussed in detail the heroes and heroines of three of the novels and stressed the prevailing enthusiasm for the books, concluding:

We take our leave of these books with the highest respect for the writer. The fireside is her field of fame; no one has ever equalled her descriptions of its blessings, and her skill in tracing out the sources from which they flow. Home is a word soon spoken; but there is no end to the variety of incident and condition which it embraces, of moral instruction which it may teach, or of mournful and affecting tragedy which can be seen in it by a prophet's eye. Since that high gift is bestowed on this author, may she use it with a sense of her responsibility, so that now, since her talent has made her equal to the highest, her conscientiousness and power of moral impression may set her above all other writers of the day.[34]

The Boston Christian Examiner also published in July a long article by Mrs. L. J. Hall on "Novels of Fredrika Bremer." It mentioned that some readers were at first annoyed by the "foreign peculiarities" and by what appeared to them as "oddities of style" in the translations. Mrs. Hall further remarked that *The H— Family,* in which one incident deals with the love of a blind girl for her married guardian, had been received with "an universal murmur of disapprobation."[35] Despite the critical attitude shown by the *Christian Examiner* on moral grounds toward the triangle depicted in this story, the reviewer lavished praise on the author:

The most striking attributes of Miss Bremer's character, as a writer, are those grand ones, genius, and moral excellence. We see her genius as she brings scenes and human beings vividly before us, and throws herself into different characters with that instinctive adaptation of act and speech which is the power of genius alone.[36]

The American edition of *Morning Watches,* a short religious work by Fredrika Bremer, was published 1843 in Boston. It is the confession of faith she felt impelled to write after reading the skeptical work, *Das Leben Jesu (The Life of Jesus;* 1835-36), by David F. Strauss. She disagreed with him as strongly as with Paine, disputing Strauss' statements that the Gospels are myths and that miracles do not occur now. She warmly defended Christianity and the Bible, though admitting that she herself had gone through a period of doubt. *Morning Watches* was discussed in S. Osgood's study on "Fredrika Bremer's Theology" in the *Christian Examiner* (January, 1844). Osgood said Miss Bremer was decidedly Unitarian in her way of explaining the Divinity of the Saviour but, regarding the doctrine of the Atonement, the Swedenborgians would say it agreed with theirs. He thanked her for "a precious statement of religious experience rather than for oracles of theological wisdom."[37]

The *North American Review* published in April an unsigned article entitled "New Translations of the Writings of Miss Bremer"; it was probably written by James Russell Lowell.[38] The reviewer pointed out that the Swedish edition of some of the Bremer novels had been in the Harvard College Library five years when Mrs. How-itt's first translation appeared, and that her claim to have "discovered" Miss Bremer was, therefore, ridiculous. (Longfellow had bought the books during his visit to Scandinavia in 1835.) The article also considered in detail *The Bondmaid, A Diary,* and *Strife and Peace;* her fireside style, her universal characters — as much at home in Boston as in Stockholm — and her delineations of children were discussed. Interspersed with the praise were some adverse comments, such as that Miss Bremer often became confused in her metaphors, and that occasionally she was overeager to utter profundities.

One of the early newspaper reviews of the Bremer books is dated August 1, 1844. John Greenleaf Whittier, then editor of the *Middlesex Standard* in Lowell, Massachusetts, no doubt wrote the editorial "It Is Never Too Late."[39] The title alluded to the widow in *Strife and Peace*, Astrid Hjelm, who had suffered much but believed it was never too late to have faith in God and in a new future. Whittier began by quoting two paragraphs from the novel, including the sentence: ". . . I am now firmly convinced *that there is no fruitless suffering, and that no virtuous endeavour is in vain.*"[40] He then commented:

There are truth, and power, and beauty in the above extract from the writings of the gifted FREDERIKA BREMER. It is worthy the attention of every one who feels the load of life growing heavy, and who is ready to cry out "my burden is greater than I can bear." The great secret of rising above sorrow, of conquering misfortune, of reconciling disappointments, is to be found in a resolution to do good to others — to make others happy. Once firmly entered upon, this resolution will save us. In the pure and healthful excitement of some great and good object of benevolence and duty, we forget ourselves, and our sufferings; the weary woe which has been settling around our hearts melts away like mist in the sunshine; the troubled and haunting thoughts which have maddened us give place to "the peace which passeth understanding."

Frederika Bremer has experienced all this — and hence her ability to "minister to minds diseased." — She has made herself happy while contributing to the intellectual enjoyment of others — and her writings, especially her admirable *Strife and Peace*, are characterized by democratic sentiment, and a clear appreciation of the equal claims of humanity. She is a decided ABOLITIONIST; and, like her gifted English sister Harriet Martineau, evinces a deep interest in the progress of anti-slavery sentiment in America.[41]

Whittier's linking of Fredrika Bremer with Harriet Martineau was relevant in that these women were kindred spirits. Miss Bremer eagerly read her British contemporary's works and, as early as 1837, had engaged in a discussion with friends about Miss Martineau's advocacy of political rights for women. Though firmly believing in equality, the Swedish author thought that if women participated in government life as men did, their femininity might be destroyed. She wanted women to take part in educational and philanthropic work, however, because she felt they possessed a power which should be freed and used for the good of society.

In 1844 the American *chargé d'affaires* in Sweden, George Washington Lay, together with his wife, visited Fredrika Bremer. They wished to make her acquaintance in order to tell the reading public in the United States about her. Lay recorded the interview in a letter to the New York *Commercial Advertiser,* October 1, and said in part:

. . . Miss Bremer in conversation is exceedingly interesting, but always seems inclined to talk upon questions of political economy, philosophy, morality or religion. She is well read on all these subjects, and in whatever she says there are a purity of thought and earnestness of manner which carry conviction to the heart that she feels deeply every word that falls from her lips.[42]

He went on to describe her study and said that her tables were covered with elegantly bound, recent books in five languages. Many were presentation copies from the authors and they included several works by Americans. In the *Advertiser* was printed a word picture of the novelist by Countess Ida von Hahn-Hahn, besides two long letters Miss Bremer wrote to Lay. In the first she told, in heartfelt and poetic language, of her early years. In the second she said that she was grateful for the "expressions of regard" from her readers in the New World, and she asked him to convey her thanks for the attention and favor shown her works there.

In April, 1845, a commendatory seven-page review appeared in the *Universalist Quarterly* and its author declared: "I would place her [Fredrika Bremer] among the best of those who instruct the public mind, through fictitious delineations of life; because she seeks to win us to the love of right enjoyment, by most amiable manifestations of individual freedom and social truth."[43] A year later the Brooklyn *Eagle* referred to Miss Bremer in its editorial entitled "Something About the Children of Early Spring." At that time Walt Whitman[44] was editor and doubtless wrote it himself;[45] he concluded:

. . . Miss Bremer tells us a beautiful and sublime thought which she learned from flowers. — In the resemblance, as they are widely and incessantly drawing life, beauty, and virtue from the sun, *while yet that luminary lessens not in those qualities which it is constantly bestowing on other things* — so the Almighty, the fountain of good-

ness, truth and all vitality, though throwing off that vitality and
truth forever, yet stays eternally the same, and loses nought.
—Ah, we may learn many a fine moral from the flowers![46]

In the August 17 issue of this paper a quotation from the Bremer
short story called "The Solitary" appeared on page one with the
caption "The Love Dream." "The White Dove" from *The Home* was
subsequently featured. An editorial on "Miss Bremer's Novels" was
printed on August 18 in the *Eagle;* Walt Whitman referred to
Harper's one-volume edition of *The Neighbors, The Home, The
President's Daughters, Nina, Strife and Peace,* and *Life in Dalecarlia.* After a short general discussion of novels pro and con, he
stated that half the imaginative books published in America were
unworthy of praise, either for their style or their intrinsic merit.
Whitman continued:

And yet there are many novels which can be read, and profit
reaped from them. We particularly allude to Miss Bremer's novels,
as translated by Mary Howitt. These charming works, making no
pretension to great intellectual merit, are probably, taking them
altogether, the best books the whole range of romance-writing can
furnish. The stories are unusually full of interest, and the reader
retains his anxiety to know what is coming, till the very last page.
The affected sentimentality of Bulwer, and the verbose weakness of
James, are not the faults of this sweet authoress. If she has, indeed,
any fault, it is, that in one or two of her novels there is a little in-
fusion of transcendentalism; but we can easily pardon it, for it can
do no great harm. The mild virtues — how charity and forbearance
and love are potent in the domestic circle — how each person can
be a kingdom of happiness to himself — how indulgence in stormy
passions leads invariably to sorrow — and depicting in especial the
character of *a good, gentle mother* — these are the points upon which
Miss Bremer labors like some divine painter, who revels in his art,
and whose work is in a double sense, a work of love. Honor and
glory to Peace! and double glory to all who inculcate Peace, whether
among nations, politics, or families!

If we ever have children, the first book after the New Testament,
(with reverence we say it) that shall be made their household companion — a book whose spirit shall be infused in them as sun-warmth
is infused in the earth in spring — shall be Miss Bremer's novels. We
know nothing more likely to melt and refine the human character —
particularly the young character. In the study of the soul-portraits
therein delineated — in their motives, actions, and the results of
those actions — every youth, of either sex, will be irresistibly impelled
to draw some moral, and make some profitable application to his or

her own case.   . . . We recommend every *family* to have a copy of these novels, as a household treasure.[47]

Walt Whitman was twenty-seven in 1846 and it was his first year as editor of the Brooklyn *Daily Eagle*. He introduced the literary miscellany column, in which he reviewed and quoted from a great many books during the two years of his editorship. (He had not yet published *Leaves of Grass*.) The following descriptive column from the *Daily Eagle* of August 29 contains a reprint from a Newark *Daily Advertiser* story three days earlier:

Miss Bremer.

As everything relating to this deservedly famous woman, (whose works at present, have a *"better* circulation," in this country than those of any other writer,) is interesting, we copy the following from the foreign correspondence of the Newark *Daily Adv.* "I must not forget," says the writer, "to tell you of an interview we have had with our favorite authoress Miss Bremer. We were fortunate enough to find her at home; to a message we sent that four Americans would be pleased to call upon her we received a favorable answer. At the hour which she appointed, we went to her house and found her apparently pleased with us. She speaks tolerable English, and in course of a half hour's conversation, she made many inquiries about the United States, and spoke with much familiarity of our writers, especially the women, who have done so much honor to American literature. Her inquiries concerning social life in our country, reminded me of her own pleasing delineations of those scenes in Sweden; and when we spoke to her of the extensive circulation of her works among us, she alluded with much feeling to the kindness of the American people, and expressed the hope that she might soon be permitted to visit us. Miss Bremer is a woman apparently between forty and fifty years of age. Her stature is short, her hair dark, turning gray, her brow expansive, and her eyes blue. While there is nothing in her features which would be called handsome, there is a pleasing sweetness in her look and conversation, an attractive homeliness about all she says and does, which cannot fail to please."[48]

In succeeding years Miss Bremer was to receive still more publicity here; the American periodical which printed the most articles was *Sartain's Union Magazine of Literature and Art* in Philadelphia. The first of these appeared in February, 1849: "Christmas Eve and Christmas Matins," a Bremer tale about Swedish holiday customs, translated by Mary Howitt. An allegorical short story entitled "The She-Eagle" and "Leaves from the Banks of the Rhine," the latter in three installments, also came out that year.

While Fredrika Bremer's writings were appearing in *Sartain's*, she was making preparations for her voyage. Her main purpose in traveling to the United States was to study American homes and family life, the status of women, and the influence of democratic government on the development and happiness of the individual. Fredrika felt that this journey was written in her book of destiny, and the following words express her thoughts:

Yes, I am going to America to see the human being in the new home, in the free state, and from this point to cast a glance at the future and what we can hope from it, all we people who are going in the same direction as the American people have gone and are going. From the strong religious spirit in this New World I anticipate a great deal, as well as from the treatment of women there.[49] (Tr.)

Fredrika Bremer was drawn by a "feeling of *inward necessity*"[50] and, as she also later phrased it, she felt "magnetized by the western world."[51] She was soon to reap a bountiful harvest of hospitality and popular favor, the seeds of which had been sown by her novels. Miss Bremer could not fully anticipate, however, the warmth and spontaneity of the reception that awaited her across the ocean.

CHAPTER II

Travels and Literary Activities*

Fredrika Bremer Arrives in New York

THE THIRTEEN-DAY VOYAGE aboard the Cunard steamship *Canada* was the longest Fredrika had ever embarked upon. The passage cost thirty-five sovereigns (approximately $155.00), first class; she was the only Swede among some sixty passengers and one of the dozen women. In her private cabin the author rested, wrote letters, and read several books. Among them was Longfellow's *Evangeline,* a parting gift from William Howitt in England. She felt that this epic poem belonged to America's history and to its natural scenery. It introduced her to the works of Longfellow, whom she was to meet that December.

During the first week of the voyage the ocean was calm, but then the weather changed and a gale brought rough seas. Although many of the passengers became seasick, Fredrika proved to be a fairly good sailor. The ship was delayed because of the storm, but reached Halifax safely and made a brief stop there. Two days later, on Thursday, October 4, 1849, the *Canada* entered New York harbor. Fredrika described her first sight of it:

The day before had been cloudy, the heavens and the sea had been gray, the waves lead-colored; but when we came into the large, beautiful haven of New York, which inclosed us like an open embrace, the sun broke through the clouds strong and warm, and every thing far around was illuminated. It was a glorious reception by the New World; besides this, there was a something so singularly full of vitality, so exuberantly young, which struck me deeply: there was in it something of that first life of youth, such as is felt at fifteen or sixteen. I drank in the air as one might drink in water, while I stood on deck looking out upon the new shore which we were rapidly approaching.[1]

---

*The notes to Chapter II begin on page 301.

A long-cherished dream was coming true and Fredrika was eager and excited as she stepped down the gangplank onto American soil. A family from Georgia helped her through the customs and dispatched her luggage to the Astor House. Shortly afterwards Andrew J. Downing greeted the author at the hotel. The refined, dark-haired man made an instantly favorable impression upon her; she wrote to her sister that he looked like a poet and had the handsomest brown eyes she had ever seen. Downing, who was fourteen years her junior, became her best male friend in America. (The prominent landscape architect later designed the gardens around the White House, the Capitol, and the Smithsonian Institution in Washington, D. C.)

New York Public Library
BROADWAY IN 1850 WITH BARNUM'S MUSEUM AND ASTOR HOUSE

Impressions of the new city crowded in upon the visitor. Broadway, with all its traffic proceeding "at an uninterrupted rapid rate," bewildered her, and her main thought was to get across the street alive. On her second day Fredrika received callers from morning until night, shaking hands with almost eighty people, among them Lydia Maria Child and Anne Lynch. Several of her countrymen greeted her, including the pioneer Gustaf Unonius. He had just arrived from the Midwest and earnestly begged Miss Bremer to warn the Swedes against emigration. The perils and sufferings he had undergone in Wisconsin made him feel that prospective emigrants should be told of the hardships new settlers faced. She was to travel there the following year and form her own opinions.

Invitations, letters, and requests for autographs poured in. It was no wonder that she exclaimed upon hearing a tap at the door: "O! I wish I was a little dog that I could creep under the table and hide myself."[2] Anne Lynch gave a soiree in honor of Fredrika, who despite her fatigue came to meet the literary friends of her hostess. Early on the third day Downing and his other guest, Miss Lynch, were waiting at the Astor House to escort her to the Hudson steamboat *New World,* which was to take them to Newburgh, the home of the Downings. The colorful autumnal foliage made the banks of the river a beautiful sight and Fredrika responded with the soul of an artist. She even liked the steamboat, which she called "a little floating palace." To quote her further: "I saw here none of Dickens' smoking and spitting gentlemen. We floated proudly and smoothly on the broad, magnificent Hudson."[3]

Newspaper Publicity

The arrival in New York of Sweden's Miss Bremer was, of course, a noteworthy event promptly reported in the press. The New York *Herald* announced it on October 5, 1849, and two days later elaborated somewhat:

The celebrated Swedish authoress, Frederika Bremer, whose *Neighbors, Home,* and numerous other works, which have become so thoroughly naturalized in our language — who has just arrived in this city — was, while in England, the guest of William and Mary Howitt. Of course an intense desire to make the acquaintance of a lady whose writings have diffused so much happiness through so many homes and hearts, manifested itself in the literary and reading world. Miss Bremer's stay in that country was brief, as she was on her way to the United States, which she has, for a long time, had a lively desire to visit. She proposes to remain here for about twelve months.[4]

The Brooklyn *Evening Star* reprinted part of this "Personal Column" in the New York *Semi-Weekly Express* of October 9:

—MISS BREMER, has already become the lioness of the town, from her gentleness and great good sense, and is in all respects

worthy of the attention she is receiving at the hands of our countrymen. — Many of our distinguished ladies and gentlemen called upon
her yesterday, at the Astor House, and also many from abroad. Miss
B. visited GREENWOOD yesterday, and will leave for Newburgh
to-day, as the guest of Mr. Downing, the eminent Horticulturalist,
for a time. She will, we understand pass the winter in Boston.

      —MISS BREMER left the City Saturday, for Newburgh, but
will spend a week in the city with Miss Anne C. Lynch before going
to Boston. Miss B. has spent most of the year past in Denmark, and
will pass the better part of a year we learn in the United States. She
speaks English sufficiently well to make herself agreeable and intelligent to all.[5]

      Both the New York *Observer* and the New York *Weekly Tribune*
of October 13 heralded her arrival and the latter added: "She will
be welcomed by a grateful multitude in this country, who are indebted to her admirable writings for so many hours of the purest
enjoyment."[6] A witty and entertaining article was featured on the
New York *Herald's* front page October 18:

FASHIONABLE INTELLIGENCE

      MISS FREDERIKA BREMER. — There are two Swedish ladies
who have recently electrified the world — Jenny Lind and Frederika
Bremer. The former, known poetically as the Swedish nightingale,
has enchanted Europe as the queen of song; while the latter has shed
a sweet light around almost every fireside of the civilized world. She
is the author of a new style of literature; and probably, at the present
moment, has more readers than any other female writer on the globe.

      By a recent steamer, this celebrated lady arrived on our shores,
and we announced her as a guest of the gentlemanly hosts of the
Astor House, who are always so kind and attentive to the press and
politicians. There was at once a general flutter among the *literati*
and fashionables of the metropolis. The equipages of the codfish
nobility came rushing down from Union Square, and the Avenues,
and "set down" many a bejewelled dowager and elegant heiress at
the steps of the Astor House; scores of servants in livery, crowded
the passages, with cards and bouquets for the illustrious stranger.
Such was the scene being enacted at the private entrance. Meantime,
the public entrance and stair ways, were lined with a large army of
seedy looking gentlemen in black, (the aristocracy of letters) each
with some book, pamphlet, or newspaper under his arm, and all
talking in strains of unbounded enthusiasm of the wonderful genius
of the Swedish lady — each and all palpitating with expectation of
some kind and gracious word from the distinguished guest. Of
course, Miss Bremer would be flattered by their attentions, and delighted beyond measure; and it was equally a matter of course that
she would graciously receive all visitors who came to offer incense

before her shrine. But the codfish nobility and the knights of the pen were all destined to meet with disappointment. Miss Bremer did not receive calls that day! A general murmur of discontent, surprise, and half-concealed irritation mounted to the cheek of more than one fair creature — and one, in particular, a very young lady, with a charming pouting lip, exclaimed pettishly, "La! who cares — she's only an upstart!" The carriages rolled away. After the crowd had dispersed, towards evening, the tall form of one of our ex-Mayors, who became almost as notorious in his day by his triumphant crusade against the apple and pie women, as old Zack afterwards did for his achievements on the field of Buena Vista, was seen (by one of the sweeps at the crossings) quietly but rapidly stealing into the private door of the epicurean temple of Charley Stetson. In a loud voice the apple stand hero requested a waiter to hand a note up to Miss Bremer. It was done. In a few minutes, the waiter re-appeared with a reply, which the gentleman slipped into his breeches pocket, and then withdrew as quietly as he had entered. What was the nature of the correspondence our readers may conjecture. The incident became known to a select few. But we are happy to be able to make an announcement which will be read with delight by thousands. It is rumored that the mammoth house of Harper Brothers, the Napoleons of cheap literature, particularly of the romance school, are preparing to present the celebrated Swedish novelist with a costly and superb memorial, in the form of a massive silver vase, (with $10,000 in California gold dust inside) on one side of which is to be engraved her own portrait, crowned with a wreath of laurel, and surrounded with exquisitely wrought scenes from her works. On the other side, much less conspicuously, (with that modesty which so conspicuously characterizes that great house) will be grouped the portraits of the illustrious brothers, John, Jim, Fletch and Wesley. This act of munificence may surprise some who are unacquainted with the numerous instances of the generosity of the Cliff street publishing house to the authors whose works they print; but although they have hitherto complied with the divine prescription of not letting their good works be known to men, yet, in this case, if the public find it out, there is nobody to blame but the industrious sweep at the crossing. We shall keep the run of this affair, and furnish our million readers with early and authentic information.

We forgot to say, in the proper place, that when the second rush of fashionables came down on the Astor House, Miss Bremer, it was announced, had left town. She has gone up to pass a few weeks at the residence of Mr. Downing, on the Hudson, where she will be free from the officious and troublesome intrusions of the codfish nobility, who fawn around every celebrated foreigner who lands on our shores. We understand that among this codfish class — the same clique which succeeded so well in making themselves and the immortal Boz such inimitable asses — a plan had been cut and dried, before Miss Bremer's arrival, of enacting over the scenes of the winter of 1841, when the city fathers began the great farce which ended in Dickens writing the meanest book any foreigner had ever perpetrated about this country or any other. But Miss Bremer seems to have got wind of it, and she has given the codfish nobility the slip. She certainly must be a woman of sense, as well as genius, which renders her a very remarkable character, since those qualities are very seldom united in the same person.[7]

The Boston press rivaled that of New York in publicizing Miss Bremer. The day after she arrived in New York the *Daily Evening Traveller* and the *Daily Evening Transcript* carried items about "the celebrated Swedish writer." The former published October 15 more than a column on "Fredrika Bremer and Her Compeers," a reprint from *Chambers' Edinburgh Journal* of August 4. It elaborated upon how much interest Miss Bremer had created in Swedish literature and compared her with such contemporary novelists of Sweden as Emilie Flygare-Carlén and Sophie von Knorring. The *Transcript* on October 16 informed its readers about the newcomer:

FREDRIKA BREMER is plain looking, short in stature, with fair complexion, light hair, and blue eyes. There is a great deal of goodness in her countenance: but not much passion; so, it is hoped, poetical young gentlemen will not go crazy.[8]

Littell's Living Age joined the chorus of newspapers by printing an autobiographical statement, translated by Mary Howitt, in its October 20 issue. The author told about her family circle, her Årsta home, and other personal details. It was not until December, however, that *Sartain's* published "A Salutation to Frederika Bremer"; part of the greeting to the "Lady of the Norseland" reads:

But when FREDERIKA BREMER declared her resolution to cross the world of waves which roll between us and the Norseland, and the papers, circulating in the huts and hamlets all over our broad land, echo that intention, an emotion of a different kind is stirred, and thousands of glad young voices from the cabin as well as from the villa, exclaim, "Welcome to her!" There is no need to explain who she is, or whence she comes — there is not a hamlet in all the land where the question could not be intelligently answered, accompanied with a hearty "God bless her!"[9]

Literary Contacts

Fredrika Bremer on her third day here learned how enterprising Americans can be. In Newburgh she was surprised by a visit from John Seely Hart, an editor of *Sartain's*, which had printed some of her stories, previously published in Sweden. He had set out from Philadelphia as soon as he heard that she had landed. Professor Hart asked for the sole rights to publish all articles Miss Bremer might write in America. Taken somewhat off guard, she consented, though at the moment she was not sure whether she would write for publication while on her travels. She wanted mainly to observe, but later she did feel inspired to express her thoughts in writing.[10]

A prominent novelist of the time, Catharine Maria Sedgwick, arrived at the Downing home a few days later. Fredrika had read some of her novels, which stressed the importance of the home. The two authors proved congenial and their conversation became animated as they discovered mutual literary and social interests. Miss Sedgwick at the time was preparing a new edition of her collected works and she consulted her friend on some proposed alterations. Fredrika advised against them, saying that she herself would never change anything she had written long ago, even where she saw faults. She felt that an author's works were portions of an autobiography which should not be altered.[11] To the first volume in the new edition, *Clarence,* Miss Sedgwick added a Preface paying general tribute to the excellence of some native and foreign writers, particularly naming Miss Bremer: "A new mine has been opened in the north. Frederika Bremer has electrified us with a series of works that have the richness, and raciness of European literature, and the purity, and healthfulness of our own."[12] A letter to a Mrs. Minot dated October 13, 1849, has this to say:

She has wisely stipulated that her mornings are to be sacred, and will probably thereby save herself from being sent to a madhouse by American hospitality. Lafayette's heroic humanity and French blood saved him; but poor Miss Bremer, of the nature of the sensitive plant, or a lily of the valley, that would hide herself under a green leaf (and could, she is so small), how could she resist a twelve-hours' siege from the "incessant" Yankee nation?[13]

Catharine Sedgwick also told her friend that Fredrika played Swedish airs and taught her and the Downings native folk dances. They made excursions along the Hudson River and once had a capon-and-champagne picnic. Another evening Per Erik Bergfalk, professor of law at the University of Uppsala, and also a visitor to the United States, came to dinner and, as he knew Fredrika from Sweden, it was an especially happy occasion.

This passage from the same letter continues Miss Sedgwick's observations on Fredrika:

I think she has some expectations that will be disappointed. She expects a more distinct individuality, a development of originality unmoulded by precedents or imitations, or Old World conventionalities, that she will not find in a country saturated with canals and penetrated by railroads. There is a dignified, calm good sense about her, with a most lovely gentleness and spirituality. She occasionally tells us pleasant stories, as of a poor lady whose husband often beat her. She one day took up a horse-shoe lying on the floor, and straightened it with her hands. Her husband was amazed. She said, "This force is a gift in my family." "And possessing it," said the husband, "you have suffered me to beat you." "Yes, it was my duty not to resist." He never beat her afterward.[14]

Some years later Catharine Sedgwick was to publish an article anonymously in *Harper's New Monthly Magazine* entitled "A Reminiscence of a Foreign Celebrity's Reception Morning."[15] It was a personal recollection from the autumn of 1849, while "the fever of national welcome was at its height."[16] On the morning Miss Sedgwick described, one woman had offered to mesmerize Fredrika, but the "Star of the North," according to the story, declined with thanks. Fredrika had discussed the suffering which exists in nature, saying she was always upset by it. When someone said that predatory animals extinguish life with the least possible suffering, Fredrika had retorted heatedly:

"It is a lie!" she said, "a dam-ned lie!" And then laughing at her own vehement expression (and it was in ludicrous contrast with the soft and pathetic voice that uttered it), she added, "You must excuse me; I am a Scandinavian, and I must *swere* when I am incen-sed!"[17]

Her English was grammatical and idiomatic, but obscured by her Swedish accent, said the writer.

During Fredrika's stay with Andrew and Caroline Downing they read aloud to her from such works as Bryant's "Thanatopsis" and "The Prairies," Lowell's *The Vision of Sir Launfal,* and Emerson's essays and poems. Even before meeting Emerson Fredrika filled pages of her letters to Agathe with comments about his work. She affirmed that although she had never yet gone one step to see a literary lion, she would go a considerable way to see the "Sphinx of Concord." Of him she said: "The divining-rod of genius is in his hand. He is master in his own domain."[18] She did not agree with everything he wrote, however:

. . . I often object to him; I quarrel with him; I see that his stoicism is one-sidedness, his pantheism an imperfection, and I know that which is greater and more perfect, but I am under the influence of his magical power. I believe myself to have become greater through his greatness, stronger through his strength, and I breathe the air of a higher sphere in his world, which is indescribably refreshing to me.[19]

ANDREW JACKSON
DOWNING
by
Fredrika Bremer

Fredrika-Bremer-Förbundet

Fredrika spent several weeks at Newburgh. She made a fine sketch of Andrew Downing in her album and on either side of the figure she drew books, flowers, and fruits to represent some of the things he liked best. She called him her "American brother." When Mrs. Downing objected to the terms of endearment in the author's letters to them, Fredrika wrote:

"Je[a]lous" Caroline?! Oh no, my sweet Caroline that word and that feeling is not for your mind. No, that little heart of yours is too great and angelic for such a thing. No, you shall let me love your husband with you, and take my hand and be my sister soul in that feeling. Thats a settled affair. Is it not? Its "all right," my dear Caroline.[20]

Fredrika and her hosts attended a dinner given by the James Alexander Hamiltons — he was the third son of Alexander Hamilton — in their villa on the Hudson. Many guests were present, among them Washington Irving, who was then sixty-six. Through his successful books, which had been translated into Swedish and other languages, he had received wide recognition abroad. Fredrika wrote that Irving, together with James Fenimore Cooper, "was the

WASHINGTON IRVING

by

Fredrika Bremer

Fredrika-Bremer-Förbundet

first who made us in Sweden somewhat at home in America."[21] At the time she met him he was working on *The Lives of Mahomet and His Successors.*

At the dinner table Miss Bremer sat next to Irving, whom she found to be a charming conversationalist. Afterwards she made a sketch of him while a young lady entertained him, lest he doze off. Irving invited Fredrika to visit his home in Tarrytown, which she did the very next day. Later she described his study in these words:

"Within, the room seemed full of summer warmth, and had a peaceful and cheerful aspect. One felt that a cordial spirit, full of the best sentiment of the soul, lived and worked there."[22]

His opinion of Fredrika was later repeated in a letter by the American scholar Willard Fiske: "I heard a warm eulogy of the authoress from Mr. Irving, when I had the happiness of being at Sunny Side, and I shall not soon forget his saying that she was a most amiable woman."[23]

After the refreshing time Fredrika spent with the Downings — her "honeymoon in the New World,"[24] as she called it — they brought her back to New York late in October. Soon she accepted an invitation from George Palmer Putnam, the publisher, to visit his Staten Island home. Mrs. Putnam was a charming woman and there were three children, Mary, Herbert, and George Haven. (The daughter later became the noted physician, Mary Putnam Jacobi.) Mr. Putnam offered to print new editions of some of the Bremer novels, and the first volume became available to the public before the end of 1849. Fredrika's special preface to *The Neighbors*[25] reveals how much she appreciated the warmth of the reception accorded her:

. . . For, strange indeed, and wonderful it seems, that a mere stranger, coming from shores far remote, should be received by a great nation as in a dear and loving home. Yet, if I had doubted that wonder, the first day of my arrival at New York should have convinced me of its reality, in seeing family homes opened to me, in a manner I never shall forget, nor ever be able fully to acknowledge, feeling as I, even here, at this moment do, all the blessings of a perfect home. . . .[26]

She would not be able to visit all the homes opened to her, but would send her books as representatives. She praised the New World for its natural beauty and for being the home of true freedom.

In *George Palmer Putnam: A Memoir* (1912) George Haven Putnam remarked concerning Fredrika Bremer:

I remember her as a graceful little woman with bright eyes, grey hair, and a genial smile and with attractively broken English. She had brought with her very little money, having the impression that by means of "lecture-talks" about life in Sweden and through the sale of American editions of her books (books which had made a very substantial success in Sweden), she could not only pay her expenses, but ought to be able to take back some proceeds to her Swedish home.

She remained with us for some weeks while my father was busying himself in arranging for the lectures and in planning for the American editions of her books. The first lectures were a success, but some other more exciting lecturers engaged the attention of the public, and Miss Bremer found, after visits to Boston and Philadelphia, that it would not be wise to attempt to interest, in her quiet narratives and pictures of rural life, the kind of audiences to be found in the Western cities. . . .[27]

Since George Haven Putnam was only five years old in 1849, his account may not have been entirely based on personal recollections of Fredrika.[28] His reference to lectures given by her is interesting, for she did not mention them in her book on America.

The next family Miss Bremer visited was that of Marcus Spring, a successful wholesale merchant in Brooklyn. She soon found that she preferred Brooklyn to New York and made that preference very clear:

. . . New York is the last city in the world in which I would live. But it is also to be regarded merely as a vast hotel, a caravanserai both for America and Europe. Besides, it is true that I always felt myself there in such a state of combat and so fatigued, that I had not time to look around for any thing beautiful. But, thank Heaven! I know Brooklyn, and there I could both live and sleep.[29]

The Springs were to be numbered among Fredrika's best American friends; in fact, she corresponded with them for the rest of her life and always displayed a warm interest in them and their three children.[30] Marcus and Rebecca Spring drove Fredrika to the North American Phalanx near Red Bank, New Jersey, so that she could observe this experiment in socialistic living. Marcus Spring's brother-in-law was president of the phalanx, which was then prospering after great initial difficulties. The approximately seventy members had advanced $1,000.00 each for land purchase, and they worked hard to raise salable crops. Even visitors entered into the activities, and Fredrika made buckwheat cakes for breakfast, played the piano, and entertained the children. Although in some respects she liked the enterprise, she thought the lack of religious services regrettable. An account of her visit was printed in the New York *Weekly Tribune* and other newspapers:

FREDRIKA BREMER AMONG THE FOURIERISTS. — We are allowed to copy the following from a letter received from the *"North American Phalanx,"* in New-Jersey:

"Miss Bremer paid us a visit last week. She seemed quite pleased, and entered very genially into all that was going on, —

mixed a batch of bread, sewed hominy bags, and would have gone out to dig potatoes, if it had not rained.

"There was an old Swedish officer with her, whom we liked mightily; he came to compile some of the beauties of our Republican customs for home use; the King, he says, being inclined to anticipate revolutionary tendencies.

"Miss B. charmed all by her musical gifts. The girls cried and laughed like wild creatures, as they are, under the influence of the delicate magic of her notes, as she played the 'Sea-king's Bride' and other national airs."[31]

By 1850 more than forty of these communities existed in the United States; Fourierism was introduced from France about 1842, but few phalanxes endured. One of the most famous — Brook Farm near Boston — closed as early as 1847. A correspondent of the New York *Herald* expressed concern in December, 1849, over Fredrika's interest in the New Jersey phalanx:

MISS BREMER AND THE SOCIALISTS. — Miss Frederica Bremer, who has come over to see and enjoy the pleasures of American society, seems to have taken a particular fancy for the Fourierites and other ultra people, whom the Chinese would classify among the "outside barbarians." At a Fourierite phalanx, somewhere along the sea shore in New Jersey, she assisted them in making a batch of bread, and in boiling a big pot of potatoes. She has since gone Down-East, and spends a large portion of her time among the model establishments of the socialists. If Miss Bremer confines her intercourse to this class of people, she will get but a sorry and distorted view of American society from her travels. These ultras, political and social, are not strictly American. They are but the rickety imitations of the fine-spun romances of the French and German schools of philosophy; and are about as near to practical society as moonshine to broad daylight. As a matter of taste, we trust that Miss Bremer will cut these people, and say nothing about them when she returns to Sweden.[32]

Fredrika nonetheless was later to describe her visit in *Homes of the New World.* She also perpetuated the names of Marcus and Rebecca Spring through the book and her private letters. The Springs were friends of Emerson, William H. Channing, and Margaret Fuller. They had taken Miss Fuller with them to Europe in 1846; she remained several years in Italy and married the Marquis Ossoli. In a letter to the Springs from Florence, December 12, 1849, the Marchioness mentioned that she had read a newspaper notice about Fredrika Bremer's visit to the North American Phalanx and added: "Write of Miss Bremer. I think she will see many things in the U.S. to please her kind heart, and trust she will give the benefit of many wise suggestions & reproofs. Sauced by her kindly playfulness they will be digested even by the conceit of Jonathan."[33]

It was probably at the home of the Springs that Lydia Maria Child, author and abolitionist, again met Fredrika. In a letter to Ellis Gray Loring, the Boston lawyer, Mrs. Child wrote:

I spent most of last Sunday with Fredrika Bremer; four or five hours entirely alone with her. Mrs. S. very kindly invited me to meet her there. What a refreshment it was! She is so artless and unaffected, such a reality! I took a wonderful liking to her, though she is very plain in her person, and I am a fool about beauty. We talked about Swedenborg, and Thorwaldsen, and Jenny Lind, and Andersen. . . . I particularly liked her for one thing; she did not attempt to compliment me, either directly or indirectly. She never heard of J. R. Lowell till she came here. His poetry has inspired her with strong enthusiasm. She said to me, "He is the poet prophet of America." Emerson seems to have made on her the same vivid impression that he makes on all original and thinking minds. What a fuss they will make with Fredrika in Boston! She will have no peace of her life. I hope they will not be ambitious of burying her by the side of Dr. Spurzheim.[34]

The celebrated Quaker poet John Greenleaf Whittier was inspired to compose a poem in Fredrika's honor. First published in the *National Era*, a Washington, D. C., newspaper, it was widely reprinted.[35] "To Fredrika Bremer" appeared on November 15, 1849; later Whittier made some changes before including the following version in *The Chapel of the Hermits, and Other Poems* (1853):

To Fredrika Bremer

Seeress of the misty Norland,
  Daughter of the Vikings bold,
Welcome to the sunny Vineland,
  Which thy fathers sought of old!

Soft as flow of Silja's waters,
  When the moon of summer shines,
Strong as Winter from his mountains
  Roaring through the sleeted pines.

Heart and ear, we long have listened
  To thy saga, rune and song,
Till a household joy and presence
  We have known and loved thee long.

JOHN GREENLEAF
WHITTIER

From an etching by
S. A. Schoff

By the mansion's marble mantel,
   Round the log-walled cabin's hearth,
Thy sweet thoughts and northern fancies
   Meet and mingle with our mirth.

And, o'er weary spirits keeping
   Sorrow's night-watch, long and chill,
Shine they like thy sun of summer
   Over midnight vale and hill.

We alone are strangers to thee,
   Thou our friend and teacher art;
Come, and know us as we know thee;
   Let us meet thee heart to heart!

To our homes and household altars
   We, in turn, thy steps would lead,
As thy loving hand has led us
   O'er the threshold of the Swede.[36]

Whittier added a note when the poem appeared in *The Chapel*: "It is proper to say that these lines are the joint impromptu of my sister and myself. They are inserted here as an expression of our admiration of the gifted stranger whom we have since learned to love as a friend."[37] Fredrika met the poet while staying with the James Russell Lowells in Cambridge — on Christmas Day he called on her. She liked Whittier's smile, his black eyes so full of fire, and his tall, slender figure. His manner with her apparently had a certain nervous bashfulness but, as she wrote to the Downings: "If you can set him at ease, he is very agre[e]able, and you see in him so true and noble a soul."[38] She called Whittier a champion of freedom, truth, and justice.

Fredrika always had a close affinity for poets; she often expressed herself poetically and others felt inspired to dedicate poems to her. Anne Lynch's verses resulted from reading "An Autobiographical Letter" in which Fredrika had exclaimed: "Hereafter, when I no more belong to earth, I should love to return to it as a spirit, and impart to men the deepest of that which I have suffered and enjoyed, lived and loved. . . ."

Lines To Frederika Bremer.

Hereafter! — nay, thou hast thy wish e'en here;
  To many a striving spirit dost thou come,
  Sweet lady, from thy far-off northern home,
Like a blest presence from another sphere,
  And love and faith, the night-lamps of the soul,
  Have burned with brighter flame at thy control.

A friend and sister art thou now to those
  Who weep o'erburdened with life's weary load,
  And faint and toil-worn tread the desert road;
To them thou beckonest from thy high repose:
  Thou'st gained that steep where endless day appears,
  That faith whose followers are baptized with tears.

There came no voices from thy distant shore;
  We heard no echo of thy country's lyres,
  We saw no gleaming of her household fires;
A cloud had hung thy land and language o'er,
  Until thy pictured thoughts broke on our eyes
  Like an Aurora of thy native skies.

Thy name is loved through all our fair wide land:
  Where the log-cabins of our western woods
  Are scattered through the dim old solitudes,

> Where, glowing with young life, our cities stand,
>   There go thy white-winged messengers, as went
>   Of old the angels to the patriarch's tent.
>
> My harp is tuneless and unknown to fame;
>   A few weak chords, alas! chance-strung and frail,
>   O'er which sweeps fitfully the passing gale.
> Would it indeed were worthier of its theme,
>   That it might bear across the distant sea
>   The homage of unnumbered hearts to thee.[39]

Delighted with the poem, Fredrika in turn composed one for Anne Lynch; she sent it to her written in a copy of *The Neighbors*.[40] Miss Lynch taught English and she also knew many prominent literary figures, including William Cullen Bryant. Fredrika wrote her sister that she had seen a whole crowd of people in Anne Lynch's home, "and among them Bryant the poet, who has a beautiful, characteristic head, with silvery locks."[41] The American historian George Bancroft was also introduced to her by Miss Lynch. Fredrika drove one day with them to visit a number of people whose homes overlooked the Hudson River. Wherever they stopped, they were all lionized and besieged for autographs. Fredrika later read with great interest Bancroft's *History of the United States* and quoted passages from it in her book on America.

The life of a literary lioness was beginning to fatigue Fredrika, however, and oft-repeated questions, such as "How do you like America?" "How long have you been here?" "How long are you going to stay?", presently became irritating. In reply to how she liked this country, she declared that America was a long novel requiring time to read.

While in New York Fredrika attended lectures on Christian Socialism by Henry James — father of William and Henry James, who were then small boys — and William H. Channing. In November the *Spirit of the Age*, a magazine edited by Channing, reprinted from the New York *Express* this account of her activities:

> Miss Fredrika Bremer is yet in our city, visiting or being visited by large numbers of admirers, who have been pleased with her literary productions. On Friday evening she is to be hospitably entertained in the mansion of an ex-Mayor of our city, and on Saturday, the Lady Hostess takes her to the High Bridge.[42]
>
> Miss B. was welcomed by a large party at Miss Anne C. Lynch's on Wednesday evening, which is her home for the present we

believe. A brother countryman, Prof. S., from Stockholm, was also
a guest, with a number of distinguished citizens, among the artists,
literati, and others of the city and country. Miss Bremer will spend
some time in the city and Brooklyn before leaving for Boston. She
contemplates a tour over the country before returning home, and
wishes especially to see the "Big West."[43]

New England Welcomes Fredrika Bremer

Late in November Fredrika accepted an invitation from Marcus and Rebecca Spring to go to Massachusetts and spend Thanksgiving with their relatives in Uxbridge. On the way they stopped
a day at Hartford to visit Lydia H. Sigourney. A large reception
had been planned for the Swedish author in the Connecticut capital
— she wrote later that there she shook hands with the whole town.
The very same experience was repeated in Worcester, Massachusetts, where Mayor Henry Chapin gave an affair in her honor.
Among the many guests was Elihu Burritt, the self-taught linguist
who had formerly been a blacksmith. He was an earnest advocate
of international peace and a lecturer on pacifism. *Burritt's Christian
Citizen* published an account of the hospitable manner in which
Fredrika had been received. Her writings had made her name beloved in all lands, said the newspaper. In Worcester she also met
Edward Everett Hale, writer and Unitarian clergyman, who discussed her in a letter to Frederic Greenleaf:

. . . Then we had Miss Bremer. Did I write you of her? Very short,
very old, very plain, but very bright and goodnatured. She looks as
if she were every day of 60, — is said to be, — *is*, I think forty-eight.
She says by the way, that she shall die when she is sixty-six years
old. She had a revelation to that effect from a friend, a gentleman
who died some years ago, — who promised if he could he would
return to tell her of the other world and give her a sign.[44]

In the same city she was asked what she thought of having so
many people come to see her. " 'I wish that I were handsomer!' replied I, simply, and with truth."[45]

The Thanksgiving holiday appealed to Fredrika and won her
wholehearted approval. At Uxbridge she ate with much enjoyment
a New England roast turkey and pumpkin pie dinner. The following
day she visited the Hopedale Community, a socialistic settlement
near Milford, founded in 1841 by a small group of Unitarians under
the leadership of the Reverend Adin Ballou. Fredrika liked it better

than the North American Phalanx because Hopedale stressed the Christian religion.

From Uxbridge she went to Boston and took lodgings at the Revere House December first. The Boston *Daily Bee* said that on Sunday she had heard Theodore Parker preach — he was then minister of the Twenty-eighth Congregational Society. Fredrika did not agree with Parker's stand on miracles, the divinity of Christ, and revelation. He had an intuitional, transcendental philosophy; his anti-supernatural Christianity had, in fact, antagonized fellow Unitarian ministers. She later wrote that they had "a good deal of quiet controversy"[46] on theological matters; on one thing, however, they were in complete accord — the slavery issue.

In a few days Fredrika journeyed by train to Concord with the Springs and Professor Bergfalk at Ralph Waldo Emerson's invitation. Coming bareheaded out of his house in the snowstorm, Emerson assisted them inside. He appeared younger than Fredrika expected, and his strongly-marked features, dark hair, and quiet demeanor imprinted themselves on her memory. During this visit with the Emersons and their three children she formed the impression that the savant was too strong and healthy to understand the weaknesses and sufferings of others.[47]

Again the following month she was a guest in their home, as shown by Emerson's note to his wife from Boston, January 15:
Dear Lidian,

I saw Miss Bremer this morning, & she will come home with me on Thursday, leaving Boston at 11 o'clock, A.M. & arriving at Concord at 12 noon. She is in feeble health & I found Dr Osgood with her, homoeopathically advising.

She sends a heath flower "to the beloved ones." . . .

Yours R. W.[48]

He also mentioned her visit three days later in a letter to Abby Larkin Adams: "I brought home Miss Bremer with me, yesterday, and we find her very good company."[49] She spent five days there and, despite her indisposition, had some weighty discussions with the philosopher. Said Fredrika: "I feel also a little desire for combat with him; for I never see a lion in human form without feeling my lion-heart beat. And a combat with a spirit like that is always a pleasure even if one wins no victory."[50] Fredrika's religious views differed from Emerson's but, as one critic wrote: "It is curious how this essentially heathen intellectual could attract an evangelical soul like Fredrika Bremer."[51]

She told about her visit in a letter to the Downings:

. . . I felt so weak and unwell the day when Emerson was to take me to his home that I meditated not to go. But my old good doktor was positive that I should and so I went. And was it his little nothings of powders or was it the strong and bracing intel[l]ectual atmosfere of Emerson, but I grew better at his home, and enjoyed intensely the com[m]union and contact with that noble eagleborn spirit. His thought I can master and soar above, but his mind, his noble and strong spirit, his severe stoicism —oh! for that I bow with a mingled feeling of delight and pain, and wish that I was true to my higher nature and calling as he is to his. I can find fault with him, easily, ask of him larger sympathies, a greater and to humanity more tender heart. But is it for the well who ripples at every breath of air, who reflects every cloud in the firmament, to quarrel with the granite-rock, which towers over its waters, that it is so hard and strong? Such breasts must be for abodes to strong metalls. Let the well be content that it is in its power to reflect the images of the stern rock and the delicate flowers and of the stars in the heavenly dome that encloses all earth. Let it thank its maker that it can supply its waters ever fresh from the mysterious fountains that the high mountains suck.

Emerson is now lecturing in New-York. When he comes back to Boston I shall see him again and have a talk with him over the futurity of this rising world.[52]

Emerson was the leader of the transcendental movement, some of whose members were Amos Bronson Alcott, Margaret Fuller, Theodore Parker, and George Ripley. The philosophic ideas of this group were influenced by German idealism and Oriental thought, and contained a large element of mysticism. Stressing the validity of spiritual intuition as a means of knowing truth, and claiming that it transcended reality and experience, the transcendentalists believed that all knowledge comes from the divinity within. Fredrika felt that they had not reached "to the highest," that it was not enough to show the ideal; one must also attain it. With gentle sarcasm a contemporary viewed her association with this group: "Miss Bremer is visiting around among our literary people and others. She rather *cottons* to the transcendental set. She is a lady of very distinguished worth and talent notwithstanding. — Boston *Letter.*"[53]

Walt Whitman told an English friend, Mrs. Anna Gilchrist, about an incident in connection with the Sabbath which had been related to him. One Sunday evening in Emerson's home, when Swedish music happened to be the subject of discussion, Fredrika went to the piano to show that the music really had certain qualities someone present said it lacked. This caused a stir and she was asked not to play. Even Emerson said: "No, Miss Bremer, this is Sunday evening, I would rather not."[54] She blushed, but soon recovered and laughed.

Fredrika's drawing of Emerson's "eagle-featured face" is among the best profiles she ever made. She later showed her sketchbooks to George Eliot in London; the British author wrote in 1851 to a friend: "I wish you could see Miss Bremer's albums, full of portraits, flowers, and landscapes, all done by herself. A portrait of Emerson, marvellously like; one of Jenny Lind, etc."[55] George Eliot continued:

I must tell you a story Miss Bremer got from Emerson. Carlyle was very angry with him for not believing in a devil, and to convert him took him amongst all the horrors of London — the gin-shops, etc. — and finally to the House of Commons, plying him at every turn with the question, "Do you believe in a devil noo?"[56]

One afternoon Emerson read to Fredrika from his manuscript about meetings with Carlyle, later included in *English Traits*. She also listened to Emerson's lectures, among them "The Spirit of the Times" and "Eloquence." She praised his deep and melodious voice, brilliant phraseology, calm and reposing strength.[57] On March 15 she dined with Emerson in New York, together with Henry Bellows, the Unitarian minister, and Caroline M. Kirkland, an author whose book on Michigan pioneer life (*A New Home — Who'll Follow?;* 1839) Fredrika had read in Sweden. She described the occasion to Andrew Downing:

. . . It was a pleasant dinner more than usually dinners are. Bellows and Emerson most sunny and agre[e]able. E. sweet and charming. He came to see us at Irving place in the evening, (rather attracted, I think, by Mrs Kirkland) and stayed till late. I read to him "the Emperors new Clothes" by H. C. Andersen, which amused him much. To night we will hear him lecture again. Why! You should have been there also![58]

Miss Bremer considered Emerson less "spiritual and angelic" than William H. Channing, and to her he was "a Magician."[59] She understood the independent nature of his mind, as shown by her comment to the Springs:

RALPH WALDO EMERSON
by Fredrika Bremer

. . . [Tell me] if the Brooklynians have redeemed their right to ears and other fine organs by crowding Emersons lectures. I will lose my esteem for them if they dont! Tell me also a little how E. and Beecher[60] went on in their hookings in their mutual minds. I suspect B. had in mind to preach to and convert E. But that wont go for him. E--s star runs not his way, and must make out its own course.[61]

Fredrika later introduced Emerson's works in Sweden and, according to Lawrence Thompson, she was the first person to translate Emerson into a foreign tongue.[62] The Swedish edition of *Homes of the New World* contained passages from such essays as "Self-Reliance," "Friendship," "History," and "The Over-Soul," and parts of the poems "Give All to Love" and "The World-Soul." She found it difficult to do full justice to Emerson's poems because, like the character of the poet, they had an extraordinary rhythm and spirit of their own.[63]

Emerson gave her a volume of his *Essays* dedicated "To my dear friend F. B."[64] and she presented him with Geijer's *History of Sweden.* Before leaving New England she gave the poet's wife *The Bondmaid,* which had been translated by Mary Lowell Putnam, Lowell's sister, and Fredrika inscribed it: "To Mrs. L. Emerson, with the love of Fredrika Bremer Feb. 1850."[65] The Swedish visitor met Mrs. Emerson's brother, Dr. Charles T. Jackson, one of the discoverers of surgical anesthesia. She congratulated Dr. Jackson on his great contribution to humanity, and he showed her the medal he had received from King Oscar I of Sweden.

A note from Downing to the James Russell Lowells resulted in an invitation for Fredrika to visit Cambridge that December. She was welcomed into the family circle and spent happy weeks there. She thought Lowell "a perfect Apollo in appearance"[66] and sketched both the thirty-year-old bard and his wife. On Christmas Eve the two ladies were alone at Elmwood and Mrs. Lowell read aloud from her husband's works; her guest received a copy of Lowell's *Poems* as a Christmas present, affectionately inscribed "to the dear Fredrika." A few days later Lowell also gave her his satirical work, *A Fable for Critics,* dedicated: "With the author's love to Fredrika Bremer, who will read it by the light of her own kindheartedness."[67] That she endeared herself is apparent from Lowell's comment to Charles F. Briggs, the journalist:

Fredrika-Bremer-Förbundet

JAMES RUSSELL AND MARIA LOWELL
by Fredrika Bremer

Fredrika Bremer stayed three weeks with us, and I do not *like* her, I *love* her. She is one of the most beautiful persons I have ever known — so clear, so simple, so right-minded and -hearted, and so full of judgment. I believe she liked us, too, and had a good time. . . .[68]

How much Fredrika liked the Lowells was later revealed in her book on America, for in it she sang their praises. She wrote of Lowell's youthful ardor and his brilliant, witty conversation, especially in the evening, when it was like "an incessant play of fireworks."[69] The fair and gifted Maria Lowell was one of the most lovable women she had met in this country. Unfortunately, Mrs. Lowell's health was delicate and she lived only until 1853.

Fredrika herself suffered from migraine and dyspepsia, and frequently felt indisposed during her Boston stay. She placed herself under the care of a homeopathic practitioner, and when they met for the first time David Osgood said: "Miss Bremer, no one can have read your *Neighbors*, and not wish to help you!"[70] She felt that the powders and diet he prescribed improved her health; in one of her messages to Mrs. Lowell she related a humorous incident which occurred after taking a sedative:

Do not, my lovely Maria, do not let your kind and sympathising heart be distressed for me. Yesterday, when you saw me, I was under the influence of a homeopat[h]ic powder which would make me sleep just at the time my visitors began to pour in, and the inward battle between the torpor of sleep, and need of it (then I had not slept well the past night) and the necessity of keeping awake and bright to the company made me uncomfortable. My strength rose as the flood rose, and that kept on rising till three oklock when it subsided, but not untill it brought me the dearest sight I had had that day after I had seen you. I slept at Alcotts conversation in the evening, yea soul and body.[71]

In another letter to the Lowells Fredrika wrote words of sympathy upon the death of their younger daughter, Rose (Appendix, p. 164). She made a special trip to Cambridge to comfort the grieving parents. Hers was a great capacity for friendship, reflected in acts of kindness and in letters full of warmth and sincerity. On her travels she continued to write to the Lowells, recounting her activities.

Fredrika visited Harvard in December and she was impressed by the fine collection of Scandinavian books, also by Audubon's *Birds of America*, which she considered a work of genius. She enjoyed meeting the orator and statesman Edward Everett and members of the Harvard faculty, among them the naturalist Louis Agassiz — who presented his betrothed to her — and the professor of natural history, Asa Gray. With the latter she had "a little botanic conversation." Fredrika made several visits to Cambridge, and after one of them the Cambridge *Chronicle* reported: "The arrival of Miss Bremer has been hailed with delight by all the literati of Cambridge, and the enthusiasm with which she has been welcomed here has not been exceeded in any other city or town where she has sojourned since her arrival in the country. . . ."[72]

A visitor at her Boston hotel on December 6 was none other than Henry Wadsworth Longfellow.[73] He was then forty-two years old and professor of modern languages at Harvard. He was already familiar with her works, having bought *Teckningar utur hvardagslifvet* (*Sketches of Every-day Life*)[74] for himself and for the college library during his visit to Sweden in 1835. Longfellow and Fredrika Bremer were to meet at least a dozen times, and each time he mentioned her in his journal. He described their first meeting:

Called on Miss Bremer at the Revere house. A kindly old lady, with gentle manners and soft voice. We talked of Swedish authors. Nicander has long been dead. He died miserably. Tegnér she spoke of with affection — much moved — with tears in her eyes. She comes to Cambridge to-day to stay with Lowell.[75]

On December 8 he wrote that she had "a lovely face, reminding one of Keats."[76] Five days later: "Last evening we were at Lowell's to see Miss Bremer, who is a very quiet little body, and sat sewing lace on to her handkerchief all the evening. She weareth spectacles."[77] December 17: "A lovely Spring-like morning after yesterday's rain. Met Miss Bremer with the Lowells in the College Yard. She said 'How beautiful the weather is! I am quite tipsy with the air!' "[78] That evening Mr. and Mrs. Longfellow dined at Elmwood and three days later the Longfellows were hosts to the Lowells:

We had a nice dinner-party to-day. Lowell, his wife and sister; — Miss Bremer the Swedish author, Miss Cushman, the tragic actress, Miss Hays the lovely translator of George Sand; — Jewett, Sumner, and young Furness, son of the Philadelphia clergyman; — a whole table-full of authors and authoresses! We fed them upon canvasback ducks, quails, Roman punch, and three kinds of American wines, Sparkling Catawba, Gabella, and Scuppernong. It was all very charming.[79]

Charlotte Cushman, to whom Longfellow referred, was then appearing in her native Boston. Fredrika heard her as Lady Macbeth and as Meg Merrilies (in *Guy Mannering*) and liked her so well that she suggested Miss Cushman portray the role of Kumba in her play *The Bondmaid,* but this never materialized. Fredrika also enjoyed hearing Fanny Kemble, the British actress, give readings from *Hamlet, Antony and Cleopatra, Henry V,* and *Julius Caesar.* Miss Kemble sent her complimentary tickets and, on occasion, the author invited the Lowells and other guests to the Kemble interpretations of Shakespeare.

At Christmas Longfellow sent Fredrika Bremer a copy of his latest work, *The Seaside and the Fireside;* her note acknowledging it is still at Longfellow House:

Cambridge the 24 Dec. 1849.

Receive, my dear Sir, my heartfelt thanks for the welcome gift of your *Seaside and fireside,* whose songs — I know it well by the voices of the night and Evangeline — will charm my fireside these dreary vintry nights, and render it more bright and genial. Let me also thank you and Mrs. Longfellow for your kindness and hospitality to me! It will ever be to me a dear remembrance. I hope to see you again, to see more of you and to gain the privilege to be remembered as your friend.

with most true respect and regard

Fredrika Bremer.[80]

She quoted from memory in a postscript her Swedish poem, "Axel till Anna,"[81] in response to the poet's request. Fredrika later sent Longfellow a copy of Johan Ludvig Runeberg's *Fänrik Ståls sägner* (*The Tales of Ensign Stål*). This cycle of poems about the heroes of the war with Russia, 1808-1809, interested the American poet, who read Swedish well. She inscribed it: "Fr. Bremer to Mr H. W. Longfellow, with affectionate regard."[82]

Longfellow entered in his journal for January: "Wednesday 23. A party at Harriet's for the Reeds. Miss Bremer was the lioness, however, though all modesty and humility."[83] Longfellow called several times on her and he wrote in his journal February 12:

Went to Miss Bremer's, who made a sketch of me in her sketch book. While there, Ellen Crafts, the slave woman who ran away in man's clothes, as a young master her husband going as her slave, came in. When Miss Bremer told me who it was, and spoke of "man's clothes" Ellen hung her head and said she did not like to have it mentioned, "some people thought it was so shocking!" Miss Bremer

Fredrika-Bremer-Förbundet

laughed at this prudery, as well she might; and we both urged her to be proud of this act of heroism. . . .[84]

Fredrika's sketch of Longfellow, begun that day, was not worked on again until a year and a half later because of her travels. Meanwhile the poet and his wife had asked her for a keepsake; what they wanted was a cast of her dainty right hand:

Tuesday 19. To town again. Found the Bremer with her homeopathic doctor Osgood; and looking brighter than yesterday. We went down and had the hand moulded in plaster. Then we went to Thompson's room, and saw sundry portraits.[85]

Fredrika referred to the cast in a February letter to the poet:

. . . I certainly think that the hand you kindly say you "hold" will not prove false to my wishes to come once more to you and enjoy your company more truly than I have been able to do it in this time of my eclipse. Then indeed I have not been half alive these past three months. But they are past, and, thank God, I feel the spring returning in body as well as in mind.[86]

The replica is still at Longfellow House; once broken by a careless maid, it has been skilfully mended and remains a graceful object.

Fredrika received many letters and invitations; she needed a secretary those busy days and, as it was, on December 11 she had to ask the *Daily Evening Transcript* to print this message:

A CARD FROM MISS BREMER. Feeling the impossibility to answer, as I should and would, letters and notes which are sent to me, many of which are precious to me, not only as to what concerns me personally, and which I treasure in my heart as things dear and beautiful, I wish by these lines to make known to my benevolent correspondents, that if I do not answer them, it is that I cannot find time and leisure to do so, during my time of traveling in this land, where there is so much to see and to learn. I would tell them that my thankfulness is not the less for that it is not now expressed in words. And I would add, that though I am well aware that, in saying all this, I may incur the charge of vanity, I will rather incur that, and bear it, than bear the thought that any heart in the United States of America should suspect mine of ungratefulness or disregard.
Boston, Dec. 1849.   FREDRIKA BREMER.[87]

The notice was copied by other newspapers, among them the Brooklyn *Evening Star,* where it appeared three days later, preceded by these words:

ANSWERING THEM AT ONCE. — Our fortune is to have so many people of education and literary taste, that the rush of correspondents is too great, when a favorite author comes among us. Poor Miss Bremer, has her basket full of letters every day from the admiring crowds of the ladies who have read the delightful novels of "Home" and caught the freshness of the Norwegian Mountains, from her inimitable descriptions. . . .[88]

During her stay in Boston Fredrika had her portrait painted by the young artist William Henry Furness, Jr. The engraving made of it was widely circulated here. She also attended some of Amos Bronson Alcott's "Conversations"; two of them were called "Temperament and Complexion" and "The Times." Fredrika considered the educator an idealist and a dreamer but was in accord with a few of his ideas. For instance, she felt his theories on eugenic marriage worthy and important. His rather extreme views on diet, on the other hand, did not find favor with her. Alcott was a vegetarian and, said she: "He should drink wine and eat meat, or at least fish, so that there might be marrow and substance in his ideas."[89] She commented to the Downings:

FREDRIKA BREMER
by W. H. Furness, Jr.

I have been to three of Alcotts conversations, and he has called
on me in private to state more closely his theories. Alas! For the good
man. He is not to be helped. He drinks to[o] much water and
breads [breeds] only vapory and misty images. I have done with him,
and I wonder only how people can sit and listen to his childish and
yet very conceited talk. Tete a tete he is better, and you can come
to something with him.[90]

Alcott's daughter Louisa May, later to become the noted novelist, was then seventeen. She must have read Fredrika Bremer, because Petrea, the heroine of *The Home*, is referred to in the following passage from *Little Women*:

If anybody had asked Amy what the greatest trial of her life
was, she would have answered at once, "My nose." When she was
a baby, Jo had accidentally dropped her into the coal-hod, and Amy
insisted that the fall had ruined her nose forever. It was not big, nor
red, like poor "Petrea's"; it was only rather flat, and all the pinching
in the world could not give it an aristocratic point.[91]

The Swedish author had in childhood been sensitive about the
size of her nose, but mature years gave her a saving sense of humor
and she was able to joke about her own "offending feature." Occasionally the press made a thrust in the direction of Fredrika's appearance, though on the whole its treatment of her was kind. She could
not have read all that was said about her, because she received publicity before and after her arrival in each city, and newspapers in
various places copied from each other.[92] Numerous notices kept the
public informed, such as the following from the Boston *Daily Evening Transcript*:

FREDRIKA BREMER did not spend "New Year's Day" in Goth-
am, as was reported. She is at present the guest of a distinguished
Swede, of this city, where she will remain for some time. (January
3, 1850)[93]

FREDRIKA BREMER, the Swedish authoress, visited the State
House yesterday, in company with Charles Sumner, Esq., by whom
she was introduced to the President of the Senate and several of the
members. She spent some time in listening to a debate in the House
of Representatives. (January 24, 1850)[94]

A new novel by Miss Bremer is announced, entitled *The Light
House, or Scenes in the North*. (February 2, 1850)[95]

MISS BREMER. We learn from the *Christian Register*, that
Miss Bremer still remains at the house of Mr. Benzon, the Swedish
Vice Consul, in Pinckney street. She will shortly start for the South,
linger awhile at Washington, pass a few weeks at Havana, to enjoy
the summer of the tropics, then visit New Orleans, sail up the Missis-

sippi and Ohio, visit the Mammoth Cave, touch at Niagara and come back to the Atlantic coast in season to return home by the close of autumn. She has been sitting for her portrait to Mr. Furness, son of Rev. W. H. Furness of Philadelphia, a young artist of promise. (February 9, 1850)[96]

FREDRIKA BREMER AT THE NAVY YARD. The *Courier* states that Miss Bremer visited the Navy Yard at Charlestown yesterday, and was received in a becoming manner by Commodore Downs, and other officers of the station. She looked at all the public works going on, and partook of a collation at the Commodore's quarters, to which all persons attached to the yard were admitted. The band of the receiving ship *Franklin* performed sweet music, and the visit was one of the happiest which this distinguished lady has made during her stay here. (February 16, 1850)[97]

The Boston *Daily Bee* also followed Fredrika's activities closely and this notice on February 12 was the eighteenth to appear in that newspaper since her arrival:

MISS BREMER AT THE WARREN STREET CHAPEL. — According to a promise made some time since to Mr. Barnard, Miss Bremer visited the Warren street chapel, on Sunday afternoon last. There was about three hundred and fifty children present, their ages varying from six to sixteen, besides a large number of young gentlemen and ladies, who would hardly be willing to be called children. She appeared to be highly gratified with their good attention, and excellent deportment. The choir sung a hymn welcoming her among them, composed by Whittier. After the service, Mr. Barnard presented her with a circular wreath, composed of evergreen moss, gathered from the rocks of Norway and Sweden. Many of those present then pressed around her, to take by the hand one who has done so much towards making home agreeable and life happy.[98]

Fredrika had a special interest in Lowell, Massachusetts, because it had furnished inspiration for a theme used in *Brothers and Sisters*. Her February visit was reported locally:

MISS BREMER, who passed a few days in Lowell last week, was very much surprised at the appearance of our city. We are told that she remarked that she expected to see a small place with some five hundred inhabitants![99] Although Miss B. was here but a short time, she visited several of our factories and boarding houses. She went among the girls while at work, and in their boarding houses while they were taking their meals — sociable, pleasant and chatting with them, as if they were so many sisters of her own.

The girls, too, regarded her as an old acquaintance, and conversed with her as familiarly as if she were a long absent friend just returned. They told her they had long been familiar with her works, and how much pleasure they had derived from them. . . .[100]

The same month a fantasy entitled "Miss Bremer's Visit to Cooper's Landing" by "One Who Was There" appeared in *Godey's Lady's Book*. In a light and satirical vein the tale poked fun at the overeagerness of the ladies at Cooper's Landing, who bustled a Mrs. Frederick Beamer to their reception by mistake. Many humorous misunderstandings occurred when this lady failed to recognize the allusions to "her" novels, and "One Who Was There" concluded:

JULIA WARD HOWE

by

Fredrika Bremer

Fredrika-Bremer-Förbundet

And so it was, dear reader; and a lesson for all who rush with impertinent curiosity to look upon a distinguished man or woman, as if they were wild beasts caged for the occasion; for all who "patronize" genius, or wit, or beauty only because it is the fashion, and that they may thereby share in the notoriety. And though America does, indeed, welcome Fredrika Bremer with warm hearts and earnest sympathy, we should remember that, as a woman, she must shrink from coarse flattery or attentions devoid of feeling.[101]

In the middle of the nineteenth century American literature took on a golden glow, and it was a distinguished group of men and women of letters whom Fredrika Bremer met. As a European writer widely read in this country, she had entree wherever literary people gathered; they sought her out and in turn she delighted in making their acquaintance. Fredrika's eventful sojourn in New England marked an auspicious introduction to the American scene. Besides such luminaries as Emerson, Longfellow, Lowell, and Whittier, she learned to know many other noted Americans. In Boston, for example, she met Dr. Samuel Gridley Howe and his wife, the latter a social reformer and poet now best known for her "Battle Hymn of the Republic." Fredrika made sketches of Julia Ward Howe and of her husband's blind, deaf-mute pupil, Laura Bridgman. (In 1862 Mrs. Howe sent Fredrika a collection of her poems entitled *Passion-Flowers,* dedicated "with kind remembrance from Julia Ward Howe."[102])

There were, of course, some authors whom Fredrika did not meet, among them: Edgar Allan Poe, who died the same month she arrived; James Fenimore Cooper, though she had read some of his books; Herman Melville, whose *Moby Dick* did not appear until 1851; and Henry David Thoreau, who had not yet published *Walden.*

Fredrika returned to New York the end of February. In Brooklyn, at Plymouth Church, she heard Henry Ward Beecher preach on "The Positive in Christianity." She found him full of life and energy, earnest, convincing, and witty. Later she met the thirty-six-year-old minister socially and enjoyed hearing about his missionary experiences. He described nocturnal camp meetings and scenes of baptism along river banks. Preaching beneath the open sky and making his solitary treks in the wilderness, he had achieved an inner peace and order.

While a guest at Mrs. Kirkland's home Fredrika met Bayard Taylor, the young writer and traveler then recently back from California. He had much to relate about the gold rush, the scenery, vegetation, and climate. Fredrika had been following the heated debate in Congress about California, so she was especially interested. (Before the end of 1850 it became the thirty-first state.) Fredrika did not reach the West Coast on her momentous tour; to her the "Great West" was the Mississippi Valley, the vast and fertile central part of the country. She was to visit the Midwest later that same year, but her plans called first for a journey to the South.

CHAPTER III

Further Travels in the United States*

Visit to the South

FREDRIKA DECIDED TO LEAVE New York by boat in mid-March, 1850, for Charleston, South Carolina. To her astonishment one captain refused her passage when he learned her name, saying he did not want any authors on board who might scorn his accommodations and "put him in a book." When she had waited eight days for the next boat, she remarked that she had Mrs. Trollope and Dickens to thank for that delay.[1]

The weather was cold, but Fredrika promenaded on deck; she saw when the ship passed the lighthouse at Cape Hatteras "in the shining night." Shortly afterward she declared: "Then I was *well*, so well as when I first crossed the ocean, and felt again the spirit of the Vikings all alive in me."[2]

When Fredrika came, Charleston was a city of approximately 43,000 inhabitants. It was so friendly and hospitable that she made it her headquarters in the South, returning there after trips to Georgia, Florida, and Cuba. She received a warm welcome from Mrs. William Howland, who insisted that Fredrika come to live in her home. Mrs. Howland introduced her to many people,[3] among them Dr. and Mrs. Samuel Gilman; Mrs. John E. Holbrook, wife of the naturalist; and Mrs. Peder Hjalmar Hammarskjöld, a Swedish woman and an accomplished musician. It soon became known, however, that Fredrika needed a rest from social life:

The first thing she did was to beg not to be lionized any more, to have no entertainments given in her honor and no invitations accepted for her. This determination on her part naturally produced only the more curiosity to see her in the good city of C———, and

---

*The notes to Chapter III begin on page 306.

resulted in a very provoking attempt to entertain and exhibit her. She acquired the habit of driving every morning to the other end of the town to take a seabath with some pleasant acquaintances who strongly pressed her to accept an invitation to breakfast at the house of a relative. She accepted, stipulating that only the family should be present. Accordingly on her return from her bath one fine morning and accoutred as she was in a wrapper or morning-robe, Miss Bremer stopped at the house in question and was ushered into the drawing-room to find herself surrounded by more than fifty guests and the centre of all interest. Dismayed and mortified and with a feeling of excusable resentment, she resolved upon nothing less decided than flight. With some plausible excuse she left the gayly attired guests, who had donned their best in honor of her, and leaving the house rushed to her friend's home, where she exclaimed: "Don't scold me! don't scold me! I have done something very dreadful — I have run away!"[4]

Fredrika's first visit to Charleston lasted a fortnight. In letters to her sister she told of strolling along the fashionable "Battery," making excursions to the Ashley River and Sullivan's Island, and visiting the large markets. She attended a Methodist camp meeting in the forest, listened to some good singing by a Negro choir, and even spent the night at the camp, sleeping in a tent.

April and May saw the city in full bloom. Magnolia trees, orange blossoms, and roses combined to create a picture of beauty; the author mentions also the cypress and sycamore trees, the live oaks festooned with Spanish moss, and the tulip trees. Joel Roberts Poinsett — for whom the poinsettia plant is named — extended an invitation which Fredrika accepted. The former American Ambassador to Mexico was a friend of Andrew J. Downing, and he asked Fredrika to visit him and Mrs. Poinsett at their plantation north of Charleston, near Georgetown. The septuagenarian enjoyed having long talks with his visitor, and among the topics they discussed was, of course, slavery. Fredrika interviewed the Negroes on Poinsett's plantation about their living and working conditions, and she admitted that sometimes the slaves were well treated. When she wrote to the Springs from the Pee Dee (Appendix, p. 171), however, she expressed in rather strong language her feelings about the unrighteousness of the institution, saying among other things: "God bless the good Master, and *God — damn* the bad one!"[5] In conversations with Southerners she told them that she belonged to the Abolitionist party.[6]

JOEL ROBERTS POINSETT

by

Fredrika Bremer

Fredrika-Bremer-Förbundet

When Fredrika's visit with the Poinsetts came to an end, she returned by boat to Charleston. Soon after her departure her host wrote to Mr. Gouverneur Kemble in Cold Spring, New York:

White house April 26, 1850

My dear Sir

The peaceful banks of the Peedee have been enlivened for a fortnight past by the presence of the fair swede Miss Bremer. I mean fair haired and fair skinned, for she is not at all pretty. She sent me a letter from Mr. Cottinet endorsed by Mr. Downing and as we would not descend from our perch we frankly told her so, and asked her to come here. A little to our surprise and greatly to our gratification she accepted the invitation and steamed up to the White house and yesterday I drove down with her to Georgetown where she embarked with a host of Idolaters on their way to worship at the shrine of the departed autocrat of South Carolina.[7] . . . But to return to Miss Bremer. I do not know who her associates were in Boston & New York; but either her preconceived notions of this country & government were very erroneous or she has been misled by impracticable minds. She sympathized with the poor Negroes, although obliged to confess that they were better fed & clothed than her Swedish peasantry and even better treated for the power of the Master over the labourer in Sweden is very great as long as the agreement between them lasts. He may & surely does beat the idle and careless workman and if the latter ventures to transgress Malthus' law so far as to have more than two children the family starve for his utmost exertions cannot maintain them. Here all who are married long enough have from five to ten. This year we are in a fair way to increase this description of taxable property full ten per cent. Seven women are strutting about in this interesting condition and as the rule is that during this period their work is so light as you would consider merely gentle exercise they are very proud & happy. Miss Bremer was greatly edified. She seems charmed with the blacks and asked them all sorts of questions. Unfortunately they could not understand each other very well. A circumstance she attributes to their want of education! She raves about one Emerson and read me some of his essays which I greatly shocked her by pronouncing exaggerated in style & thought. On the whole however we were much pleased with her visit and entertained with her talk. Thought & language are equally quaint & amusing. . . .[8]

Fredrika witnessed the funeral of John C. Calhoun; as mourners lined the streets, regiments of soldiers paraded by and banners waved aloft. The visitor was greatly impressed and she felt there must be many who did not share the prejudice her recent host had expressed to her against the departed. A few days later she left Charleston and traveled by steamboat to Savannah, Georgia. She went directly to Pulaski House and the next morning entrained for Macon, having been invited by Bishop Stephen Elliott to visit the Montpelier Female Institute outside the city. Professor Emmanuel V. Scherb, whom she had met at Emerson's home, conducted her to the school. The carriage ride was an uncomfortable one, "on roads of which hardly too much ill can be said, as well as of a government who leave[s] such breakneck things alone."[9] At the school, where English, French, Latin, music, drawing, and painting were taught, Fredrika was an interested spectator at some of the classes, and she felt compensated for the rough journey.

After the stay with the bishop and his family, she retraced her route to Macon and Savannah, where the local press reported her arrival. Invited to the home of Israel K. Tefft, she saw his famous autograph collection, which occupied a whole room in his house, but she said it would take six or seven months to examine it fully. (Two of her letters were to be added to Tefft's collection — Appendix, pp. 173 and 180.) While in Savannah Fredrika also visited an orphanage, probably the Bethesda Orphan Asylum, and two Baptist churches for Negroes.

Laden with gifts, she left presently aboard the *Oregon,* which sailed up the Savannah River to Augusta. The 250-mile journey past luxuriant, semitropical foliage appealed strongly to the artist in Fredrika. She was, however, disappointed not to see even one alligator in the course of the week-end trip, nor were the birds disposed to sing. In Augusta she was met by Mr. and Mrs. John Bones, whom she had known aboard the *Canada,* and was a guest in their home, as reported May 21 by the *Daily Chronicle & Sentinel.* Fredrika passed several pleasant days and she found time to visit some nearby plantations, also some poor whites called "clay eaters" who lived in the forest. A perverted appetite for clay turned their complexion gray and gradually destroyed them.

Fredrika heard the Negroes sing their spirituals and folk songs to banjo accompaniment; she liked the rhythm of their singing and welcomed every opportunity to listen. Among her favorite melodies were "Carry Me Back to Old Virginny" and young Stephen Foster's "O Susanna." Her memories of Augusta were happy, although the slave market appeared to her as a blemish on the fair state of Georgia. By the end of May the heat became somewhat oppressive and she decided to return to Charleston, via Columbia. May 23 found Fredrika in the state capital, a small, attractive city, and the *Tri-Weekly South Carolinian* informed its readers:

MISS BREMER. This distinguished literary lady arrived in town on Saturday evening, and is stopping at Hunt's United States Hotel. She has already received many calls from our citizens.[10]

Although her stay was brief, she met among others a well-known German, Professor Francis Lieber, who held the chair of history and political economy at South Carolina College; he had also been responsible for the first edition of the *Encyclopedia Americana.* Fredrika had a good knowledge of German, so they probably conversed in that language.

About this time Fredrika commented in a letter to Agathe that Columbia was remarkable for its great number of colonels, and that this American passion for titles did not seem in keeping with the aims and ideals of a democracy.

Returning once more to the Howland home, she stayed nearly three weeks, until June 15. At one social gathering she was introduced to the novelist William Gilmore Simms, whose love for the natural beauties of the South she shared, but whose proslavery views she opposed. (Simms was in his early forties and numbered among his published works: *The Yemassee, The Partisan,* and *Southern Passages and Pictures.*) Fredrika went to a ball given for some five hundred people by William Aiken, former governor of the state, and the lovely Mrs. Aiken. The profusion of flowers, the crinolined "southern belles," and the music helped to make this affair one of the most beautiful she attended during her American visit.

It was with reluctance that she bade farewell to the Howlands, but she was to see these friends again and to correspond with them in the months and years to come. A poem appeared in the Charleston *Courier* just before Fredrika left which paid tribute to her books:

[For the *Courier*]

To Miss Frederica Bremer

Authoress of *Home* and *Neighbors*

"Home" had attractions, long ere thou didst write;
    "Neighbors" were kind before thy face we knew;
'Twas left for you to give each more delight,
    "Neighbors" and "Home" are best when shar'd with you.
Your Swedish "Home" we long desir'd to see,
    Your "Neighbors" too we all had hoped to know;
Where'er you go, mansions that welcome thee,
    With "Home" and "Neighbors," love and friendship glow.
Expand the circle of your generous faith,
    A faith to virtue and to peace so dear;
Teach every "Home" to gather round its hearth,
    Whate'er humanity with friends may share:
As a bright landscape, glowing on the sight,
Leaves on the heart for aye its living light;
So shall a "Home" be found, where'er you stray,
A "Neighbor" still, however far away.

                                  B. F. P.[11]

Philadelphia and Washington

Fredrika took the boat for Philadelphia June 15, a guest of the steamship company. When the *Osprey* docked, Professor Hart was on hand to meet the much-traveled Fredrika and to take her to his home — as reported by *Cummings' Evening Telegraphic Bulletin*:

Among the passengers in the *Osprey*, which arrived this morning from Charleston, was Frederika Bremer, the Swedish authoress. There are thousands, who will read this announcement, who have long loved this estimable woman for the excellent sentiments her writings inculcate; and who will now learn, with pleasure, of her arrival among us. In the novels of Miss Bremer there is a purity and depth of feeling, which, apart from their merit as pictures of Swedish life, have made them cherished in all hearts chastened by religion or instructed by the experiences of life. Other novels, as a general rule, impair the moral tone, either by openly outraging it, or by a sickly sentimentality; but the fictions of Miss Bremer strengthen every good resolution, spiritualize the nature, and cultivate the best affections of the soul. We welcome her most cordially among us. Few strangers have ever visited us deserving of a more kindly reception, and by that we mean also a considerate one; for few have done so much good. We understand she is to be the guest of Professor Hart of the High School, editor of *Sartain's Magazine*.[12]

The *Public Ledger and Daily Transcript* announced Miss Bremer's coming in a somewhat shorter account and on June 19 the *North American and U. S. Gazette* said in part: "She will be welcomed heartily, and she deserves a generous reception from those to whom her writings have afforded profit and pleasure."[13] Responding to this publicity, Philadelphians called at the Hart home and it soon became necessary to issue a press notice:

MISS BREMER. — We are requested to state that Miss Bremer receives visitors only in the evening, being engaged all the day in visiting the various public institutions of the city. She will remain only this week, being on her way to Washington. She will return to this city in the autumn.[14]

Among the institutions Fredrika inspected were: Girard College for white orphan boys (founded 1848), the Sailors' Home, the Philadelphia Almshouse, the insane asylum, and a penitentiary. Some of these institutions were run by Quakers, and her admiration for the Friends grew as she observed their good deeds. Their simple way of life and worship appealed to her and she felt an affinity with their ideas, including the Inner Light belief, a guiding influence in their lives. Fredrika remarked: ". . . the more I see of the Quakers the better I like them."[15] She attended several of their meetings and heard a lecture by Lucretia Mott, advocate of women's rights, universal peace, and the abolition of slavery. Fredrika also dined with the Motts, their children and grandchildren, and later Mrs. Mott posed for her, wearing the traditional Quaker bonnet.

On Midsummer Day — always celebrated in Scandinavia — Fredrika made a special pilgrimage to Old Swedes' (Gloria Dei) Church, built in 1700. There she met some descendants of the early New Sweden families, according to an account by the Philadelphia correspondent of the Baltimore *Sun*:

LUCRETIA MOTT

by

Fredrika Bremer

Fredrika-Bremer-Förbundet

. . . Yesterday afternoon, in company with her host and Mrs. Sarah J. Hale, she paid a visit to the ancient Swedes church in Southwark, and was received by the Rev. Jehu C. Clay, the pastor of the congregation. By the request of Miss Bremer, many of the descendants of the Swedish settlers were assembled at the church, and had the pleasure of a personal introduction. Miss Bremer is contemplating a visit to Washington designing to return here in October.[16]

Fredrika read the Declaration of Independence at Independence Hall, and she laid a wreath on the grave of Benjamin Franklin, whose life and achievements she deeply admired. Of her visit she retained a host of favorable impressions and expressed regret at being unable to remain longer: ". . . it goes much against me to leave so soon the City of brotherly love, then I am perfectly charmed by the public institutions here, so grand, so good, so glorious to humanity and to the people whose work and mark they are. . ."[17] Fredrika said goodbye June 26 and she must have given Professor Hart permission to print the following poem, for it appeared in the July *Sartain's*:

The Man and the Rose
By Frederika Bremer.

The Man.

Thou art so fair, oh Rose, so pure and tender,
I am unmeet to touch thee, even to place
My lips endearingly anear thy beauty.
How, in this sinful world, cam'st thou so fair?
Guiltless of sin! ne'er shall a sinner's hand
Destroy thee for his own poor, transient pleasure;
No, live in joy; live to be loved, caressed
By dew and breeze, by sun and butterfly,
By all things fair and innocent as thou,
And blossom brightly in the eye of God.

The Rose.

Ah, freely pluck my bloom, oh Man, for thou
Art greater far, and better far than I;
Thou, of a truth, may'st suffer and may'st combat,
But 'tis that striving after the eternal,
Which to the great Eternal brings thee nearer
Amid eternity. For one brief hour
I brightly bloom, and then — wither and die,
And no ascending dawn awakes the dead.
Then, freely pluck! Rejoice in me, and let me
For one short hour delight thee and refresh thee,
And then in silence wither at thy feet.
If I have served thee, I have lived enough.

Great Nature's Genius heard the noble contest
And smiled; because she saw, in time to come,
(When the new heaven brings forth the fair, new earth),
That roses nurtured in the human heart
With it will pass into eternity,
And blossom there anew in Eden's groves,
A joy to man, well-pleasing unto God,
And lovelier than on earth — if that may be![18]

Fredrika proceeded to Washington, D. C., and stayed at the National Hotel, as the *Southern Press* and the *Republic* announced. President Zachary Taylor gave a reception June 29 on the White House lawn and on this occasion the Baltimore *Sun* chronicled:

Miss Bremer, the Swedish authoress, was among the visitors at the President's grounds, in Washington, last Saturday evening. She has as many followers in Washington as at the East, but her own knowledge of human nature, which is the same every where, teaches her to esteem such attentions at their true value. She is yet to take an extended journey to the Far West, it is said.[19]

She thought that President Taylor was kind and agreeable; however, to her womanly eye, Vice President Millard Fillmore looked more like a president than the former general of the Mexican War. Less than two weeks later Fillmore did, in fact, become chief executive and she witnessed the installation ceremony. The *Sun* had a further report:

Miss BREMER gave a "reception," at the National Hotel, Washington city, on the evening of the third, which was brilliantly attended by the elite of the metropolis, Senators, M.C.'s &c. She is now visiting in Prof. Johnson's family, in that city, and is much attended to.[20]

On July 4 the Washington *Daily National Intelligencer* conveyed the following news:

Among the visitors just now gracing the seat of government with their presence are several literary celebrities of the better sex. We fear to venture their names in company with the less interesting elements of news and politics; but there is one, a stranger from a far land, whose pen and whose virtues have shed lustre on her own country, and endeared her to the whole world of letters; we allude to Miss FREDERIKA BREMER, of Sweden, who arrived in the city a few days ago, and is still here; information which will, we know, be very interesting to many of our readers who are also hers.[21]

Fredrika visited the capital at a critical time in America's history. Dissension between the North and South over the extension of slavery in the territories divided the country; the conflict, destined to break into civil war a decade later, was already sharp and bitter. To Mrs. James Russell Lowell Fredrika wrote:

. . . Here dear Maria I am in the midst of the political strife shaking hands with Senators and representatives, list[e]ning to the speakers in the Capitol and hearing different opinions on all sides about the great golden kalf who of age was a creator of discord. Alas! Alas! When one is not in humour to laugh at the vanities of men one feels sad and sorry.[22]

She attended sessions of the Senate and House of Representatives, and listened to several eloquent speeches by Daniel Webster and Henry Clay. The latter, in a private conversation, inquired about King Oscar I of Sweden and his standing with the people. This question pleased Fredrika, who told Clay that the king was a good and noble-minded monarch, loved by the Swedes. She remarked: "By what the American statesman knew respecting him and our Swedish political affairs, I could see the glance of genius, which re-

New York Public Library

WASHINGTON, D. C., IN 1851

quires but little knowledge to enable it to perceive and comprehend much."[23]

Miss Bremer thought that Clay's Omnibus, or Compromise, Bill would pass. In August and September of 1850 five measures were enacted: Slave trade in the District of Columbia was abolished, California was admitted as a free state, a fugitive slave law went into effect, New Mexico and Utah were organized without prohibitions against slavery, and Texas was awarded a monetary settlement of its claims to adjoining territory. The Compromise lasted ten years, but gradually it intensified the friction between the slave and free states.

Fredrika met both Clay and Webster socially several times; she described the latter in these words:

. . . He has extraordinary eyes; when they open and fix their gaze upon you, you seem to look into a catacomb full of ancient wisdom; but not much of this comes out into every-day conversation and social life, and that depth lies deep enough in that magnificently-formed head.[24]

The senator from Massachusetts was then in his sixty-ninth year and his political opponent Clay in his seventy-fourth. Their long and distinguished careers were drawing to a close, but they were great Americans and it was a high-light of Fredrika's visit to meet them and listen to their speeches. Among the other senators she heard were: Thomas Hart Benton (Mo.), Salmon P. Chase and Thomas Corwin (Ohio), Stephen A. Douglas and James Shields (Ill.), Henry S. Foote (Miss.), Sam Houston (Texas), and William H. Seward (N. Y.). Some of the senators took Fredrika Bremer for afternoon drives; one day when Mr. Seward escorted her, he told her why he was an unwavering opponent of slavery.

Abraham Lincoln had finished his term as Representative from Illinois in March, 1849, and had resumed private law practice in Springfield. In *Swedish Immigrants in Lincoln's Time* Nels Hokanson observes:

Nor could Lincoln overlook entirely the Swedish population which drew attention from time to time. He was aware of the activities of Fredrika Bremer, Jenny Lind, and John Ericsson who were receiving favorable mention during the fifties in the American press.[25]

Fredrika visited the Library of Congress with Georgia's Senator John M. Berrien and while there she met Dorothea Dix, a vigorous worker in such causes as the improvement of prison conditions and the care of the mentally ill. Of her Fredrika said: "The activity and influence of this lady is one of the most beautiful traits of female citizenship in the New World."[26]

Also in Washington at the time was Anne Lynch, who introduced Fredrika to important people. On the Fourth of July they went to Mount Vernon, accompanied by Senator Corwin and Mr. Israel Andrews, an American consul in Canada. They carried a letter of introduction which Henry Clay had written and, at the home of the first president, a grandnephew of George Washington received them. Fredrika laid a green branch on Washington's tomb. In her book on America is an interesting comparison:

Washington has always appeared to me in life and character to have a resemblance to Gustavus Wasa; although his life was less romantic, and his character more phlegmatic, less impulsive, than the Swedish liberator. Wasa is a more dramatic, Washington a more epic figure; Wasa more of the hero, Washington more of the statesman; Wasa king, Washington president. Large, powerful, kingly souls were they, both worthy to be the governors of free people. Washington, perhaps, stands higher than Wasa, in his pure unselfishness, as the supreme head of the people.[27]

These were busy days but Fredrika did not forget her other friends nor lose sight of future visits she planned to make. She wrote to the Springs, urging them to accompany her and the Lowells to the White Mountains, New Hampshire, and to Niagara Falls (Appendix, p. 175). She mentioned her summer plans in a letter to Elizabeth Peabody, sister-in-law of Nathaniel Hawthorne.[28]

On July 9 Fredrika was sitting in the Senate, listening to Senator Butler of South Carolina, when Daniel Webster interrupted to announce that President Taylor was dying. The message stunned the entire audience. Following a public appearance on the Fourth of July, the president had suddenly been taken ill and he died the same day Webster made his announcement. Fredrika watched the funeral procession July 13, and she wrote to the Springs:

. . . The bells are tolling to day for the funeral of the good deceased President. I can't help looking upon his death as almost providential at this moment. It will proba[b]ly settle the great question about California etc. at once, according to Mr Clays compromise bill. Next week will probably be of stirring interest in Congress. Oh! my dear friends how much how much of interest and stirring life has not been and is within my grasp in this country! It seems that my mind is bending and labouring to widen to take it in all. But alas! —[29]

In September *Sartain's* published Fredrika's "Tribute to the Memory of General Taylor." She told of her two meetings with the president, at the White House garden reception and at another White House party, when the late president had entertained the ladies with stories about Indians. Her article was a warm eulogy of President Taylor, the man; one would not have suspected that, from a larger historical perspective, she regarded his death as "almost providential."

The same issue of *Sartain's* also contained a biographical essay by Anne Lynch on Fredrika Bremer, together with an engraved portrait of her made from the one by W. H. Furness, Jr. In praising the Bremer novels Miss Lynch compared them with the works of George Sand, Bulwer-Lytton, and Scott. She also said:

When it was announced, a few months since, that Fredrika Bremer had landed upon our shores, the intelligence was received by the thousands who have read her works, with an interest that admiration of literary talent or genius alone could never have inspired. More than almost any other writer, Miss Bremer seems to have become a personal friend to every reader, and the cause of this is to be found in a far deeper source than mere admiration for the novelty and vividness of her narratives, her quiet pictures of domestic life, or her strong delineations of the workings of human passion. Her large and sympathetic heart is attuned to such harmony with humanity, or rather she so expresses this beautiful harmony of her own soul with God, with nature, and with humanity, that the human heart that has suffered or enjoyed, vibrates and responds like a harp-string to the master-hand.[30]

A book of poems by Anne Lynch was reviewed during Fredrika's Washington stay. The *Daily National Intelligencer* of July 16 quoted one poem and added: "We select her lines to FREDERICA BREMER, whose presence among us is a source of sincerest satisfaction to the thousands of admiring friends in all our country; for who that has read her works (and who has not?) but feels that Miss Bremer is their own especial friend?"[31]

Fredrika also met Professor Joseph Henry, physicist and secretary-director of the Smithsonian Institution, which had been established in 1846. Another new acquaintance was Henry R. Schoolcraft, ethnologist and authority on American Indians. He had participated in or led explorations in the central part of the country and since 1822 had been Indian agent for the Great Lakes tribes. (His six-volume work on the Indians was published in 1851-1857 by Congress.) Fredrika looked at his curios, among them the small flutes which the Indian braves used in their courting. One of the paintings she received from Schoolcraft depicted a wooing scene, with the warrior outside the wigwam of his beloved, blowing on a flute.

Among the Americans who made a profound impression upon Fredrika was Horace Mann, then in Washington as Representative from Massachusetts. Speaking with the great educator, "a man of strong, immeasurable hope," she became a more fervent believer than ever in America's future. The impulse which Mann was giving to universal popular education could not fail to stimulate progress and take the country along the path to greatness. His was a heroic nature, she felt, and he inspired her with new courage. She saw in his countenance the "beam of genius" and later called him the "Education-man par excellance in the New World."[32]

Fredrika indeed met a galaxy of American stars, including such men as Asa Whitney, railroad engineer and inventor, and Henry C. Carey, the economist. She carried with her vivid memories of the capital, marred only by a slavepen located near the Senate.

Accompanied by Dorothea Dix, Fredrika traveled to Baltimore July 23 and the ladies were guests of General Steuart, whose home overlooked Chesapeake Bay. (The host had read Hans Christian Andersen's autobiography and was much moved by it, Fredrika wrote in a letter to the Danish storyteller.[33]) One evening when the two feminists were alone, Miss Dix told her Swedish friend the fascinating story of her life. Fredrika was deeply touched, and later she called Dorothea Dix a wonderful woman.

Leaving Miss Dix in Baltimore, Fredrika went by boat to Philadelphia, where she spent a few days in the home of Professor Hart and his family. While there she received two calls from a Finnish gentleman named August F. Soldan, who was on his way to assume a chemistry post at Harvard. A portrait of Fredrika hung in the Hart parlor and Soldan thought it a good resemblance, except that it showed no sign of the eyestrain caused by much reading, often by lamplight. The Finnish professor attended a party for Fredrika and he observed her while surrounded by admirers. He wrote in his diary: "It is wonderful to see, how she does not in the slightest become dizzy by all the incense-offering; she is and remains sincere through and through."[34] (Tr.)

A few days later Fredrika accompanied John and Amelia Hart to Cape May, the fashionable New Jersey summer resort. When she ventured into the ocean, Mr. Hart held her hand; it was the custom then for a gentleman to invite a lady to go in bathing, much as he asked her to dance. The scene was gay and colorful, with men, women, and children disporting themselves on the beach and in the water. They were attired in costumes of all colors, but Fredrika's brown woolen dress was not the same blouse-shaped, pantaloon style worn by the others. (The Bloomer costume was introduced in 1850, incidentally, but Fredrika considered it unfeminine and preferred dresses.)

Newspapers of the day reported that on July 19 Margaret Fuller Ossoli, together with her husband and small son, had drowned in a shipwreck off Fire Island, New York, as they were coming in from Europe. In a letter to the Lowells Fredrika commented:

. . . They are in the Spiritual world together, the real world, as the Swedenborgians say, and how happy that they were allowed to depart together, to be united in life and death! It is only the horror of the moment which causes us to shudder. These three long hours on the wreck — looking death in its horrid face![35]

Fredrika spent several weeks at Cape May and, as she prepared to leave, she wrote to Mrs. Downing: "And now ap[p]ro[a]ch-es my birthday, the time when every year I am as born anew to life."[36] She bade goodbye to the Harts on August 16 and the following day celebrated her forty-ninth birthday. About this time the Swedish visitor decided to prolong her stay in the United States. She felt that she could not leave without seeing the rapidly-growing midwestern territory, that great "land of promise," as she was later to call it. Returning to New York, Fredrika again met her good friends the Marcus Springs. With them she went bathing at Coney Island, which she described as solitary and having a wild charm.

En Route to Niagara Falls

At the end of August Fredrika left New York and with the Springs took a Hudson River steamboat to Castleton-on-Hudson, where they all debarked to visit the Shaker community in New Lebanon, New York. This religious sect had been introduced in America from England in 1774, and its first communal enterprise was established by Anne Lee in Mt. Lebanon. The group's real name was "The United Society of Believers in Christ's Second Appearing," but the members were called "Shakers" from the shaking movements which formed part of their worship. Fredrika was cordially received and had an interesting visit. The thriving community, then numbering between seven and eight hundred members, shared equally in the profits from livestock and agricultural products. A hard-working, peaceful group, it had ideals of celibacy which gradually diminished the number of Shakers. Miss Bremer was favorably impressed by the sincerity and industry of the sect.

Marcus and Rebecca took leave of Fredrika at Lebanon Wells. With James and Maria Lowell, who had joined her there, she continued her journey north to Albany, by steamboat and railroad. Three newspapers announced her arrival; this is the notice from the Albany *Evening Journal* of September 3: "Among the strangers of distinction in the City are FREDERIKA BREMER, the Swedish Novelist, and Judge Wayne, of the U. S. Supreme Court. Both lodge at Congress-Hall."[37] A heavy downpour hindered Fredrika in her sightseeing of the New York capital, much to her disappointment. She and the Lowells remained only one night, then proceeded to Utica through the Mohawk Valley. On September 8 she wrote to the Springs describing the journey:

. . . Next day, oh! what a treat it was to drive in the glorious sun and genial air through the beautiful valley of Mohawk, and follow the running river upwards. It was a day of thankgivings for me. I felt myself wrapped up in the cloak of your kindness, and my heart all warmed by it, was more alive than ever to that beauty and goodness in nature which mirrors that of Man, boath reflecting that of their source, their invisible creator.[38]

Fredrika and the Lowells made an excursion from Utica to Trenton Falls and spent a tranquil day admiring the beauties of nature. Next the travelers entrained for Rochester and passed "infant cities" — as Fredrika called them — such as Rome, Oneida, Syracuse, and Auburn. A fire broke out on the train, but they arrived safe at their destination. Rochester, a manufacturing city, was growing rapidly. It was also a center of antislavery agitation and the home of Frederick Douglass, a mulatto who had run away from Maryland. He worked for the abolitionist cause and edited the newspaper *North Star;* he also aided the "underground railroad" for fugitive slaves. Douglass had written his autobiography in 1845, *Narrative of the Life of Frederick Douglass, an American Slave.* In the Swedish edition of *Homes of the New World* Fredrika translated a few paragraphs from it. While in Rochester she wanted to meet Douglass, but he was ill and could not call on her. She went to his home, only to find that he was almost unable to speak because of a sore throat. Nevertheless, he expressed his bitter feelings about the evils and injustices of slavery.

Fredrika tried to reach her old friends Mr. and Mrs. George W. Lay. The former *chargé d'affaires* in Stockholm lived in the nearby town of Batavia, and she went to the Rochester telegraph office to send a message. Soon a reply came that the Lays were in New York, but that other members of the family would welcome her. Fredrika, incidentally, was delighted with Samuel Morse's new invention. The operator wired to Buffalo: "Miss Bremer is in the office," and the answer came at once: "The operator at Buffalo sends his compliments to Miss Bremer, and hopes she is pleased with the experiment."[39]

In Rochester at the time certain "spiritual manifestations" or "knockings" were being widely discussed, and Fredrika was induced to try to communicate with the spirit world. Her comments were scornful: "In the afternoon I went to hear the celebrated Rochester-knockings, spoke Swedish with the spirits, and became perfectly satisfied that the spirits are false spirit[s] or rather *no spirits at all,* and that the women who make the knockings are great rogues. But how they contrive to knock about I do not understand or even guess."[40]

The *Daily American* of September 7 announced the visit of Fredrika and the Lowells in Rochester:

FREDERIKA BREMER. — This popular and distinguished author-ess, arrived in this city on Thursday evening, and took rooms at the Eagle Hotel. She is travelling in company with the poet, James Russell Lowell, and Lady, of Cambridge, Mass. The party left for Niagara Falls in the steamer last evening.[41]

The ship sailed up the Niagara River to Niagara Falls, where the travelers took lodgings at Cataract House, uncrowded in September. In a letter to the Springs (Appendix, p. 177) Fredrika described her sensations on seeing the majestic waterfall. Like other tourists, she also viewed the falls from the Canadian side and took the *Maid of the Mist* boat ride. She went sightseeing in the vicinity and visited some Seneca Indians.

During the Niagara stay Fredrika gave James Russell Lowell a gold pen. Accompanying it was the following verse, which found its way into the September 17 issue of the Albany *Evening Journal*:

To James R. Lowell, with a Gold Pen.

A gold pen is a little thing —
But in thy poet hand
It will take life; it will take wing —
Become a magic wand,
More powerful, more wonderful,
Than Alchemy of old;
It can make minds all beautiful,
And change all things to gold.

Fredrika Bremer.

Niagara, Sept. 11, 1850.[42]

Later, in a letter from Cincinnati dated December 12, Miss Bremer mentioned the popularity of Lowell's poetry: "In Madison (Visconsin) in Galena, at St. Paul, etc I met with warm friends and admirers of James poetry, and I am glad to find in such always the best heads as well as hearts of the land."[43]

On the first of September Jenny Lind had arrived in New York City, where she received a tumultuous welcome. Fredrika Bremer anticipated how great the enthusiasm of Americans would be for Miss Lind and she hoped her friend would be able to withstand all the receptions. The suggestion had been made to Maria Lowell that she invite Jenny Lind to Cambridge; Mrs. Lowell said she would gladly do so, if Miss Lind wanted a place to rest, but it would be like inviting Niagara into her house. Fredrika Bremer had written a long article about Jenny Lind's life — published in *Sartain's*, June, 1850 — and it became especially timely upon Miss Lind's arrival. Widely quoted and reprinted, the article concluded:

. . . She is again to leave her native land to sing to a far remote people. She is expected this year in the United States of America, and her arrival is welcomed with a general feeling of joy. All have heard of her whose history we have now slightly shadowed out; — the expected guest, the poor little girl, of former days, the celebrated singer of now-a-days, the genial child of Nature and Art is — JENNY LIND![44]

Fredrika composed a song for a contest P. T. Barnum was conducting. The prize of $200.00 for lyrics to be sung by Miss Lind at her first concert in Castle Garden was won by Bayard Taylor for his "Greeting to America." Fredrika mentioned her song in a letter to the Springs (Appendix, p. 179) and again when she wrote from Chicago: "Do how you will with my little Jenny Lind-song, dear Marcus, but dont let it be printed."[45] Nevertheless, her "Greeting to America" was published in *Sartain's*, February, 1851:

Greeting to America
BY FREDRIKA BREMER.

O, LAND of promise, fair and free,
　　Earth's opening morning-glory,
Columbia, hail! Fame tells of thee
　　A short, but wondrous story.
From Vasa's land to Washington's,
The way is far, but freedom's songs
From land to land, o'er rolling sea,
　　Ring with true heroes' glory.

I see thy peaceful dwellings rise
　　O'er boundless territories;
I hear thy children good and wise,
　　Proclaim thy future glories,
That "blessed are the rich in peace,
The merciful!" they will increase,
So says the prophet, — they will rise
　　To rule earth's territories.

In gold and silver rich thou art,
　　Thy crops are great and growing;
But richer still I know thy heart,
　　Its treasures overflowing.

To the oppressed thou callest, Come!
To homeless ones thou giv'st a home,
To hopeless hearts a hopeful heart,
    To every growth a growing.
So mayst thou grow more strong and free,
    America, for ever,
A blessing to all peoples be,
    A blighted hope — O, never.
But may thy eagles farther fly,
With cries for light and liberty,
Till hearts and thoughts, as eagles free,
    Thy glory hail for ever.[46]

Meanwhile the Lowells accompanied Fredrika to Buffalo, but there had to leave her. The bustle of the Great Lakes port was confusing; she boarded the *Ocean* the same evening without having done much exploring. After a pleasant journey across Lake Erie she arrived the following day at Detroit. On this stage of her travels she was assisted by Judge Bond, an elderly gentleman who had called on her at Niagara with a letter of introduction from Mr. Ellsworth, American *chargé d'affaires* in Sweden. The judge had been a pioneer in the West, so he was an excellent cicerone. They proceeded to Ann Arbor and there Fredrika received callers. Later she and her new friend took the train across Michigan; Judge Bond left at Niles, his home town, and Fredrika found her way to Chicago.[47] Lake Michigan was crossed by steamer and it seems to have been a smooth and enjoyable passage to that "great unknown West" which drew her adventurous soul with an irresistible force.

Fredrika Bremer in the Midwest

The Chicago *Daily Journal* had informed its readers of Miss Bremer's stay in Albany and her departure from Detroit. On September 17 it reported:

FREDERIKA BREMER. — The owner of this name, one which has found a welcome and a home at many a fire-side, arrived in this city yesterday.

With what pleasant hours and pleasant thoughts is the name of this gifted daughter of dusky Norland, associated in the minds of thousands. Like that voiceful sister of hers, who is now charming the new world as she stands, singing entrance upon its threshold, Frederika Bremer has the gift of song in its noblest acceptation; for the musical flow of her musical thoughts, timed and tuned to a gentle spirit, will linger in memory, making sweet harmony there, long after the twin "daughters of music are brought low."

Even here, upon the hither shore of Lake Michigan, she will find that her thoughts have gone on before her, like the flowers from Eden, and throughout the whole west, her heart will be inditing the poet's line anew:

Be it ever so humble, it is everywhere home.[48]

Chicago was then a pioneer town (population 28,269) situated on the edge of the rolling prairies. Shortly after Fredrika's arrival her hosts, Mr. and Mrs. John H. Kinzie,[49] took her for a drive about eighteen miles outside the town. Her enthusiasm for the vast meadowland is expressed in a letter she wrote to the Springs (Appendix, p. 181): "The view of the prairies impressed me more than even Niagara."[50] Chicago itself, however, was swampy, smelly, and windy. Fredrika said in the same letter that it was one of the roughest cities she had seen in America, but that it had some most agreeable people.

In 1850 the future second city of America could not begin to compare in housing or comforts with the cities Fredrika had visited in the East, but the main streets had been recently planked and other public improvements were under way. Frame houses predominated and these were not especially attractive; it could not be imagined then that great buildings would one day rise upon the shores of Lake Michigan. People without vision prophesied obliteration for the struggling town, and perhaps a cholera epidemic or other disaster could have destroyed it.

In this "gateway to the West" Fredrika made new friends and set out upon her customary tour of the various institutions. The Chicago *Daily Democrat* reported September 24 that Miss Bremer had visited the public schools. She found that much emphasis was being placed upon education, and because of this she foresaw for Chicago not destruction but future progress. The press eulogized Fredrika:

BEAUTIFUL TRIBUTE. — We find in this morning's *Tribune,* an exquisite "offering" to Frederika Bremer, by "M. A. M.," whose reluctant fingers too rarely touch the harp of song.

We copy three stanzas of the poem:

Charmed hath my vision met each bright-hued limning
    Of Home and Fireside by thy pencil drawn, —
For love was there, whose beauty knew no dimning,
    And Faith, that brightened as the night came on.

Pale "NINA" smileth in her mournful beauty,
    As death comes onward, making hope secure,

And calm "SERENA," linked to home and duty,
    Goes on before me, whispering, "Endure!"
Clothed in the radiance of her self-denial,
    The loving "SISTER" moves amid her own —
I see the "ARTIST-MAIDEN" end her trial,
    And rise triumphant from the life-like stone.[51]

Fredrika did not meet Gustaf Unonius, for he had gone to New York to request funds from Jenny Lind for his Chicago church. She met his wife, however, and also the Johan Carl Fredrik Polycarpus von Schneidaus, other Swedish pioneers. The following lines are from a letter by Fredrika:

Chicago also is so full of Jenny Lind as a city so far remote from New-York well can be. All talk of her and read articles about her. The Swedish captain Mr Schneidau came yesterday with news and a portrait of her, in daguerreotype well executed but unfavorable as all daguerreotypes are to women. I shall be his victim to day, and I see in anticipation the coming forth of my nose in an exalted form. Then large noses are always made larger by the daguerreotype. But I must submit in good humour. The Swedes are not many here. I expect to meet more in and about Milwaukee where I am going soon.[52]

After a visit of twelve days Fredrika left Chicago September 25 by lake steamer for Milwaukee. A Swedish immigrant, Olof Gottfrid Lange, met her and took her to his home, where his wife cordially welcomed her. The Milwaukee *Daily Sentinel and Gazette* knew of her coming:

DISTINGUISHED ARRIVAL. — The world renowned authoress, MISS FREDERIKA BREMER, is expected here from Chicago this morning. She will sojourn with one of our Swedish fellow-citizens for a few days, and then make a journey into the interior to Pine Lake.[53]

The Milwaukee *Daily Free Democrat* announced her arrival and published September 27 an interview worth quoting in its entirety:

MISS FREDERIKA BREMER.

We have seen Miss Bremer, and, fresh from an interview with her, we sit down to write out our impressions.

Miss B. is small in stature, about forty years of age, we should judge, with nothing, at first sight, particularly interesting in her external appearance. Handsome, she is not. Those who go to see her for the charms of beauty alone, will go away disappointed. It is only in social conversation, when you commune with her finely organized and cultivated mind — when you see the mild beaming of her eye — the glow on her countenance — the lights that play upon her high, full brow — that you really see and appreciate the superiority of the woman above most of her sex.

The same characteristics that have made the *Home, Nina,* and *The President's Daughters* such universal favorites — a quiet, charming grace — a fine play of fancy — a heart warm with truth and goodness — she displays in her own person. Affable, apt, ready in conversation — with vast stores of information, few are better able to delight the sympathizing visitor. She rejoices in forming acquaintances with those who have read and loved her in her works, but who, four thousand miles away, little expected ever to behold the gifted authoress, face to face.

She has a fine, soft, sweet voice. She does not speak English fluently, but much broken. She exhibits a strong desire to become acquainted with the manners and forms of our people — though she retains, in all respects, the peculiarities of her loved "fader-land." — Upon her return to Sweden, she will write a book of her travels. It will be eagerly sought for by all who have seen and known her.

She says that to visit America — to see her countrymen and countrywomen here, and to ascertain if they live as well and as happily here as they did at home — has long been the object of her desires. She has now witnessed what she longed for, and as she beautifully expressed it, she found them as happy beneath the shade of the young and vigorous tree, as under the venerable, tall, and wide-sheltering pine of her Swedish home.

Her habits are simple, quiet and unostentatious. You feel as much at home in her company, and as much of a personal interest — aside from her celebrated character — in her, as if she were an acquaintance of years. In short, she is a noble, truthful, kind-hearted, talented woman. And these characteristics, aside from personal beauty, will invest any one with charms of a peculiar and lasting nature.

Miss Bremer feels a strong interest in the schools of our country, and Miss Beecher, with whom she had become acquainted in Chicago, had strongly enlisted her sympathies for the success of her designs of education. — The peculiarities of this system were a subject of conversation. She had some doubts of its entire success, but she liked it and had strong hopes of it.

Miss Bremer performs beautifully on the piano, and she played some ancient airs of her native country, that were of exceeding simplicity and tenderness. Connected with one of them, was a legend of olden times, which she related in a style exquisitely beautiful, and so much better than *Home,* that the interesting incidents were told with her own soft and sweetly modulated voice.

Withal, Miss Bremer is a wonderful woman. She seemed to us, even in our brief conversation, as one whose mission is to do good — one of those kind and active spirits, true and noble souls — whose genius has gained them renown — and the purity of whose character

— the truth, benevolence and goodness of whose lives are equal to, and worthy of their fame.[54]

This column was among the most laudatory printed about Fredrika Bremer during her American wanderings. The Milwaukee *Daily Sentinel and Gazette* also gave a firsthand account September 28 of some of her activities:

FREDERIKA BREMER. — The celebrated authoress of the *Home, Nina, The Neighbors*, &c., after an extensive tour through the United States, has reached our city, where she has been spending two or three days, at the house of one of our Swedish fellow citizens. Yesterday afternoon and last evening, Miss Bremer was the guest of our Mayor, and received calls from many of our people. A select party, by the invitation of the Mayor, met her at his house in the evening and were highly pleased with the genuine, unaffected simplicity of the guest of the occasion. — Though not conversing as yet with perfect command of our language, she was still abundantly able to interest, instruct, and amuse, by turns, those to whom she addressed herself, with the same good old-fashioned, home-feeling which is the charm of her published works.

She leaves our city to-day for the Swedish settlement near the Mississippi, surprised and gratified with the appearance of our growing city, but most of all gratified to find that her Swedish brothers and sisters who have cast their lot among us have found pleasant and happy "Homes" in the West.[55]

Milwaukee had great appeal for Fredrika and she tired herself sightseeing. At a large school for girls she made a speech in which she congratulated the pupils on being Americans. Through the efforts of Catharine Beecher, sister of Henry Ward Beecher and Harriet Beecher Stowe, reforms were being made in western schools for women. Concerning the common interest Catharine Beecher and Fredrika had in women's education it has been stated:

. . . While Miss Beecher was still visiting the Milwaukee Normal Institute and High School, Fredrika Bremer, the famous Swedish writer, came to the city. It is thought that she influenced Miss Beecher towards her national system of calisthenics, which later became a marked feature of the students' training.[56]

Fredrika's call at the girls' school and a comment on her speech are recorded in the *Daily Free Democrat* of October 17:

MISS BREMER — INCIDENTS AND VISITS. —

While Miss Bremer was in this city, she visited the Normal Institute for Young Ladies, and manifested a great interest in Miss Beecher's Educational enterprise. In a few remarks to the scholars, she reminded them of the superior advantages they possessed over those of any other country, and of their obligations to appreciate and improve them.

On entering a private dwelling she was asked to sit near the fire where some other ladies were seated, but replied, "No, no; you American ladies are very handsome, but you are too *white*. You sit down by a fire of your own making, and neglect the great fire that God has placed in the heavens, which would give you health and a better color."

She left this city, in company with Mr. O. G. Lange, and visited a Swedish settlement at Pine Lake, in Waukesha County, where she spent the Sabbath. She entered into all the sports and plays of her country, with all the zest of a school girl, and appearing, like herself, a truly happy, kind-hearted, though extraordinary woman. She expressed herself highly pleased with the people of Wisconsin, and remarked that her visit to Milwaukee and Pine Lake, had been the most pleasant of any she had made since she left Sweden.[57]

As indicated, Fredrika visited the settlement her countrymen had established at Pine Lake, about twenty miles away. Mr. Lange drove her there in his carriage on a Sunday and she received a warm welcome. The Swedes lived in log cabins built in the woods adjoining the small lake; only half a dozen families remained, however, for the soil was not fertile and the other settlers had moved away. Fredrika saw the farms round about and the deserted homes of Unonius and von Schneidau. The evening was enlivened with the singing of Swedish songs, dancing, and playing of games. Fredrika read aloud "The Pine Tree" by Hans Christian Andersen. Her feelings after her visit were eloquently expressed to the Springs (Appendix, p. 184). Later, in *Homes of the New World*, Fredrika told about Pine Lake and praised the beauty of the region. She prophesied: "A new Scandinavia shall one day bloom in the valley of the Mississippi in the great assembly of peoples there, . . ."[58] According to Unonius, however, she did not stress sufficiently the great hardships of pioneer life. He considered her account too "poetic" and in his memoirs contradicted it to some extent; he took exception, for example, to her intimation that some of these settlers had not chosen the best quality soil for their homesites.

After Pine Lake Fredrika's next stop was Watertown and there she learned that the Public Conveyance Company had provided her with free transit in Wisconsin. The Watertown hotel also made her its guest. She spent a pleasant evening with some Danes, and the very next day the indefatigable traveler set out via stagecoach for Madison. The road was bumpy; the carriage almost overturned and at times was partially submerged in water, but Fredrika reached her destination intact.

One advance publicity item in the Madison press — the *Wisconsin Argus* of October 1 — compared Fredrika Bremer with Jenny Lind:

> Miss FREDERIKA BREMER. — This amiable lady and accomplished authoress, we learn from the Milwaukee papers, will pass through our place in a day or two, on a trip to St. Pauls. We trust she will find it convenient to stop a short time, and take a look at the charming lake scenery of this section of the country. Her works have preceded her to this western region, and will often be met with in the rude cabins of the wilderness, a cherished literary treasure on the hearth-stones of the pioneers. Unlike her distinguished countrywoman, Jenny Lind, she comes with no sound of trumpets, but her talents have shed a fragrance more grateful and enduring than the warbling of the Nightingale; and her memory will be cherished long after the songs which now thrill the nerves of a portion of our people, shall have died away and been forgotten.[59]

On October 3 the *Wisconsin Express* announced that Miss Bremer was stopping at the U. S. Hotel in the village of Madison; two days later the *Wisconsin Democrat* said that her fame as an authoress was unknown to few in this country and that she had visited some Norwegian settlements in the Koshkonong section, about twenty miles from Madison. There she found that land had been cleared to make farms and build log cabins; the settlers had chosen good soil for their farms, and had built neat homes and two churches. Fredrika spoke to them in their native language, and she met two grandchildren of Bishop Johan Nordal Brun, the celebrated Norwegian poet and composer of hymns. She also obtained copies of a Madison newspaper published in Norwegian.

The *Wisconsin Statesman* of October 8 described her:

> FREDERIKA BREMER.
>
> This accomplished and charming female writer paid our village a visit, on her way to the Minnesota country — and for the past few days has been the guest of Mr. J. C. FAIRCHILD, where she has received numerous calls from our citizens. Miss BREMER is a lady somewhat advanced in years, but possesses the vigor and vivacity of youth. She takes a lively interest in all that relates to American institutions and manners, and during her sojourn in the United States and Territories will find abundant opportunities to form a correct idea of our peculiarities as a nation, as compared with those of the Old World.[60]

The *Wisconsin Argus* the same day praised her "electrical" nature:

MISS BREMER. — This distinguished authoress has been spending several days in our town, and many have availed themselves of the opportunity to make her acquaintance, and all agree that her manners in social intercourse, correspond with the simplicity and naturalness which characterize her writings. The facility with which she commands a choice selection of words, indicates a good knowledge of English, though her pronunciation betrays the want of early practice in speaking it. When interested in conversation, her countenance is animated and intellectual, and the romance of her nature darts forth like sparks of electricity from a highly charged battery.

During a brief interview with which we were favored, Miss Bremer spoke of the beauties of western scenery; — the woodlands, the openings, the lakes and the prairies, the latter of which seemed most to excite her admiration; — they looked so wild and free, and were so rich in beautiful flowers! But she lamented the absence of *mountains* to bound the prospect and afford a resting place for the eye, for which nothing else, she thought, could fully compensate. A lake was *beautiful,* but a mountain was *grand!* She spoke of the country as the ancient home of the Indians, and alluded to the wrongs they had suffered at the hands of the whites, but quickly added that she could readily overlook those wrongs in the Americans when she observed their many noble qualities, and especially the respect and kindness so universally bestowed upon women.

She left our village yesterday on her way to Galena, from whence she proceeds to Minnesota.[61]

Before leaving Madison Fredrika visited the University of Wisconsin, where Chancellor John H. Lathrop conducted her on a tour of the campus. Presently she continued her westward journey and arrived at Galena, Illinois, October 11. The *Weekly North-Western Gazette* was most complimentary:

MISS FREDERIKA BREMER.

This celebrated lady arrived in town on Friday from Chicago. She is on her way to visit Minnesota. Her fame has gone before her, and is interwoven with all the better, purer and finer sensibilities of the human heart. Fame like hers *is* fame.[62]

The Swedish visitor stayed several days and rested up after the rigorous stagecoach rides. She also had to wait for the steamboat *Nominee,* which was to take her up the Mississippi to St. Paul. It was October, a beautiful time of the year, and the river banks of Iowa, Wisconsin, and the Minnesota Territory were aflame with color. Aboard the *Nominee* Fredrika had the pleasure of conversing with the Representative to Washington of the Minnesota Territory, Henry H. Sibley, who was returning home with his family. He knew the Sioux Indians well from having lived among them and he told her about their customs. Some Indians were on the boat, and their villages dotted the shores of the Mississippi. On October 17 the *Nominee* reached St. Paul; the trip from Galena, first class with private stateroom and meals, had cost only $6.00, and the captain had been courtesy itself to Fredrika. She felt inspired to write Mrs. Lowell:

. . . And oh! Maria! that I could have had you with me on the upper Missis[s]ippi, from Galena to St. Paul, on the passage through the great scenery on its shores! It was a great treat to behold those high bluffs and natural ruins from the times when the Mammoths and Megatheriums walked the earth, and see the play of the clouds and sunbeams round them! And then the stillness, the solitude of those wast [vast] lands, inter[r]upted only by the flight of ducks and wild Geese, and by the log cabin here and there rising at the foot of the hills, with a little corn acre around it for a garden.[63]

When the steamboat docked, Governor and Mrs. Alexander Ramsey came aboard, and they invited Fredrika to stay at their home.[64] St. Paul was then a busy trading center with about 2,000 inhabitants, and many new houses were being built. The *Minnesota Pioneer* of October 17 said it was gratified to notice the arrival of the novelist, and the *Minnesota Chronicle and Register* mentioned her October 21:

The *Nominee* arrived at 4 P.M., with a large cargo and crowded with passengers, among others, Miss Frederica Bremer, the delightful Swedish writer, the authoress of *Nina, Home, The Neighbors*, &c. Our readers have frequently been favored with extracts from some of her writings, from which they will have learned her deep sympathy with every thing noble and beautiful. The following gem is a fine example of her style of clothing the useful and instructive in the garb of poetry:

"One fountain there is," says Miss Bremer, "whose deep vein has only just begun to throw up its silvery crops among mankind — a fountain which will allay the thirst of millions, and will give to those who drink from it peace and joy. — It is knowledge; the fountain of intellectual cultivation, which gives health to mankind, makes clear his vision, brings joy to his life, and breathes over his soul's destiny a deep repose. Go and drink therefrom, thou whom fortune has not favored, and thou wilt soon feel thyself rich! Thou mayest go forth into the world, and find thyself every where at home; thou canst cultivate thyself in thine own little chamber; thy friends are ever around thee, and carry on wise conversations with thee, while nature, antiquity, heaven are accessible to thee." . . .[65]

Governor and Mrs. Ramsey were gracious hosts and they made Fredrika's eight-day visit a memorable one. The governor kept a diary and his entries about her begin October 17:

. . . "*Nominee* in after dinner. Mr. Sibley and Miss Fredericka Bremer, the Swedish authoress on board. The latter a guest at our house." The next day: "With Miss Bremer took a drive up to the falls of St. Anthony. . . . Walked over to Mr. [John W.] North's residence on the Island. Miss Bremer remarked, as a characteristic of the Americans, they were gentle in manner, but had a great energy of purpose and will. They are less pleasing than the English." On October 20: "After dinner walked out with Miss Bremer over the bluff back of St. Paul. The day was warm, thermometer at 60 degrees, the atmosphere hazy, as is the case in Indian summer, and she was most delighted with the views around." Another visit was to the St. Peter's Indian agency and the Little Falls, as Minnehaha was then called. "Miss Bremer sketched the likeness of Moza Hota and Wauhpa, his wife. We visited the Indians in their tepees, which gave her much pleasure."[66]

Mrs. John North a few days later told her parents in a letter that Fredrika Bremer and the Ramseys had been her guests. Fredrika had played the piano well but had refused to sing, saying "I never sing, only to children, and to God in the church — the little ones, and the Great One are not critical."[67] Another of Fredrika's remarks was that she had found the mass of American people more intelligent than she had expected and was much pleased with them.

The Indians never failed to interest Fredrika and she went with Governor Ramsey and an interpreter to see one of their villages. She observed their living quarters, tasted their food, and asked the squaws whether their babies were *hoksidan* (boy) or *winona* (girl). These were the only Indian words she knew, so she had to rely on the interpreter for other questions. Occasionally she received gifts, like the white fur bag with beadwork which she brought back to Sweden. Some of Fredrika's more vivid impressions of Minnesota and the Indians are contained in her letter of October 28 to the Springs (Appendix, p. 182).

Fredrika's enthusiasm led her to say in *Homes of the New World* that this was just the country for a new Scandinavia.[68] Her report was widely circulated and played a part in causing emigrants to leave Sweden and Norway for America. Large numbers of Scandinavians settled in the midwestern section and, despite great difficulties, thrived. They cultivated the soil and tamed the wilderness. At the time Fredrika visited the Minnesota Territory some Swedes

GRAY IRON,

SIOUX INDIAN CHIEF

by

Fredrika Bremer

Fredrika-Bremer-Förbundet

and Norwegians were already there, but the great influx was yet to come. The immigrants' experiences were, of course, very different from Fredrika's. She came as a literary celebrity and distinguished visitor; she was warmly welcomed into the finest homes. Those who left their native land to seek their fortunes in the New World arrived as unknowns, unfamiliar with the English language, and usually very poor. Fredrika did not share the problems of the immigrants, but it cannot be said that she lacked understanding or sympathy. She could also envision the good life that lay ahead for them and their children in this promised land, if they survived initial hardships and dangers.

John H. Stevens in his recollections of Fredrika's visit to the future site of Minneapolis remarked: "Miss Bremer was perhaps among the first of her countrywomen who visited us; and it would seem that she has been a guardian-angel to her people in the city, for they have prospered in the new land of their adoption."[69] She made excursions from St. Paul, and on the way to Fort Snelling and Fountain Cave she saw the Little Falls. She said goodbye to the Ramseys October 25 and re-embarked on the *Nominee,* to travel down the Mississippi. The *Minnesota Pioneer* of the preceding day published a long editorial, expressing the desire to have her remain in America and especially in Minnesota:

FREDRIKA BREMER

Right glad, were we to learn, that Fredrika Bremer, whose portraitures of domestic life in Sweden, have been admired by all, who love a happy home, came up on the *Nominee*. Since she has been in this Stockholm of America, she has been the guest of Governor Ramsey. Though far away from her native land, she is not a stranger to us, for she is one of those individuals whom all lands love to claim, and whose birth place is soon forgotten, because her presence is felt every where. Her manners are natural and her expressions candid. Unlike those literary women, whom Byron hated, and called "Blue Stockings," she makes no display, and loves not to talk about her own productions, but desires to place herself, in the attitude of a learner. From a biographical sketch recently published in one of our magazines, we gather the following particulars of her history. She was born in Finland, but when a mere child, removed with her parents to Sweden. During the summer, her father resided in the country, but passed his winters with his family in the city of Stockholm. Her country residence is called Arsta. The house is built of stone, venerable with age, in sight of a meadow, where the great Gustavus, whose services in the cause of religion and civil freedom will not soon be forgotten, reviewed his army; and not far distant may be seen the dark waters of the Baltic. Her mother is still alive and dwells with her. Generous by nature and possessed of an ample fortune, many a poor man and woman in her neighborhood are ready to call her, blessed.

If our steamboats, railroads and hotel parlors were to contain more readers of *Home, Nina, The Neighbors,* and other productions of this sound-minded and pure-minded authoress, instead of the works of Eugene Sue and that Amazon, Sand, there would be less faithlessness, fewer broken hearts, and more happy firesides. While a perusal of the latter corrupts the soul as effectually as the Maelstrom wrecks the ship, the influence of the former is as soothing and as freshing, as walking upon the shores of one of the many lakes of her native land upon a moonlight summer's eve.

On last Sunday, she worshipped with the church of which the Rev. Mr. Neill, is minister.

Her reputation has brought her in contact with all classes and conditions of men, and therefore, it is not to her casual associations, but to her writings, that we must look for an index to her religious sentiments.

In her *Morning Watches,* she gives evidence that she has hopes that extend farther than this life, and that she has a reason for such hopes.

Right valiantly in that work does she battle against the German Strauss, and others of the rationalistic school, who would pare off all that was divine in the nature, or miraculous in the works of the God-man, our Blessed Redeemer. Says she speaking of Christ, "But this *man*, who so lives, so suffers, and so dies for the benefit of mankind, and even for my good, is he not more than God? Is he not in this work, a far higher and more noble being than the God, who sits calmly in his everlasting blessedness, while a sinful world under his feet sighs in darkness? And he its Creator, takes none of its burdens on himself, divides nothing of its suffering; touches not a finger to its salvation; he only sends another to bear and suffer; another to save and redress. What and who then is God? Is he a cold, heartless potentate? The beautiful life of the *mere man* Jesus, and his mournfully dark death makes not God more clear to me but darker."

We are sorry to learn that she leaves us today. If she did not so love Sweden with its dark pine forests and deep tranquil lakes, we would love to see her cast her lot with the people of America; more, with the people of Minnesota.[70]

The same issue of the *Minnesota Pioneer* reprinted Fredrika's poem to James Russell Lowell and her "Tribute to the Memory of General Taylor." The *Minnesota Chronicle and Register* recorded her departure and added: "Miss Bremer, by her kind cordiality and simplicity of manner, made many friends while here, and she has the best wishes of our community for health, happiness and prosperity."[71]

Fredrika sailed down the Mississippi to Galena, stopping there a few days, and the *Weekly North-Western Gazette* reported November 5 that she had returned from her trip north. She left again on the *Minnesota*, which docked briefly at Rock Island, Illinois. There she was met by some Swedes from Bishop Hill who asked her to come and visit their colony.[72] She declined for several reasons, but listened with interest to a report about the group. She said it numbered some seven or eight hundred; the colony had lost many of its members that summer in a cholera epidemic. Since the recent murder of the tyrannical leader, Eric Janson, the settlers were being governed by two men whom they had selected. Fredrika approved of the means the Swedes were taking to improve their economic condition; their principal error, she felt, was in continuing to have faith in the sinner Janson. She chose not to attend the trial of the slayer scheduled for the next morning. Instead she continued the river journey, and a Davenport, Iowa, newspaper printed this item November 7:

Miss Fredrika Bremer — This distinguished Swedish author-ess came down on the steamer *Minnesota* last Friday and dis-embarked at Rock Island, with the intention of visiting the colony of her country people located in Henry county. A friend who had the pleasure of a few minutes interview with her, describes her as a lady of medium height, rather masculine features, large nose and an eye beaming with intelligence. She speaks our language not fluently and when addressed upon the subject of the great West, declared that she had been very *hungry* (had a great desire) to see the West![73]

Later the steamboat was grounded on a shoal; the passengers had to debark and Fredrika crossed the Iowa prairie in a covered wagon. At Keokuk she boarded a ship for St. Louis. The *Intelligencer* of that city announced November 6:

Frederika Bremer. — This distinguished authoress is now sojourning at the Planters' House, and we trust she will receive from our citizens the consideration to which she is so eminently entitled.

Of all modern writers of fiction, we know not one, whose works are so true to nature and abound so much in genuine benevolence and kindly sympathies, as those of Miss Bremer. Her novels are all gems in their way. Unlike most works of fiction, they not only con-tain nothing that is hurtful to morality or inimical to the christian virtues, but they are replete with touching sentiments of piety and goodness, and present the most admirable pictures of peaceful, af-fectionate and virtuous domestic life. No one can read her books without feeling his heart expand, and his sympathies go forth with renewed vigor and warmth. None but a genuine, christian, loving, womanly heart, could have conjured up the scenes which are so beautifully described in her pages.

We hope she will be welcomed to St. Louis with a cordial hos-pitality which will cause her to remember it with a grateful feel-ing, when she returns to her distant home in the North.[74]

During her stay Fredrika visited several Catholic institutions and the German section of the city. After a few days at a hotel she moved to the home of Senator Thomas Allen, who lived in Crystal Springs, near St. Louis. On November 10 she wrote a letter to Mar-cus Spring, painting a word picture befitting a seeress:

. . . With what interest have I looked, from my rolling Cabin, on the river, out on the shores of Wisconsin, Iowa, Illinois, Missouri, on the great Valley of Mis[s]is[s]ippi, the future abode of millions of men, of the people of peoples! It is a broad vast country, immense views, not the country I should like for my home, but splendid in its way. And so are the views about St. Louis on a sunshiny day. The mind seem[s] to expand looking on them — will the human mind expand here, become larger and better? I ask so of heaven and earth — but their responses are rather oracular t. i. [that is] dark. We may long continue to pray: "thy Kingdom Come!"[75]

The novelist resumed her journey and it took six days on the *Asia* to reach Cincinnati, the "Queen of the West." At Cairo the ship turned northeast, going up the Ohio River. Fredrika's coming was awaited, according to a notice from the *Daily Cincinnati Gazette*: "Frederika Bremer is expected here on every St. Louis steamer. She was announced as leaving that city on the 13th inst. While here, we learn that she will be the guest of Charles Stetson, Esq."[76]

She stayed at the home of Mr. Stetson, the financier, and his wife for more than three weeks. A local newspaper of November 26 wrote: "Fredrika Bremer is quietly making daily excursions over the city."[77] She enjoyed strolling about, though sometimes she made a hasty retreat. It was slaughtering time, and when she encountered a herd of swine being driven through the streets on the way to the abattoir, she quickly changed her route. On the whole she had words of praise for the city. She celebrated her second Thanksgiving in America and attended a Baptist church service. The sermon dealt with a solution of the slavery problem proposed by the American Colonization Society. This organization had been founded in 1816 for the purpose of repatriating Negroes to Africa. The state of Ohio had purchased land in Liberia, which was then being colonized by former slaves; it had become a republic headed by a president. Fredrika's interest in the plan is revealed by a notice published in the *Daily Cincinnati Gazette* December 16, and by her letter to David Christy, Ohio agent of the Colonization Society:

MISS FREDERICKA BREMER AND AFRICAN COLONIZATION.

Messrs. Editors: — Miss Bremer, the distinguished Swedish authoress, at present in the city of Cincinnati, attended the public services in one of our churches on Thanksgiving Day. The pastor, in compliance with the request of the State Committee, introduced the subject of African Colonization, and pointed out its bearings upon the ultimate civilization and evangelization of the hundred and sixty millions of native Africans now sunk in the depths of heathenish barbarism. In supporting his position, the speaker drew liberally upon the statistics of the Colonization Lectures of Mr. Christy, the Agent for Ohio. At the close of the services, Miss Bremer waited upon the pastor, and expressed a wish to obtain a copy of Mr. C.'s lectures; stating that she supposed they would afford to her reliable statistics upon which great practical principles could be based.

This request was communicated to Mr. Christy, and he forwarded his three lectures to Miss Bremer, expressing, in a written note, his regret at not being able to call upon her on account of the severe illness of his eldest daughter, who was lying in the last stage of consumption. On receiving and reading the lectures, Miss Bremer addressed to Mr. C. the following note, which I take the liberty of making public, as an indication of the value which "the gifted Norse woman" attaches to the labors of our agent, and the great work in which the friends of Colonization are engaged.

A.

Cincinnati, 9th Dec., 1850.

My Dear Sir: — Receive my heartfelt thanks for your letter and lectures, and still more for your views and working in the question about emancipation and slavery! They are the first ones I have met, which inspired me — I mean, have made me feel inspired, glowing on the subject — and opened to me great views, great possibilities in the cause. They have made me truly delighted. — My nature is too averse to polemics, to have been able to sympathise or be warmed by the ultra abolitionists. But I adore the ideal, the perfect and true, and only from that central point can all relative points come out in their true light, true relations; and only from that point is any strong organizing power to be exercised. I congratulate you most sincerely on the view of the cause you have taken up, and the way you are working it out, and myself to be instructed by your writings.

May this great work be a comforter to you in the sorrows of your heart! May your young daughter pass away without bitter pains or pangs, and I will say with the old saying — which to me seems very true — "Those that the Gods love are taken away in their youth!"

Yours, very truly,
FREDERICKA BREMER.[78]

Fredrika's name appeared December 16 in the *Daily Cincinnati Gazette's* list of "Lions in Town," along with those of Governor Wood and Cassius M. Clay. The latter called on Miss Bremer; she also heard him give a lecture in which he denounced Daniel Webster for supporting the Fugitive Slave Bill. Clay — a distant relative of Henry Clay — had freed the slaves on his own plantation. He published his antislavery newspaper, *The True American,* in Cincinnati after his plant in Lexington, Kentucky, had been destroyed by a proslavery mob.

Fredrika recognized the need for a book exposing the evils of slavery. She longed to write the story of a fugitive pair herself, but realized that she lacked the necessary knowledge of the country. She said that an "American mother" should take up the subject, not knowing that Harriet Beecher Stowe, who had lived in Cincinnati 1832-1850, was soon to publish *Uncle Tom's Cabin*. Mrs. Stowe's book was first printed serially in the Washington *National Era*, beginning June, 1851, but it is unlikely that Fredrika started to read the novel while here.[79] These words in *Homes of the New World* seem pertinent:

I have heard histories of the flight of slaves which are full of the most intense interest, and I can not conceive why these incidents do not become the subjects of romances and novels in the literature of this country. I know no subject which could furnish opportunities for more heart-rending or more picturesque descriptions and scenes. The slaves, for example, who fly "the way of the North Star," as it is called, who know no other road to liberty than the road toward the North, who wander on by night when it shines, and conceal themselves by day in the deep forests, where sometimes gentle Friends (Quakers) carry out food to them, without which they would probably perish: this journey, with its dangers and its anticipations, its natural scenery and its nocturnal guiding star — what subjects are here for the pen of genius![80]

(Among the letters Mrs. Stowe received after the publication of *Uncle Tom's Cabin* in book form was one from Miss Bremer.)

In Cincinnati Fredrika found time to admire statues created by Hiram Powers; she mentioned particularly his "Greek Slave" and "Ginevra." She met Joseph R. Buchanan, writer and phrenologist, of whom she made a sketch. He was also a popular speaker and she attended one lecture of his on the activity of the brain and its relationship to free will.

Fredrika was, of course, asked for her autograph; one reads: Dear Sir!

In answer to your request for an Autograph I send the following translation of a Swedish proverb who is capable of beautiful application: "Listen to the murm'ring tree by whose root thy roof is fixed!"
Fredrika Bremer.[81]

On several other occasions she had written Swedish words, then the English translation:

"Gör rätt, gör väl i döden, det öfriga gör Gud."
Transl. "Do the best thou canst, and leave the rest to God!"
Fredrika Bremer.[82]

"Du skall glömma, Du skall glömmas!"
Transl. "Thou shallt forget, Thou shallt be forgotten!"
Fredrika Bremer.[83]

The following sentiments, each accompanied by her signature, are typical of those she often wrote for American friends: "Names are nothings / seek for real things!"[84] " 'The *shadow* of God *wanders* through nature,' but in the noble heart, in the happy home He steps in Himself and — *dwells*."[85] Another was: "*Iduna vare med dig!*"[86] ("May Iduna be with thee!")

Fredrika's outlook was constantly expanding; she said that what was transpiring in the valley of the Mississippi had given her much to think about. Some of her impressions are summed up in a letter of December 12 to Mrs. Lowell:

. . . As to the futurity of the human race, in this great Central valley of America, I have of it both a serious and a comic view. The latter one has been imparted to me by Mr Dewitt, an amiable man (who dined with you and James not long ago by Mr Longfellow). With him I look upon the Valley of Missis[s]ippi as the great Jotunheim[87] where the heroics and Comiks of old Thor and the Jotuns are still going on; and many a feature and many a fact, which else would be disagreeable and an[n]oying, is from that point of view amusing or c[h]arakteristic; and every day furnishes us with new anecdotes in that line. I was considerably annoyed on the steamboats of the Missis[s]ippi by some wifes and daughters of the Jotuns, who smoked their pipes, blew their noses in their fingers, and then asked me a hundred questions, particularly "how I liked America"; so that I had rather dark thoughts about the race they were perpetuating. But, I have also seen *Iduna* the goddess of eternal youth and goodness, among the sunflowers of the great West, and Baldur the Good build there with Freij and Freija — so that I see some hope that when the Jotuns and Jotunesses will be driven off into Utgaard (Nebraska) then may come the golden age, when the earth shall give crops without beeing laboured, the time when the lion shall lie down with the lamb, the eagle protect the dove, — (and I suppose — the Cat feed the rat) and all good men enjoy peace and joy unmolested under the clear sunny sky. Amen![88]

The "Mr. Dewitt" referred to was really Mrs. Longfellow's cousin Isaac Appleton Jewett. He happened to be reading Longfellow's translation of Snorre Sturluson's *Edda* when he met Fredrika in Cincinnati, hence the references to Norse mythology. She seemed to enjoy the comparison; the very "wild" West was to her Utgård, the home of the giants. Mammoth Cave in Kentucky was called "Skryme's glove," an allusion to the episode in Snorre's *Edda* when Thor mistook the giant's glove for a huge house.

Fredrika left Cincinnati December 16 on the *Belle Key*, with New Orleans her destination.[89] It was a long voyage on what she called "Noah's Ark"; aboard ship were more than a thousand head of livestock being sent for sale at the Christmas fair. In bleak December she saw Tennessee, Arkansas, and Mississippi; along the shoreline she noted the canebrake, cottonwood trees, and cotton fields. Fredrika went ashore at one point and picked some bolls of cotton, which she later took back to Sweden. On the *Belle Key* she made acquaintances; among them there was a handsome, middle-aged man who in her opinion resembled Sweden's Gustavus II Adolphus. She confided to her sister: "Yes, if I were younger, and if my life's purpose were less decided than it now is, I confess that there is here and there one of these American gentlemen, with their energy, their cordiality, and chivalric spirit, who might be dangerous to my heart."[90]

As the *Belle Key* passed Memphis, Vicksburg, and Natchez, Fredrika was intrigued by the constantly changing scenery. Presently Baton Rouge came into view and in the distance, on a height, stood the capitol of Louisiana. The Mississippi River widened, sandbanks and green islands appeared, and ships of many different kinds lay at anchor or sailed in the port of New Orleans.

Arrival in New Orleans

The *Belle Key* docked December 23 and Fredrika was glad to leave the "ark" with its bleating animals. She stopped first at the St. Charles Hotel, but her room happened to be small and cold, so she moved soon to a private boardinghouse overlooking Lafayette Square. Christmas Day the *Daily Picayune* listed Miss Bremer's name among the new guests at the St. Charles and the following day it "took pleasure in announcing" Fredrika Bremer's arrival.

At this festive season she felt homesick. She missed her family and the Swedish Yule celebration to which she was accustomed; she longed for the pine woods, for snow, sleighs, and the familiar church service at daybreak. Far away, among strangers, her thoughts turned to Årsta and Stockholm, and the Christmases of other years.

Printed in the correspondence column of the Natchez *Courier* and quoted in the New Orleans *Weekly Delta* of January 6, 1851, was the following droll episode:

Miss Bremer arrived in the city on Tuesday last. She is now staying at Mrs. Hurd's in Camp street, opposite Lafayette Square, but I believe that rooms are to be prepared for her at the St. Charles Hotel. Since she has been in our city she has been made the invol-

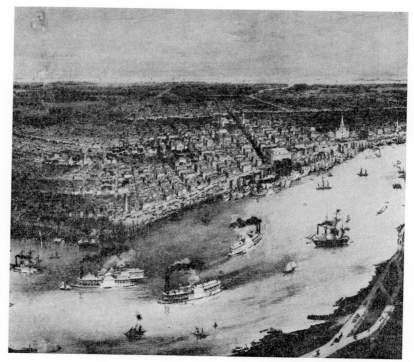

New York Public Library

NEW ORLEANS IN 1850

untary recipient of a large quantity of adulation and admiration, which had been kept bottled up for the occasion, by sundry ambitious literary ladies and gentlemen. A ludicrous scene occurred in the parlor of Mrs. Hurd's house two or three evenings ago. Miss Bremer had been sent for by a select company, composed of a physician and his wife, a blue stocking young lady, an inquisitive young man, and one or two matronly ladies, as spectators. The programme of reception was arranged beforehand with all due solemnity; the Doctor was to occupy one end of the sofa, and Mrs. Doctor the other end, whilst the centre was to be reserved for Miss Bremer. The inquisitive gentleman was appointed to a chair near the fireplace, and the young lady was to receive the Swedish lioness, and conduct her to her seat.

When everything was arranged, the performers took their places and awaited the awful moment in the most anxious suspense. At last Miss Bremer came; the young lady C. rushed forward, oversetting a chair in her haste, to lead the great authoress to the sofa, but the fallacy of human hopes, and the fallibility of human plans was vividly illustrated. Miss Bremer did not like the seat on the sofa; she preferred to sit near the window, and so she did — thus breaking up the nicely arranged programme. For a moment an awful silence prevailed, when Mrs. Doctor could restrain herself no longer, "Miss Bremer" she exclaimed, "we are all glad to see you; we love you; we adore you. You must visit our plantation in the country. You will there find friends who know you through your works, and dote on you. Here is a young lady who loves you, yes, worships you, she thinks of you night and day; she sleeps with you; she kisses you."

Miss Bremer could stand it no longer. She arose and presented her cheek to be kissed. The interesting young lady seized this opportunity to throw her arms around the neck of Miss Bremer, and to exclaim in passionate tones, how much she was loved. Mrs. Doctor followed suit, the other ladies imitated the example, and when I left, Miss B. was about to be overwhelmed by the affectionate embraces of five or six ladies and three ambitious gentlemen.[91]

A new series by Fredrika Bremer entitled "Northern Loves and Legends" began to appear in *Sartain's,* January, 1851. In the third "Fireside-Talk" she told of her travels to Niagara Falls and the Midwest. Her comments on America's wide expanses and future promise are as worthy of careful reading now as they were a hundred years ago:

THE PRAIRIES.

If you have seen the sun-embraced earth in one of those immense Western landscapes; — if you have seen the Prairie, in the great valley of the Mississippi, all covered with sunflowers, seen, during a clear autumn day, the sun rising over it, wooing it, as it were a bridegroom his bride, till evening came, and he sank down on the bed of sunflowers to the bosom of the well beloved, — have you not seen a vision of the marriage of heaven and earth, a glorious prophecy of that which is to come? . . .

And again I looked about me, saw the little homes and cottages of men rising over the fertile grounds, saw the schoolhouses for the education of all classes rising among them, and, in the schoolhouse (even the log cabin), schoolbooks that, though wanting in centrality, opened to the scholar (even the ragged one), a view over the whole world, and the choicest gems of literature, and I saw that a building was going on, of a great temple, a spiritual temple to the sun; I saw that America was laying the basis to a pyramid of dimensions the world has never before seen. And who will tell how high the top will rise, how near the heavens? Something earth must do, something heaven, to make the day come on when the two will be one. Be ye but as sunflowers, souls of men! Then of you will the millennial Church be built up.[92]

She went sightseeing in New Orleans, visiting the French market (which brought back memories of Paris), the Catholic Orphan Asylum, a hospital, prisons, and the French burial ground. She attended auctions at the slave market and indignantly watched human beings bought and sold. She sympathized with one pretty mulatto girl whose mouth was opened by a prospective buyer to observe the condition of her teeth and gums. The price of a strapping male was $2,000.00, a mother and child brought $700.00, and a young Negress $350.00. Fredrika deplored the cruelty of separating parents and children and the fate of slaves sold to brutal masters. To quote her: "No sermon, no anti-slavery oration could speak so powerfully against the institution of slavery as this slave-auction itself!"[93]

On the lighter side of life, she spent an evening at the theater, according to the New Orleans *Weekly Delta* of January 6:

AMERICAN THEATRE — MISS BREMER — *The Last of the Incas* is rapidly winning on the admiration of the playgoers, as was shown by the full attendance at the American last night. Among those present, we noticed the celebrated Swedish authoress, Miss Frederika Bremer, who is now sojourning in the city.

Miss Bremer is rather under than above the middle size. Her features are extremely plain, and already do they begin to exhibit traces of Care's unhallowed furrowings. Her nose is large, her eyes of a light grey color, and her hair of an auburn hue. The complexion generally is rather florid than otherwise, and the expression of the countenance, though indicative of great force of character, does not betoken that high intellectuality for which Miss Bremer has become distinguished.

Miss B. was dressed in the most plain and unostentatious manner imaginable. Her dress was of dark silk, her bonnet of white satin, trimmed with flowers, and her fan was a very unaristocratical combination of turkey feathers. Such is Miss Bremer, in reading whose works of fiction so many have been rendered oblivious of care.[94]

Fredrika took passage on the *Florida* that day across Lake Pontchartrain to Mobile, Alabama, as the steamship company's guest. Mrs. Octavia Walton Le Vert, the social leader who had invited her, was at the pier when the ship docked after the overnight run. Fredrika stayed at the home of Mrs. Walton, mother of Octavia Le Vert and widow of a former governor of Florida. Both mother and daughter introduced their Swedish guest to some of the best families; she later voiced her approval of the southern city:

"Beautiful quiet days! I like Mobile, and the people of Mobile, and the weather of Mobile, and every thing in Mobile; I flourish in Mobile."[95] While there, Fredrika attended the theater several times. She saw Julia Dean, a popular young American actress, in *Daughter of the Stars* and praised the performance in a letter of thanks to Joseph M. Field, director of the Mobile Theatre (Appendix, p. 188).

In the daytime Fredrika's artistic pursuits were not forgotten. Mrs. Le Vert and her mother posed for profile sketches, as did a mulatto maidservant and a Choctaw Indian couple. Glancing back a little, we might also note Fredrika's culinary interests.

In South Carolina she had learned to like bananas, though at first she said: "I could have fancied I was biting into soap. I have a notion that we shall not become good friends, the banana and I."[96] Later, however, she exclaimed, "Long live the banana!"[97] Fredrika tasted gumbo creole soup in New Orleans and this elicited another exclamation: ". . . gumbo is the crown of all the savory and remarkable soups in the world — a regular elixir of life of the substantial kind. He who has once eaten gumbo may look down disdainfully upon the most genuine turtle soup."[98]

This curiosity about the foods of other peoples almost landed her in difficulties, at least once. The story is told of Fredrika's walking one day through the Choctaw camp outside Mobile. She picked up the stick used to stir a pot of stew, when an old Indian fired such a stream of invective at her that she hastily retreated. He, of course, did not know she wished to compare his food with that of the Minnesota Indians.

The many-sided Fredrika enjoyed discussing with Octavia Le Vert such subjects as Christianity, Mormonism, transcendentalism, and literature. Incidentally, more than six years earlier (September 1, 1844) Mrs. Le Vert had commented on Miss Bremer's novels in her diary:

The writings of Bremer: How I love her writings! She displays to you the world in a pure and radiant light, exalts every thing that is noble, good, and generous in the human heart. One feels elevated in his own eyes after reading her descriptions. There is a tenderness, a consoling feeling in the mind as you read. A gentle sadness steals over you. If a deep grief is cradled in your heart, you feel lulled to rest by her simple and touching narrations. There is a religion so holy shining out from her pages that we must believe in its truth. In the afflictions of the excellent and good we see the type of this world everywhere. In the punishment of the guilty a soft pity springs up in the mind, tho we feel it is just. She never startles you with the reflections of your own thoughts as Bulwer, who often makes you feel as tho you had positively seen or felt before some scene or event he describes. It is like holding a magic mirror to our bosom and seeing therein reflected our own emotions. But it is like being soothed by the gentle fall of waters or by distant music or by the softness of moonlight. A quiet sweet feeling takes possession of the soul; it is also a melancholy feeling. We see the pure oppressed and suffering, and we feel such must be the lot of created beings; then the rays of joy play over the heart when we find the good rewarded. Her writings have one great object — the improvement of the heart and submission to the Divine Will. Much may be learnt in her works and in hours of affliction and gloom the mind recalls the gentle admonitions to pray and be content with whatsoever God shall give us.[99]

Soon the two women were fast friends and planned to travel together to Cuba, but the ship on which they sailed for New Orleans ran aground, hence they missed the *Pacific,* which left January 14 for Havana. Fredrika and Mrs. Le Vert took lodgings at the St. Charles Hotel. However, the former received an invitation to a private home and moved there the following day. On January 18 a fire broke out in the St. Charles, completely destroying the ornate building. It started near Mrs. Le Vert's room, but that morning she had left the hotel to visit Fredrika; she described the day's dramatic occurrence in her journal:

I quietly sat to Miss Bremer until she had completed the picture, and then drove down to the St. Charles, accompanied by a friend. When we were within six squares of the Hotel, we were compelled to leave the carriage. Mrs. E. endeavoured to persuade me to return home with her. But I said "no, no. If the St. Charles is doomed to ashes, I am resolved to be in at the death." We wended our way slowly through the crowd. Thousands and tens of thousands of persons filled the streets. When we neared the noble edifice, I looked at the magnificent dome. A deep black mass, like a funeral pall rested upon it. Soon a bright, serpent-like flame sprang through the cupola, high into the heavens. The cloud parted, and rolled away. The sun shone forth, and its beams lingered lovingly upon the glittering dome. As I gazed upon it, there came a crash such as ears have rarely heard. The dome had fallen! Then arose a wild wail of sorrow, from the multitude (numbering more than 50,000 persons). Above the terrific crash was heard this cry of despair. Thus in early day was destroyed this graceful dome![100]

By the time Fredrika arrived at the fire the dome of the St. Charles had fallen and flames were enveloping the beautiful

OCTAVIA LE VERT

by

Fredrika Bremer

Uppsala University Library

colonnades; soon the hotel lay in ashes. Only two days later the Swedish visitor was amazed to read in the *Daily Picayune* of a meeting that night to be attended by citizens and former stockholders interested in rebuilding the famous landmark.

Fredrika, of course, visited churches and various institutions in the "Crescent City"; her tour of the schools was reported January 27 in the New Orleans *Weekly Delta*:

Miss Fredrika Bremer's Visit to the Public Schools.

This distinguished authoress was invited by the Board of Directors of the Schools of the Second Municipality, to visit the places of education under their charge. Miss Bremer notified Recorder Caldwell that it would be agreeable yesterday to pay the intended visit. Mr. Caldwell, owing to continued indisposition, was unable to pay his personal respects, but he appointed a committee from the Board, composed of Messrs. R. M. Carter and Wm. Monaghan, to introduce Miss Bremer to the Schools. In company with these gentlemen she visited the Young Ladies' High School, the Washington, and Fiske Schools. The time allotted for the visit prevented her examining the other Schools. She appeared pleased and delighted with the condition and order of the Schools — the singing exercises elicited the warmest commendation. The high range of studies pursued in the Young Ladies' High School, and the interesting and intelligent appearance of the pupils, could not fail to excite approbation. The Washington and Fiske Schools were in perfect order, and showed good scholars and good teachers. It was to be regretted that the engagements of Miss Bremer prevented a more extended visit, so as to embrace all the Schools. The library was visited, and at the suggestion of Mr. Monaghan, Miss B. left her autograph. They ought to keep a book of autographs here.[101]

This rapid visit clearly disproved the assertion that the Schools were disorganized; but, on the contrary, all was industry, order, and regularity.

Miss Bremer also visited the principal rooms of the Municipal Hall. In the Hall of the Council she found much to interest her, in the portraits of the eminent statesmen and patriots which adorn that room.[102]

Mrs. Le Vert decided, after all, not to accompany Fredrika to Cuba and returned to Mobile. Before Fredrika left New Orleans she received letters from the Downings, Lowells, and Springs, who were following her travels with keen interest.

CHAPTER IV

Visit to Cuba and Last Months in America*

Impressions of Havana and Meeting with Jenny Lind

FREDRIKA LEFT NEW ORLEANS on January 28, 1851, aboard the *Philadelphia* bound for Havana. She made the usual shipboard acquaintances; among the passengers were a number of men, including two Swedes, going to California (via Panama) to prospect for gold. On the third day the beautiful Havana harbor came into view with Morro Castle silhouetted against the sky. Fredrika, standing on deck as the ship drew closer, gazed upon the panorama before her. The distant palm trees and pastel-colored houses lent an air of tropical splendor to the scene.

Before the passengers could disembark, a delay occurred because one of the leaders in the Narciso López revolutionary expeditions, Colonel White, happened to be on board. He was on the way to California, and the Spanish military officials (Cuba then belonged to Spain) made sure that he did not leave the ship. Afterwards some gentlemen assisted Fredrika ashore and through the customs.

One of the first things she did upon arriving at a hotel was to write a note to Jenny Lind. The singer had given four concerts in Havana but was to leave soon for New Orleans. The Swedish ladies had not met since they were in Stockholm several years previously. That very evening they had a memorable reunion[1] — Fredrika described it later in a letter to the Springs:

Yes, dear Marcus, I met Jenny Lind, here, and hardly did I hear her voice, and see her radiant, beaming face turned up to me (I was going up stairs, to my room, she stood below) than all former clouds and unpleasant impressions were shere [sheer] forgotten /I saw her only in her beauty, in her peculiar loveliness,/ and I must directly

---

The notes to Chapter IV begin on page 309.

Brady-Handy Collection, Library of Congress
JENNY LIND

stoop down to kiss her. She was charming to me the days we passed here together and lately I have heard from my sister in Sweden of some beautiful charities that she is doing there, even during her stay and working here. Still Marcus, she is the last person on earth that *I* would ap[p]ly to for any thing like a favor.[2]

Fredrika had been one of the first to forecast Jenny Lind's success, but strained relations had resulted when Fredrika did not remain neutral in a matter involving Miss Lind and the Adolf Lindblads. The young singer lived for over three years in the home of her teacher, the eminent composer Adolf Lindblad. In 1843 Jenny

Lind, then twenty-two, left for personal reasons[3] and went on a concert tour in Finland. She evidently feared that the friendship between her and her instructor would develop to the point of breaking up his marriage. Fredrika was a good friend of the Lindblads and, in fact, she said in a letter dated October, 1844: "That the enchantress and tormentress J. L. is gone is a blessed thing for them."[4] (Tr.)

When Fredrika Bremer and Jenny Lind met in Havana the past seemed to have been forgotten and a cordial friendship was quickly established. No doubt the two women were homesick, and this helped to heal the breach. Miss Lind wrote: "I met Fröken Bremer at Havana . . . and my heart was refreshed by interesting talk, and drew ever sweet and bitter memories from my country, always so *dearly, dearly* loved; and from my early life so full of inner struggles."[5]

Fredrika wanted to hear details of Jenny Lind's triumphant tour of the United States, but the singer preferred to talk of Scandinavia and their mutual friends, among them Hans Christian Andersen and the late Erik Gustaf Geijer. They may also have discussed Jenny Lind's meeting with Longfellow in Boston, September 28, 1850. Fredrika had written him a letter of introduction to the singer, and an accompanying note said: "As I cannot have the pleasure of seeing you again this fall, as I had hoped, I send here the letter of introduction to Jenny Lind that you wished for, though I do not think that the Poet Longfellow needs annother introduction than the mentioning of his name."[6] After hearing Jenny Lind's first concert in Boston the poet had called upon the singer and spent an hour with her.

Perhaps the "Swedish Nightingale" did not tell about it, but Fredrika would have enjoyed hearing of the tribute paid Miss Lind by the Swedish Society of New York. The forty-eight members of this organization, founded in 1836 and still in existence, visited Jenny Lind at her hotel October 31, 1850. The secretary, William Scherman, greeted her in her native tongue and in his speech mentioned other Swedes who were an outstanding credit to their homeland, among them Miss Bremer:

. . . Through her writings of genius Miss Frederika Bremer had made our pleasant life and wonderful felicity known, but all this, however great and excellent, seems to be far exceeded by the effect

Miss Lind's fame, conduct, and song have had on the American people. . .[7] (Tr.)

From time to time during her travels Fredrika told her American friends about Jenny Lind's glorious voice, which she could well do because she had heard her at the Stockholm Opera House many times. Fredrika had been present when Miss Lind made her debut in 1838 as Agatha in *Der Freischütz*. She had also mentioned "the captivating Jenny Lind" in *The Home* (1839).

When both met in Havana, the gifted singer was thirty years old and at the height of her career. Fredrika wrote her sister that she believed Jenny Lind was rather tired of the strenuous tour, and that they had discussed marriage and domestic life. Fredrika thought it likely that her friend contemplated a change, but doubted whether marriage would be sufficient to fill her life. The following year, in Boston, Jenny Lind was to marry her accompanist Otto Goldschmidt, a talented conductor and composer. Fredrika did not meet Goldschmidt, but she referred to him in a letter to Hans Christian Andersen after her return to Europe:

Jenny Lind I met in Havana, where she was infinitely kind and friendly to me. Under the Cuban palms we spoke only about Sweden and cried over the friends we had lost, over the sorrows in our homeland. In our tears we drew close to one another; closer than ever before; at least I felt so. Her nature became clearer and more understandable than previously. It was also clear to me that she was tired of the life she led and wished to withdraw herself from it to the tranquility of private life; and I had reason to believe that a man who was then with her (not Goldschmidt; he was not along then) would be the one chosen to lead her there. But it happened otherwise. However it may have happened — may she be happy! She is entitled to it because through her beneficence she has made thousands happy, and in her choice she has not followed worldly considerations (titles and names of the highest reputation were available to her), nothing else but the free choice of her heart. Religious enthusiasm may even have been a factor, for she in all probability influenced G.'s conversion to Christianity. He was a Jew (as you probably know) but was baptized two hours before he was married to her. He is supposed to be several years younger than J. but is said to be a fine and gifted young man, and from a good respectable family, in addition well-to-do. In America she has everywhere been a credit to Sweden, and has done much good, infinitely much good, here as elsewhere, often in the finest and most amiable way.

She spoke heartily and gaily about you, as of a very good friend; and we agreed on that topic as on almost all subjects we discussed during those three days. For only three days were we together. During them I saw her often and we visited together some of the beautiful gardens under the tropical sky. Jenny Lind introduced me to the nature of the tropics.[8] (Tr.)

At a dinner party Fredrika met P. T. Barnum, his daughter, the singer Giovanni Belletti, and other members of the company. More than a week before Fredrika's arrival Jenny Lind had given her final Havana concert, a charity event, but she sang privately for Fredrika a Swedish song by Adolf Lindblad.

Paseo de Isabel II, Habana, Cuba

HAVANA IN 1851

The two ladies took long drives in Havana along avenues lined with palm trees and flowers, and dotted with fountains and statues. All too soon it was time for Jenny Lind to leave and continue her tour; Fredrika saw her off, February 5. Aboard the *Falcon* she gave her friend a bouquet of roses and, as Fredrika returned to shore, Jenny Lind stood at the railing and waved.

About a year before the Havana meeting a song had been dedicated to Miss Lind entitled "The Dream":

I dream, I dream of my Fatherland,
As fancy my slumber beguiles,
Where the spell of beauty each heart enthralls,
Where the home of my childhood smiles.
Ah yes! I dream of wealth and pow'r,
The wildest of visions could will.
But I wake to the truth in affliction's hour,

Of the heart that loves me still.
/ :I dream, I dream of my Fatherland,
I dream of my Fatherland.:/⁹

The arrangement was by Karl Müller, and the song had a second
stanza. The sheet claimed "Words by Frederica Bremer," but this
was very strange. She did not write the words and, in fact, disliked
them, as indicated by this passage written in Brooklyn, March, 1850:

. . . I also heard here a song, with which, to my shame I say it,
I have been greeted two or three times in this country, because the
words, in which I can not discover a grain of sense or connection,
have been dedicated [ascribed] to me (they begin, "I dream, I
dream of my fatherland"), and the music to — Jenny Lind! *C'est
imprimée!*¹⁰

FREDRIKA BREMER

AND AN AGAVE PLANT

by

Fredrika Bremer

Uppsala University Library

Jenny Lind's departure from Cuba and the sale of the furnish-
ings in the house she had rented were announced in the leading
newspaper, *Diario de la Marina*. Fredrika's activities in Havana were
not reported during her sojourn, for she led a quiet life. Presently

she left her hotel to stay in turn with several private families, both in Havana and in the nearby towns of Serro, San Antonio de los Baños,[11] Guanabacoa, and Matanzas. From Matanzas she wrote to the Springs, February 20 (Appendix, p. 189), and she mentioned her visit to the Valley of Yumurí. Fredrika sketched this valley and many tropical flowers, trees, and birds, filling about thirty pages of her album. She said that she arose early in the morning to go on her sketching jaunts, for then she was less likely to attract the curious.

Fredrika appears to have done a good deal of letter-writing, as well as sketching. A paragraph from a letter to Dorothea Dix indulges in somewhat idealistic fancy:

"ST. AMELIA ESTATE, CUBA, *March* 17, 1851.

"If I had rule on earth, Cuba — this beautiful Antille — should be transformed into a great Maison de Santé, a home for the sickly and feeble. There they should sit in their rocking-chairs under the palms and the tamarinds, and breathe the delightful air of this island (which I cannot think was better in Paradise), be caressed by the soft, loving breeze, and drink in it, as in Olympian nectar, new health, new life. And you should be the queen here, and have a cabinet of ladies, kind and beautiful, such as I know several in the United States, who should chiefly officiate as nurses for the sick, as noble Valkyrias and healing goddesses for those slain or wounded in the battle of life."[12]

The Cuban breeze made a lasting impression. Some months afterward, on August 2, while vacationing at Nahant, Massachusetts, Longfellow wrote in his journal:

Miss Bremer is here, staying with Mrs. Bryant. We called in the evening and there she is, the same bland, quiet little woman, after her long travels by sea and land. What she remembers with most delight is the breeze of the tropics! "Ah that breeze! that breeze!" such is the burden of her song.[13]

During her stay in Cuba "la señorita Bremer" learned some Spanish words, and a Spanish grammar is preserved among her books in Stockholm. She met a number of English and French people while there; she also knew the Swedish-Norwegian consul, so she could manage without knowing much Spanish. In her letters she interpolated Spanish words and explained what they meant. Fredrika sent a long letter to Caroline Amalie of Denmark in April describing conditions in the United States and Cuba. The existence of slavery and the slave trade with Africa were Cuba's "night," the natural beauty of the tropics was its "day." The letter is printed in

Homes of the New World, which devotes 220 pages to the "Queen of the Antilles." Fredrika says that Cuba has much to offer; she gives reasons why the philosopher, poet, artist, and statesman, as well as the aged, weak, and suffering should go there.[14] More of her vivid impressions appear in her letter of April 9 to the Springs (Appendix, p. 191). Elsewhere Fredrika told of enjoying Cuban music and the dancing of the Negroes to the beat of drums.[15] She especially liked the rhythmic dancing of a slave named Carlos Congo and made a colorful sketch of him.

The vacation benefited Fredrika; her American friends said on her return that she looked healthier and younger. She remained longer than she had expected in Cuba, "a heavenly oasis between the two hemispheres." Later she wrote in a letter: "North America made me better understand the real earth but Cuba made me better understand heaven."[16] She spent Easter in Havana, where the ostentatious religious processions evoked her strong disapproval; at the end of a personal letter to the Springs, never intended for publication, she made some adverse comments (Appendix, top of p. 193).

Departure from Cuba and Visit to Florida

The American steamer *Isabel* left Havana for Charleston May 9, 1851, with Fredrika on board. From a passenger list in the Savannah *Daily Republican* of May 12, it seems that a stop was made at Key West: "Per steam-ship *Isabel,* from Havana and Key West . . . Mrs. Cail and son, Miss Frederika Bremer, . . ."[17] On May 11 the author arrived in Charleston, but this time stayed only a day with the Howlands.

Two of Fredrika's friends, members of the McIntosh family, were going to travel to Florida that month. Fredrika and Mrs. Howland decided to make the trip with them and both ladies went to Savannah on May 12. There Colonel W. J. McIntosh, his daughter, and Dorothea Dix joined them. Fredrika's spirits are reflected in this passage:

The weather is glorious, the moon is at the full, and I am full of the desire for traveling, and the desire to see Florida, the flower of the Southern States, the land of which the delicious balmy odors made the Spaniards believe that the fountain of eternal youth was hidden there. And now — thither, thither, to taste its nectar![18]

The group of five boarded the *Magnolia* and sailed for Jacksonville, but on the way the ship went aground. The mishap, caused by an inexperienced pilot, delayed them more than two days. One steamer they had hoped would help just ignored them, but on May 18 the *St. Matthew* picked up the disgruntled passengers and brought them south to Palatka. A lady aboard the *Magnolia* was so provoked over the conduct of the captain who had passed them by that she drew up a "declaration of indignation." With Fredrika's signature it appeared in the *Florida Republican.*

FLORIDA MONTAGE

by

Fredrika Bremer

Uppsala University Library

The journey on the St. Johns River aboard the *St. Matthew* reminded Fredrika of her trip up the Savannah River to Augusta the preceding year. She drew a landscape called "Florida, St. John (Welaka)," the latter word being the river's Indian name. The sketch is quite unique; the upper part of the tropical scene is dominated by a tree laden with Spanish moss, and at the lower part is thick vegetation. A snake curls in the foreground, an alligator and a turtle swim in the river. Fredrika also described the scene to the Springs in prose that bordered on poetry (Appendix, p. 193).

The group continued to Lake Monroe but could not journey farther inland by boat. They returned north to Jacksonville, stopping overnight in a hotel; the *Florida Republican* announced May 22:

Among the arrivals at this place on Sunday last, are Miss Frederika Bremer, the admired Swedish authoress, and Miss Dix, our countrywoman, who has won for herself a noble reputation by her efforts towards the amelioration of the condition of the insane. These strangers make a short visit to this portion of Florida, and are at present guests at the retreat of one of the principal planters in our vicinity.[19]

Another newspaper commented: "Miss Bremer and Miss Dix are in Florida. Both are tireless in pursuing their object, the one in searching out the condition of the prisons, hospitals and poor houses; the other, to see all that is beautiful in animate and inanimate nature."[20]

Dorothea Dix went on alone to St. Augustine, and the rest of the party accepted an invitation from a relative of the McIntoshes to the Ortega plantation. Fredrika spent a few days there and later visited the Cooper plantation in Darien, Georgia. From there she returned to Charleston, where she stayed in Mrs. Howland's home for the last time. Before leaving on June 12 Fredrika gave her hostess a guest book in which she had written: "From a good home it is not far to heaven."[21]

Another Charleston lady, Mrs. John E. Holbrook, accompanied her to North Carolina, where they took the train to Richmond. Fredrika remained in the Virginia capital for several days, while Mrs. Holbrook traveled to Saratoga, New York. The Richmond *Enquirer* of June 17 announced: "Miss Frederika Bremer, the distinguished Swedish authoress, reached Richmond from the South on Saturday, and took lodgings at the American Hotel."[22] She wrote to Mrs. Howland:

17 June. I am now battling — all in love — with my good friends in Richmond that will not let me have peace. Their friendly good will is gratifying to my heart though I can accept but little of its courtesies. — Yesterday I passed the evening, very agreeably, with some very pleasing German friends; and will pass this evening with some American ones. It is now so cold here that it is a wonder and — a shame, cold and vindy and dusty. Still Old Virgin[n]y looks

green and friendly, and I hope to enjoy her natural beauties with very friendly feelings towards her.[23]

Last Months in America

Next on Fredrika's itinerary was Charlottesville, Virginia. She had been invited by Maximilian Schele De Vere, a Swede who had emigrated in 1843 and was teaching modern languages at the University of Virginia. Professor and Mrs. De Vere showed their guest around the campus and also took her to see Thomas Jefferson's Monticello. Fredrika knew Professor De Vere from Sweden, where he had called upon her at Årsta. Much later he described her activities in Charlottesville:

. . . near the window, on a smaller stand, were carefully laid out drawing papers and colors, and a little rough but faithful sketch of the beautiful view from the window gave evidence of the indefatigable industry of the new occupant. For she knew no rest. Now she would saunter out to fill her portfolio with outlines of the rich mountain scenery with which that region abounds, from the gentle swelling hill to the loftier height of Jefferson's chateau-like home on Monticello Mountain, and thence higher yet to the soft but imposing outline of the Blue Ridge, which closes the horizon. In these wanderings she met no one, young or old, black or white, but she would give him a friendly greeting, and, if not actually repelled by timidity or haughty reserve, enter into a lively chat full of intelligent questions and kindly words of interest and sympathy. As soon as she returned, the sketches were arranged, some left for a future day, and others to be filled up at once; then the diary for her sister's use was carefully written up, notes were made for the book that was to pay the expenses of her journey, and then only she would come down to us in the sitting room, as fresh and ready to hear or to speak as if she had but just begun her day's work.[24]

During her stay with the De Veres Fredrika took a carriage ride through the Blue Ridge Mountains. When she visited the grottoes at Weyer's Cave near Staunton, Virginia, she was the only tourist and spent two hours looking at the rock formations. It seems that she also visited the Western State Hospital for the Insane at Staunton. The inmates occasionally wandered off by themselves, and after Fredrika left the institution she was somehow mistaken for one of them. Professor De Vere narrated the rest of the episode:

. . . So the poor lady had to trudge back to town, a prisoner once more, and escorted by two sturdy men, who watched her peaceful blue eyes as if they expected a fearful explosion at every moment, and who bore their stout cudgels with an air as if their prisoner, little over four feet high, might suddenly acquire a giant's strength and endanger their precious lives.

Her second entrance into the pleasant town, if not as stately as the first, was surely not less ludicrous, and a sketch in her portfolio, representing her as she appeared, thus accompanied, before the authorities of the asylum, is worthy of a page in Punch. Of course explanations were given to the worthy but suspicious countrymen. Apologies were offered with that courtesy which is characteristic of the people, and nobody laughed more heartily at the whole adventure than Miss Bremer herself.[25]

Fredrika attended commencement ceremonies at the University of Virginia. She liked especially an address in which a young student protested the injustice of slavery and showed, with historical examples, how it degraded both master and slave. After Fredrika said goodbye to Professor and Mrs. De Vere two days later, she returned to Richmond and spent some additional days visiting the city's institutions.

She made excursions to Baltimore and then to Harpers Ferry, where she remained three days. Fredrika received a marriage proposal from a young Irishman named Jim, who earnestly sought to attach himself to her; aside from that she had a tranquil stay.

She traveled by rail and boat to Philadelphia, where she was the guest of a Quaker couple, Mr. and Mrs. Elisha Townsend. Although the July heat bothered her, Fredrika accomplished a good deal during her week's visit. For one thing she revisited the School of Design for Women.[26] Located the previous year in the home of its founder, Mrs. Sarah Peter, the school now had its own building. Fredrika thought it excellent that young ladies could receive instruction in drawing, painting, designing, and lithography, and she praised the school.

Fredrika also went to the Female Medical College of Pennsylvania which, founded only the year before, had an enrollment of some seventy students. While there she heard about Dr. Elizabeth Blackwell, the first woman to become a doctor of medicine in the United States, having received her degree in 1849. Fredrika was very much interested in the young physician's career and struggles; she saw great possibilities in the opening of the medical profession to women and felt that the college was a credit to the New World.

About July 21 Fredrika left Philadelphia. Mr. Townsend accompanied her to New York, where she had a short visit with her friends Marcus and Rebecca Spring before continuing to Boston and Concord. It was her earnest desire to see Emerson once more, so she journeyed to New England and found her way to his home. In her book on America Fredrika relates that he drove her to a little forest lake and then to see his mother, who was confined to her bed with a broken leg. During their ride she asked Emerson if he considered the New England culture had reached its acme, but he did not think so; a number of foreign ideas were then being introduced and these would produce new developments. Fredrika felt again the energizing power of his mind. When he gave her a glass of pure water from a forest spring, she compared it with all that was refreshing, crystal clear, and invigorating in his nature and writings. She would never see his equal again; when she was old and gray she would still yearn toward Emerson and want to receive from him a draught of cold spring water.

In Concord Fredrika saw several other friends, including a younger sister of Margaret Fuller, Mrs. Ellen Channing, wife of the poet Ellery Channing. Fredrika thought Mrs. Channing had aged much after the tragic drowning of her brilliant sister. Fredrika also made an excursion to West Newton with Elizabeth Peabody to see the Normal School established by Horace Mann. She spoke with the educator and his wife, Mary Peabody Mann, in their home.

At Nahant, a seaside resort outside of Boston, she was a guest of Mrs. William Cullen Bryant and was also introduced to the historian William H. Prescott. She saw Longfellow for the last time and put additional touches on her sketch of him. Before leaving Nahant Fredrika sent a note to Mrs. Marianne Silsbee, whose invitation to Salem she accepted (Appendix, p. 198). The trip went well and from Salem the Swedish author wrote to Marcus Spring August 5:

. . . I am extremely well dear Marcus, keeping bravely up with a good deal of fighting with society and other pleasant but fatiguing things, beeing sometimes in three different places many miles distant from one annother, in one day, talking with different persons on different subjects from 7 oclock in the morning till eleven or twelfe oclock at night. But every body is good to me and every thing turns out well and pleasant in the [long] run. And so I am now to run to the white mountains with one of the most pleasing witsches of Salem Mrs Marianne Silsbee (at whose home I now am) and her son to care for us on the way. It could not be better to my taste. . . .[27]

Fredrika visited the Shakers at Canterbury, New Hampshire, and received a good impression of the well-ordered community, with its dairy, weaving room, school, kitchen, and "medical" garden. She compared this Shaker settlement with the one in New Lebanon she had previously seen. When it was time to leave, Shaker sisters escorted Fredrika and Mrs. Silsbee to the railroad station, and they took the train to the shore of Lake Winnepesaukee. They crossed the lake by boat, admiring the view of the White Mountains and especially Mt. Washington.

CATHARINE M. SEDGWICK

Engraving of Sketch

by

Fredrika Bremer

Harvard College Library

The ladies continued their journey by wagon, seated on buffalo hides, and stopped at Franconia Notch, New Hampshire, before traveling to Burlington, Vermont. There they were guests for several days in the home of a Mr. Wheeler. The house overlooked Lake Champlain, and it was in this setting that Fredrika reached her fiftieth birthday on August 17, 1851. It is a Swedish custom to make much of this milestone, but Fredrika seems not to have recorded any special celebration.

The ladies went on to visit Saratoga Springs, New York. Rainy weather had somewhat spoiled the season, but Fredrika attended a fashionable ball; during her short stay she met some old acquaintances and made new ones. She and Mrs. Silsbee continued to Lenox in western Massachusetts, where the American lady left for Salem and Fredrika spent a day with Catharine Sedgwick. She also visited Nathaniel and Sophia Hawthorne at their cottage nestled in the Berkshires, and came upon a happy family scene. An air of domestic tranquility pervaded the little red house. Baby Rose was nursing and Sophia beamed upon her child and husband, whom she deeply loved. She called him the best of husbands and seemed to read "his very soul."

NATHANIEL HAWTHORNE

Engraved from painting by
C. G. Thompson

Conversationally Fredrika did not get on well with her diffident host. Nathaniel Hawthorne caught about one in ten of his guest's words and could not reply with any confidence that he had understood. Later Emmanuel V. Scherb wrote in a letter to Longfellow

that Fredrika had described her conversation with Hawthorne thus:
" 'Sere vas nossing bot seelence. I never met sush seel-e-n-c-e.' "[28]
She elaborated on the occasion:

. . . I had to talk by myself, and at length became quite dejected,
and felt I know not how. Nevertheless, Hawthorne was evidently
kind, and wished to make me comfortable — but we could not get
on together in conversation. It was, however, a pleasure to me to see
his beautiful, significant, though not perfectly harmonious head.
The forehead is capacious and serene as the arch of heaven, and a
thick mass of soft dark brown hair beautifully clustered around it;
the fine, deep-set eyes glance from beneath well-arched eyebrows
like the dark but clear lakes of the neighborhood, lying in the sombre
bosom of mountain and forest; the nose is refined and regular in
form; the smile, like that of the sun smiling over the summer woods;
nevertheless, it has a bitter expression. The whole upper part of the
countenance is classically beautiful, but the lower part does not
perfectly correspond, and is deficient in decided character.[29]

Hawthorne was then forty-seven years old and *The Scarlet
Letter,* published in 1850, had brought him renown. Fredrika had
not yet read it, but previously, in Boston, Charles Sumner had read
to her Hawthorne's short story "The Great Stone Face," which
she called a poem in prose. He wrote *The House of the Seven Gables*
at Lenox and it had come out early in 1851.

Fredrika returned to New York. Once again she set out to see
more of the city's institutions and to learn as much as possible about
the life of the metropolis. She had earlier asked Andrew J. Downing
to take her to the notorious slum section known as "Five Points," but
he had refused. Ugliness had no appeal for him, a lover of beauty.
She went with Mrs. Abby Gibbons, daughter of the Quaker Isaac
Hopper who had helped more than a thousand slaves to escape.
Fredrika declared that she did not see anything worse at "Five
Points" than she had seen before in Paris, London, or Stockholm.

The two women also visited several institutions on Randalls
Island and the Tombs prison. Fredrika had some criticisms to make
of prison conditions, and even thought that some of the jailers themselves should have been behind bars. On the other hand, when she
found an establishment that was especially well run, like the Bloomingdale Asylum, she was quick to praise it. She mentioned the
flowers, the library, and the music that was heard in many of the
rooms. The methods employed in the treatment of mental disease
at Bloomingdale were to her enlightened steps forward.

Fredrika found time to pay a final visit, accompanied by Marcus Spring and William H. Channing, to the North American Phalanx. She noted that more buildings had been erected and that the membership had grown. The Reverend Channing conducted a discussion meeting on the social position of woman; that Sunday he spoke about the relationship between religion and the community. Fredrika remained three days in New Jersey and then returned to her Quaker friends in New York. Incidentally, she wanted to meet Horace Greeley, editor of the New York *Tribune*, and Peter Cooper, businessman, inventor, and philanthropist — but perhaps did not. A letter reveals her wish:

When I again shall be with you, I shall ask of you, dear Marcus, to give me the opportunity of conversing with Griley [Greeley] and with Mr Cooper of New York, (the Merchant). With them and you I long to steady my thoughts about the social formations and reformations going on, and must try to concentrate my ideas, clear away doubts, clear up questions! . . .[30]

Fredrika's American visit drew to a close in September of 1851. It was very difficult to say goodbye to the Downings, Springs, and other close friends she had made during her stay. As she wrote from the Downing home to Mrs. Howland September 7: "I leave you, I leave your land, with a sorrowful heart though I am glad to go home."[31] The Downings and Fredrika made an excursion to West Point to see the United States Military Academy; the New York *Herald* informed its readers that Miss Bremer was at West Point.[32] Upon returning to New York, she bade a fond farewell to Andrew Downing, her "young American brother," at the Astor House, where he had welcomed her two years before. As parting tokens he gave her Susan Fenimore Cooper's *Rural Hours* and also *American Scenery*, illustrated by William Henry Bartlett, and with text by Nathaniel Parker Willis.[33]

The press reported Fredrika Bremer's imminent departure — for instance, the New York *Morning Express* announced September 13: "For Europe. — The steamship *Atlantic* sails from this port to-day, for Liverpool. Among her passengers will be Miss Frederika Bremer, the well known Swedish authoress."[34]

Marcus Spring brought her to the ship, where admiring friends showered her with gifts and kisses. Fredrika's final moments in New York were indeed moving. As the *Atlantic* slowly left its Canal Street pier she gazed for the last time at the shores of America. Memories of the past two years, so rich and rewarding, doubtless came to her. The visit had been eventful, stimulating, and fruitful beyond anything she had imagined. Her expectations had for the most part been fulfilled, and she had seen with her own eyes much of the New World for which she had yearned. In a letter to her old friend John S. Hart the "Seeress of the Northland" exclaimed with feeling:

Whether I shall ever tell you and my American friends something more of that absorbing love-story of mine in America; — its joys and sorrows, expectations and disappointments, new hopes, new lights, its last visions, its last crop of evergreen hope and faith, — will depend on the Spirit that rules the mind of man, and on — circumstances that rest with the will of no man.

. . . .

Good bye, great Western world! world of promise, of hope, of boundless resources, of immense futurity! land of the setting sun, blessed with all the riches, the Hesperian fruits, of earth! — good bye for ever, for I shall see thee nevermore! But I thank God that I have seen thee!

As I saw thee last, — from the Atlantic, by the setting sun, — an immense crescent on the blue waters, opening its arms to the Eastern world, while glowing lights and purple shadows, melting by the horizon in the soft, warm colouring of the peach, — sunbeams and showers were descending over thee, — the sun, in setting, piercing through the clouds, as a great, godly eye making its way through the darkness, — so I see thee yet, so I know thee, so I love thee, so I bless thee![35]

Her letter was published in *Sartain's*, preceded by one from Professor Hart, who said of Fredrika: "Her mission to America, as often explained by herself, was to learn, rather than to teach; to gain, not to give; to enlarge her own soul by seeing a new people and a new state of society."[36] In October *Sartain's* published "A California for Women; Better than Silver and Gold" by Fredrika Bremer. The article praised the new opportunities open to American women, giving as examples the schools of design in Philadelphia and Boston. She believed that widened horizons for her sex were of far greater importance and future significance than the material riches of California:

American women have in the realm of nature a field more vast than any other women on earth. From the Atlantic to the Pacific, from the Arctic zone to the tropics, what a variety of climates, of products of the soil, of plants and animals; what richness in forms, characters, colours, embraced by the United States!

In that variety, is opened an unbounded field to American art and inventions. And we expect to see the pine and the elm of the North, the palmetto and the live-oak of the South, the stately corn, the richly-coloured leaves, the numberless vines, flowers, and fruits of the different States, and THE VINE running through them all, from Minnesota to Louisiana, from New Hampshire to Florida, enlacing them, as it were, all in one bond of love and beauty, reminding at once of the name given to the land by the Scandinavian sea-kings, the good old name, Vine-land, — and of the promise of the Scripture for the promised land, that there, "Every man shall sit under his own vine tree"; . . .[37]

Nor did Fredrika neglect the male sex. Four days after her departure from America the Hartford *Daily Courant* published a revelatory statement on husbands, probably never intended for publication:

FREDERIKA BREMER ON MARRIED MEN.

I confess, then, that I never find, and never have found a man more loveable, more captivating, than when he is a married man: that is to say, a good married man. A man is never so handsome, never so perfect, in my eyes, as when he is married — as when he is a husband, and the father of a family — supporting in his manly arms wife and children, and the whole domestic circle, which in his entrance into the married state, closed around him, and constitute a part of his home and his world. He is not merely ennobled by this position, but he is actually beautified by it. Then he appears to me as the crown of creation, and it is only such a man as this who is dangerous to me, and with whom I am inclined to fall in love. But then propriety forbids it. And Moses, and all the European legislators declare it to be sinful, and all married women would consider it a sacred duty to stone me. Nevertheless I cannot prevent the thing. It is so and cannot be otherwise; and my only hope of appeasing those who are excited against me is in my further confession, that no love affects me so pleasantly; the contemplation of no happiness makes me so happy, as that between married people. It seems to me that I, living unmarried, or mateless, have with that happiness little to do — but it is so, and it always was so.[38]

On her travels the author received presents from admirers in virtually every place she visited. In addition to the hospitality, flowers, and complimentary tickets freely bestowed upon her, Fredrika's gifts ranged from a gold nugget pin presented by a Californian, to a packet of chewing tobacco given her in a Richmond tobacco factory. Books by American authors, Indian paintings, ivory figurines (from the Poinsetts), and such personal items as a beaded bag, a fan from "Fanny" (Frances) Osgood, to mention but a few, were among her American souvenirs. Fredrika brought home pine-cone sewing baskets from Georgia and orange-tree canes from Florida.

She wrote that during her two years in America she had experienced more than in an ordinary decade. She had hoped to make other trips, but these did not materialize. It is nonetheless remarkable that of the thirty-one states then in the Union Fredrika visited at least twenty-seven. She missed seeing California and Texas. Though she was invited to Maine and Rhode Island, she apparently did not go to either state. It was not necessary for her to cover every mile of the young republic in order to sense what Van Wyck Brooks has called the "national mood of self-realization." Fredrika was extremely receptive to the vital currents of the day and, in fact, found life here "overpowering."

Views on American Social Questions

Fredrika Bremer was a keen observer of the complex social scene in mid-nineteenth century America, and she took the country's problems to heart. Her fields of interest were broad, encompassing slavery, women's rights and education, and all aspects of human betterment. She might be called a pioneer sociologist. She spent a total of approximately ten months in the South and Cuba, during which she studied the problem of slavery. Before her first trip south, however, she had spent nearly half a year in New York and New England. There Fredrika had come into contact with a great many people holding strong antislavery sentiments: Henry Ward Beecher, William H. Channing, Maria and James Russell Lowell, Theodore Parker, and Wendell Phillips, to name only a few. It was natural that her opinions should be somewhat influenced by them, but Fredrika did not become an extreme abolitionist. She had this to say of William Lloyd Garrison:

Speaking with him, I told him candidly that I thought the extravagance in the proceedings of the Abolitionists, their want of moderation, and the violent tone of their attacks could not benefit, but rather must damage their cause. He replied, with good temper, "We must demand the whole loaf, if we would hope to get one half of it!"[39]

While in the South Fredrika observed that there were good and bad masters, contented and extremely unhappy slaves. Sometimes she was a guest in homes where the colored servants were treated like members of the family. In these cases they might fare better than some free whites in the North, and Fredrika felt that she should report truthfully that not all Negroes were suffering under what she called the "baneful institution." However, she freely professed her antislavery views and protested against slave auctions. This did not satisfy the abolitionists; they wanted her to denounce slavery without any qualification whatever and to fulminate against it.[40] Even to hint that kind masters existed was treason. Later Fredrika was falsely accused of having betrayed the antislavery cause; Wendell Phillips went so far as to say publicly in 1852 that she had "half ignorantly" laid incense "on the demon altar of our land."[41]

One attempted solution of the problem was the African colonization plan, which Fredrika supported. The work of the American Colonization Society presented only a partial answer, however, for all the Negroes could not go to Liberia. For the rest Fredrika favored a gradual rather than an immediate emancipation. She felt that the slaves should first be prepared for freedom through education and Christian instruction. After her stay in Cuba she advocated for the United States a law similar to the one in force there. Cuban Negroes were permitted to purchase their freedom ($500.00 for an adult) and were given opportunities to earn wages. This idea is also expressed in a letter to Rebecca Spring: "Such a law combined with the workings of Christian preaching and teachings would ensure a gradual emancipation, prepare the slaves to free work and self control, and be the best safety valve and ventilator through whom that curse of your country could be removed. At least I believe so."[42]

Civil war was a horror which wise heads tried to avert. Fredrika suggested that a convention, or high tribunal, composed of the best men of the North and South, should meet to deliberate on the slavery question.[43] She felt also that Christian settlements of free Negroes could be formed, and that these should exist independently of the larger communities. Fredrika disagreed with Harriet Beecher Stowe as to the mode of emancipation. She thought the South should handle the problem alone, without northern interference, and in so doing would achieve unfading glory.

A second social question which had Fredrika's keen sympathy was the women's rights movement; indeed in her time she was the "unafraid apostle of human rights and women's freedom."[44] Her report on the American progress toward equality of the sexes is especially valuable.[45] Some male observers in the United States frowned upon this trend, Unonius among them. The first Women's Rights Convention took place in 1848, with others following annually, but it was not convenient for Fredrika to attend any of them. However, she rejoiced in the number of good women speakers for the cause and in the facts they made public. She was also glad that such men as Channing, Emerson, and Whittier sympathized with the movement and gave it their support.

While in America Fredrika associated with both men and women leaders. She heard Lucy Stone speak at an antislavery meeting in Boston; she knew Catharine Beecher, Paulina Wright Davis, Dr. Harriot Hunt, Lucretia Mott, and the Peabody sisters. From her contacts Fredrika formed a high opinion of the status of her sex in America. She felt women were permitted to become all that nature had intended them to be. She believed that even those who did not become wives and mothers could lead full lives in some other way; for instance, they could find self-expression in educational and philanthropic work. She wrote to Miss Howland in 1853: "It is a privilege of American women that they may more than the women of Europe take interest and part in the great general life of their land. Ah! if I was not a Swedish woman, how happy should I feel to be an American woman."[46]

In one conversation Fredrika affirmed the right of women to become soldiers, if they so chose. When she asked why they should not fight, Fanny Kemble held up the author's delicate fist and retorted: "Because of this!"[47]

An article later published in the *Monthly Religious Magazine* contains this interesting passage:

During her entire visit, she watched every thing that was done for and by woman. It has been claimed by some of Miss Bremer's friends, that she was not, in the ordinary sense of the word, a "woman's rights' woman"; — "she was feminine," they say, "and exerted her influence only through books." But Miss Bremer would have scorned such a defence: she very plainly told a lady, now well known as one of the foremost of those who demand the suffrage, but in 1850 somewhat undecided in regard to that point, that her labors would be useless, until she claimed the power of self-protection. "Do you think," she said, "that daughters would be as wretched as they are in Sweden, if women had the right of suffrage? No woman ever became a mother, without knowing that a woman, even more than a man, requires a certain freedom."[48]

Fredrika's attention was called to the Washingtonian Temperance Society (founded in Baltimore, 1840), which had gained considerable influence. Meetings were held throughout America at which reformed drinkers lectured to large crowds; often "the pledge" was taken in an atmosphere of religious fervor. While Fredrika was not a total abstainer — occasionally she liked a glass of wine with dinner — she sympathized with this organization's aims and favored curbing the misuse of alcohol.

Miss Bremer was, of course, greatly interested in the religious life of the United States and attended services in Baptist, Calvinist, Congregationalist, Lutheran, Trinitarian, Unitarian, and other churches. She genuinely admired the Quakers and went to some of their meetings. She studied the religious history of America, starting with Puritanism and including Mormonism, but did not think the New World would produce a perfect society: ". . . we must not expect a Utopia from America, but rather a day of judgment; and to no nation so much as to this does the admonishing word of Christ seem so applicable — 'Watch!' "[49] Looking upon the abundant, powerfully increasing life of the United States, Fredrika confessed that her heart was full of hope. She believed the country would remove the anomaly of slavery, and earnestly endeavor to realize the kingdom of Christ on earth.

She deplored some other conditions besides the existence of slavery. She protested the government's past treatment of the Indians, while granting that they were currently given more justice and consideration; for instance, land was purchased from them instead of confiscated.

Another criticism was leveled at the American pride in material possessions:

The aristocracy of wealth is the lowest and commonest possible. Pity is it that it is met with in the New World more than it ought to be. One can even, in walking through the streets, hear the expression, "He is worth so many dollars!" But the best people here despise such expressions.[50]

Fredrika was rather astonished at election campaign tactics; the rivalry between the Whigs and the Democrats was something she had never seen before:

. . . The nearer the day of election approaches, the stronger becomes the agitation, the more violent the cry, the personal abuse, and the threats. One might imagine that the torch of discord was about to be lighted in every city, that the Union was at the point of being torn to shreds, and that every citizen was in danger of being attacked by his neighbor.[51]

She wrote, however, that this type of electioneering could be regarded as a sort of safety valve. The Americans would, she hoped, try to obtain more stability in their government and extend the tenure of elected officials.

Fredrika Bremer formed a wealth of impressions of the American scene from October 4, 1849, to September 13, 1851. She sought to understand the true life and environment of the people. Did they thrive in their democracy? Were they happy, and did they have an opportunity to better themselves? Could they solve their problems? She had come "with a thousand questions" in her soul, and it is certain that she found answers to a great many.

With prophetic eyes Fredrika looked ahead. Optimistic about America's future, she felt that its vigorous people were destined to make remarkable progress. The great westward growth was predicted by her, and particularly the success of Scandinavian settlements in Minnesota, Wisconsin, and Illinois. Fredrika was happy to have made the long journey from Europe to see for herself how the young nation was taking shape, and the love that she acquired for America was deep and genuine. In the course of her extensive travels she gained knowledge that could be obtained only through personal experience. The New Orleans *Weekly Delta* had informed its readers: ". . . she will proceed to England, and thence to Sweden, after having performed the most wonderful tour for a woman, on record, and within a period of twenty-four months."[52] Not only this, but Miss Bremer left behind her a trail of good will; she was a credit to herself, to womankind, and to Scandinavia.

Following the ten-day voyage to Liverpool, Fredrika remained a while in England. Among the people she met there were George Eliot, Mrs. Elizabeth Gaskell, William and Mary Howitt, and Charles Kingsley. She was not informed until she reached Sweden early in November that her beloved sister Agathe had died on September 30. It was a bitter blow and made Fredrika's homecoming sad. In time work helped to alleviate her sorrow. Early the next year she wrote *England om hösten år 1851* (*England in the Autumn of the Year 1851*) and after that began to edit the letters she had written to Agathe and others during the American odyssey.

CHAPTER V

Later Contacts with America*

Publication and Reception
of "Hemmen i den nya verlden" in Europe

A T THE TIME Fredrika journeyed to America, she did not plan to write a book about her experiences. During two years of travel she communicated her impressions in letters to Agathe Bremer and a few friends. When she consulted Andrew Downing as to the fitness of publishing these letters, he approved, saying that "they would give the most true and lifelike image of the inner life of a people but little known and commonly misrepresented in Europe."[1] Downing also suggested that she use her sketches of prominent Americans, but she later decided against this idea.

Fredrika wanted in some way to repay the kindness that had been shown her and felt that the story of what she did here — a description of the people, their life and activities — would help acquaint Europeans with the country. She sensed that her letters would give a more spontaneous picture than could be achieved in any other genre. The title for the work appears in a letter to Downing, January 7, 1852:

Have I told you that my work on N. America is Christened: *the homes of the new world!* It will give matured and in extension the views that have been bred in your homes, in the com[m]union of minds between the dear inmates of these homes and myself during my life of love and confidence with them. An earnest holy work it will be to me, — more holy than any thing I have yet written. Nor will it be the less so, as these letters from your homes to my home, to my *Innermost* there, now will be written over again before eyes looking on me out of eternity, out of the eternal final home![2]

The notes to Chapter V begin on page 311.

That summer Fredrika heard news which deeply grieved her. She learned that Andrew Downing had died in a steamboat accident July 28. He and Mrs. Downing were returning to their Newburgh home on the *Henry Clay*. The captain engaged in a race with another Hudson River steamboat and this so overtaxed the *Henry Clay* engines that the ship caught fire. Caroline was saved, but Downing perished while trying to rescue some drowning passengers. He was only thirty-seven years old, but had already attained recognition; a memorial stone vase in his honor was later erected on the Mall in Washington, D. C. Upon receiving the sad news Fredrika wrote Caroline a letter of condolence, which also acknowledged the lock of Downing's dark hair the widow had sent.

Fredrika paid tribute to Downing's memory in a letter "To the Friends of A. J. Downing," published in the 1853 edition of his *Rural Essays.* In it she avowed: ". . . I loved him better than all, save *one* — the sweet wife who made all his days days of peace and pleasantness. And the eye of love is clairvoyant."[3] The Preface declared: "No man has lived in vain who has inspired such regard in such a woman."[4]

Work on the manuscript of her forthcoming book occupied Fredrika. She edited forty-three long letters written from America and supplemented them with additional data. The Swedish edition, *Hemmen i den nya verlden,* in three volumes, was published 1853-1854. When Mary Howitt's translation appeared in London, it was called *The Homes of the New World; Impressions of America.* Harper & Brothers of New York published an American edition in 1853 — earlier than the complete Swedish original. Five printings were exhausted the very first month[5] and there were several later editions. The book was also translated into Danish, Dutch, French, and German, receiving numerous reviews in Europe. One French critic said: "By showing us America in all its grandeur, and making us love it, and by imparting to us the secret of that vigor and youth which astonish us, she has served both worlds at once and nobly repaid the debt of hospitality."[6] (Tr.) A German reviewer noted her intuitive approach and said that she "writes with her heart."[7] An American scholar then visiting Sweden, Willard Fiske, saw the advance proofs of Fredrika's work; he described it as one "which will do special honor to our land and essentially heighten the Swedish opinion of our customs and literature."[8]

American Reviews of "Homes of the New World"

Newspaper advertisements like the following began to appear in the autumn of 1853:

FREDRIKA BREMER'S VISIT. THE HOMES OF THE NEW WORLD; OR, IMPRESSIONS OF AMERICA By Fredrika Bremer. Translated by Mary Howitt. In 2 vols. 12 mo. Cloth, 1,200 pages, $2.

"I have wished to present to your Majesty, from the soil of the New Wor[l]d, some very beautiful spiritual flowers, not unworthy of those roses your Majesty's own beautiful hand gave me at parting."
[Letter to the Queen of Denmark.]
For sale at EVANS & BRITTAN'S, No. 697 Broadway.[9]

A few passages in the Swedish are not to be found in the American edition, as, for example, an interesting two-page comparison between England and America. John Bull and his younger Yankee brother, Jonathan, both want to humanize and civilize the world, but the latter goes about it more zealously and wants to go further. John Bull is an aristocrat, Jonathan a democrat; both desire wealth, but Jonathan is more liberal in sharing it with everyone. He is always busy and does not laugh as much as John Bull, nor does he enjoy his meals in the leisurely fashion of his English brother. As Fredrika humorously puts it, Jonathan eats quickly and soon leaves the table to found a city, dig a canal, or construct a railroad.[10]

Norton's Literary Gazette and Publishers' Circular reviewed her work on America October 15. The critic described it as entertaining for foreigners to read but wished that Fredrika Bremer had instead written a novel based upon American characters, manners, and scenery. Two days later Longfellow wrote in his journal: " 'We have Miss Bremer's book on the *Homes of the New World;* full of soft and very lady-like indiscretions; but written in the tenderest spirit.' "[11]

Newspapers also reviewed Harper's release; for instance, the Washington *Daily National Intelligencer* mentioned it October 26 in its "Notes on New Books." *Homes of the New World's* pictures of life were graphic and sketched with warm colors, said the newspaper. Miss Bremer had seen all the magnates of the land, the lions and lionesses. She had some minor criticisms, such as the necessity at receptions to reply to the same questions until she felt like a parrot. However, the visitor had been very kind and had made the best of everything.

The editor of *Putnam's Monthly Magazine* in New York had this to say the following month:

. . . The book will be much more entertaining on this side of the world than on the other, for the amiable little author has been so personal in her remarks, and so piquant in her descriptions, that only those who know well the scenes and persons she alludes to can fully appreciate the value of her observations. It will be a great comfort to the admiring crowds who hovered about her wherever she went, while she was in this country, to know how much they annoyed her, how indiscriminately she lumps them together, and what she thought of them at the time. She makes very free with people's names, although a good many are only alluded to by their initials, and falls into a good many amusing blunders about persons and places. But she is never querulous nor ill-humored, and we fear that we shall never have a traveller among us better disposed towards us, or who will make a milder report of our shady side, and a more genial one of the bright side of our national character. She is the first foreigner who has complimented the male part of our popula-tion on their good looks; she has the eye of a sculptor for the good points of manly beauty, and is never so warm and enthusiastic as when describing the fine looking men. . . . The *Homes of the New World* is not so good a book as the *Neighbors,* but it has some of the best qualities of that popular novel, which served as the introduction of the author to the homes which she has so genially described.[12]

In December *Putnam's Monthly Magazine* published a second review — five pages long — with a number of quotations. The re-viewer, Charles F. Briggs, expressed some mingled sentiments:

. . . The curiosity to know what Miss Bremer would say about us was never more intense since European notorieties first began to publish their opinions of what they saw and heard on our side of the Atlantic. The little, sentimental, "potato-nosed" Swedish lady, had captivated our entire reading population, which includes nearly our whole people, by her quaint and romantic pictures of society in her native hyperborean home, and it was very natural that those who had tried to dazzle her by their attentions should wish to know how they had succeeded. The little lady has not left us in the dark, or doubt on the subject. No one can complain of a want of frankness and transparent thinking on her part. To make use of a Westernism, she records her impressions "with a perfect looseness"; and appar-ently with a most amiable unconsciousness that there is any thing at all improper in her doing so. She is, in fact, the *enfant terrible* of travellers in the United States; and her sayings are all the more valuable and entertaining from their innocent freshness. They were made on the spot, and have none of the dubious indistinctness and hesitancy of second thoughts or remembered impressions. When she slept in a cold bedroom she notes it on the spot, if she was bored by a formal dinner down goes the fact, with the names of those who bored her, while they vainly imagined they were giving her an entertainment. We have no fault to find with her on this account. It is very well for people to see themselves as others see them. The motive of the borer might plead in extenuation of the offence, in some minds; but Miss Bremer only knew that she was bored, and didn't regard the homage to herself, which it implied, as a sufficient offset. She was a Sybarite in pursuit of comfort, and rebelled against being killed with kindness. Her aim was enjoyment and not sacrifice. And who shall condemn her for it? Must one be grateful for an unsought dinner that inflicts dyspepsia? . . .[13]

The critic went on to mention that Fredrika Bremer frequently misspelled the names of persons and places, and also misquoted book titles. Summing up her impact on Americans, he said:

Many querulous remarks have been made by our contemporaries of the Press, about the imprudences of Miss Bremer, in her revelations of domestic society, but her amiability and overflowing love for every body with whom she came in contact, should be considered as a sufficient apology for her unreserve. As to the other complaint that she elevates into importance personages whom we had never before heard of, and makes heroes and heroines of quiet people who had never been suspected of heroic qualities by their acquaintances, it does not strike us as a very serious offence; if she sees a park in a little inclosure of two or three city lots, shadowed by one or two ailanthus trees, it does not follow that her other descriptions were all in her eye, for she seems to have been fully impressed by the grandeur of our river scenery, and she has given some very graphic sketches of the rural districts, both of the East and the West. It is inevitable that travellers should make mistakes in their description of foreign countries; but, when as in the case of Miss Bremer, they are all in favor of the country visited, the people whom she describes should be the last to complain. We do not believe that her book will have a tendency to make us less respected in Europe, that it will cause Americans to be received with diminished consideration abroad, or that it will cause a single Scandinavian to change his purpose of emigrating with his family and household gods to the wilderness of the New World. . . .[14]

Harper's New Monthly Magazine of November, 1853, also carried a detailed review; part of it read:

. . . We will say at once, that she looks at the homes of America in the most flattering light — with a few important exceptions, her descriptions are of the deepest rose-colored tint — she admires our institutions of government, education, and domestic life — and toward numerous individuals in different parts of the United States, whom she honored with her friendship, her heart appears to overflow with a perfect gush of enthusiasm. . . .[15]

The reviewer had some derogatory comments to make, among them that Miss Bremer vainly endeavored to make lions out of very ordinary domestic animals. He said, however, that he thought the book would be received in the same friendly spirit it had been written.

Other critiques appeared in such magazines as the New York *Literary World,* the Boston *Christian Examiner,* and *Graham's Magazine* of Philadelphia. *Graham's* was a diatribe against the book, although the critic admitted that people were "Bremer mad" and that the popularity of her novels was an "open sesame" for her. He felt that she had violated some implied confidences — the use of initials did not sufficiently mask the identity of many of her hosts, whose family life she revealed. He did not think the "personal gossip" worthy of translation and publication:

. . . Irving, Bryant, Longfellow, Emerson, Lowell, Parker, Alcott, Sumner, Downing, Miss Lynch, Channing, not to mention others, are the objects of her insatiable gossip. Undoubtedly many of her descriptions exhibit a shrewd insight of character, and, occasionally, a quality of mind, or disposition, or person, is happily caught and embodied. She, however, necessarily makes mistakes. Had she informed these persons that she intended to sketch their portraits for the public, they would have been on their guard. Those who did not escape from her altogether, would have appended to their conversation explanatory notes. They would have said, after hazarding a careless remark, "I beg you to consider this as not being my whole philosophy of life"; or, "Miss Bremer, you will have the kindness to consider this as a joke"; or, "Miss Bremer, as I shall probably forget the observation I am now going to make the moment after it has passed my lips, I beg you to consign it to a similar oblivion." As it is, however, they are held responsible before the world for trifles, chance sayings, capricious expressions, and all the little nothings which so readily escape from a man in conversation, but which appear ridiculous in print. . . .[16]

Fredrika regretted that Mary Howitt's translation contained a number of embarrassing mistakes; she felt that her friends in America and England ought to know she was not to blame. She sent therefore "A Card" to the London *Times,* printed on December 23, and she also forwarded another to the *Daily National Intelligencer* in Washington, D. C., which printed both the card and her note to the editors:

GENTLEMEN: The wide reputation of the *National Intelligencer,* and the character of benevolence which belongs to you personally, induce me to address you, in order to request that the included note from me may be admitted into your paper for the purpose of circulation in the United States. Confiding to you this address to the good sense and just feeling of the American public, I am confident, gentlemen, that I cannot leave it in better hands.

Yours, sincerely,
Fredrika Bremer.

Stockholm, December 12, 1853.

A CARD.

Having obtained a copy of the English translation of my late work, Homes of the New World, and having recently looked through some parts of it, I feel myself compelled to say a few words in reference to the same to my American readers. Although I certainly think the translation faithful and good on the whole, as far as I yet have seen, and in many parts even excellent, especially in the latter parts of the work, still there are in several places, and chiefly, as I think, in the first volume, misconceptions and mistakes as to words and meanings of the Swedish original, which must convey to the reader not acquainted with this impressions equally far from my intention and unjust to the persons or cases concerned. The great difficulty in the translation of such a work, and the very unfavorable circumstances under which it was carried out, are enough to explain and excuse these mistakes. Still I owe to my friends and to myself to state that there are such. . . .[17]

Fredrika was especially distressed by the passages about the Hamiltons and the Poinsetts. She let it be published that the Hamilton ladies had somewhat too spare figures, and that the family served highly seasoned foods — she said cayenne pepper spoiled both meat and stomach. The "classical honey" from Greece served at breakfast did not impress her; it did not seem any better than that of Northern bees. James Hamilton and his family were offended and found her account "shocking." Fredrika wrote a conciliatory letter (Appendix, p. 226), also telling the Hamiltons that she had received invitations from English families to stay with them, though they knew well "the danger they may incur from so dangerous a guest."

Part of her story about the Poinsetts would have displeased the diplomat, had he lived to read it, and Mrs. Mary Poinsett probably resented this passage:

. . . The evenings spent alone with my good old friends are somewhat tedious. One can not be always talking American politics, and the old statesman takes an interest in nothing else, nor can one always have stories and riddles at hand to amuse the old lady, who sits dozing by the fire, and sometimes persuades her husband to do the same, sitting opposite, while I amuse myself as well as I can, which is not very well, as I am not able to read, and as there is no piano, and it is then too late to go out. It is time, therefore, to be going.[18]

In her card in the *Daily National Intelligencer* Fredrika endeavored to soothe ruffled feelings:

. . . She (Mrs. Poinsett) was one of the kindest and most sweet-tempered of women, their home, a home of peace and comfort; their union so perfect as often to remind of that old celebrated classic pair of ancient Greece to whom the Gods of Olympus came as guests. And so I have said.[19]

Other remarks must have been embarrassing to the George P. Putnams, in whose home she had an unpleasant experience:

I was frozen in my bed-room, because the weather is now cold, and they do not heat the bed-rooms in this country. It is here as in England, not as in our good Sweden; and I can hardly accustom myself to these cold bed-chambers. It was to me particularly hard to get up and to dress myself in that chilly room, with my fingers benumbed with cold.[20]

A few examples of Mary Howitt's errors in translation may be cited. Lydia Maria Child was called too "angular" to be happy, whereas Fredrika said "delicately sensitive" (*finkänslig*). Horace Mann was described as having "one of those vernal foreheads which are arched upward with aspiring ideas,"[21] but Fredrika had written that he had "one of those two-storied foreheads. . ." ("*en af dessa tvåvånings-pannor. . .*"[22]). The Swedish word for "spice" (*krydda*) was translated as "cream": "I receive every sentiment of cordial liking which is evinced toward me, by man or by woman, with calm gratitude, as a cream on the good food of life, . . ."[23]

In an introductory "To the Reader" Fredrika admitted that the letters suffered from "egotism — the offense of all autobiography."[24] She apologized for excessive reference to her illnesses and for the endearing terms used toward her favorite sister. She claimed to know the faults of her work better than anyone else and, in a special preface "To My American Friends," wrote: "That which I saw and found in the New World has been set down in these letters. They are, for the most part, outpourings from heart to heart — from your homes to my home in Sweden."[25]

In a candid message to Justina Howland Fredrika affirmed:

. . . My letters on America are offerings on the altar of love and of truth. Had I to write them again I should make some shortenings and cut off personalities, but on the whole I should leave them as they are. I look upon them as fated. I have no right to write them otherwise, and I neither could nor would. You think, dear friend, that I have read all that has been written in the papers about them, both criticism and praise. Indeed I have not. I never seek to read reviews about my writings, fearing thereby to encourage the touchiness and selfishness of the author. And to this work I felt that whatever was said about it, it was something — a word that God had given me to say, and that I must say so, the world may say what it would. . . .[26]

The London *Times* card said that Fredrika had no one to whom she could turn for information while writing *Homes of the New World*. However, it appears from the following letter that she consulted Francis Schroeder, the American *chargé d'affaires* in Stockholm, who wrote to George Bancroft May 24, 1853:

We see a good deal of Miss Bremer, and she applies to me frequently for facts, dates, and local details. She tells me her book will exhibit her to *us* in America, as an abolitionist; but not *enragée*. I fear however I have seen on her remarks that she has not a just understanding of the obligations of the Federal Government in regard to Southern affairs. I have had many conversations with her, in which I have carefully endeavoured to set this matter in the light in which I derive it from the great commentators at home; and although she does not choose I think, to abandon some fixed ideas, I am sure she is writing in a different tone from that which has been set in a blaze by Mrs. Stowe. There will be some notice of the work of this lady in Miss Bremer's book; — and I hope in a juster sense than prevails elsewhere in Europe. . . .[27]

Fredrika had written an Appendix saying that her original intention had been to add a section on slavery, but that the publication of Harriet Beecher Stowe's *Uncle Tom's Cabin* in 1852 made this unnecessary. In these words she paid tribute to Mrs. Stowe:

Honor be to the noble, warm-hearted American woman, who has stood forth in our day — as no other woman in the realms of literature has yet done — for the cause of humanity and the honor of her native land, and that with a power which has won for her the whole ear of humanity. Honor and blessing be hers! What will not that people become who can produce such daughters![28]

Correspondence with Americans

Fredrika followed American affairs with the greatest interest as long as she lived. During the remaining fourteen years of her life, from 1851 on, she wrote to friends made while in the New World, some of whom she considered almost as close as brothers and sisters. After her homecoming, grief for her sister Agathe left her temporarily unable to carry on her voluminous correspondence. In January of 1852, however, she wrote to the Downings, George Putnam, Mrs. Howland, and Mrs. Holbrook. Later — March 20 — a communication to the Springs reveals that she received much mail from America:

Dear Marcus, I have to you a request; And that is to put in the tribune a card requesting that *strangers* to me in America who wish to send letters or books to me, will send them *to you* to be forwarded to Sweden. And when such come, dear Marcus, *do not send them,* but keep them till some good opportunity offers to send them without postage; or break them and see if it is worth while to send them at all. Several troublesome messages make it to me necessesary to take that measure; and beg of you to be my safeguard from beeing annoyed by letters and packets w[h]ich are to me disagreeable to receive as the writers ask of me things impossible for me to do.[29]

At that time postage on foreign letters had to be paid by the recipient, and Fredrika complained to Anne Howland about the high fees.

Fredrika was instrumental in having some works by Hawthorne and Harriet Beecher Stowe translated into Swedish. In November, 1852, she wrote to Sven Adolf Hedlund, editor of *Göteborgs Handelstidning,* suggesting American literature suitable for publication in serial form. Recommended were Mrs. Stowe's early work, *The Mayflower, or Sketches of Scenes and Characters Among the Descendants of the Pilgrims,* Hawthorne's short stories and his novel *The House of the Seven Gables.* She said of her contemporaries: "Hawthorne is, like Mrs. Stowe, a real American national writer, and their works give a true insight into N. America's private life as well as natural scenery."[30] (Tr.)

Miss Bremer also indicated that *Littell's Living Age* had many good stories. In a letter to Hedlund she recommended Catharine Sedgwick's tales, "which are distinguished by their local color and general interest. She is N. America's most loved and most widely read novelist up to the present."[31] (Tr.) Thus Fredrika played a role in acquainting Swedes with the works of contemporary American authors.[32] She encouraged several of her friends to translate this literature, among them the poet Thekla Knös, who published a book of American poems in Swedish. (Hawthorne's *The Scarlet*

Letter appeared 1853 as a serial in *Aftonbladet;* Longfellow's *Evangeline* came out in Swedish 1854 and *Hiawatha* two years later.) *Uncle Tom's Cabin* was widely read in Sweden and Fredrika mentioned it to Justina Howland:

. . . America begins more and more to attract the attention and interest of Europe and even that of my polar land. Your three great modern lions, *Uncle Tom,* President Pierce and the caloric machine invented by the Swede [John] Erikson, have this year drawn up our eyes to you, and out our tongues to speak about your doings. I am most glad of the caloric machine, first as it will make an end to many dreadful accidents and losses, and then as it is a Swede that has done the thing. Of Pres. Pierce I don't as yet know what to say, but of *Uncle Tom* I say that it is a most charming, touching and excellent story, only I think in fault as to the method and means of emancipation from slavery. There emancipation previous to education will never do. The thing must begin by the other end.[33]

When Fredrika's friends traveled to the United States, they frequently asked her for letters of introduction, which she gladly gave. For example, she sent Longfellow a note introducing two Danish acquaintances of hers. Occasionally American friends came to Sweden; in 1853 Fredrika received Mrs. Marianne Silsbee of Salem and Dr. and Mrs. David Osgood of Boston. After the visit of the Osgoods in Stockholm she accompanied them via the Göta Canal to Gothenburg. To Fredrika's joy, Marcus and Rebecca Spring came to Europe and in the summer of 1854, after traveling on the Continent, arrived in Sweden. Their visit gave Fredrika the happiest days she had known since her own journey to America. She no longer could entertain at Årsta, as the estate had been sold, but she proudly showed the Springs around Stockholm, Uppsala, and Gothenburg. She was also their cicerone in Denmark, where they met the Dowager Queen Caroline Amalie and Hans Christian Andersen.[34]

In March, 1855, Fredrika's mother died after a long illness. Fredrika was now left completely alone except for a married sister, and she continued to live in Stockholm. Her numerous activities occupied her, including much philanthropic work. One of her American friends, Dr. Harriot Hunt, received a communication later that same year and in it Fredrika asked for news of the women's movement and for Dr. Hunt's views on "the elevation of woman to her true character and social position." To quote Fredrika: "The more I live and see of the world the more I feel that this indeed is the question on which depends the true liberation of mankind. I long to learn

what you do for the great cause in America, and I will tell you by
and by what I try to do and want to do for it in Scandinavia."35

Social Welfare and "Hertha"

Miss Bremer was very active in the organization she headed,
the Stockholm Women's Association for Child Welfare (*Stockholms
fruntimmersförening för barnavård*), which had been formed to
care for over five hundred orphans, survivors of a cholera epidemic
rampant that winter. She wrote that in organizing this society she
had patterned it on the United States Constitution. In the course
of Fredrika's humanitarian endeavors she addressed audiences, as
she herself told friends across the ocean:

. . . I have spoken several times before large assemblies, and I cannot but thank America and ladies in America to have been able
to do so with calm and self-posses[s]ion. Their example has guided
and sustained me. I have thought especially of Lucretia Mott and
of Rebecca [Spring]. And I have enjoyed to speak out my heart
and mind before multitudes and to feel the electric response of the
hearts and minds of those to whom and for whom I spoke.36

Fredrika wanted the women of the world to unite for peaceful
purposes and suggested that they form an alliance. The London
Times published August 28, 1854, her "Invitation to a Peace Alliance," which outlined a plan to care for destitute children, the
aged, the sick, prisoners, and others in need. She proposed that a
committee in the capital of each country gather data on its women's
societies and exchange such information with committees in other
countries. One paragraph from her appeal follows:

Sisters, then, whom we do not know as yet, but in whose existence we believe and hope, here and there among the ancient
kingdoms of Asia, the steppes of Siberia, or in the Imperial cities
of Russia; sisters of the western countries of Europe, who have
lighted and guided us a long time by your bright example; and you,
sisters in that vast new land beyond the Atlantic Ocean, whose
homes we have just learnt to know as nurseries of all Christian
virtues; and you, Christian women among the nations of Africa;
Christian women in the isles of the South Sea; mild, loving sisters,
all over the earth, in whose existence we believe, though we have
not seen you, whom we love without even knowing you — give us
your hands! May the earth thus become encircled by a chain of
healing, loving energies, which neither ocean nor event, neither
discord nor time, can interrupt! Let us unite to form an alliance
eternal as God's own being; for war shall come to an end, and

"tongues shall cease, and knowledge shall vanish away, but charity shall not fail; charity abideth for ever."[37]

Fredrika felt that if the Christian women of the world formed one bond and sisterhood, great charitable works could be performed. To an American friend she expressed herself: "The women of America — to whom the God of love has given in a rich measure the heart of the *Mother* — will, I venture to prophesy it, stand forth in that capacity applied to the young generation at large, nobly and gloriously among the nations of the earth."[38]

The social ideas Fredrika had gleaned during her sojourn in the United States matured further in her mind; by 1856 she was ready to impart them in novel form to her Swedish public. The previous year she had written to Böklin saying she was working on *Hertha eller en själs historia* (*Hertha, or the Story of a Soul*), which she described as: ". . . the first harvest of the New World's spirit wedded with Swedish conditions in my soul. A woman is the focal point, and woman's just development the thought about which it revolves."[39] (Tr.) She said she had never given more serious homage to truth.

The English edition of *Hertha* appeared in 1856, before the Swedish one, in fact. Fredrika was imbued with the possibilities of her sex and the book advocated education and emancipation of women. It caused widespread discussion on both sides of the Atlantic. Some readers thought she had sacrificed a little of her popularity by presenting such pronounced feminist views. The Springs, however, received the work with enthusiasm: "We are all delighted with *Hertha;* it is full of fresh rich thought — and it also contains great principles. It must have been a pleasure to write as we find it a pleasure to read such a book."[40]

The hero, Yngve Nordin, spends two years in the United States and tells his sweetheart, Hertha, about life there. He also reads aloud to her from American authors, among them Lowell. Yngve speaks of the women's rights conventions, and through him Fredrika voices her own opinions. He is in a steamboat accident, similar to the one which caused Downing's death. (Fredrika Bremer dedicated the American edition of *Hertha* to Downing.) Unlike the prototype, however, the fictional Yngve Nordin survives, after dramatically rescuing women and children. An American critic saw a parallel between Hertha and Margaret Fuller:

In America, Miss Bremer had been greatly disappointed not to see Margaret Fuller. Not only was her imagination kindled by what she heard from the group of friends who had clustered about her in their girlhood, but she wished to thank the woman who had written *Woman in the Nineteenth Century*. It was while she was here that the storm-tost waves closed over that tost and wandering life. Perhaps the circumstances kindled still farther a pathetic interest; but when, after she had carried her book of travels through the press, she published, in 1856, her *Hertha*, it was impossible not to see how she had mingled in that wonderful appeal the bitter experience of her own youth with the glowing traditions of her American friends. Hertha, among her pupils in the "Iduna Hall," is Margaret Fuller in the midst of her "Conversations," so far as a foreigner could seize and transpose the life.

This book, less entertaining to read than those tales in which Miss Bremer bound herself by no definite, practical purpose, will remain immortal, perhaps unique, among the books of women; for it changed, in a most important respect, the laws of a great nation.[41]

Fredrika's bold presentation of her ideas aroused protests in Sweden. *Hertha* was criticized because long passages expounding the author's opinions weighed down the plot. Reports of the adverse criticism reached Fredrika in Switzerland, but she felt the cause which the book espoused was more important than the displeasure of some of her contemporaries:

. . . *Hertha* is but the *first part* of a work or representation whose other half is yet to follow, and will follow in a year or two if God so pleases. To be able to carry out that I have left Sweden and my manifold occupations there for a time to travel and live qui[e]tly in Switzerland, perhaps in Piémont and then wholly for my litterary pursuits. After this I shall return to my own dear land and work in my part till my day is over. Ah! how gladly would I not once more comme over to America to see those friends I hold so dear, and to think and work with them in what I could, but ah! there is the great ocean between, and ap[p]roaching age, and so much to do in Sweden, and time and life so short! I fear I cannot come.[42]

She wrote the above to Justina Howland from Brussels, where she attended the Congrès de Bienfaisance in September, 1856. An address prepared in French, dealing with the welfare of European women of the poorer classes, was read for her by Auguste Visschers. At the closing banquet a toast was proposed to Fredrika Bremer, Florence Nightingale, and Harriet Beecher Stowe. Later Fredrika had a three-hour audience with King Leopold I of Belgium, who had read all her works.

Meeting with Hawthorne in Italy

Fredrika spent five years traveling extensively in Switzerland, Italy, Palestine, and Greece. She recorded her impressions in *Two Years in Switzerland and Italy* (1860), *Travels in the Holy Land* (1861), and *Greece and the Greeks* (1863). Interested in religious thought, she studied Alexandre Vinet's ideas in Switzerland, and she also had a long audience with Pope Pius IX in the Vatican.

In Rome, in the spring of 1858, Fredrika met Nathaniel and Sophia Hawthorne. This time the conversation flowed more easily than at their first meeting:

Miss Bremer called on us the other day. We find her very little changed from what she was when she came to take tea and spend an evening at our little red cottage, among the Berkshire hills, and went away so dissatisfied with my conversational performances, and so laudatory of my brow and eyes, while so severely criticising my poor mouth and chin. She is the funniest little old fairy in person whom one can imagine, with a huge nose, to which all the rest of her is but an insufficient appendage; but you feel at once that she is most gentle, kind, womanly, sympathetic, and true. She talks English fluently, in a low quiet voice, but with such an accent that it is impossible to understand her without the closest attention. This was the real cause of the failure of our Berkshire interview; for I could not guess, half the time, what she was saying, and, of course, had to take an uncertain aim with my responses. A more intrepid talker than myself would have shouted his ideas across the gulf; but, for me, there must first be a close and unembarrassed contiguity with my companion, or I cannot say one real word. I doubt whether I have ever really talked with half a dozen persons in my life, either men or women.[43]

About a month later the Hawthornes were invited to tea at Fredrika's unpretentious abode near the Tarpeian Rock. The Swedish Minister had preceded them and after warmly bidding him goodbye, Fredrika chatted with her American guests. From her window they admired the glorious sunset and view towards St. Peter's. She accompanied them on a promenade when they left; that Hawthorne remembered the Tarpeian Rock is indicated by the fact that he used it as background for a scene in *The Marble Faun* (1860). He also wrote of Fredrika:

... There is no better heart than hers, and not many sounder heads; and a little touch of sentiment comes delightfully in, mixed up with a quick and delicate humor and the most perfect simplicity.[44]

. . . .

She is a most amiable little woman, worthy to be the maiden aunt of the whole human race. I suspect, by the by, that she does not like me half so well as I do her; it is my impression that she thinks me unamiable, or that there is something or other not quite right about me. I am sorry if it be so, because such a good, kindly, clear-sighted, and delicate person is very apt to have reason at the bottom of her harsh thoughts, when, in rare cases, she allows them to harbor with her.[45]

After her visit in Italy Fredrika continued to travel for several years and did not return to Sweden until 1861. She was heartened to find that some improvements had taken place in the status of women; for example, unmarried women had been granted legal majority at the age of twenty-five. A training school for women teachers had also been organized; girls could study at the Academy of Music, the Academy of Fine Arts, and the Industrial School in Stockholm.

Letters About the Civil War in the United States

When the Civil War began in 1861, Fredrika's sympathies were deeply involved, for she had good friends on both sides. However, she favored the North, as shown by a letter written that August to Justina Howland, a Southerner:

Out of the peace of my country and home I send many an anxious glance over the ocean to the great new world which I have felt as the home of generous hearts, and now, alas, the scene of civil war! God be praised that you and your family are no more in the South, where to live now would be next to death to such minds as yours, and where every day must be full of fear and terror as I think of it. God be thanked that you are in the free north linked to it in welfare as you always were in sympathies. I feel no doubt as to the issue of this war, but much blood and much bitterness may come of it ere it results in peace. I feel for my friends both north and south, feel for the generous hearts in both parts of the disunited union, and for the putting off of the good works of peace. But works of charity and moral fortitude will take their place; public and private calamity will work more seriousness, a higher tone of life, nobler views of man's and woman's calling in the public mind, and, I have no doubt, a better state of society. Much do I hope for a nobler turn in the aspirations of American women throughout the land.[46]

Fredrika's genuine interest in American political affairs long after her visit is revealed by a message dated March 30, 1862, "To My American Friends," which she sent the Springs (Appendix, p. 263). A personal letter accompanied it and both were published in the New York *Daily Tribune*. The heading was "Fredrika Bremer on Emancipation," and she used the opportunity to thank for the many gifts sent to her during her five-year travels in the Old World. She told of the sorrow she felt on seeing the Civil War "pollute a country gifted beyond all others with all the blessings of this earth." She hoped for peace and rejoiced over President Lincoln's plan for gradual emancipation and for compensation to the states willing to abolish slavery. (On March 6, 1862, Lincoln had sent a message to Congress recommending that the Federal Government give financial assistance to any state desiring to free its slaves.)

The Emancipation Proclamation was not delivered until January 1, 1863, but Fredrika considered Lincoln's plan of the previous year a "measure of high politics" which could make the United States Government rise to the dignity of a high moral principle. She said that President Lincoln had aligned himself with all the honest, unselfish hearts in America for right, freedom, peace, and the good of all. She concluded by saying to her American friends: "never more than in this hour did I feel myself so truly and entirely yours."[47] Her sentiments were supported with a contribution of $100.00 toward Lincoln's 1862 plan of emancipation:

. . . Small as is the sum, it may yet serve to free a poor elderly black woman working under the lash. I saw in South Carolina and in Cuba two or three such old faces, whose looks of settled despair will forever haunt me. During the Summer the money will be sent to you in a check from London. I cannot tell you with what joyful sympathy I shall henceforth follow the triumphs of your arms, for I see justice and generosity to your white as well as your black brethren going with them.[48]

Early in 1863 Fredrika wrote a long and eloquent letter to the Springs about the Battle of Fredericksburg (Appendix, p. 268). She mentioned the conflict again in November:

. . . Marcus last dear letter says about the present civil war many a thing to which I, with all my heart, subscribe. Impossible to understand and *to bear* this war if not by taking a high moral view of it and the will of Providence working through the works of man. Materially we see woe and destruction, spiritually we can discern the building up of a greater and nobler realm than was the former one, now shattered and ruined; we can discern the new Phoenix rising out of the ashes of his ancestors funeral pile. America shall still accomplish her great destination as the promised land of humanity.[49]

Fredrika discussed events in the United States with her friend Per Bergfalk, who lived in Uppsala, and they often exchanged American newspapers. If there was any special news, they sent telegrams. Fredrika followed the progress of the war on a map of the United States. A letter to Anne Lynch from Stockholm in February, 1864, voices some of her deepest feelings:

. . . Cheering and refreshing one, many things you tell about the regeneration of your people, — about its rising to manhood! Alas! that so bloody a baptism was needed, and still seems needed for it! I need not tell you with what intense interest I have followed, and do follow, all phases of this American war, which certainly is one of the most remarkable in modern, and perhaps also in ancient, history: next to the religious war of "thirty years," which closed the middle age and founded a new order of things in Church, State, and Society. I know of no war except the present one in America where so great and so life-teeming principles are working for the future of still unborn generations. And to have lived to see its probable issue, its certain fruits, is a great privilege. . . . But my heart and mind will never be absent from America. One of my last books of love and blessing will be for that country where I have lived so much, enjoyed, loved, and learned so much; and on which still my fondest hopes for a better and more happy humanity do repose. . . . Alas! when will this war cease? Though every pulse of my being beats for the success of Northern arms and ideas, I do suffer with the South, with its brave men and its much-suffering, self-sacrificing women, with its *good* slaveowners and *happy* slaves, — for such there are, though now they are confounded with the cruel and unhappy. . . .[50]

In 1864 many "Sanitary Fairs" were held in American cities to raise funds for sick and wounded Union soldiers, and contributions were also solicited in Europe. New York had a Sanitary Fair that spring and Fredrika sent an autograph statement to be sold with other such items. The American envoy in Sweden, William Widgery Thomas, Jr., had asked her for it:

I feel happy to offer, — alas! only in poor words — my humble tribute to the sanitary fair in New York, a most noble contrivance of the great christian heart which in face of human suffering knows neither f[r]iend nor foe, neither north nor south, only the bleeding, help needing neighbour! "Blessed *are* the merciful; for they will obtain mercy!"

Stockholm 18 febr. 1864

Fredrika Bremer[51]

Thomas wrote a chapter about Fredrika in his book, *Sweden and the Swedes;* he said that whenever she heard of the arrival of an American in Stockholm, she would invite the visitor to her home. The envoy learned to know her well and wrote that she was a greater woman than author. "Her heart was full of love for every human creature, and this love manifested itself wherever she knew of a sufferer to be comforted or a poverty-stricken home to be made bright and joyous."[52]

A forty-nine page section entitled *Det inbördes kriget i Amerika* (The Civil War in America), dated May, 1864, was appended to a condensed Swedish edition of *Hemmen i nya verlden;* it reveals how closely Fredrika followed events in the United States. She discussed the presidency of Abraham Lincoln, told about his humble beginnings, and said: "He was regarded in the North as a man of truth and moderation, a worthy representative of the Union."[53] (Tr.) She described the Confederacy, the early battles of the war, and the history-making naval engagement between the *Monitor* and the *Merrimac*. She ended with a prayer for peace and reconciliation between the North and South. Her sympathy was deep and her prayer prophetic:

. . . My heart bleeds when I think of those flourishing cities, those beautiful homes, where I enjoyed beyond words the hospitality of the people and the characteristic beauty of nature in the South, — when I see them laid waste, their owners fugitive or exposed to all manner of want, to all kinds of sacrifices. — I know that in America all Christians pray for them, just as for all who are involved in the great struggle; I know that in France, Switzerland, also in England people unite in praying for them. In Sweden at least one voice, one heart shall continually pray: Good Lord have mercy! Let Thy truth, Thy love enlighten the hearts of the fighters. May they find means of reconciliation, so that they can lay their weapons down upon Thy altar, Father of us all! May that day come soon, O Lord! — Then, O country blessed more than other continents with everything which can make human life rich and happy, people great and independent, each person a completely developed personality, — then shalt thou once again open thy ports for people from the whole world; social laws, which were founded at Plymouth Rock, shall be valid for all thy states from the Atlantic to the Pacific, and thou with all thy inexhaustible spiritual and material resources shalt become a new and regenerating home for children of the whole earth, those who wish to live sincerely and vigorously in the light of the universal consciousness!

Of this life, even during its unfinished development, my letters in *Homes of the New World* can bear witness.

May I be permitted to live to see its new morning rise and then
— be permitted to die in my own country!
Stockholm in May, 1864.

F. B.[54] (Tr.)

Fredrika received the news of General Sherman's victories
somewhat late. The newspapers the Springs sent her were delayed
because of the severe winter, but on March 20, 1865, she acknowledged their receipt. In the same letter (Appendix, p. 274) Fredrika
wrote that although her heart bled for Charleston and other ravaged
southern cities, she rejoiced in the northern victory. She realized
that the Civil War was nearly over; as the end approached she
wrote to the Springs again: "And W. H. Channing, and the Furnesses
and the Beechers, W. [J.] R. Lowell and Whittier and all those noble
friends of right and humanity how happy they must feel! And how
happy should I feel to have a look at them, a shake hands with
them at this very moment."[55]

A letter from Årsta in her last autumn sums up Fredrika's
feelings:

. . . And then *the poor negro!* They will have much to suffer ere the
new order of things can bring out effective blessing to them. But a
great, a glorious victory is now won, a great work is achieved by
your free people, not only for its future life but for the whole earth.
. . . Greatly as I glory in the noble victory gained, I still feel for the
sufferings of the vanquished party.[56]

Fredrika Bremer's Death in 1865

The new owners of the Bremer family estate had invited Fredrika in 1864 to come there again, and this was a comfortable arrangement for her. More than a year later, on a Christmas morning, she
caught a cold going to church. The seriousness of her condition was
not immediately recognized; pneumonia set in, and she passed away
after a very brief illness. Her sister Charlotte and brother-in-law
Per Quiding were with her when the end came, December 31, 1865.
(Mrs. Quiding was the sole survivor among Fredrika's sisters and
brothers.[57]) The author was buried in the churchyard at Österha-
ninge and a large cross marks the grave. Years later a statue of her
was erected in *Humlegården,* a Stockholm park.

The Swedish people and the many who had known her in other
lands mourned her passing. Those who knew her best loved her
most, affirmed *Harper's Weekly* in an obituary. "To the people of
this country the career of Miss BREMER is especially interesting from

the fact that she has lived among us, and is so well remembered here by thousands of loving friends."[58] An American in Stockholm, Juliet H. L. Campbell, wrote to Longfellow January 23, 1866:

... My friend, no longer with us, Fredrika Bremer, being a daughter of the people was enthusiastic for the [legislative] reform.

Did you know her? — She was of the stuff that angels are made of. I can criticize her as author, but her true greatness was in her noble womanhood. — Her large kind heart asserted itself in her last deeds. — She had a christmas tree for a party of dependent children — danced with them about the tree — gave them all gifts and delighted in conferring as much pleasure as possible on her humble guests and neighbors — Xmas day she went to church — took cold which settled on her lungs, and died the last day of the year. In her death she was honored by her countrymen and the papers have been filled with beautiful tributes to her memory.[59]

Fredrika's friends in America sorrowfully received the news of her death. The announcement was delayed almost a month, as shown by the New York *Daily Tribune* obituary of January 26:

DEATH OF FREDERIKA BREMER

Yesterday's European steamer reports the death of Frederika Bremer, the Swedish novelist, one of the best known women of the century. She was born in 1802 on the banks of the Aura, near Abo, in Finland. Her family, which was wealthy, removed into Sweden when she was about three years old. She was carefully educated, spent a year in Paris, and was afterward a teacher in a female seminary in Stockholm. In 1842 her novel *The Neighbors* was translated into English by Mary Howitt, published in England, and immediately became popular. Subsequently Mrs. Howitt translated *The Home, The Diary, The H. Family, The President's Daughters, Nina, Brothers and Sisters, Life in Dalecarlia,* and *The Midnight [Sun]*; all of which were republished in America, and widely circulated. In 1850-51, Miss Bremer visited America, and was very warmly welcomed. She had previously traveled widely on the continent of Europe and in England. On her return from the United States, she published a book made up of letters to her sister, entitled *Homes of the New World,* which appeared simultaneously in Sweden, England, and America. *England in 1851* appeared at Altona in 1852. In 1856 she wrote *Hertha,* in 1858 *Father and Daughter,* and after a residence in the South of Europe she published in 1860 *Two Years in Switzerland and Italy.* This was followed by a journey to the Holy Land, whence she returned by way of Turkey and Greece, and in the latter country prepared her books on the Holy Land and Turkey. At the time of her death she was residing in Stockholm.

Miss Bremer will be very generally regretted in the United States, where her books are widely read, and where she made many personal friends during her visit. The most complete edition of her works was published at Leipsic in 20 vols., from 1841 to 1853; and many of them have been translated into German, French, and Dutch, as well as into English.[60]

The New York *Daily Tribune* printed another article about her on February 5:

The recent decease of the celebrated Swedish novelist, Fredrika Bremer, which has already received a passing notice in our columns, affords the occasion of recalling the deep and affectionate interest which she cherished in American affairs, especially since her visit to this country, about fifteen years ago.

Her admirable works of fiction had won for her a host of friends on this side of the ocean. Their fresh and vivid pictures of Northern life were a novelty in literature; they opened a new world to readers who had become weary of the stale incidents and common-place plots of much of the popular fiction of the day; they produced a deep impression no less by the artlessness of their style, than by the fidelity of their portraitures; and for a long time, her name was the subject of universal encomium.

Her purpose of making an American tour was widely announced before her arrival. She was expected with grateful and almost tender interest; her coming was welcomed with eager delight by many who had known her through the medium of her writings; and when she landed on our shores, many hospitable firesides grew brighter at her approach, and in the intimacies of friendship she was never permitted for a moment to feel the loneliness of a stranger. Her frank and cordial manners, combining a simplicity which sometimes amounted to an almost childlike naiveté with a womanly dignity that was never laid aside, her kindliness of disposition, and her noble unselfishness of purpose, procured her access to more than one choice family circle, and surrounded her with friends, with whom her cordial relations closed only with her life.

On returning to her own country, she published an interesting record of her experiences in America, showing her appreciation of our national character, and her attachment to our institutions. Her active temperament did not permit her to remain long in the enjoyment of repose. Five years were devoted to extensive journeys in the Holy Land, Greece, Italy, and Germany, the fruits of which appeared in six volumes of travels, which enhanced her high reputation both in this country and in England. She passed two years in the family of the chaplain of the Queen of Greece in friendly intercourse with the royal family. The King put at her disposal his yacht in which with a party of chosen friends she visited the principal Grecian islands.

Upon the breaking out of the war of the Rebellion her sympathies were deeply enlisted in the success of the American arms. With the aid of our leading journals, and a careful study of the map, she kept herself fully acquainted with the progress of the struggle, and never lost her faith in the triumph of freedom and right. In the last edition of her work on America, she has added an appendix, describing the character and effects of the war. Her intelligent and lucid exposition has doubtless had no inconsiderable influence on European opinion, and contributed to a favorable view of the nature of the cause. "The assassination of Lincoln," she says, "opened the eyes of the people of Europe to the serpent nature of the Rebellion, and in the shock and shudder electrically felt from this serpent sting, a pedestal rose under the feet of the victim, raising him and the cause for which he died so that he became visible to all nations."

The latter part of Miss Bremer's life was quietly passed in her old family castle, Arsta. She continued to take a deep interest in public affairs. She felt great joy in the progress of this country toward a high ideal, and watched with anxious sympathies the course of moral and political reform in her own. In a recent letter to an American friend, which we have been permitted to use, she says: "From one of the high windows of this large high room, your Swedish friend sees rise on the western horizon the spire of the parish-church, pointing upwards, and to her telling of the place of repose where the body will in no long time be laid down with those of her parents, brothers, and sisters." She has now passed away in the ripeness of a pure and honored age, crowned with an abundant harvest of pleasant fruits, and golden grain, and healing leaves, while her memory will long be cherished in gracious esteem by many who were her debtors for the sweet beauty of her character, and the reviving influence of her works.[61]

The two quotations at the end were taken from Fredrika's letter of September 8, 1865, to the Springs (Appendix, p. 277). These true friends performed a final service in publishing some of her last words about the United States, words which reveal that only a few months before her death her thoughts dwelt on the country's destiny. As she had written in *Homes of the New World*, she wanted to return in spirit a hundred years later:

When homes such as those of Andrew Downing and Marcus S[pring], and of my good friend Mrs. W. H[owland], which is almost a Swedish home, stand upon the heights of the Mississippi and St. Peter's; when church spires shine out and scalp-dances are no longer danced there; when voices such as those of Channing, and Emerson, and Beecher, and Bellows, lift themselves in the councils, and when Lucretia Motts speak there also for freedom, peace, and the rights of woman; when the Christian Indian States, Nebraska, &c.,

stand peacefully side by side of Minnesota, then — it may be in a
hundred years — then will I return to Minnesota and celebrate a new
feast of the spirits; and I will return thither in — the spirit![62]

Fredrika Bremer's Name Perpetuated in America

More than a century has elapsed since Fredrika came to
the United States, but her memory lingers on. Although her novels
do not have the same appeal to readers now as they did in the mid-
nineteenth century, they are to be found, of course, in many libraries. When she wrote them, they were in tune with the sentiment and
taste of the times. *Homes of the New World* is more frequently referred to and quoted. It is interesting to note that one set of this
work at the Library of Congress belonged to Mrs. James K. Polk,
wife of the eleventh president of the United States; her signature
is on the flyleaf of both volumes. Another set was presented by
Susan B. Anthony in 1902. The leader of the American suffragist
movement, then eighty-two, inscribed Volume I: "This noble woman
from Sweden gave her impressions of America in 1853. We have
improved some since then, but this goes to the Congressional Library, Washington, D. C."

"Frederika Township" and "Bremer County" in Iowa were
named for her about 1853 at the suggestion of Stephen Hempstead,
second governor of the State. In Des Moines the Fredrika Bremer
Elementary School existed from 1883 to 1914, and a Minneapolis
public school bears her name now. Some years ago Dr. Henry God-
dard Leach, president emeritus of the American-Scandinavian Foundation, wrote in a letter to Henry Wadsworth Longfellow Dana: "I
have just returned from lecturing in Minnesota, where Fredrika
Bremer is not a maiden aunt but a goddess."[63] At Upsala College in
East Orange, New Jersey, a women's dormitory is called Fredrika
Bremer Hall. Her name is also inscribed on a plaque at the Woman's
Medical College of Pennsylvania.

A room at the American Swedish Historical Museum, Philadelphia, is named in her honor. When the tercentenary of the arrival of the Swedish settlers in Delaware was celebrated in 1938,
the visit of this great woman was publicized. On the recommen-
dation of Dr. Amandus Johnson, then curator, a committee had
been formed in 1936 by the National Council of Swedish Women
to initiate a fund-raising campaign for a "Fredrika Bremer Room."
In June, 1938, the room was dedicated and opened by Crown Prin-

FREDRIKA BREMER ROOM IN THE AMERICAN SWEDISH HISTORICAL MUSEUM

cess Louise, later Queen of Sweden. Located next to the Jenny Lind Room, it contains a copy of the oil portrait by Södermark, statuettes and photographs of Fredrika Bremer, early editions of her books, the complete manuscript of *Hertha,* and framed reproductions of some of her sketches. On one wall is a large tapestry woven by Swedish women, with quotations from her writings. Very interesting are some of the letters on display, most of them written to American friends, but also one to Hans Christian Andersen. Miss Bremer's map of the Western Hemisphere is there, and the carpet-bag she used on her American travels. Presentations have been made to the Museum of souvenirs she received, as well as her letters, and the Bremer collection continues to grow.

In 1954 a new Bremer Committee was formed at the Museum, with such patronesses as Mrs. Dwight D. Eisenhower, Madame Erik Boheman, Mrs. Lennart Nylander, Mrs. Walter G. Nord, Dr. Esther C. Meixner (chairman), and with other distinguished women as members. Besides maintenance of the Fredrika Bremer Room, the work of the Committee includes strengthening the ties of friendship between the women of Sweden and the United States.

Fredrika's pioneer efforts in the social field have been continued in Sweden by *Fredrika-Bremer-Förbundet,* founded 1884. Since then the Society has expanded and in 1954 there were over 12,000 members; headquarters are in Stockholm and many branches operate throughout Sweden. "To work for the betterment of women intellectually as well as practically, through the cooperation of experienced women and men" is the Society's purpose. It publishes a magazine called *Hertha* and also awards scholarships to Swedish women amounting to more than $7,000.00 annually. In 1951 the women's organizations sponsored a celebration to commemorate the one hundred fiftieth anniversary of Miss Bremer's birth; it was held in Stockholm and speakers paid homage to her memory.

In December of the same year the *UNESCO World Review* broadcast a radio program entitled "Women's Rights in Scandinavia — the Story of Frederika Bremer." From time to time lectures about her have been given, and articles have appeared in such periodicals as the *American-Scandinavian Review,* the *American Swedish Monthly,* the *Bulletin* of the American Swedish Institute in Minneapolis, *Minnesota History,* the *Swedish Pioneer Historical Quarterly,* and in the publications of the American Swedish Historical Museum. In 1951, just a hundred years after Miss Bremer's visit to Cuba, the sketches she made while there were reproduced in the quarterly of the Cuban National Library.

The name of Fredrika Bremer still has a familiar ring in many parts of the United States and, though not heard with the same frequency as a century ago, continues to find responsive hearts in each generation. The spirit of prophecy which moved this dedicated woman to predict a great future for the New World lives on; time has proved the clarity of her vision and the soundness of her words. Whittier truly called her "Seeress of the misty Norland, Daughter of the Vikings bold."

Appendix

Introduction and Letters

Introduction to Letters

THIS APPENDIX contains seventy-five letters by Fredrika Bremer, only two of which are included in the four-volume collection of *Fredrika Bremers Brev* edited by Klara Johanson and Ellen Kleman (Stockholm [1915-1920]).[1] All in English, they were written during the years 1846 to 1865 and are here arranged in chronological order. Forty of them were sent to Americans while Miss Bremer was in the United States and Cuba. The rest are also addressed to Americans, with the exception of one to Charles Kingsley and three to Mrs. Samuel Carter Hall. In the course of time these letters have inevitably passed from hand to hand; the present location of each is indicated in a footnote. For a list of abbreviations used, see page 299.

In editing the letters I have tried to reproduce the original text as accurately as possible. Fredrika Bremer's marginal notes have been placed within /. . ./ immediately following the word to which they refer, instead of using asterisks and footnotes. Undated letters have been placed in their approximate sequence, according to internal evidence. Where excerpts from these letters have been quoted in the preceding text, a cross reference is given. Only the most necessary additions have been made — all insertions within square brackets [ ] in the text are mine. In a few cases where Fredrika obviously omitted a word, I have supplied a logical one within brackets. The first time an orthographical error occurs, the correct spelling is given, if the meaning of the word is not readily apparent. It will be noted that certain English words are generally misspelled, for example, *agreable, aquaintance, ennough,* and *excellant.* The author's

---

1. See Vol. III, pp. 191-212, and Vol. IV, pp. 533-549, for letters written by F. Bremer in America. (These four volumes contain a total of 1,486 letters.)

capitalization was quite individualistic — in one letter in the Huntington Library *sweden* is written with a small *s,* and *Corn* with a capital *c.*

Miss Bremer was not a perfect speller even when writing her native tongue, so it is not surprising that she had difficulty with some English words. Certain Swedish influences on her spelling can also be detected, among them: omission of apostrophes in possessive nouns and contractions (*Emersons, oclock, dont*), confusion of *v* and *w* (*walley, Visconsin*), and *c* and *k* (*Amerika*), as well as the occasional insertion of a Swedish word (*hade, och*).[2] This author knew French and German well and some of her spelling reveals the influence of these languages. Other orthographical lapses (*beeing, joyn, dooings, exept, heartely, scool*) might have been due to haste rather than lack of knowledge, for she often spelled the words correctly. Despite some errors, one must admire Fredrika Bremer's ability to express herself in English with such clarity and originality. She seemed to overflow with thoughts and impressions which she wanted to impart to her friends. One letter — dated Athens, October 10, 1860 — covers fourteen handwritten pages. Quite often she turned a letter sideways and continued it across the lines already written, making such letters difficult to read.

Thirty-five letters are addressed to Marcus and/or Rebecca Spring, who were interested in the literary and social movements of the time. Fredrika had this to say about them to the Downings:

. . . Indeed Rebecca is noble and excellant; but the beauty of Character of Marcus S. is surpassing. I say this with the more certainty as he had no kind of magnetic charm to me, which often comes in in friendship between men and women and gives it a higher spice, and som[e]what of the haze of your Indian summer; I looked upon him as a beautiful child a flower yet fresh with the dews of Paradise. I never saw a more perfect goodness, and simplicity of mind and purpose together. I never saw so angel-like a man; though his touch of absentmindedness made me a little impatient with him at times. With both — Marcus and Rebecca — I had often to be on the defensive, but always against their — generosity.[3]

---

2. Constructions showing Swedish influence are not uncommon, e.g., ". . . what tragic plays she uses to perform" — (cf. Sw. *brukar*); ". . . and work in it after my power" — (cf. Sw. *efter förmåga*).

3. Johanson and Kleman, *Fredrika Bremers Brev,* IV, p. 553.

Mrs. Spring lived to be almost a hundred years old and died in Los Angeles in 1911.[4]

This Appendix contains thirty-six of Fredrika Bremer's letters owned by the Henry E. Huntington Library, which purchased them in 1934. Eleven others are from the Harvard College Library collection, most of them written to Mrs. James Russell Lowell. Also included are the texts of five Bremer letters at the American Swedish Historical Museum in Philadelphia, three at the Historical Society of Pennsylvania, four at the New York Public Library, two at the Boston Public Library, and one at the Minnesota Historical Society. Not all the unpublished letters listed in the Manuscript Bibliography are included in this Appendix; for example, only two belonging to *Fredrika-Bremer-Förbundet* are given.

The extent of the correspondence with Americans which has been preserved is indeed remarkable. Though the ink may have faded with the years, the luster of Fredrika's bright, often prophetic, mind shines through, fulfilling once more her desire to "Sing unto the Lord a new song." Like her book on America, where this Biblical theme is quoted, the letters also reflect an inspired sense of mission. She felt that the American journey was altogether necessary for her moral and intellectual development, and these letters show the extent to which Fredrika Bremer's horizons expanded in the New World.

––––––

4. For a picture of Mrs. Rebecca B. Spring in her ninety-fourth year with Susan B. Anthony and two other pioneers in the suffrage movement, see *The Story of a Pioneer* by Anna Howard Shaw (New York and London [1915]), opposite p. 270.

Fredrika Bremer Letters

(*The pertinent footnotes appear at the end of each letter.*)

1. To [Andrew Jackson Downing].[1]

Årsta the 28 Okt. 1846.

It was on the eve of my departure for Germany that I had the pleasure of receiving your letter and your book,[2] my dear Sir! I had not leisure in the hurry of that moment to write to you my thanks; but now, just returned from my voyage[3] it is one of the first and dearest duties I long to accomplish. Your book is a most beautiful and interesting work, your letter full of friendliness and goodness, but what makes book and letter so very precious to me so touchingly interesting to my heart is the kindness of the intention manifested through them to the far off stranger. Indeed it fills me with a most delicious feeling of joy and gratitude. And those endearing hands stretched over the great ocean in good will and benevolence how eloquently do they bear testimony to the coming of that Spirit which bids space and time vanish that its work of love and union may be accomplished throughout the world.

To your gift you have also joyned a most friendly invitation. I sincerely hope to be so happy once to say you personally my thanks for it. . . .[4] A specimen theireof is even your book in the sfere it embraces. We should very much need such a work in Sweden to help some of us to plant and b[u]ild and others to open their eyes with understanding to the objects that surrounds them and be a little less drowsy.

Allow me now to ask you: have you no thought of coming to Sweden and see our romantic land, its cottages and old mansions? There is one of the latter sort who would gladly open its doors to welcome you. It is on the coast of the atlantic,[5] three swedish miles from Stockholm; its name is *Årsta*. And happy should one of its inmates be, there to make you "les honneurs" of her native land and — let me whisper it — to have your counsels about a most unlucky and misst[h]riving plantation, in no style at all, which she there has undertaken. Allow her, my dear Sir, here to intreat you to pay a thought or two to this affair, and to hope a joyful result! in the mean time she subscribes herself

Your obliged and thankfull

Fredrika Bremer.

------

1. MS, Minnesota Historical Society. Andrew J. Downing, 1815-1852, American landscape gardener. He married one of the nieces of John Quincy Adams.

2. Possibly *Landscape Gardening* (1841).

3. F. Bremer, with her mother and sister Agathe, visited Marienberg, a bathing resort on the Rhine, during the summer of 1846.

4. See p. 2 for omitted passage.

5. She meant, of course, the Baltic.

2.   To Lydia H. Sigourney.[1]

Newburgh on the Hudson, Oct. 18, 1849

Dear Mrs Sigourney!

Heartily do I thank you for your kind and cordial welcome and invitation! How grateful do I feel for all the goodness and hospitality which have cheered my arrival to the shores of Amerika, and how glad I am to be here, to see, to feel, to live and learn. I am most happy now in Mr Downings charming home, and in the truly inlivening company of his wife and himself. And so shall I be, my dear lady, on my ro[u]nd from New York to Boston (as I believe in November) to pay you my respects, to converse with you, to thank you! — Nature is beautiful here and home seems as kind in the new world as nature is beautiful. I can only enjoy and be grateful. More when we meet my dear Madam and most truly Yours

Fredrika Bremer.

------

1. MS, ASHM. Lydia H. Sigourney, 1791-1865, popular American poet and author.

3.   To Charlotte Cushman.[1]

New York. Astor house. 31 Oct. 1849.

Dear Miss Cushman!

I am very much dissap[p]ointed on my arrival from Newburgh to New York not to find you here. I wished to thank you for your friendly note, to make your a[c]quaintence and to talk with you — over many a thing. I shall remain here about three weeks. Can I hope, dear Madam, to see you here during that time, and if so that you will give me notice of your arrival at New York and tell me what time it will be convenient to you to see me? If so, a note from you, left at M^r and Mrs Spring, *Brooklyn, State Str. Pink-Cottage,* will always find its way to me, even if I should not then be living with them as I now am going to do for a week or so. Indeed I hope not [to] leave this city ere I know more of *Miss Cushman.*

Truly Yours
Fredrika Bremer.

————

1. MS, owned by S. Rooth. Charlotte Cushman, 1816-1876, American actress.

4.   To Rebecca Spring.[1]

Dear dear Rebecca! A thousand thanks for your little note. I have written one to you, to day, taxing your motherly care for me. Dear Rebecca, take me home friday morning and let me be with you and yours till we go to New England! I am so weary. But I shall be well again when I am with you, and to see and hear Channing[2] is to me repose and refreshment at once. God bless you! I can but thank you!

Fredrika.

Wednesday.

————

1. MS, *s.l. et a.,* HL. Probably written in November, 1849, since the Springs accompanied F. Bremer to New England before Thanksgiving.

2. William Henry Channing, 1810-1884, one of the transcendentalists and nephew of the Unitarian clergyman William Ellery Channing. An idealist, reformer, and eloquent preacher, W. H. Channing spent the years 1854-1861 in England.

5.   To Marcus and Rebecca Spring.[1]

Boston, 9 Dec. 1849.

Oh Marcus, Oh Rebecca, Oh my dear friends, how glad, how very glad I am! Dear little Baby "out of danger;" thank God! And thank you, dear Marcus, who made it so swiftly known to us here, who were sorrowing for you. How delightful! See Rebecca, it was my story over again. You came home in the morning, and the night was passed and danger and darkness with the night. Oh! it is almost worth to have much sorrows to be able to feel such joy. It was on returning from Mr Parkers[2] sermon, yesterday, that that beautiful, joyful line from Marcus met us. Oh, it was a treat indeed. And we should have *Thankgivings* together, from the first to the last of our autumn frolic, after all my dear friends; is it not charming?! Mr King[3] came to know about you and was quite relieved and was happy with me by the good news.

At the concert I missed you so! Beethoven, with his harmonies, came to me consolator, and comforter. Oh! who has learnt that man the secrets of the beating heart, its woes and delights and aspirings, its downfalls and its final liberation. He made me cry with delightful emotion. Parker in his pulpit, on sunday, was grand in his moral, but not so in his theolog[y], and roused my spirit of contradiction. He came to see me in the evening, and we had a good talk, and he was noble and — lovely. I hope to see him again. Yesterday with Bergfalk[4] and Mr King we had the reading of [the] Whipple[5] /I believe that was the name. —/ speech and had a good deal of talk about it. It is interesting but not so original and powerful as Emerson et Com. made me think it. Mr Channing brought me "Archi Moor"[6] from the Author and with Benzon[7] I am incessantly talking about slave stories. To day I shall go to Cambri[d]ge, to the Lowells.[8] And now I shall leave you my dear friends. I would thank you for your wonderful goodness and kindness to me but I cannot. Words cannot tell how deeply and strongly you have bound me to you by what you are and what you have been to me. To think of that, to think of you will always be a sunshine to my soul. My dear friends, God bless you for that, and for what you are, and make your children and dear little baby grow up to by[be] like you! Your friends arround me send their love, and mine is with you, and so I would fain be myself,

your
affectionate
Fredrika.

Dear Rebecca! will you tell me your homeopat[h]ic Rec. for a cold? t.i. [that is] such a cold that affects the nose —

------

1. MS, HL. Marcus Spring was born 1810 at Uxbridge, Mass., and died 1874 at Eagleswood, Perth Amboy, N. J. Rebecca Buffum Spring was born 1811 in Providence, R. I., and died 1911 in Los Angeles, Calif. They were married in Philadelphia 1836 and had three children: Edward Adolphus (b. 1837), Jeanie (b. 1843), and Marcus Herbert (b. 1848).

2. Theodore Parker, 1810-1860, American preacher, theologian, and social reformer.

3. Mr. King was a young lawyer and friend of the Springs.

4. Per Erik Bergfalk, 1798-1890, Swedish professor of law, an old friend of the Bremer family.

5. Edwin Percy Whipple, 1819-1886, American critic and author; in HNW F. Bremer wrote that the speech was entitled "Essay on the American Mind."

6. Archy Moore: pseudonym of Richard Hildreth, 1807-1865, American historian. His novel, The White Slave: Memoir of Archy Moore, was republished in 1837 under this title.

7. Swedish-Norwegian vice-consul in Boston.

8. James Russell Lowell, 1819-1891, and his wife, Maria White Lowell, 1821-1853.

THE SPRING FAMILY
by Fredrika Bremer

6. To Marcus and Rebecca Spring.[1]

Cambridge, 21 Dec. 1849.

My dear, Excellant friends, Marcus and Rebecca! I can to day but just write two words to you, but these I must write to thank you for your welcome letters, for the good news about dear little Baby! God be thanked that all again is well in your beautiful home. The thought of it has made me enjoy the sun of these bright days as I should not have done had it been otherwise with you.

Dear Rebecca! You know what a pleasure to me it is to do any thing you wish, and that it then becomes my wish also. And so I think I shall have a bit of a letter about socialism, or my view of it, ready for Channing when he comes to Boston, and shall give it up first to his criticism, afterward to his paper if he so wishes.[2] I am invited to be at Concord with Emersons the 15 Jannuar[y] and I suppose Channing will by that time go there also. As to our young poet here[3] he said after reading Rebeccas words for him that it needed no birds to make him sing for Channings, that he had long thought of it etc.

He is a charming young man, there! no mistaking that! And I like and love him and his wife and the old Gentleman[4] more every day. Now I shall leave them and go about with my trunk to three or four places before I can be at rest for a little while. But I feel this will not do longer. I grow wearied to death, and you will have to lay me to sleep at Greenwood on the Ocean Hill. Then there I would lie. My dear kind friends I am melancholy to day, then[5] I want sleep. To morrow I hope it will be better. I am so thankful for my letters from home. Mother and Sisters perfectly well, and happy about my letter from New York and my American friends. Other things with family-relations were not pleasant, and political strifes make hearts sore and spirits bitter at home! Alas for that! But thank God for what is good and comforting!

Now Good bye and God bless you my kind excellant friends! Ever Yours

Fredrika.

Kiss Eddy and Jenny and Baby for me!

----

1. MS, HL.

2. W. H. Channing edited *The Spirit of the Age* (New York), but no letter by F. Bremer appeared in January-March, 1850.

3. James Russell Lowell.

4. James R. Lowell's father, Rev. Charles Lowell, 1782-1861, pastor of West Congregational Church in Boston.

5. Miss Bremer frequently used "then" in the sense of "because," presumably doubly influenced by the German "denn" and the less frequent Swedish "då," both conveying this meaning.

7.   To Lydia H. Sigourney.[1]

Cambridge 26 Dec. 1849.

Dearest Mrs Sigourney!

I was just in the act of writing to you, to day, when I received your new gift and your note. A thousand thanks, dear Mrs Sigourney, for this kindness, as well as for that I enjoyed at your house, in Hartford! I should have written long ago if not — well, the excuses your own kind and considerate mind will suggest. Dear Mrs Sigourn[e]y, I shall probably stay at Boston the whole month of Jannuar[y]. I have been so fatigued, almost to illness, with going about and seeing much company during more than two month[s] that I must have a time of quiet and retirement to get up again and be able to go on afresh. Such a time I shall be able to have at Boston, and I do not know now when I shall begin to travel again, nor if it shall be possible to me to make the visit to Hartford and to you that it would have been my wish to pay. I feel very "Bearish" at this cold season and would, if I could help it, hardly leave my warm den. When I shall go southward, then dear Mrs Sigourn[e]y I shall take the liberty to write to you and tell about my movements and if I shall be free to come and see you. Give my love to your Daughter, and my cordial thanks and compliments to those who have sent invitations to me and wished to see me. I regret truly that I should have so little time. Young Miss Todds letter made me smile indeed, and when she will be of my age, and especially if she should happen then to be an author she may smile too, on looking at her girlish thoughts about the stuff authors are made of, — but with a feeling she now may be little aware of.

The young man who brought me your note this afternoon pleased me much, and I should be glad to see him more. Your "Whisper to a bride" I shall bring over the ocean to the brides in Sweden. Your kindness to me I never shall forget, but keep it in a thankful heart.

respectfully and affectionately Yours

P.S.   Fredrika Bremer.

M. Longfellow has received his part of your letter. He is a very agre[e]able man. And a truly charming man is the young and noble poet, James Russel[l] Lowell, at whose home I now am staying. He and his wife are a charming and happy pair.

───────

1. MS, owned by S. Rooth. (Presented by Gustav Wetterstrom, New York.)

8.   To Rebecca Spring.[1]

Concord the 19 Jan. 1850

My dear good Rebecca!

I should have written earlier to you if I had been so well as (thank God!) your little baby is now. But I have not been nor am, nor know when I shall be again. Alleopathie [allopathy] failed with me, though I had one of the first alleopathes in Boston, and I have taken to Homeopathy and have felt it work well at some times but not yet steadely so. I have an excellant kind and wise old doctor (Mr Osgood[2]) who through good will and science will make me well, if possible. And if he will succeed, then my dear friends I shall see you again before the middle of Februar[y], and from New York I shall go with Anne Lynch[3] to Washington and after some stay there proceed to the south. If I should not be better than I am now — well dear Rebecca, then I shall ask Marcus to give me his kind and protecting hand just to carry me on board of a steamer that will go right down to Cuba, and once there I shall lie quietly down among the flowers, and ask the kind heaven and the air and the earth to give me annother feeling of life and existance than now is mine; I shall lie down in the quiet and *wait* as "the friends" would adwise me to do. And I am sure I shall not wait in vain. I feel certain that nothing serious is the matter with me, and that the feeling of weakness from which I suffer will give way when a time of perfect repose and perhaps change of air will permit my good nature to rise again as is its nature to do. Do not, dearest Rebecca, look out for any escort (as you call it for me). I love to be alone on the great waters (and never feel less lonely as then); and a companion who should not be a very good and congenial friend would now only make me suffer.

I write to you from Emersons house. I did not believe myself able to go there, but encouraged by my good doctor I went and am glad of it, then I enjoy extremely E.-s society and his strong, logical and poetical mind. On monday I shall again be in New York and be for some days a poor lioness on evening parties which I cannot escape. But after these I shall keep doggedly to rest and homeopathy. To Mrs Kirkland[4] I shall very soon write. A little note to H. W. Channing I enclose here. Give my love to Mrs Child.[5] I hope to see her when I come to New York.

Dear Rebecca I have forgotten to thank you for sending my vintercloak. I do so now very heartely. I could not do without it. And now I have still a request. Dear Rebecca, would you look through the books that I left at your house and find out a thin light blue book of Swedish poetry with title: *Fänrik Ståls sägner* af Runeberg;[6] and if you find it there would you be so good to send it to me at Benzons house? I have promised the book to Mr Longfellow.[7] Excuse!

Now I am going to make a little sketsh of Emersons eagle-featured face, and leave you for the present. My love I also leave with you and Marcus; let it play among your children, in your home, as one of them! Yours

Fredrika

Benzon has been most kind and excellant to me. I sorrowed over his departure as over that of a good and faithful friend.

––––––

1. MS, HL.

2. David Osgood, a homeopathic practitioner in Boston.

3. Anne C. Lynch, 1815-1891, American author noted for her literary salon in New York. She moved there in 1845 and taught English composition at the Brooklyn Academy for Women.

4. Caroline Matilda Kirkland, 1801-1864; American author who wrote about her experiences as a settler in Michigan.

5. Lydia Maria Child, 1802-1880, American author and reformer.

6. Johan Ludvig Runeberg, 1804-1877, Swedish poet born in Finland. *The Tales of Ensign Stål* is a collection of narrative poems.

7. F. Bremer presented it to Longfellow in February, 1850; now at Longfellow House.

9.   To Marianne Silsbee.[1]

Boston 25 Jan. 1850.

Dear Mrs Silsbee! Let me thank you heartely for your kind little note and invitation, and let me tell you that since I have seen you I feel strongly drawn towards Salem and to your home there, and am not without hope to be able to go and sit down with you there. But next week it cannot be. I must be stronger in health than I now feel myself to be. I must try a little while more what homeopathie and my kind doktor can do for me to put me up again, and that, and some engagements also, will detain me here next week. When I feel myself stronger, when I see my horizon cleared up, and feel I shall be able to enjoy the company and the home so kindly offered me in Salem, then, dear Mrs Silsbee, you shall hear of me again!

Affectionat[e]ly Yours
Fredrika Bremer.

––––––

1. MS, ASHM. Mrs. Marianne Cabot Devereux Silsbee, 1812-1889, author of *A Half Century in Salem* (1887).

10.   To Maria Lowell.[1]

Boston. Tuesday Af. Noon.

. . .[2] To day I feel extrem[e]ly well after a delightful night; I have enjoyed Emersons conversation one hour and Alcotts two in the morning, and should have enjoyed you and James, so as I can enjoy the company of belowed [beloved] beings, when I am well. And I shall be well my sweet Maria, fear not. Homeopathy will do it, and that kind good man of a Doctor who looks upon and almost into you with so benignant and so keen good-willing a look, that if a look could cure that certainly should. And it certainly has its power too. And so has your kind sympathy. Bless you for it.

To Concord I shall go first on thursday. Emerson will go there with me. On Monday next week I shall return. One day that week I should wish to visit the sc[h]ool of your sister in law Mrs Lowell with you, or with Mrs Putnam.[3] And that will be my first visit in the sc[h]ools of Boston.

And now, good Night. Bless you dear Maria and all which is yours! And then I must be in the company as one of yours

Fredrika.

----

1. MS, *s.a.*, HCL. Probably written in January or February, 1850.

2. See p. 46 for beginning of paragraph.

3. Mary Lowell Putnam, 1810-1898, sister of James Russell Lowell; she had translated F. Bremer's work *Trälinnan* into English (*The Bondmaid;* 1844).

11.　To Maria Lowell.[1]

[Boston, February, 1850?]

What's the matter Maria, dear Maria, that I hear nothing from you, nor see a line answering my questions, and why do not you or James ever come to Boston? Is Cambridge revolutionized, barricaded, blown-up? Or are you — well I don't know what to suggest, to invent, to fall down upon to account for this silence and nonapparition of yours since a week. Dear Maria let me now very soon hear of you by letter or personally!

I heard Mrs Kemble[2] last night and was truly delighted with her reading. I have conversed with her to day, and am so[3] with her true and honest mind. She was kind ennough to give me a billet of introduction to her readings for me and my friends. On Saturday morning at elleven o klock she is to read *Julius Caesar.* Now, I can think of no friends I should be so delighted to be with at that reading, as you, dear Maria and James. And now I ask you, my dear young friends if you will not give me the pleasure to go there with you? If you should come here at about 10 o klock I should have a carriage ready to take us there in good time, then to have good places it is necessary to go about an hour before the reading begins.

Now, do come if you can. It should be so pleasant to hear that beautiful thing (the play) together, read by so true an artist. (Very bad english this, I suspect!)

Good bye, and let me hear from you!

Fredrika

Thursday.

----

1. MS, *s.l. et a.*, HCL. Address: Elmwood. Probably written either late in January or early February, 1850.

2. Frances Anne Kemble, 1809-1893, English actress and author.
3. F. Bremer forgot to insert a word after *so*.

12.   To Maria Lowell.[1]

Boston 9 Febr. 1850.

I have been thinking of you, talking to you, all the time since saturday last, dearest Maria, and only not writing to you because an excursion to Lowell, much company, and afterwards illness (but only an obstinate migraine) has hindered me. To day well again and alone for a little while, I must write to you the talk of my soul with you. Thanks dearest, sweetest Maria for your little note of yesterday, which comforted me for you, then I was in fear of your beeing sick, and which let me see your feelings, so natural; then sad and sorro[w]ful they must be for a while, and wrap your thoughts in shadows. Though not beeing a mother I can deeply sympat[h]ize with you. I can feel the rising bitter wawe [wave] of longing to that little bit of flesh and blood arrayed in beauty, flesh of your flesh, which so recently lay warm at your breast and now lies cold in the cold earth.[2] Oh! yes, I can feel and weep for you with you, then I have lost all those who were dearest to me and have closed their eijes [eyes] and seen them laid to sleep in their graves, and many and many a time have felt as if I would stre[t]ch myself and lye down on those graves never to rise more. Yes, I can feel with you, and yet I must feel that your sorrow is such as heaven sends to its favorites. It is hallowed and hallowing. The frozen snowflake falls but it melts to the ray of day, and lo! it is changed in a clear tear in a radiant eye who looketh upwards and mirrors the lights of heaven. How different from those barren griefs which produce barren[n]ess which as bitter northwinds blowing incessently from day to day freeze up all the generous flowing rivers of the heart; — seemingly at least, and for this space of time which we call earthly life. Then I do not, cannot believe in any everlasting winter. I have experienced in my own life how even on earth paradise lost changes in the glories of paradise regained. Then I will not say it is lost, but only it is obscured, obscured in the shadows of night, and waits for a new day. Earth has a glowing hearth — and the heart out of which it came forth — oh! ever glowing with love, everlasting and all powerful will not permit any spark connected with its life to close in darkness, to escape the fulfilment of its heavenly instinct, its hopes and its love.

Still there is a great difference in the missfortunes of life, there are such for whom we must shed the tears of anguish, and call on death as a benefactor. Not so yours my sweet Maria. For such are the sweetest hopes and consolations of heaven. And even in your grief I must call you blessed. Yes, blessed are you in the innocence and beauty of sorrow, blessed in your love, blessed in that beauty which draws to you the hearts of fellow beings and makes your own being harmonious in its whole life; blessed are you in the love of your good and nobleminded husband — in the deep harmony with him and his noble and expanding career, — blessed in beeing to him a blessing and making even sorrow, and the snowflakes of winter turn to roses to laurels round his brow. Oh! in sorrow as in joy, yours is a noble lot dearest Maria! May you feel it and let your drooping head gently rise in the consciousness theirof, and gaze serenely again on that heaven to whose darling children you belong. For ever I shall be glad to have seen you and known you. Your dear image I treasure in my heart, and feel it to be there a blessing.

I hope to see you again at your house, but know not if before I leave Boston this time. In summer I must come and look in upon you before I go home and see you and James happy and joyful again!

ever Your

Fredrika

———

1. MS, HCL.

2. Rose Lowell, third daughter of the Lowells, died February 2, 1850, aged six months.

13. To James Freeman Clarke.[1]

Tuesday morning 12 Febr. 1850.

My dear Sir! You and I have both been sufferers since a time, you bodily, I more mentally. We are now both recovering, thank God! Permit me to send you a neighborly greeting and Congratulation, and to tell you how truly glad I am to know you are better. I take the liberty to send you some flowers, and wish you would look upon them as emblems of sweet joys that are waiting for you in life, and of the kind feelings and good wishes that blossom for you in the hearts of many friends. As a true partaker in these wishes, and in the feelings of these friends for you, allow me to be numbered among them!

Fredrika Bremer.

———

1. MS, s.l., HCL. James Freeman Clarke, 1810-1888, Unitarian minister and author. Because of ill health he left Boston for Pennsylvania in August, 1850.

14. To Marcus and Rebecca Spring.[1]

Charlestown, South Caroline
28 March 1850.

My dear, kind, rose coloured friends (observe that I write to you on rose-coulored paper!) hear I now verely aim [am], happy and well, indeed so well as well can be, and thankful to God and men, but most especially to the rosecolored couple at rose Cottage! Dear Marcus, dear Rebecca! I cannot well thank you, but I wish you could but see how happy I am in the thought of you!!

A little while after you left me on the Steamboat, I laid down my aching head and tried to sleep, and slumbered slightly, always fancying again and again that I saw you coming in my room, and I thought "well! there they are! They have not left me after all! They are going with me!" But alas they were not! I walked much on deck in the afternoon and was better. Read Davis book "on special Providance,"[2] almost with indignation. /on account of the dictatorial and oracular tone he assumes in the poorness of his reasonings./ What a poor undigested thing! Whatever of genuine aspiration and vision has been in the man it is now cramped and confused by undigested metaphysics. With a little of Parker he tries to dogmatize over christian religion and dogmas, ap[p]ealing magnificently to the "laws of Nature" as ultimate standard of criticism, without seeming in least aware of how little the laws of Nature in their final causes and their relations to spiritual nature and spiritual laws are known by us as yet (and the greatest as well as the most true minded of natural philosophers of this age: Berzelius,[3] Örsted,[4] Humboldt[5] would tell him so). With a little of Fourier[6] he tries to patch up what is wanting in this "perfect system of nature" in contradiction to what he just before asserted. And he crowns the whole work by a dissertation to prove that the sin against "the holy Ghost" means sin against *nature* which can never be pardoned; t.i., must always be punished *in proportion* (?) to the sin. For the rest it strikes me with D..s visions as with those of Swedenborg[7] and St. Theresa,[8] that they [are] reverberations of their own moral and intel[l]ectual perceptions. But D. is, compared to these mystics, as a moth to a Mammoth. But this is to[o] long a talk over so little a thing!

In the evening that first day of my voyage, my companion (the young lady) was brought in to me, very sick. I welcomed her kindly and should have felt althogether so to her, if not as soon as her eyes were opened in the morning she had not come out with that most dreadful of all questions to me (perhaps for that I have heard it so many hundred times): how do you like America! Question who was invareably repeated by every one on board who accosted me. But I was so intent on beeing in peace and silence, and manifested so clearly, that I was permitted to be so, and had but short scraps of talk with my fellow passengers except with a young man who pleased me through his expression and ad[d]ress and did not ask me "how I did like Amerika?"

Tuesday: bright sun, but still cold till about noon; then at once spring, and the most delightful day. The Ocean was all gold and the sky full of beauty. Oh! this was a treat indeed. I sat on the upper deck almost alone, and enjoyed the great lonely ocean, and the air

so fresh and soft, saw the sun go down and the moon rise in mild
majesty with Jupiter as for[e]runner, I sat turned to the north star,
now removing farther and farther away from me, and saw the con-
stellations coming out all arround. On the deck below, the young
men also came out with there [their] young women (we have no
old ones on board; I think I am one of the oldest) in the beautiful
moonshine; they seemed fond and loving as doves, and there also
sat side by side the friends[9] M^r and Mrs A. in the quiet as doves,
looking up to the moon silently, and the moon looking down upon
their innocent and somewhat unmeaning faces. I sat alone but I
could not help thinking myself the happiest of the party, thus I
enjoyed all and conversed delightfully with the things in heaven
and the creatures and things on earth. So we rolled on in the shining
night on the shining deep towards Cap[e] *Hatt[e]ras,* whose phare,[10]
gleaming as a great star on the southern horizon announced that
we would soon come in the mexican gulph and in the warm waters
and warm winds. But that was a "sham" promise. Next Morning
storm and rain, and sky and ocean so gray and dismal as possible.
Under a roof, on the lower deck, part of the company sat down to
a merry play of card[s] (great part was seasick). I sat somewhat
apart with the two friends who were silent and looked thoughtful
or — thoughtless, I dont know well which. However they both soon
went to sleep. I was keenly awake that day with an essay of Emerson, (afterward with Bankrofts history[11]), the Ocean, and in fact a
world of thoughts. Then I was *well,* so well as when I first crossed
the ocean, and felt again the spirit of the Vikings all alive in me.
Colder and colder grew the day, and *to day* on coming to the land
of promise for summer and paradisi[a]cal we[a]ther it was almost
as cold and disagreeable as the day I left New York, and *no Sun.* But
the shores covered with dark firs and greening leaftrees looked
strange and pleasant. Mrs Howland had sent her brother and a
carriage for me, but I preferred going to a hotel with the friends.
And here I am now, at the Ma[n]sion house, very comfortably,
writing to you my dear, excellant friends. The sun has come out of
the grey clouds and though the wind is chilling I have enjoyed a
stroll of two hours all alone through the city, looking at the strange
trees now putting forth their young leaves as if a little afraid of
the cold, and the roses and lilys nodding from out the gardens and
teracces. I have also heard the mocking-bird in a cage and its curious song maid [made] up of all other birds notes without any
original strain — at least so it now seemed to me. Two thirds of the
population in the streets are coloured. Many merry looking but
ragged men. Children rather pretty and stout.

    29. Well! how wonderfully things turn out sometimes! I cer-
tainly never expected Mrs Howland (judging from her letters[)]
to turn out into a hearty and truly comfortable sort of person with
whom I should be most pleased. But so it is. And to morrow I shall

go to her house and stay with her some days, and go with her to several plantations "rich and poor that I may see both kinds;" and go with her to "a botanising and sensible lady." The Gilmans[12] I have seen, and like prodigiously the old Gentleman, very well the young son in law and the ladies also; shall go with them in the woods and to Sullivans island. My dear friends, the sun shines, I am well, have just eaten a Bananas, and love you, and hope the slaves may be happy and will be free!

Dear Marcus dear Rebecca when health and spring are coming we cannot help hoping all things. Now write to me (to the care of Doctor Gilman) and tell me how you are all, and the Children and the cow, and. . .[13]

I enclose a letter for Sweden, dear Marcus, with a boon[14] to you to see it forwarded by next steamer.

Love to the Children, to your good and beautiful Channing, to that beautiful and noble Stoic Emerson also, though I am sure he cares not a farthing for it. But he has it yet. Thats a fact. And a fact it also is, and a more true there never was, dear Rebecca, dear Marcus that I am your grateful and loving friend

Fredrika.

I shall write to morrow to Mrs Kirkland.

-----

1. MS, HL.

2. *The Philosophy of Special Providences. A Vision* (Boston, 1850) by Andrew Jackson Davis, 1826-1910.

3. Jöns J. Berzelius, 1779-1848, Swedish chemist.

4. Hans Christian Örsted, 1777-1851, Danish physicist.

5. Alexander, Baron von Humboldt, 1769-1859, German naturalist and explorer.

6. François M. C. Fourier, 1772-1837, French socialist.

7. Emanuel Swedenborg, 1688-1772, Swedish scientist, philosopher, and theologian.

8. St. Theresa, 1515-1582, Spanish Carmelite nun and mystic.

9. Quakers.

10. Phare: lighthouse.

11. *History of the United States* (1834+) by George Bancroft, 1800-1891, American historian and statesman.

12. Dr. Samuel Gilman, a Charleston minister, and family.

13. See p. 44 for rest of paragraph.

14. Boon: request (obsolete meaning).

15.   To Maria Lowell.[1]

White House on the Pee Dee South Carolina,
21 April 1850.

And so, dearest Maria, the Angel of death has again visited your sunny home and spread gloom over its life! But I see the flowers round the pale face of the deceased,[2] and in that beautiful symbolic language I read the words: "o grave where is thy victory?" But your poor father! Still that pious and true christian, will soon have lifted himself up to read the answer to his prayer, though the characters were written in greater proportions than well fits our common mortal eye. I have myself often been studying and wondering over the manner in which God answers the prayers and questions of his creatures. How paternally sometimes, how familiarly and homely, just as if he would say: "I am not only the lawgiver of the world, I am also a father, *thy* father entering in all thy concerns, feeling for thee, and ministering unto thee as a father, that thou may know me as such." Then at other times how grandly and dreadfully, in the events of individual life or of history, as if he would say: "My kingdom is not of this world!" — And ther[e]by opens to us the realms of annother life, the space of the universe. Once he seems to speak to you directly in the revelations of your mind, in the closet of your heart, filling you with grace and joy; annother time you ask and he answers not, you beg for a drop of spiritual grace — and your mind is dry as the desert. But after a while — perhaps a new view of the world or of life, new intel[l]ectual treasures are opened to you, in which your mind expands and renews itself, and you find that the bread which was withheld for a moment and in a special manner is given indirectly and in a grander style. It seems to me that in my own life I have, at different periods, received all these different answers, and I have concluded that it must be so, that these different modes of Gods conversation with man makes part of his education, and that we by them must learn to adapt ourselves to the style and manner of the great speaker, happy if in the *general* providence as well as in the *special* one we have learned to believe in, to love the good, the loving Father! To some minds this seem[s] to be wonderfully easy, to be as it were *inborn,* and I think yours, dear Maria, is among these.

Thanks for what you told me of you and yours, your sorrows and hopes! May the lovely spring make all these latter ones come out in fair flowers!

When we meet I shall have much to tell you about life here in the south. I write now to you on the banks of the little river Pee Dee, on a plantation belonging to Mr Poinsett[3] where I have been lingering a time for the rare opportunity I have to study here and on neighboring plantations, the condition and life of the Negro slaves. In Charlestown I heard much of the late Indian Chief O[s]-ceola[4] and have gathered elements of a story which to become a most beautiful poem needs only to be treated by J. R. Lowell. But of this we will speak by the waters of Niagara.

My life in the Palmetto state has hitherto been a very happy one, nature has been beautiful (though dimmed by much bad weather) and men kind. I have intensely enjoyed some very beauti-

OSCEOLA:

Fredrika Bremer's Copy

of a Portrait by

Robert John Curtis

now in the

Charleston Museum

Fredrika-Bremer-Förbundet

ful days, and the company of one of the most intel[l]ectually interesting women I ever met with — Mrs Holbrook.[5] The naturalist Mr
Bachman,[6] and the old amiable statesman, Mr Poinsett, are to me
very agre[e]able and instructive a[c]quaintances. Among the Negro slaves I have also such, though in annother manner. Mr and
Mrs Gilman are good and agre[e]able people. I had the pleasure
to meet at their house a sister of yours, dear Maria, and must kiss
her heartely for that merit. In the family of Mrs Howland, in
Charlestown, I found a most agre[e]able home and a good and
pleasant family. Now, I am soon going to Savannah, and from thence
to Augusta, after which I think to go back to Charlestown again
and from thence to Washington through Virginia, by the middle
of May. There dear Maria I hope to have that letter from you which
as yet has not reached me, but whose words I seem to know, then
I know you.

    And now good bye, dearest Maria! May all the sweet powers
of the spring in the sky and on earth, all the good spirits of youthful
nature conspire with your young lover and poet and husband to
make you well and happy!

Kindest regards to him, to your father and Rebecca from your affectionate friend

Fredrika.

––––––––

1. MS, HCL.
2. Lowell's mother, Mrs. Harriet Brackett Spence Lowell, died March 30, 1850.
3. Joel Roberts Poinsett, 1779-1851, American statesman.
4. Osceola, ca. 1804-1838, Seminole Indian chief.
5. Mrs. Harriott Holbrook (d. 1863), wife of the American naturalist and professor of anatomy, John Edwards Holbrook, 1794-1871.
6. John Bachman, 1790-1874, American naturalist, associate of Audubon.

16.   To Marcus and Rebecca Spring.[1]

White House on the Pee Dee
22 April 1850

Thank you my dear friends Marcus and Rebecca for your welcome letters and the news about you and yours! Charlestown should be a dear place to me only for its merit of having restored you, dear Marcus, to life and health, but it is endeared to me also now by many most pleasant associations. Then though I have had here a great deal of cold and rainy weather I have highly enjoyed nature on some beautiful days and felt happy in the kind and pleasant family which has given me a home in Charlestown. I have also highly enjoyed the company of Mrs Hollbrook, one of the most intel[l]ectually interesting women I have ever met with, and a day alone with her, at her farm, will range among my most pleasant memories of my life here. The Naturalist Mr Bachman and the old statesman Mr Poinsett are to me also very agre[e]able and instructive a[c]quaintences.

I now write to you from his plantation on the little river Pee Dee, some miles from Georgetown, a very retired and solitary place where I have lingered more than a week for the rare opportunity I have here, during my solitary rambles, to study the condition and life of the Negro slaves, then about 6 (six) plantations, belonging to different masters, lie here about clustered together in the woods, and I roam about and see the negroes on the rice-fields and by their dinner, in their villages and by their firesides and talk freely with them. ["]I have dust in my eyes, about slavery!" Oh no Rebecca, that is not possible! It is not possible for an unsophisticated mind to blunder[2] to the unrighteousness of the institution, and the evils necessar[i]ly resulting from it. But neither is it possible for any one, with open and clear eyes, to look about here, /And in Charlestown —/ and see these good-humored, grinning faces, the fat and portly matrons, the quantities of merry children, to go in the Negro villages

SCENE FROM THE

POINSETT PLANTATION

by

Fredrika Bremer

Fredrika-Bremer-Förbundet

and behold the Peach trees and poultry and pigs surrounding each house and belonging to the family there, with an enclosed garden ground, it is not possible to see the people there by their firesides with their pipes and their meat, to hear their merry jests and laughs when at work, and not to be aware of, that, even under that baneful institution, more wellbeing and happiness is possible than is commonly believed. Of course that will be different under a bad master and chances, och [and] rather, necessity has already made me see some of the worst as well as some of the best features of slavery. Much I will have to tell you when we meet again. Meantime I write down to you here what I openly say every where in the south: "God bless the good Master, and *God — damn* the bad one!"

With Mr Poinsett I have had great pleasure to talk of several objects relating to this country, also of slavery. He is a trueminded man who frankly and fearlessly faces the subject. Many other[s] I have met who talk of slavery in a manner to convince me that they themselves are the slaves of Mammon.

I am soon going to Savannah, and will hardly leave the south for Washington before the middle of May. Dear Marcus! will you take in your care and send to Europe the enclosed letter? Dear Rebecca I send herewith a copy of the little sketsh of Jenny Lind. But do not let any other person enjoy it! Certainly I must have left my book *Margaret*[3] at your house. If so, dear Rebecca take care of it then it belongs to Mrs Hooper in Boston. And now good bye dear kind friends! Ever Yours affectionately

Fredrika.

Your pleasing and amiable relation Mrs Taft I have seen and hope to see again. She has been very ill in health and was when I saw her last.

––––––––

1. MS, HL.

2. F. Bremer probably confused the English word *blunder* with the Swedish *blunda,* meaning "to close one's eyes."

3. Sylvester Judd, 1813-1853, was the author of *Margaret, A Tale of the Real and Ideal, Flight and Bloom,* a transcendental novel published anonymously (1845).

17. To Israel K. Tefft.[1]

Savannah 17 May 1850.

Mr I. K. Tefft!

Writing with your pen and on your paper — mine by grace and gift of you — let me express to you, my dear Sir, how thankful I feel for the hospitality and kindness shown me by you and yours! The generous kindness I have experienced in America, and which I have experienced in your house anew, makes me feel the wealth of this people more than all the gold of California could do; and here I must repeat what I already have said and will say of America: happy the land where there are such hearts and such homes!

respectfully and thankfully
Yours
Fredrika Bremer.

––––––––

1. MS, NYPL. Mr. Tefft, 1794-1862, noted autograph collector of Savannah.

18. To Rebecca Spring.[1]

Philadelphia 22 June 1850.

Dear kind Rebecca! A thousand thanks to you for your letter breathing all love and spiritual life! It drew tears to my eyes to see how good you and Marcus are to me how you have thought for me! How have I come to such sweet love and goodness? Only by the grace of God. And Him I thank for it. God be thanked also that you, dearest Rebecca, are restored again to those who love you so well and that you love, and that you, though feeble still, are improving in health! Marcus, in his little note, gave me hope to see him during my stay here. How glad should I be! I will not leave Philadelphia before Wednesday when I must proceed to Washington, though it goes much against me to leave so soon the City of brotherly love, then I am perfectly charmed by the public institutions here, so grand, so good, so glorious to humanity and to the people whose work and mark they are; and I am charmed also by the people about me, particularly *the friends,* who also are extremely friendly to me. I have been at one of their meetings but this one was very dull. The spirit moved nobody. One member coughed, I sneezed, and that was all action I heard or saw. But I liked the earnest and thoughtful faces. Lucretia Mott[2] came to see me and I have been at her house and am taking a little sketsh of her. Beautiful and bright little woman!

I am not sure yet dear Rebecca if I shall go back to Sweden this fall. I wish to stay in America one winter more, see the tropics and be a time with you, kindest and best of friends! But my Mother and sister seem to long for my return, and ask me much when I will come to them again. And if they strongly express that wish, after my having written to them asking if they can spare me one winter more, then — *I must go,* and you dear Rebecca will also say so. But at all events I shall have some quiet days with you before that time; and perhaps — perhaps may I be permitted to see the winter fires kindle in your chimney and enjoy them with you!

I cannot write more, then a severe headache compells me to lye down on my bed! God bless you and yours dearest Rebecca and make you soon all well!

Your loving
Fredrika.

Dear Rebecca! I left in your little wardrobe up stairs (right hand) a little bottle with homeopathic pills. Would you send them to me with Marcus or with the post in a letter?! I need them much and dont know their med. name so I cannot procure them.

Poor Bergfalk has been sick to death in Philadelphia but has been restored to health through care and kindness. He writes of it with a heart melting with thankfulness. He is going home, from Boston.

––––––––

1. MS, HL.

2. Lucretia Mott, 1793-1880, Quaker social reformer, a leader in the abolitionist movement.

19.   To Maria Lowell.[1]

Washington 3 July 1850.

Dearest Maria! The Month of June is at an end, and — where is our Niagara-party? Mr Downing has run off to London, and I am in Washington and you and James, where are you? I write to Cambridge and hope my letter will find you somewhere by that way. Dear Maria I have been retarded and retarded on my way till I find that I shall hardly be able to be at Niagara falls before the middle or end of August. Then I must from here go to the see [sea] shore to recruit my strength in the waters of the ocean after which I shall go to Maine and New Hampshire and from [there] to Niagara. Shall I find you there. I should be so glad! But perhaps that time will be to[o] late for you and for the health of Maria not so conveniant.   . . .[2] You speak, dear Maria, (in your little welcome letter which I received here) of my serenity of humour. Alas for that. I feel often very morbid, and am sorry for it then that is an unhappy feeling. Still I am not very anxious for it nor for anny morbidness in my friends, then I know that it so very often is the effect of bodily defect and disease, which we will drop when we shall drop off this poor mortal clay. There is — but more of this, sometime and somewhere, when we shall be at peace. Will it be [by] the falls of Niagara?!

[End of MS]

————

1. MS (incomplete), HCL.
2. See p. 65 for omitted passage.

20.   To Marcus and Rebecca Spring.[1]

Washington 13 July 1850.

My dear, kind friends! Thanks to you for your friendly, welcome and welcoming notes! How glad I shall be to see you again, and then — — and then if you could be induced to take a trip to the White mountains, or to go with me and the young Lowells to Niagara! — As it now seems to me I will be in New York (or Brooklyn) about the 10 or 12 of August, and soon after start for Niagara with J. R. Lowell and his wife who will go up the Hudson with me. From thence I shall proceed to the west. And if I cannot take just a *short* trip to the White mountains, I must allthogether give up to visit Maine and New-Hampshire, till after my return from the West, for fear beeing to[o] late there and at the falls. If, — If I only can have time! It is pity that time cannot be manufactured. I should need it so much.

Tell me, dear friends, do you think it possible that you about the middle of August could take that trip to Niagara with the Lowells and myself? Indeed I think no four persons could come together more fitted to be happy in one anothers company than you and the Lowells. And I should be so happy to be with you. Mr Downing is gone to London on *Buissness* and his little lady is gone to the sea shore so their part in our party is broken up.

Now I should have much to tell you about things here, but much you know already through the papers, and the rest I must spare till we meet. . . .[2]

Here in Washington I have made some most interesting a[c]-quaintances among whom I count Miss Dix,[3] Professor Henry,[4] Mr Carey[5] of Philadelphia and several others. Many people I must also see of no interest at all to me. But that is a tax to be paid every where.

I shall leave Washington for Philadelphia about the 22d July, and from there go to Cape May with Professor Hart[6] and his wife to take the sea baths a forthnight, and from thence go to New York. And now I must go to see the funeral procession,[7] so Good bye, my dear friend[s] love to the children from your

affectionate friend
Fredrika

———

1. MS, HL.

2. See p. 68 for rest of paragraph.

3. Dorothea Lynde Dix, 1802-1887, pioneer in the reform of prisons, alms-houses, and insane asylums.

4. Joseph Henry, 1797-1878, American physicist, first secretary and director of the Smithsonian Institution.

5. Henry C. Carey, 1793-1879, American economist.

6. John Seely Hart, 1810-1877, American educator and author.

7. President Zachary Taylor had died July 9, 1850.

21.   To James and Maria Lowell.[1]

Philadelphia 26 July 1850.

Now for you, my dear young friends and for a clearing off of the mist which has hung over our Niagara tour this long time! then I feel it clear in my mind to day, and I must tell you as I feel it. Thanks for your letter, dearest Maria! It came to me just as I was leaving Washington and I did read it next day, in a beautiful place, on the shores of the Patapsco.[2] I had written to you some time before from Washington but dont know if you had got my note.[3] I spoke there of our starting for Niagara, from New York, about the middle of August, but I must a little alter that, as I feel the necessity for me of having some longer stay at the seashore. I am now going to Cape May, and shall from thence go to Nahant, near Boston. Now, my proposition is: that we will meet in Boston /latist week in August!/ and from thence take a trip to the White Mountains and to the green ones of Vermont, return to Boston, go to New York, where the Springs will joyn us, and go with us up the Hudson and to Niagara, where we should arrive by the 1 of September. Should you wish not to go to the White Mountains (but why should we not meet all the Giants at once?) I shall still go, and then some days later joyn you in Boston. People say that the weather generally is warm and delightful about the first part of September. Well my dear young friends what do you say to that? Will that do? Will it be agre[e]able to you? Please direct an answer to the care of Professor Hart, Sartaines Magazine, Philadelphia, and I will have it with certainty. Of all other things I wait to speak till I am with you. But I must say alas! for the gallant Sir Robert Peel![4] And Alas! Alas, for the Countess Ossoli, Marg[a]ret Fuller[5] coming to her native shore with her infant boy and husband

[Half page of MS missing]

in his little grave on desolate sandhills, and she is in the deep ocean apart from him.

But no! . . .[6]

Methink our young poets heart will make him take his harp and sing a requiem for the dead, a requiem over the once fierce but now hushed waves! - - -

[Half page of MS missing]

P.S. A still better plan would be — (supposing you take with me the trip to the white mountains and the "Verts-monts") to go from thence up to Mount Real [Montreal] and down the St. Laurence to Niagara. From thence you can go down the Hudson and so both coming and going see new ways and new scenes. I hope to enduce the Springs also to go to the white mountains.

———————

1. MS (incomplete), HCL.

2. Patapsco: a Maryland river.

3. See p. 175.

4. Sir Robert Peel, 1788-1850, British statesman and prime minister who died in London July 2, following a fall while horseback riding.

5. Sarah Margaret Fuller, Marchioness Ossoli, 1810-1850, American author and literary critic.

6. See p. 70 for rest of paragraph.

22.   To Marcus and Rebecca Spring.[1]

Niagara 8 Sept. 1850.

"Even so," and God bless you both, kindest and best of friends, for a thousand reasons and also for what you have been and are to me! You do not know, you cannot understand, Marcus and Rebecca, how much good you have done me and are doing. Nor will I now tell; but you will understand it once. Thank you, dear Rebecca, for the letter I received from you on the morning of my arrival here, and which was most welcome to me. Then more necessary to me than to see the falls of Niagara was to know that you were well and happy at home. I was ashamed, I could not well hold up my head for the sake of the deluge which came on the very day I prophesied good weather; and then to know you on the way all that time! And how Marcus must have looked down upon my spirit of prophecy! But I beg him to consider that prophets, sometimes look farther than to the nearest futurity, and so may my spirit have overlooked the deluge of the day for the glorious sun of next day. Indeed, I cannot but believe it was so. We[2] were fairly not drowned but drained by the downpouring streams, we and our Carpet bags, and had a great drying up at Albany where we remained till next morning. . . .[3]

In Utica I went out and searched for the spirit of Cato, and *found it* though in a metamorphosis which to many would have been puzzling.[4] In Rochester — oh! how I wished that you, my dear friends, had been theer [there] with me and my young friends! How I wished that you had been with us on the banks of the Genesee, opposite the range of factories, and looked with us on the streams of wasted water who after having done their work in the Mills now came gushing and dancing down the pictureske walls, bubbling as champaigne, and merry as boys who come out of the sc[h]ools for a holiday in the country. Rich verdure, shrubs, wines [vines] and flowers came up along the paths of the streams down to the river telling a hundred tales about the goodness of labor, and how beauty will follow the paths of well directed usefulness, and plants flowers in the footsteps of industry. It was charming to look upon these living tales and think upon the history of coming times such as this country will develop it, being true to its mission. Pleasure grounds were beginning to be laid out on the beautiful high meadows opposite the factory bank, and we saw in thought the laborers of the mills coming, in the evening, on this side of the river, to enjoy the innocent pleasures of life in song and dance, and plays, or repose on the green fields looking on the picturesque beauty of the opposite shore which they unconsciously had worked out.

We saw some very pleasant and kind people in Rochester, who loaded us with fruits and flowers. Fr. Douglas[5] was ill from an inflammation of the throat (bronchioles) and could not go out. So I went to see him with my young friends. I liked him much, but his difficulty in speaking, and the shortness of my time was a drawback on our conversation. But I hope to renew it some time. His wife is very black and so is his little daughter Rosetta. They were uggly, but had kind feeling looks. . . .[6]

That evening we took the Ontario-boat, and arrived at Niagara early in the morning next day. And here we now are, my dear friends, our rooms on the roaring rapids, and intending to stay some day[s] to make thouroughly a[c]quaintance withe the giant whos[e] first view we had yesterday. The impression of Niagara is to me very different from that of the falls of Trenton. /We were at the Trenton falls one whole day and night./ Trenton is a young hero, somewhat intoxicated with old Sherry,[7] and dashing on its course in blind, wild rapture. Niagara is a god[d]ess who knows her power and her will, and is calm in the highest display of that will and power. She is sweet and mighty at once, calm in the h[e]ight of action, and leaves you so. She is the holocaust of nature personified. Or I would rather say: Nature would one day offer a holoca[u]st to her creator; but she felt she could not. Her heart swelled and swelled and flowed over — in Niagara. And the smoke from the great cataract is forever arrising upwards towards heaven. That magnificent column of white spray arrising in the calm air, as I saw it yesterday evening, on the soft rosy evening sky, and coming, as it were, out of the lap of the great cataract, shining with emerald green is a most beautiful thing.

My young companions are most pleasant and kind, and will, I think, go with me even to Detroit. They enjoy with fresh and noble minds the treat of every day and every good thing.

Dear Rebecca! if my little Jenny Lind Song should fall through with the judges of the poetic com[m]it[t]ee, I do not wish it to come out a failure among a hundred other failures, but just let it fall in the portfolio of Marcus, or in yours, and be kept there. And I shall think in more honorable keeping there than — even on the lips of the renowned Nightingale, full of song and charm as they are! I send the little song.[8]

Now I must say goodbye to you, then I must write other letters — alas! When you look upon the little scandinavian genius, and when you see the fires of your camin[9] dancing over its face and make it ap[p]ear all alive let it say unto you:

"I am the spirit of beautiful humanity, the Sabbath-child who would be alive in every human mind to beautify it, to glorify its creator, to make it happy. It is obscured, it is asleep in many a bosom, but the touch of your kindness can dispell the clouds, can make it awaken, can make it alive there. And then, see your work! Then I am your work in human breasts, and the im[m]ortal sculptor lives in your own hearts and is a part of you!"

And many other words could I tell out of his mind and out of my own also, but, shall now only ask you to think of me as your loving and grateful

Fredrika

Love to Eddy and the little ones! So glad that Baby is better! I am so sorry I could not find a shaker[10] cricket to Jenny, but she shall have some little indian curiosity instead.

P.S. I see that I have taken up to[o] little money for my western tour, and have w[r]itten to Mr Heijerdahl for one hundred Dollars more. Dear Marcus, please let my note come to him and send me a draught for the money on St. Louis, Missouri Care of *Mr Thomas Allen Esq.*[11] But pray let me hear from you in Chicago, and send the letter to the care of Mr Hoffman Ogden, *Chicago!*

Dear Marcus, have the enclosed letter for Sweden posted with the first going Steamer for England!

————

1. MS, HL.

2. F. Bremer was traveling with the Lowells.

3. See p. 71 for rest of paragraph.

4. Cf. *HNW*, I, pp. 575-576.

5. Frederick Douglass, 1817-1895, antislavery orator and journalist; originally a slave from Maryland.

6. See bottom of p. 72 for rest of paragraph.

7. Cf. lines from Maria Lowell's "Memories of Waters":
   "Pour down, o Trenton, thy amber screen
   That the pool's dim surface no more be seen!
   Gay reveller, tossing away thy wine,
   Thy golden sherry, whose hue divine
   Was never sphered in the clustering vine; . . ." *The Poems of Maria Lowell*, Hope J. Vernon (Providence, 1936), p. 65.

8. F. Bremer's song may have arrived too late to be considered.

9. *Camin* (*kamin*): Swedish for "stove."

10. F. Bremer had visited the Shaker community at New Lebanon, N. Y.

11. Thomas Allen, 1813-1882, railroad builder and state senator in Missouri.

23.   To Israel K. Tefft.[1]

Niagara the 9 Sept. 1850

My dear Sir!

I cannot let Mr. Fay depart from here and go back to Savannah, without sending with him a word of greeting to my kind host and friend there. And believe me, my dear Sir, the hospitality and kindness shown me by you and your family is one of my cherished memories from the south, and as alive in my soul by the falls of Niagara as it was on the quiet river of Savannah! Even the paper I write on reminds me of your kindness. I am now on my way to the great West, and am happy to go on with the hope of remaining in America over one winter more. And so I hope once more to see, beautiful Savannah, and my friends there, at least on a flying visit. I shall be so glad to see you again, my dear Sir, and even so Mrs Tefft and my young friend, Sarah. May I see you well all and happy! From Philadelphia a portrait of me with autograph was to be sent to you, about a month ago. If it has not yet arrived, I think it soon will. My moments for writing are numbered then Mr Fay is on the point

of departing. Give my love to our friends, and think of me my dear
sir as of a sincere and grateful friend

                                                    Fredrika Bremer.

———————

1. MS, HSP. A reference to F. Bremer is to be found in a letter William
Gilmore Simms sent to I. K. Tefft in January, 1855: "Are you frozen? Are
you fat? Are you still drudging all the marrow out of your bones? Are you
frisky? Do you dream of Frederika Bremer? What are you doing, dreaming,
meditating? . . ." (*The Letters of William Gilmore Simms,* III, Columbia, University of South Carolina Press, 1954, p. 360.)

24.   To Rebecca and Marcus Spring.[1]

                                            Chicago 22 Sept. 1850.

    Now, dear Rebecca, I have seen, I have enjoyed, myself, that
beautiful vision you once saw and spoke so beautifully of, I have
seen *the Prairies,* seen the Sun-embraced earth, covered with sunflowers, dressed in splendour as a bride to meet the bridegroom who
lighted up in glory lowered down from his pure native skyes to the
bosom of the well beloved; — I have seen the wedding of heaven
and earth and, in it, a type of my own hopes for the futurity of human
kind! Oh it was a glorious sight; it was a happy day I passed on
these sunlit prairies /from morning and untill night when I saw
the sun setting down on its bed of sunflowers/ under a sky so soft
and clear as in a summers day. Little farms and loghouses are now
rising in every direction over the prairie; yet that is so immense in
its expanse that they seem only as birds nests swimming on the
ocean. And how the sunflowers rustled and nodded all over that
ocean, here and there interrupted only by a clear, little river or by
a grove or a field of Indian Corn, but stretshing beyond them far
to the horizon — it was charming to see. The view of the prairies impressed me more than even Niagara. Chicago is one of the ruffest,
moste bare and brute cities I have seen in America, but has some
most agre[e]able and even genial people, whose company has
made me very happy. Mr *William B. Ogden*[2] (*not Hoffman* Ogden
as somebody had told me) who was to be my host here, is absent
as I had not ap[p]rized him of the time of my arrival, but his brother
and sister in law and Mr and Mrs Kinzie[3] (at whose house I am
living) have made my stay here perfectly agreeable.

    Just as I was writing to you, I received your and Marcus' dear
letters. Thank you most heartely for them! But how sorry I am that
Marcus has been hurt! — I will not pardon the angels if they do not
guard Marcus from any serious accidant. And though this did not
prove serious I think they should have been better on their watsh.
Most sincerely do I joyn and rejoyce in your enjoyment of the song
of Jenny Lind. I feel again through you (and others who have heard

her) its thrilling, soul entrancing power. And I can only say: would you could see and hear her on the stage as Norma, as Agatha, as Pamina, Somnimbula![4] Without that you have no adequate idea of her powers, of the feelings she can create within the minds of the beholders.

. . .[5]

Thank you, dear Marcus for the money-paper from the Swedish Consul and other papers! Do how you will with my little Jenny Lind-song, dear Marcus, but dont let it be printed. Fr. Douglas[s], dear Rebecca, did not seem black to me. He is a fine-looking man of the colour and cast of countenance I should suppose to belong to Arabs. It was of *his wife and little daughter* I spoke, in my letter, as beeing very *black*. Douglas[s] I liked much and wish to see more of him under more favourable circumstances.

Here I hear much of the Indians, among whom my host and hostess here have much been and know well, and I have heard stories of them which would touch your hearts as they have done mine. I am glad to go a little among them, but that will be *a little* only.

Adieu! you, my Sunflowers among the minds of this land! Dear, bright spots, on whom my mind alights to rest, and rejoice in the powers of the great Sun! Blessing on you and all which is yours, — part of it in consequence on your friend

Fredrika.

Please to ad[d]ress letters to me to the care of Governor Ramsay,[6] St. Paul Minnesota till the Middle of October, and after that time to Cinncinati Ohio, Care of Mr Stetson Esq.

Dear Marcus, pray take care of my letter to Sweden and have it sent off!

---

1. MS, HL.

2. William Butler Ogden, 1805-1877, American railroad executive, elected first mayor of Chicago, 1837.

3. Mr. and Mrs. John H. Kinzie, early settlers in Chicago.

4. Agatha, heroine of *Der Freischütz*, opera by von Weber; Pamina, heroine of *Die Zauberflöte*, opera by Mozart; *La Sonnambula*, opera by Bellini.

5. See p. 77 for omitted paragraph.

6. Alexander Ramsey, 1815-1903, appointed governor of the Minnesota Territory, 1849. Later he was mayor of St. Paul and, in 1859, became governor of the State of Minnesota.

25. To Marcus and Rebecca Spring.[1]

Galena 28 Oct. 1850.

Dear Marcus! dear Rebecca! my kind friends, its autumn now, the frosts have come and the long dark evenings. I am alone in a little room in a hotel, but I am well and happy, then I *am alone*, and with me are chearful memories. Among these is your home, your pleasant cozy parlour, your fireside so peaceful so chearful and the dear people there! How well I see it all! Now I have so much to tell you out of the west, that I am just afraid to begin, and feel that I must leave the best of it till we meet. But still I must tell you how amused I have been by the Indians in Minnesota and interested in their strange customs and manners. I have visited several of their Tipis (lodges) and was agreeably surprised to see there, instead of filth and poverty as I expected, a kind of oriantal, though coarse luxury and comfort. Some of the women sitting on embroidered pillows round the walls of the tent, were, by the flickering lights of the fire, lighted in the midst of it, positiv[e]ly pretty, and one highly attractive. I did not wonder when it was told me that her young husband was so fond of her that he would allow her to do no hard labour or bear any burdens, which is a rare case. All the women looked friendly and merry. The men grave, some of them were working on stone pipes (smoking pipes), and were highly painted in their faces. In general I thought the men looked extremely coxcombish and vain, and their dignity more like the dignity of a crowing cock than that of noble man. Their paintings and plumings were gordious [gorgeous] and uggly, without a shadow of good taste but rather the reverse. I wanted to take some sketshes of the Indians, and when Governor Ramsay, through the interpreter, told the old Dakotah-chief *Mozah huntah* that I wanted the lik[e]nesses of *all the great men* of this land, to show to the people on the other side of the great waters, he vouch[s]afed to give a gracious grunt, and consented to sit to me. And one day I shall have the pleasure to introduce to the a[c]quaintance of Eddy and Jenny the Chief *Mozah-huntah* (Grey Iron) the brave war[r]ior (and great coxcomb) *Skonkah Skaw* (hvite [white] dog) and his very pretty, young wife *Moukah pedaga* (Checker[e]d Cloud).[2] And Jenny shall have a pair of pretty moccazins for her little feet. Several notions I collected about the Indians I think very interesting, though not all very to their advantage. Minnesota is, still more so than Visconsin, a great rolling prairie, with the most rich soil all ready for culture, the high, dry grass waving invitingly over hills and me[a]dows to be cut and used by hands — which now are not there. Minnesota looks as an English park in great style with fine Oak openings lovely lakes and rivers. It is one of the finest countrys for settlers, and yet almost whol[l]y unsettled. The scenery on the upper Missis[s]ippi is noble and grand though not of the grandest. /The falls of St. Anthony are nothing after Trenton and Niagara, nothing more than the falls of a large Mill damm. A little Island below the falls called the Spirit Island from a pretty but melancholy Indian tale attracted me more than the falls.[3]/ The bluffs are to[o] much of one h[e]ight, not ex-[c]eeding seven hundred feet. Still they are pictureske, and the river running amidst them of larger dimensions than the rivers of Europe. I read Emerson and Bankroft alternately as I was passing among these noble scenes and enjoyed the feast of life so highly as I believe it to be possible. And never shall I forget the sweet and majestic beauty of the evening when I came out upon the Missis[s]ippi from the little winding river of Feve[r] by Galena. Governor Ramsay and his handsome hearty wife made me happy in their home while at St. Paul. Now I am again in Galena expecting to embark to morrow for Rock Island from whence I shall go and visit the Swedish colony in Henry-County. I enjoyed 'to be among my people at Pine lake, in Visconsin, and to find them so swedish still, to hear the fine Swedish songs, to see the swedish dances, and above all to find the warm, overflowing Swedish heart at home among them. I dwellt in Loghouses among them, and at the Norvegian Settlement Kos[h]-konong, near Madison, and also at Blue mound. But alas! I am spoiled for these, and they have but little attraction for me here-after. But the great western views, — these immense expanses — how I like them! Theres elbow room and room for free respiration in them, the[y] make the heart expand. It is said that the western man is "the Yankee expanded." How it is with that I cannot yet tell. In Visconsin I was happy to see the great and liberal ideas which were working in the laws and institutions for the education of all classes, and which prepare for that State a glorious futurity. What a happy institution is that of *your States* and their freedom of government. What a great field it opens to emulation, and improv[e]-ment, to the development of individual power and excellance!

Thank you, dear Marcus for letters, papers and some dear words also! Your last ones of the 22 Oct. just received. Letters from home excellant! Thank God for them! I never had better and more comforting news since I left home. Packets who may come for me, dont send any where, dear Marcus, but please keep for me till I come to you, to my dear home in Brooklyn, before I go to my native home. If you read in Sartains Magazine some "Fireside-talk" about "Northern loves and legends," may be Rebecca will recognize a little fire-side picture and remember one evening in her home.[4] It is a sunny and lovely day, to day, true Indian summer! But the foliage is all ashy colored, not a green or even yellow leaf. The frosts are early here and have been severe. Galena is most pictureskly situated upon hills along the Feve[r] river, and it is charming to see the smoke of the little homes and the church spires rise in the calm air up in the azure sky on the rolling hills. Its living is by *lead* which is dug out of the earth all round. Some pleasant people I have seen here, /Among them a young presbyterian Minister F. G. Magoun, whose conversation and writing have given me much pleasure, then he is one of those clear largeminded divines who preach the coming of Gods kingdom not only to the heart but to the intellect, and makes philosophy as well as charity concur to glorify christianity. He is one of the builders of the coming millenial Church, in which men such as Beecher and Bellows[5] are workers as well as he./ but decline seeing many. I am well in health now, thank God, but am anxious to keep so, and must therefore avoid much company keeping. Now goodbye to you my dear kind friends. Next time I shall write to you from Cincinnati. Ever Yours

Fredrika

Autographs follow!

----

1. MS, HL.

2. In his essay on "Slang in America" Walt Whitman reproduced a list of twenty Indian names which F. Bremer gave in *HNW*, II, p. 42: "Miss Bremer found among the aborigines the following names: *Men's,* Horn-point; Round-Wind; Stand-and-look-out; . . ." (Walt Whitman, *Complete Prose Works* [Philadelphia, 1897], pp. 407-408.)

3. The legend tells that an Indian girl committed suicide when her husband took a second wife; with her two babies she plunged over the falls in a canoe.

4. See *SUM*, VIII (1851), pp. 166 f. — F. Bremer's description begins thus: "It is a pleasant, cosy parlour, — fine pictures, handsome carpet, — hundreds of little things which make a parlour pleasant. The fire is blazing merrily in the grate, and before it sits a handsome woman, . . ."

5. Henry Whitney Bellows, 1814-1882, American Unitarian clergyman.

26.   To Marcus Spring.[1]

Chrystal Springs near St. Louis
Missouri Nov. 10. 1850.

Dear Marcus!

Again a letter for Sweden, dear Marcus, for which I beg your kind care, to have it forwarded by next Steamer!

I am sorry to have let so long time go between last letter for home and this one. But — I write now, from a pleasant home[2] on the shore of the Missis[s]ip[p]i, with a beautiful view over it, though now enveloped in thick fog. . . .[3]

St. Louis is a growing and will be a very handsome City in time. I have seen there fine and flirting society, and — hospitals belonging to Catholic convents — very different scenes of life; — almost no colored people, less than in any city of America. Missouri needs no black labour and will do away with its slavery in short time, I hope. To Morrow or the day after I will leave St. Louis for Cincinnati. Adieu dear Marcus! may you and yours be all well and happy!

Ever
Yours
Fredrika

Miss Ch. Cushman writes me that she, last summer, wrote me a letter ad[d]ressed to your Care in Brooklyn. I have not got it. Dear Marcus can you recollect having seen such a letter.

----

1. MS, HL.
2. F. Bremer was the house guest of Thomas Allen and his family.
3. See p. 88 for rest of paragraph.

27.   To Maria Lowell.[1]

Cincinnati 12 Dec. 1850.

My sweetest Maria, I think so often, so much of you and of James that I think you must feel it even through my silance. But now I must say it, though pen and ink never tell well, and seem to me a kind of obstructions. Dearest Maria! I long to know of you. The time must be near at hand or is perhaps at hand when you again have to feel the sufferings and joys of Maternity.[2] God grant you a happy hour and God bless you and your little one! Oh! how glad I should be, to be able to come to you, one day of your con-valescense, and sit with you and James, and talk with you over — a thousand things, that I cannot write over, and then, not in writing, hear your remarks, your thoughts!

Dear Maria! Much have I seen and lived and thought since I last saw you. This great Valley of the Missis[s]ippi in which I still am, and what is going on there has given me much to think of — and has widened the world to me; peculiarly in Cincinnati have I found a centrality in thought and tendencies which has to me been most exhilerating. The views here promulgated in reference to slavery and the futurity of the African race have to me been inspiring, and so has Dr. Buchanans[3] views on Man — far more comprehensive and central than any I have met with — almost anywhere.   . . .[4]

A thousand thanks, dear Maria, for the kind letter that came to me from you in Minnesota. I was then among the Indians, visiting their Tipis, eating and talking (Indian of course) with them, and much amused by them.   . . .[5] The Falls of St. Anthony are, after Trenton and Niagara, only as the falls of a great Milldam; the Spirit Island in the midst of them, and the story connected with it, was to me of more interest than the falls themselves. The *little fall,* so called, in annother direction, (on the Indian territory,) is beautiful, and so is, as a great and lovely Idyll the whole country arround St. Paul. Yes, the whole Valley of the Missis[s]ippi is like an immense Idyl — a great rolling prairee fertile and full of rivers and lakes. St. Louis is the New York of the West — alas! I would it were Otherwise. Cincinnati deserves the name of the Queen of the West. It is a beau-tiful City on the lovely banks of the Ohio. I have lived there a happy time in the home of most kind and pleasant people.[6] Now I am about to leave for New Orleans, where I shall pass Christmass. Write to me there, one of you, "young and happy pair," *care of Mr Gustavus Schmidt of Sweden,* and tell me how it is with you and with the baby! I long to know it. In Madison (Visconsin) in Galena, at St. Paul, etc I met with warm friends and admirers of James poetry, and I am glad to find in such always the best heads as well as hearts of the land. I am well, dear Maria, and feel brave and thankful. At my home all is well, and I can go on with peace of heart. May God bless you, my sweetest Maria, your other half, your dear father, and all yours!

Remember me as your loving friend

Fredrika

How glad I am that you did hear and enjoy Jenny Lind so as she should be heard and enjoyed. Those who are dissap[p]ointed in her song are persons without music in their souls, and who have it only at their fingers ends.

––––––

1. MS, HCL.
2. A son, Walter, was born to Maria Lowell December 22, 1850; he died in Rome, 1852.
3. Dr. J. Buchanan, Cincinnati phrenologist and director of the Medical College there.
4. See p. 92 for rest of paragraph.
5. See p. 83 for omitted passage.
6. Mr. and Mrs. Stetson.

28. To [John S. Hart].[1]

New Orleans 30 Dec. 1850.

My dear Sir!

Only two words, to day, to say that I wrote to you from Cincinnati, at the beginning of this months, sending you two little stories about the blind Gud, proving him to be clairvoyant at times;[2] but in directing the letter I committed a mistake, and ad[d]ressed it to 27, Filbert Str. instead of 227 as it should have been. As your name must be well known in Philadelphia, I suppose that, long before this, some sensible people in 27 have corrected or redeemed my blunder by sending the letter to the right place.[3] Still, I write of it now, that in case the letter has not yet come to you, you may know the reason, and know where to find it.

I have happily accomplished my run on the Missis[s]ippi from Minnesota and St. Paul to New Orleans, Louisiana, and am very glad to have done so. But the sunny south frowns as yet upon me and pours down a constant shower of cold rain, which makes it almost impossible to be out and see any thing. This is not pleasant.

But I am well, have a pleasant room in a good boarding-house, and am thankful for the good I have, hoping for better t.i. for sunnier days.

Good friends I have found here as every where in America, and have made som[e] precious a[c]quaintences with good and free-minded men. At the end of this week I shall go to Mobile, and about the Middle of Januar[y] to Cuba.

I hope, my dear Sir, this will find you and all yours (the 500 inc[l]uded[4]) well and prospering!

Faithfully Yours

Fredrika Bremer

———————

1. MS, Boston Public Library.

2. Perhaps these were two stories in the series, "Northern Loves and Legends," printed in *SUM*, VIII (1851). *Gud:* Swedish for "God."

3. According to McElroy's *Philadelphia Directory for 1850* (Philadelphia, 1850), p. 175, John S. Hart resided at 227 Filbert.

4. The five hundred pupils in the Central High School, of which J. S. Hart was principal.

29. To Joseph M. Field.[1]

Mobile 8 Jan. 1851.

My dear Sir!

I must do myself the pleasure to express, myself, to you my grateful acknowledgment of your repeated kind attentions, which already have afforded me so much pleasure, and promises to afford me still more! If I now tell you that I was gratified far beyond my expectations and even surprised at being so moved by Miss Deans[2] playing as "the Daughter of the Stars," that I longed to take her hand and tell her that I saw greater stars shining and beckoning over her head than the shooting stars of artistical glory — you will easily guess in what c[h]aracter I should wish to see the young, gifted actress again. She must be excellent in tragedy, in that most noble and touching scene of human life. — I do not know in what tragic plays she uses[3] to perform, but Mrs Le Vert[4] speaks of one of the name *Evadne*[5] as being very impressive. But in any one good tragedy that she would make her appearance I am sure I should enjoy her beautiful, rising talent, and again I thank you, my dear Sir, for offering me a fresh opportunity of so doing!

I hope to have the pleasure of seeing her, and of seeing you soon again.

Yours very truly

Fredrika Bremer

———————

1. MS, Boston Public Library. Joseph M. Field, 1810-1856, American actor, playwright, and journalist; director of Mobile Theatre, 1850-1852.

2. Julia Dean, 1830-1868, popular American actress.

3. Uses — is in the habit (of performing).

4. Octavia Walton Le Vert, 1810[?]-1877, author, linguist, and Southern society leader.

5. *Evadne: or the Statue* (1819), play by Richard L. Sheil.

30. To Rebecca Spring.[1]

Matanzas (Cuba) 20 Febr. 1851.

You can hardly conceive, dearest Rebecca, how much your letter of the 21 Jan. (received just this morning) puts me on the stre[t]ch about your knockings! "Well though I" — reading on almost breathless — "now they, these truly spiritual and rational beeings, will they indeed believe also in these knockings." I felt quite miserable about it! But how glad, how relieved I was when I came to the *ladder!* I almost blessed the ladder. I breathed again. O Rebecca how you puzzled me! Indeed, Indeed I should have felt unhappy if any true spiritual com[m]unications (that I could not help believing in) had come *to you* by such means. And if any of the departed Spirits that I have loved, the noble and earnest minded men and women that have gone away from this stage of life should come and com[m]unicate to me by — knockings, oh! It would give me a shudder for death, for the scene behind the Earthly coulisses, that should give me a distaste for life! Then if now, beeing earthly still, we should scorn to communicate with our beloved ones by such poor means, how, when disrobed of this mortal clay, when gone in the spiritual life, how is it possible that — but I will not enlarge on this topic, you will easely understand what I mean and — feel as I. Indeed, Indeed there is more spiritual com[m]unication given us in the twinkling light of the farthest star, than in these gross knockings. I do indeed not doubt that such can be and are in fact produced (I have heard of too many facts prooving it) at times, by spirits; but I will always contend that they are produced by low Earth-bound Spirits, and not by those of higher order. Their modes of communion with us are, I am sure of, of a very high tone. In the course of our destinies, in the secret intuitions of our souls, in the depths of our feelings, our aspirations, our joys and sorrows they will be with us, work for us, — and in the paradise home that they have gained and we hope for they are preparing our place, our home with them, while we are wandering below and see it not. Oh! how often during a beautiful music — whose tones have been neither of joy nor sorrow but something above both — have I not seen or felt the spirits of departed friends — peculiarly that of *one* — come towards me, have seen that dear face, pale with the bliss of unearthly joy, (as I saw it on her deathbed) in a heavenly vision waft to me, as it were, a feeling, a vision of that existence which no human eye has seen, nor ear heard, nor mind been fully able to conceive! Very little, very poor have all earthly enjoyments seemed to me compared to the anticipations given in these rapt moments of spiritual com-[m]union.

Now, tha[n]ks for your letter, dear, kind Rebecca, and you dear Marcus for your words! It was so delightful to me to see you again — in Rebeccas graphic description, in your home, see you on the little sopha [sofa], hear you talk — it made tears come to my eyes! . .

I have written to you from Cincinnati and New Orleans. Have you received the letters? /Yes, I see it now by the lines written upside down on your first page./ And much could I have to tell you now from Cuba that wonderful land of noble, aspiring Palms and creeping, killing parasites but — but, — I feel I shall not talk freely to you but in your home, in that dear little parlour! . . Please God it will be so at the end of May, when my pilgrimage at the south has been completed. Oh! how glad I shall be again to be with you, then beautiful as many homes have been open[e]d to me, and dear and pleasant friends as I have found since I left you, and though I often have formed affections — "tents of one night" as Emerson calls them — never have I felt so fully at home, and spiritually so, never so fully in sympathy as with you both.

How glad I am that you are reading Geijers[2] history of Sweden — that is something of the best in — human history, — both the story and the genius who writes it. And you feel it as it should be felt. You will find that intense love for such a people and its great memories is very natural, when you will know more of them. And you can have no better guide than Geijer. There is a great heart in his history whose beating is felt throughout its pages.

I am well, my dear friends; I am enjoying this new scene of life and opening my mind freely to its tale. And well I see that the weal and woe, the beauty and the horror of existance is at home here as elsewhere; though here the contrasts are stronger. The Palms and the breeze are from Paradise, of that I am clear, from the unspotted one where all was good, — but the snake is here also and winds its dreadful folds round the ideals of life. I write to you from a most pleasant home — that of Mr John Bayley in Matanzas; I was Yesterday on a Coffee Estate and saw things there; and am soon to go, for some time, at a Sugar estate, some tventy miles from here. In the beginning of April I shall return to America, first go to Florida and then to Carolina and Virginia, and then farther north. Please my dear friends, when you write or have letters for me to direct them to the Care of the Swedish Consul Mr Nenninger in Havanna and after March to the care of Mrs A. C. Howland, Lynch Street, 21 in Charleston S. C. Good bye and God bless you, and all yours, my dear, excellant friends! Ever Yours

Love to the children!   Fredrika.

21 Febr. Good morning dear Marcus, good Morning dear Rebecca!
Such a beautiful morning! How I have enjoyed it during a solitary
walk in the lovely valley of Yumori [Yumurí] and conversing with
the cliffs, the Palms the flowers the humming-bird who sucks them
on the wing, and who is here as fearless and confiding as it is shy
in the united States. The beautiful valley has its bloody traditions;
but over the river where the first inhabitan[t]s, the peaceful Indians,
pursued by the cruel Spaniards threw themselves calling out "Yo
mori!"[3] over the hill and house where a father was lately murdered
by — his children, — nature breathes her "Via medicatrix," and man
can inhale it and receive inspirations to a healing, remunerating
life. Oh! if it was not for that, and for the eternal hope which fans
us during life with its Palm branches — Cuba may for me sink in
the depths of the ocean! — But I would have some sons and daughters of old Noach saved!

------ --

1. MS, HL. Address: Care of M. Spring & Co., 51 Exchange Place, N. Y.

2. Erik Gustaf Geijer, 1783-1847, Swedish historian, professor, and poet.

3. *Yo mori*: either the preterite tense of the Spanish verb *morir* (*yo morí* —
I died), or an Indian dialectal form.

31.   To Marcus and Rebecca Spring.[1]

Caffetal La Industria, near
Cardinas. Cuba, 9 Apr. 1851.

My dear friends, Marcus and Rebecca!

I turn my thoughts to the North and to you, and feel happy
soon to be with you again. Then though charmed here by the climate and the beauties of nature, in love with the breeze, the Palms,
flowers, humming-birds, Cucullos[2] and contradances of this Queen
of Islands, and enjoying highly the hospitality of its inhabitan[t]s, —
still, more than ever, I feel that my true home is in the north and its
peoples, my life in their life. And so I have enjoyed Cuba even as
an offset for the United States — or for that part of the States that
is growing towards its Ideal. In *this paradise* things are going on
that make men, such as Alcott,[3] ar[r]ayed in their robes of milk-
white innocence, seem as the Angels of earth, and makes one grow in
love with the ideas of socialism, even in their extravagances. And oh!
how beautiful seem, seen from here, the great aspirations, the harmonious formations of social life as are developing themselves
through the true, the good and rational, the men of God, the prophets
of his kingdom, of the coming time!!

. . .[4] And Rebecca, dear Rebecca! shall we not go to the Quaker-
meeting in — New Jersey (I think!) to Sarah and Angelina Grimke?[5]

I want to study with you the government of the Quakers, and to talk with you about what women *could* do in the cause of Anti-Slavery. I want to talk about it with *Mothers*, then my faith in emancipation rests on the training up of the child[r]en of the Slaves. I hope to be with you in the Mid[d]le of June. Will you then be at rose-Cottage? Will you have time for me? Oh, how glad I shall be to see you again and Eddy and the little ones! And how is it with Mrs Oakes Smith?[6] Is she gone to Mexico, or is she still in Brooklyn and could and would go with me about the end of June to her beloved Maine, and to the white Mountains? I must see the White Mountains befor[e] I go home. But I must make a short trip, then by the middle of July I must embark for England and home. I want to be about a Month in England, and to meet my sister at the bath of Marstrand, on the west coast of Sweden, in August. From Cuba I intend to go, with the Isabel, on the 22 April; and to Savannah, from whence I shall go to visit an Island on the coast of Georgia where I am invited to see the beau Ideal of a planters life. After that and a flying visit to Charleston I go on to Virginia, and from thence to Philadelphia where I want to visit and know all about the College for female students of Medecine, to have a good talk with Lucretia Mott about the rights of women, and with Mrs Peter[7] about their wrongs, after which I intend coming to you, my dear friends, and anticipate with you the time when men and women shall talk of no rights and wrongs against one annother, but be together "as the Angels in heaven."

So looks my plan for the next months. And in the mean time, I am looking on trees and flowers, sketshing all the day, looking out at night for the Southern cross, and listening to the African drum, whenever its merry sounds are heard. But alas,! this time of the year you hear only, the nights through, the stamping of the Sugar mill. But on my special request, I have several times been able to see the c[h]aracteristic dances of the children of Africa. Much even have I seen of them and their life here visited them in their Boheas[8] and s.[so] f.[forth] But of what I have seen and come to know, I will tell you verbally.

Havanna 20 April. Thanks dearest Marcus for your pleasant note, received at Mantanzas; it was so welcome! But alas! that you should have more work to do, and so hard work too! Then the working for the ungrateful or by their fault is hard work indeed! May spring and summer give you flowers ennough to cover and make you forget all the iceicles of the winter! I still hope to see you by the middle of June, though I am compelled (but pleasantly, through the charms and amiable inhabitan[t]s of Cuba) to postpone my return to the United States still somewhat longer, and not go away from here till the eight of may.

. . .[9] I am now for the eastern [Easter] days in Havanna, visiting the churches and looking on processions. All show and mummery. Not a spark of devotion, not a breath of earnest feeling. Religion is dead in Cuba. There is but one voice about that. And the ceremonies going on are its funerals. Gayety and dress and worldly show watch by the tomb of Christ, and officiate by his resurrection. The women white and colored go about (on good Freyday) dressed as to a ball, have necks and arms covered with flowers and glittering ornaments. The men go and look at the women or at the glittering ridiculous shows in churches and processions.

[End of MS]

----

1. MS (incomplete), HL.

2. *Cocuyos*: West Indies fireflies or glowworms.

3. Amos Bronson Alcott, 1799-1888, American educational reformer and transcendental philosopher.

4. See p. 117 for beginning of paragraph.

5. Sarah (1792-1873) and Angelina (1805-1879) Grimké, Quaker leaders in the American Anti-Slavery Society.

6. Elizabeth Oakes Smith, 1806-1893, American author, lecturer, and reformer.

7. Mrs. Sarah Peter, wife of the British consul in Philadelphia; she founded a school of design for girls.

8. *Bohío*: Spanish for "hut" or "cabin."

9. See p. 101 for omitted passage.

32.   To Marcus and Rebecca Spring.[1]

Charleston 5 June 1851.

Thank you, Marcus and Rebecca, my dear excellant friends, for your sweetly calling voices, that are to me as music of the Sferes! But though they made my heart start and run on to the north, still my body remains in the south detained by several things. I hardly came from Cuba when I started for Florida and took a capital run to the depths of its wildernesses. /I went up the St. John river so far as lake Munroe./ I had there some hardships to deal with, but am most glad to have seen that part of N. Amerikas realm, so that I can better appreciate the whole of the great realm that once will be filled by the people of peoples. There, in the land of eternal summer where no frost comes, no snow is seen, is still now the realm of the old heathen Pan embracing with alike love the evil and the good, there is to be seen the primeval wilderness, rich and beautiful and fearful at once with the births of a chaotic life; there you see vegetation in its exuberance b[u]ilding temples in the woods, beautiful green pillars, porticos, altars over which the high Cypruss[e]ss and magnolias in full bloom and with long flowing beards stand as priests, while under them rich bowers, (fit for the most beautiful

Najads [naiads] and Dryads), the greedy Alligator grunts for his prey, the peaceful turtle dwells with the venemo[u]s watersnakes. The deer bounds in those groves but also the Panther and black Bear; the rattlesnake and the Moccasin coil round those soft green pillars, and birds of prey pursue the birds of song. It is the feast of natural life, rich, wild, flowering, full of enjoyment and cruelty, production and destruction, without law and love ex[c]ept the animal ones. But how rich, I must say, again and again! The fish abounds so in these waters of the St. John (or the Welaka) that it keeps a perpetual jumping and dancing day and night, and so even the Alligators keep grunting or roaring and the Whippoorwills and Mockingbirds singing.

Now I am in Charleston again for a few days enjoying the beautiful home of the Howlands, fitting up my gard[e]robe[2] and preparing for my turn to the north again. I shall go through Virginia and shall make some stay there, partly to see friends, partly to see the natural beauties of "the old dominion." From there I shall go to Philadelphia and from there make an excursion to visit the little Moravian settlements of Nazareth and Bethlehem. /Would they not interest you to see also?/ I shall hardly be able to be with you, my dear friends, before the end of June; then I hope to see you at your Phalanxtery home, and there we shall talk of — many things.

Much would I have given to be with you at the inauguration of the great hall there, of which I read the report in the paper Marcus was kind to send me. It was highly interesting and touching, and could not but have an elevating character under H. W. Channings influence. I hope his discourse will be or is printed, so that it may be read in extenso. As *now* the institution of that Association is, I do not think it can, in its *Idea*, be more perfect; and if it will (as I indeed believe it will) die, as to its presant *form* still it will not have lived in vain, but has been and is now the nursery from which millions of hallowed seeds will be scattered through all the world for the growth of humanity. Barbarity, abuse of power will have no ex[c]use more. Blessing be on the home of divine justice in society! And on those who work for it!

Before leaving Cuba I was happy in meeting with two beautiful women Owners of plantations, truly motherly natures who contrived to take off, at least momentar[i]ly, from slavery its curse, for the slaves arround them; and who looked with honest, unsofisticated minds on the unhappy institution. Much did I enjoy them, and so I have here in America enjoyed some men and plantations in Georgia, that work for the presant wellbeing, and gradual education and emancipation of their negroes. Many things not good I have seen also, but of all that we will speak.

Dear Marcus, will you be so kind to take charge of the enclosed letter for Sweden! The last letters from my home were, thank God, very good and cheering, and that has made me able to extend a little more the time for my stay in Amerika (till the latter part of August) and go on with peace of mind. In a few days I leave the sunny south never more to return, and turn for ever, and more lovingly than ever to the lands where the stars shine so bright even in wintry nights, and where the whole social scale is moving upwards to them. The southern heads, good and intelligent though many of them are lack in general the bump of ideality, that some of our Northern friends have a little too protuberant. But I cannot do without it and always get on ground with people that want it. Good bye my dear kind friends, love to the children. I hope soon to be with them and you!

Ever yours

Fredrika

Dear Rebecca, if you write to that noble and beautiful Elizabeth Hoar[3] give her much love from me. I think often of her and wish much to see her and have a talk with her before I go home!

———————

1. MS, HL.

2. *Garderobe*: French and Swedish for "wardrobe."

3. Miss Elizabeth Hoar had been engaged to Charles Emerson, a brother of Ralph W. Emerson; F. Bremer met her in the latter's home.

33.   To Lewis R. Gibbes.[1]

Charleston 12 June, 1851.

Professor L. R. Gibb[e]s!
My dear Sir!

I am sorry, my dear Sir, not to have seen you, during this my short and (alas!) last visit in Charleston, and consequently not have been able to offer you viva voce my thanks for the pleasure and benefit I have derived from your a[c]quaintance. Allow me then to offer them to you autographically, as to one of the southern men to whose learning and kindness I feel myself particularly indebted! I am now leaving the sunny south, but the grateful memory of all I have enjoyed there will never leave me.

My kind regards to Mrs Gibb[e]s and best wishes for the welfare of you and yours!

Faithfully Yours

Fredrika Bremer.

———————

1. MS, owned by S. Rooth. Dr. Gibbes, 1810-1894, was a professor at the College of Charleston.

34. To an unknown man.[1]

Richmond 18th June, 1851.

My dear Sir!

Receive my thanks for the unexpected kindness with which you have provided me with letters of introduction on my tour in Virginia! Virginian hospitality is proverbial, and if I shall judge by the beginning of my visit to your state no proverb ever was more true. I shall be happy at my return to Richmond to see you and tell you of your friends.

Yours truly
Fredrika Bremer.

––––––

1. MS, ASHM.

35. To Marcus Spring.[1]

Philadelphia 16 July 1851.

Dear Marcus! I shall wait a day longer for the sake to have the company of Mr E. Townsend[2] /that I much want to make a[c]-quainted with you and Rebecca, as a most amiable man and a re-forming, advancing mind./ on my way; and first on friday night shall come to you your

Fredrika.

––––––

1. MS, HL.
2. Elisha Townsend (b. 1804), Quaker dentist.

36. To Elizabeth Peabody.[1]

Tuesday morning. [1851]

Dear Miss Pibodie!

I am sorry and half angry with myself that I do not feel well ennough to fix on Wednesday for a visit to Newton. Will you dear Mrs Pipodie allow me to postpone it to annother day perhaps in next week, when I hope to be more strong than now I am. If you would, as a compensation, give me an hour or two of private conversation in my quiet parlour to morrow (Wednesday afternoon) you would make me happy!

Sincerely Yours
Fredrika Bremer.

––––––

1. MS, s.l. et a., HSP. Elizabeth Palmer Peabody, 1804-1894, American writer and educator. (F. Bremer visited West Newton with her in the summer of 1851.)

Richmond 18th June, 1851.

My Dear Sir!

Receive my thanks for the unexpected kindness with which you have provided me with letters of intro duction on my tour in Virginia! Virginian hospitali= ty is proverbial, and if I shall judge by the beginning of my visit to your state no proverb was more true. I shall be happy at my return to Richmond to see you, and tell you of your friends.

Yours truly
Fredrika Bremer.

American Swedish Historical Museum

FACSIMILE OF A LETTER BY FREDRIKA BREMER

37.   To Marianne Silsbee.[1]
                                Nahant Sunday morning. [August, 1851]
Dear Mrs Silsbee! *Be sure I shall come,* if I am alive, and the world
goes as it now goes, and is not upset by some bump against annother
globe. But do not send your Cariole! A somewhat long ride fatigues
me a good deal, and the short one in the Cars will not at all. But I
shall take the four oclock train at Lynn, and should I, peradventure,
miss that, I will *certainly* come in the fife oclock one, then not for
all the world would I send Mrs Silsbee out of the world before her
time which of course must be long after our trip to the White Hills!
Excuse! And believe me!
                                        Affectly Yours
                                        Fredrika Bremer.

----

1. MS, *s.a.*, owned by S. Rooth. (Presented in 1951 by Vilas Johnson, then
president of the Swedish Pioneer Historical Society, Chicago, Ill.)

38.   To Marcus Spring.[1]

                                        Salem 5 Aug. 1851.
Dear Marcus! Thank you my kind friend for your little notes, en-
closing my letters! /one from my friend at Charlotte[s]ville M.
Sheele de Vere was a sad one, ap[p]rising me of the death, in child-
birth, of my kind little hostess there — his wife./ I am so glad to
hear you are all well and enjoying yourself at the Phalanx! . . .[2] A
pleasant trip I made to Concord during my stay in Boston, went with
[R.] W. Emerson in the woods and with Elisabeth Hoar in the sunshine enjoying to see her own mind come out oc[c]asionally bright
and beautifully as the sun out of its gray clouds. Emerson was well
and strong and beautiful; asked about you and yours with his kindest
and most bright expression and voice. I have also been at Nahant
at Milton /And at Newton where I went to see Mrs Child. She is
well and kind but not very happy./ etc. A sc[h]ool of Design about
to be established in Boston by an excellant master Mr Whiteacker[3]
has interessted me much. Mr Barnard[4] helps it on in its beginnings
as he does all good things, and babies.
      The little square mulatto woman to whose care you so kindly
recommended me, dear Marcus, on board the Steamer from New-
York, prooved to me a true gentleman, and cared for me in perfection
particularly in the changing from the steamer to the Cars, at half
past four in the morning, when it was well needed. My good Doctor
Osgood, so kind as ever met me at the depot, and — so every thing
has gone well and peacefully with me; and if it goes on so, I shall
as I hope be with you my best and kindest friends before the 26 or
on the 26 Aug. to have my last good time with you. To morrow I shall
start for the New Hampshire trip. Miss Hunt hunted me out, (I

say it in all kindness, then she *is* kind and good) at Nahant and with her I shall, the first day of my journey, visit the Shakers of Canterbury.[5]

There, dear Marcus, is a little outline of my dooings past and present. Now adieu and ever Yours

Fredrika.

————————

1. MS, HL.
2. See p. 113 for omitted passage.
3. For description of her visit to Mr. W. T. Whiteacre's school, see *HNW*, II, p. 567.
4. Charles Francis Barnard, 1808-1884, American Unitarian clergyman and philanthropist.
5. Illness prevented Harriot Hunt from going along.

39.   To Marcus Spring.[1]

Lennox 24 Aug. 1851.

Alas dear Marcus! As usual I am delayed, and do not come on as I expected and wanted! In your friendly note that I have just received I see, with pain, that you expected me already yesterday. But yesterday first I came from Sarratoga to Lennox (after having paraded at the great ball there till 2 oclock the night before, started from bed there at 6 oclock in the morning and driving the whole day in all kinds of carriages and manners). I intend to leave here on tuesday morning /after having given one day to the Sedgwicks[2] and one day to the Hawt[h]ornes./ with Dr. Osgood and his wife who have come here to meet me, and will follow with me to N. York. There I intend to stay, with them, at the New Yorks hotel, see Mrs Kirkland, some other persons that I must see, see the fife-points[3] and the Tombs.[4] I hope to have done with all that till freyday, or at least to Saturday, last of Sept. And then, dear Marcus — will you take me down with you to New Jersey?! Alas! the birthday will be over, and Channing perhaps gone?!. . . But — I will have my birthday wreath for Eddy with me, and cannot you keep a bit of the birthday cake (at least a spiritual one for me till I come?) And Channing Oh! keep him too, Marcus! I cannot have him go away without seeing him speaking with him in that home of his spiritual love. *I wish and need speak there with him and you,* over things and times to come. Keep him, if possible, and let my last divine Service in America be there, with him and you, my *thankgivings* day! Let me offer my thanks through him and with him! . .

On the third of Sept. Mr Downing will come for me from Washington, to take me to his home on the Hudson. It is but right that my last week in America should be devoted to my first home, my first friends there. I have decided upon the 10th of Sept. to sail for England with the Steamer for Southampton (Don't tell it in

Gath!) and will probably come the eight Sept. down with Downing, to New York and to you, to see you before I start.

Dear Marcus! will you not, if you can, come and see me at the N. York hotel, if you are in the City next Wednesday or Thursday or Freyday? and we will speak more of our movements.

Ever yours and Rebeccas in love

Fredrika

------

1. MS, HL.
2. Catharine M. Sedgwick, 1789-1867, American author.
3. Five Points: a poor and crime-ridden section of lower Manhattan.
4. Tombs: prison in New York City.

40.   To Anne Howland.[1]

New Home on the Hudson 7 Sept., 1851

How many a time, Dearest A[nne], have I longed to write to you, but my life since a month has been a constant run that has made my pen lay still, my ink stagnate and my heart heavy through the feeling of what I would but could not do. Now I must *make* time, then I must say farewell — and it is a sad word, a sad thing to me. I have taken my passage on the Atlantic for the 13th of September and will then sail for Europe. Your last little letter, kind and welcome, I received in Salem just when I was about to start for the White Mountains.

Now, my dear A[nne], I am after two years pilgrimage again in the home that first received me in America. Among the many homes that have opened themselves to me during my wanderings and given me all the comforts, all the heart-feelings of home, there are three on whom my mind dwells with peculiar blessings; much have I lived and loved and enjoyed in them. These homes, and this my first one (Mr. Downing's); the house of Marcus Spring — and *your home*, my dear kind A[nne]. Thanks and blessings to you and yours for the peaceful days I have spent there; thanks and blessings to you, A[nne], for your timely, sisterly and motherly care for me, so kind, so pleasant. I leave you, I leave your land, with a sorrowful heart though I am glad to go home. As I could not make dear little Sarah hear Jenny Lind I will make her see her in a daguerreotype of my sketch of J. Lind. I shall send it to you or leave it at Marcus Spring's till it can be sent for.

Dearest A[nne], give my love to your children and husband, kind regards to your brother and sister. I embrace you with all my heart and live forever,

Yours in love,
Fredrika Bremer.

------

1. Published in New York *World,* March 28, 1878, p. 2. Anne Monefeldt

Howland, 1804-1860, lived in Charleston with her husband, William Howland, and their seven children. Both her parents had been born in Denmark.

41. To Miss McIntosh.[1]

New home, on the Hudson, 7 Sep. 1851

My dear Miss Mac Intosh!

I was very sorry to find, when I last time was in New York that you were not there, but in the country, then I had long looked forth to see you there and to thank you, and talk with you over your southern friends, over man and woman in America. Now I must depart without meeting you. Dear Miss Mac Intosh, I can then only thank you for the kindness and good will you have shown me, the introductions to your friends in the south, that so much have contributed to my enjoyment there especially the a[c]quaintance with your relations in Savannah, the Excellent Mac Intoshes, that went with me to Florida.

Thank you, also, for the beautiful example of womans fidelity that I know and revere in you. Accept of my best wishes, and think of me as your companion in work and friend in heart

Fredrika Bremer

––––––––

1. MS, ASHM. Presumably Maria Jane McIntosh, 1803-1878, whose work *Two Lives; or, To Seem and to Be* is mentioned in *HNW*.

42. To George Putnam.[1]

Stockholm, Jan. 1852

My dear Sir!

Accept of my grateful acknowledgement for the truly generous and noble manner in which you have ac[c]eeded to my desire to make another arrangement than that proposed between us, for my intended work![2] It has given me a great satisfaction to witness a behavior so gentlemanly and, I think, so rare on such occasions. Let me also express to you my intention and hope that I shall be able to show my sense of it in a manner that will convince you and others that generous behavior may be not only a good deed but also a good speculation. As for you, I hope you will – if I succeed in my wish – look upon the thing, as I do myself only as a mark of esteem and confidance from a friend to a friend!

Truly and heartely
Yours
Fredrika Bremer

––––––––

1. MS, NYPL. Address: Broadway, New York. George Palmer Putnam, 1814-1872, American publisher.

2. Presumably *Homes of the New World,* which was subsequently published by Harper & Brothers.

43.   To Marcus and Rebecca Spring.[1]

Stockholm 20 March 1852.

Dear Marcus and Rebecca! I know that you some time ago were on the way to Cuba, and I suppose to Jamaica and St. Domingo; but now, when this note comes to Rose Cottage, you will be there also. May you be well and happy my dear blessed friends! I write these lines in haste, with young Mr Buttenskön who is on the wing from Sweden to America. Oh! could I go with him for a day or two, see you and the children and tell you about many things, and hear from you what you have seen in the tropics about slavery and free black labor. Ah me! I fear that lat[t]er can never come to much! And then —

Dear Marcus and Rebecca I am well; I thank God for many things, "there is always something to thank for"; I have health and much to do, that I like to do. That is very good. I am now living over again my life in America, my life with you in writing over my letters to my home, to make them fit for the public eye; still leaving them in there original tone and charackter, changing very little, only now and then making exclusions and additions out of my private notes. How intensely these times are coming back to me in the letters and in memory; and it seems more clear and fresh as I now enjoy the peace of body and mind that I seldom enjoyed in America. I write to you and for you and my other friends in America, as well as for the old countries. You will be my judges with my own consciense! The work seems more easy more delightful to me than I ever thought. I almost feared it.

. . .[2]

Spring is turning its blessed face to us in Sweden, and the snow is melting away in a genial sun. We have had charming days. We live on quietly, and comfortably. But were it not for life within me I should feel here the lack of life. Sweden is a good place to sleep in. My poor Northern land is chained down by the hoary Giants of frost and Snow.

I long to hear from you and yours, and your life and doings, and what is going a head in the great new world. How goes the Phalenxtery and the Womens rights conventions and Channing??? Ah me! That letter to Mrs Oakes Smith I should write. It shall come yet, dear Marcus; be sure!

Now Adieu! God bless you! dearest kindest, excellent friends. Oh! Rebecca did I ever thank you for your nice mending of my little silk sack[3] for the Sea voyage. It kept me so warm and well, and looked quite respectable through your care, dear Rebecca! How good you both have been to me! —

I long to have that dear picture of American scenery in my room. But it is still in my trunk in Gothenburg. Will not come on before summer. Adieu! God bless you and yours! Yours in love

Fredrika.

---

1. MS, HL.
2. See p. 134 for omitted paragraph.
3. Sack or sacque: a loose-fitting coat or jacket, worn by women.

44. To Rebecca Spring.[1]

Stockholm 12 June 1852.

Oh! dear Rebecca how glad and how grieved, at once, I have been by your dear, long letter written during your wanderings in the south! How dear to me to go with you, to partake of your impressions, your enjoyments and sorrows as if I was with you, but how very sad and sorry some of these last have made me! Alas! When I last was with you at Rose Cottage I had the feeling that Marcus was overtaxing himself, and that Climate and care and buissness was wearing fast on him. (And I think I spoke with you and Marcus about it.) I saw a change in him since I had seen him last time; (th[at] is he had become thinner and looked worn) and I left you lastly with an anxious feeling about his health. I thought he could not long go on in that manner. Now, the feared period has come. Dear Rebecca I have wept with you in your anxieties for Marcus, as if he was my brother. Still, thank God, that things were so arranged that he could be freed from care and take time and travelling to effect a restoration; and how good that you can go with him! I suppose that by two or three years travelling in warm climates by wintertime and in temperate ones in summer, Marcus' health must be restored, as he is young still and certainly of a good constitution. Next year you will come to Europe, then in summer you will come to Sweden. Dear friends, [that] I think you should do even for the benefit of the climate — delightful in the latter part of summer — and to try the *Swedish "Gymnastik,"* so powerful to give new life and vigor to overstrained or fatigued bodily organs. It is especially known for *restoring sleep* and the energiees of the vital organs. The scientific method of apliing [applying] the Gymenastik to the care of disease, or to renew decreasing health, has, I think, been carried out first in Sweden. Certain it is that many foreigners have come here to try it and to learn it, and that many have gone out from the Central Gymnastic-institute here as teachers of that science in foreign lands. In Stockholm the art is in constant practice; and the whole year the institution is visited especially by middleaged and old gentlemen employed in Office or buissness, and who are greatly benefited by the treatment the[y] receive. Many, — among these my brother in law, go there one or two months every year (two hours in the morning) to get fresh vigor for the year. In England that mode of cure is gaining much favor. I think it is there known under the name of *Kinnepathie*. A young Swede, M̲r̲ Georgii,[4] is now employed in that way in London. O! Marcus must come here. And how happy should I be if I who have slumbered so happily under his roof should be permitted here to smooth the pillow for his head, and prepare for him sweet repose at my good country-home during the cool and calm clear nights of Sweden! Oh! may you come, my dear friends, may you come, and share with me whatever good or pleasant I may have in this world. How thankful I should be for such a treat. And, indeed, indeed Rebecca and Marcus I think you would enjoy the fresh and quiet life of a Swedish country home, and I would have you see and live at my dear Årsta.

And then the peculiar and romantic scenery of Stockholm its life in the thousend little boats /greater part of them go with wheels turned by four stout and merrylooking Dalkarlian girls (Dalkullas) in their bright costumes. These boats are called: kull-boats and have roofs of white linnen to protect you against the sun./ running on the waters between the many islands, indeed it would interest you to see; and how I should delight in running about on the waters with you (and little Jenny with us) and show you what is worth seeing. Oh! think on it dear friends; or rather — resolve on it; and promise you will come.

This year as I have with my mother tarried longer in Stockholm than I commonly do in springtime, I have seen much of spring and summerlife here. It is quit[e] a peculiar feature of this City of Islands. Every island in the city is as a swarming beehive, sending forth swarms of people in small boats to picknick (or to go [to] cricketing parties on the pretty green islands out in the sea and the country); they go with music and baskets with refreshments, and every thing looks merry. Then the scenery is so pretty and picturesque. But not the glowing picturesque of Havanna and Cuba. I enjoyed to hear how much you and Marcus enjoyed the delightful climate, the trees and all the peculiar beauty of the Queen of the Antilles. But live there for a length of time and be happy there you could not; nor could I. There is a kingdom of darkness behind the sunny scene that will for ever hurt the mind that once has beheld it. There are happy slaves and kind masters in Cuba, as elsewhere, but there are also dreadfully the reverse. I am glad dear Rebecca that you have looked with your own eyes at things in your American south, and become persuaded that an im[m]ediate emancipation would never do, and would do more harm than good to the greater part of the slave population itself. Christianity must prepare the ground for coming freedom and is silently working out its blessed mission more powerfully spreading from year to year. The people of the south is becoming more and more aware of their duty to give the benefits of religion to their servants; and the negro people is singularly ready and happy in taking up and adapting the leading truths of revelation. "And" as the good bishop Elliott of Georgia said "when they will be our equals the[y] will cease to be our slaves. Their next step will be to wages." One thing I would ask of the southern states as a justice to themselves and their slaves, as a justice to their country; and that is a law, like that of Spain in Cuba, who should allow the negroes to bye [buy] their freedom for a certain prize [price] fixed by the law. Such a law combined with the workings of Christian preaching and teachings would ensure a gradual emancipation, prepare the slaves to free work and self control, and be the best safety valve and ventilator through whom that curse of your country could be removed. At least I believe so. /Mrs Howland — dear Rebecca — nobody can know who has not seen her a longer time in her home. There she is excellant indeed most charming and excellant in every way. Her ambition is a parasite that does not affect the core of her life. That is pure and beautiful. The parasite grows loosely hanging on the branches of the tree and makes more show than harm./

18 June. The spring is full, and a glorious spring it is. I hardly ever saw it more rich in Sweden since a severe dryness of several weeks has been relieved by copious showers of rain. And how is Marcus? Oh! that Marcus ever should become so unwell, Marcus my kind brotherly friend! But freedom from care, travelling going to northern lands in summer will restore him. Many in his case, and by his still young years have been restored so. Dear little Rose-Cottage, where I have seen you so happy, and been so happy myself, I cannot think but that it is yours still. I see you always there. And with you Rose Cottage lives for ever in my heart, in my mind. Perhaps the day will come ere long when my noble Årsta will be in the hands of strangers. Alas! I must wish it; then a great estate with heavy debts on is a heavy load. Dear kind Rebecca, thank you for your most kind and considerate wishes about the letters. But poor indeed must I be when I shall not be most happy to pay any postage for letters from you. And thank God, dear Rebecca, it is not come to that. We hope still to be able to arrange ourselves so as [to] be comfortable on earth and help some that are poorer than we. Things may even turn out better than they now look. And in the worst case even it is not *very bad,* only difficult and very different from what we had a right to expect. But — we have no children and I have few wants. My brother in law and sister are very well off by his high salary as judge at the supreme court. May he be permitted to live on, /and continue as he has well begun to arrange the management of our estates./ and all things may still be well for us. But — he is a man of very delicate health. Next year I shall have a good

income through "the homes of the new world" (your home Marcus and Rebecca!) and feel myself quiet [quite] rich. Thank God for every good thing. "There is always something to be thankful for" as you once wrote dear Rebecca, and I have much.
July 8.

Since I wrote last our economical horizon has cleared up a good deal. The wonderful goldriches of Australia filling the money market of England begin to work even here on the public mind and make *landed* property rise higher in value as the rent[3] of money is lowering down. Still it is very high in Sweden and much to[o] high in proportion of the rent of land. But a *good* sale of a good landed property becomes now more and more probable, and then thank God, all may be well for us.

How is Marcus? oh! how is Marcus? Every day I throw out that question in the wide space; but no answer comes. Dear Rebecca! I am with you in heart about him feeling with you every anguish or every joy. Oh that I had you both in my cool high Halls at Årsta, in this hot time! Even here it is hot, unusually so, and begins to be painfully so in the City. In a few days I shall be at Årsta with my Mother. Next year, I hope, — with you. Then not so soon shall we part with our old home. The earth is all alive, dear Rebecca, the great hive is swarming, and all the ends of the earth are filling with — especially the Anglosaxon race. 60 000 emigrants are next going out to Australia to dig Gold (Mr W. Howitt[4] his two sons and intended son in law are already there in quest of gold) and about 10 000 Germans come every week to Liverpool to take passage for America. So the far east and the West are through gold mines and Anglosaxon-Norman homes preparing for the golden age. Indeed it is delightful to look on the great movement of this time, clearly it seems to me ordered by the hand of providence. My land is out of the great t[h]oroughfare, and is comparatively quiet, but still the movement is felt even here. But the people who goes forth with the law and the Gospel, is the people of God and to him the dominion of Earth is given; he will prevail; and be the reigning people.

I send this letter to you with young Mr Hjortsberg (the friend and former Secretary of Jenny Lind in America) who is going over to America hoping there to advance his fortune as engineer more speedely than in Sweden, where there are no railways as yet, and seems not to be very soon. Gods choicest blessings on you and yours my dear Excellant my ever blessed Friends! Yours as long as I live!

Fredrika.

Dear Rebecca let me have your and Marcus' opinion on a subject that puz[z]les me. In writing over my letters to my sister Agathe, to make them fit for publication of course I give the pictures of home life of my friends as they are given there but — how shall I do with the names? Shall I write them out or only the Initials. Public persons known by their works as Downing, Channing, Emerson etc. I think may be fully spelled out as they are so already before the public, but more private charackters; — even though I should wish the whole world to know their names and their virtues — will they look on it with pleasure? Some may; others may not like the exposure flattering as it may be to their characters. Yet — the world is always, in cases of scandal, well supplied with facts and names; and criminal stories are detailed in papers and books; oh! why should not some of those names and virtues who sow blessings along the shady paths of life be whispered in the breeze that wafts round the earth with comforting and refreshing powers, and make men look up with joy and think: "the earth is still full of the Goodness of God!"

After all — why should I ask Marcus and you? I think I shall do as I please after all, and name and abuse even you on the ground that I just now have urged!

Give to Channing my best wishes for him; he lives in my memory as one of the purest blessings the new world bestowed on me to know. I should be happy if he would once at leisure write to me something about the revivals in the new world; if they have or had the same character in every church and sekt, and if they belong chiefly to the new world or show there any peculiar character. Channing should write well upon awakenings and revivals then he is himself a revival-man, a man whose spirit is a revival!

————

1. MS, HL.

2. Augustus Georgii, author of *A Biographical Sketch of the Swedish Poet and Gymnasiarch Peter H. Ling* (London, 1854); a copy dedicated to F. Bremer is at the Stockholm Teachers College for Women.

3. Cf. Sw. *ränta* — interest.

4. William Howitt, 1792-1879, English writer.

45. To Marcus Spring.[1]

Stockholm 12 Jan. 1853.

My dear Marcus! You are in London, and I did not know of it before the letter of Mary Howitt[2] ap[p]rized me of it! For about three weeks I had a letter from Rebecca dated *Rose Cottage* that made me so happy. You were better, dear Marcus, and all things looked bright and well with you, your family and friends. I answered the letter in the joy of my heart. Now you are in England and not well. My dear Marcus, it makes me deeply sad. Mary H. speaks only of your health as beeing delicate. But why then stay in that undelicate, foggy climate of England? Why not go to sunny Italy at once for the winter, and return north in summer? My dear

Marcus, can I hope then to see you and Rebecca in Sweden? Have you thought of it? You must by and by write to me a word about that. If you come I can hardly advise you to come before midsummer, as the weather before that time is often cold /though not *very* so. I felt more cold at midsummer time in Virginia the year 1851 than I have ever done at that time in sweden./ and unsteady. From midsummer and to September, and even the first part of Sept. the weather is generally good, even for a delicate health. If you think of coming, write to me before spring, dear Marcus, and tell me what way you will come. And when you come, my dear brotherly friend, and when we meet, if you see tears on my cheeks, you must not mistake them, but be sure that they are tears of joy, of joy at seeing you again, of welcoming you to my land, to my heart and home!

God bless you my dear Marcus, and make you well, for the sake of your many friends. None of them loves you better than your

swedish sister
Fredrika Bremer.

Later.

My dear friend I have your letter from England! God bless you my dear Marcus for writing it. It has made me both happy and unhappy, unhappy on account of the state of your health. My dear Marcus, you must not stay in England over the winter you must go south, not to Nizza [Nice], not to Florence, not to Rom[e], but to Neapel [Naples] or Palermo. Neapel and Palermo are the only places where the air is unchangingly sweet and wholesome for delicate health. O you must not stay in England over the winter. But when the summer comes you must go north and come to Sweden; and the more you travel about the better certainly will it be.

Now let me say a few words about my letters on America. Any alteration, my dear Marcus that you will suggest I heartily subscribe to. And I am happy to see corrected any thing that I may have misstated. But in relation to my friends and the manner in which I speak about some of them I think that what I shall say about it in my preface or my dedication "to my friends in America," will make them easy, and satisfy the public. There is a kind of *fate* about this work that rules it and me; but I feel it as if it was of the hand of God. I *must* give my impressions of country and people in America as they were written down in my letters to my dear Agathe, or — not write at all. To take away what has made me happy, what has made my heart beat with new fresh life and love would be to take away the life of the work, and I could not do it, Marcus. I felt pretty sure that you would object to being spoken about as I have done it in some of my letters — *but* My dear Marcus it *is written there,* and I have no power of unwriting it; — *you* must only be prescribed not to read it. I have yet suppressed many a little private thing that I keep as a gem in my heart and that seemed to my [me] too holy

to come out of home. /and that I have not written even to Agathe./
For what I still have said to[o] much for the delicacy of some of
my friends I shall ask publicly their pardon in my dedicatory letter,
and tell them, what is the truth of [the] thing, that *I could not help
it.* I hade [had] once written these things to my home and for my
home and sister alone, without any thought of making them public;
now, when she is gone and I write them over again — I cannot often
bring to my mind, or realize that I write them for the public. The
sister in her heaven is only before me — and the com[m]union of
spirits like hers. I shall be most glad to errase on yours or Mrs
Howitts suggestion any thing personal[l]y disagree[a]ble to some
persons that have intended kindness to me. It is a true blunder
that such have been preserved in the second writing. But the spon-
tane[o]us risings of the loving and grateful heart, dear Marcus,
these you must leave and — forgive! Think my dear friend that
this book is exceptional. It is written to the homes of earth and *of*
the homes. The earnestness of my object shall hallow my work.
Nor can you yet fully ap[p]reciate the bearing or meaning of many
things as you have not seen the latter parts of the work and it does
not come fully out till there. I must bring out in the beginning some
standard-homes and men, from where to criticise homes and men
in general. To the homes of the new world will be my last ap[p]eal:
"sing to the Lord a new song!"

Still my dear Marcus, my dear brotherly friend, I shall take care
of your delicacy and put you behind the curtain so much as possible.
You have seen the worst I shall say about you already. You dont
know how good you are, and — that is the best of the thing.

In my letter to you and Rebecca written some weeks ago to
New York, I wrote about my joy and hopes in your new Association.[3]
Indeed I am most heartily glad of it and have felt elated in joy at
the strong hope, faith and love of which this interprize [enterprise]
is the product. I look upon the Eagles returning to the place every
year, to breed their young anew, as prophets of the success of your
enterprize. Then unwavering faith, hope and love, patiance and
constancy — these are the eagle wings of humanity.

God bless your Bay Union!

May be once, when I have succeeded in clearing my affairs, I
shall come and joyn it, and work in it after my power — at least for
a time.

Now Marcus, I hope you will soon write to me: "I am going
to Italy and then — to Sweden."

I am well, my dear friend, and days run smooth and not un-
pleasantly with me. I live in a very comfortable home, with a very
kind and amiable old mother. In the forenoons I write at my letters,
in the evenings some friends commonly come, take tea with us
and play at whist with Mama.

God bless thee Marcus, dear brotherly friend, dearest of those still left me on earth. I hope much for thy health of the Climate of Europe. The climate of America is terribli exciting to the nerves. I was quite astonished at its influence over my nerves so strong and calm before. Now and here I am strong again. And thee shallt here become so my dear Marcus. Thine in love

Fredrika.

I am so glad your writing so long to me did not injure your sleep. Thank thee for mentioning it!

P.S. Let me say once more, my dear Marcus, that if you feel a *serious* wish about suppression of any thing particular in my letters, name it to Mary Howitt and *it shall be done.* I have also written to her about it, and thanked her as well as you for criticism about some personalities that had better not be said. Should you *seriously* advise the suppressing of full names of persons known to the public as for ex. Downing, Channing, Emerson, your wish shall be followed in the english edition. The Scandinavian one may yet follow my will and way. And it is the wish and will of my heart to have the dear name of *Spring* (and some other names) connected in the minds of men with the *spring* of love and life with all the sweet and gladdening feelings that belong to the *spring* of the year and of the heart.

I have read Uncle Tom;[4] half Sweden has read it and wept and rejoyced over that most touching, charming excellant story. Its perfection and beauty has made me truly happy. But Marcus, I am truly sorry for the views of the Authoress with regard to emancipation. Emancipation previous to education never will do with the Negro people. I shall yet have much to say about slavery and tell some dreadful things, on the Missis[s]ippi and in Cuba, but I shall take a different view of the m[e]ans of liberation. I am sorry Marcus you have only read the first Vol. of my letters then that is decidedly the weakest and most selfish one. The second Vol. contains I think the marrow of the work. But, you must not read Manuskript. I know how in America even reading of letters affected my nerves painfully. You must not do any thing now, but run about, this winter to Italy, this summer to Sweden, dear Marcus!

Have you heard any thing about my dear Mrs Howland of Charleston and her family? I am anxious at not having heard from her as the yellow fever has been in Charleston.

---

1. MS, HL.

2. Mary Botham Howitt, 1799-1888, English writer and wife of William Howitt.

3. Eagleswood or Raritan Bay Union, near Perth Amboy, N. J.

4. *Uncle Tom's Cabin* (1852), by Harriet Beecher Stowe.

46.   To Rebecca Spring.[1]

Stockholm 11th March, 1853.

Where in all the world has my letter gone, the letter that I wrote to you, my dear Rebecca, in answer to your first one last fall from *Rose Cottage,* that letter that made me so happy, and made my heart and my eyes both overflow! Oh how happy it made me! Then I had not for very long time heard from you, and Marcus, and I looked about with anxious heart to know where you were; all seemed so sorry and lonely about you; Marcus so ill, you so sorro[w]-ful, and *Rose-cottage gone!* And then, at once to receive that dear, delightful letter from *Rose Cottage* dear blessed, Rose Cottage, and all its good Angels there, and well, and working again with the Angels of Heaven for peace on earth, and good will to Man! Oh! it made me happy indeed; and made my heart bloom as summer. And now, here comes your letter of 1 Febr. telling me that I have not answered that letter of yours! But, my dear Rebecca, you should have known me better! You may as well have told me that I was dead or had lost the use of my hands and every means of writing to you. I answered your letter in the fullness of my heart when I had got yours, t.i. by the end of last December — I think it was. And as I enfranchised it and direkted it as my former letters to you, I am as astonished as sorry that it had not yet come to you by the first of febr. But the posts from Sweden are often very slow by this time of the year; your letter of the 1 of Febr. came to me first yesterday, 10 of March; and so I hope that my letter has come to you, soon after you wrote. It makes me unhappy that Rebecca Spring even for a minute could think me ungrateful or careless. Oh, my dear Rebecca, my dear Rebecca, never, never think so! Think any thing else. I *cannot* be ungrateful; nor a single moment neglectful of such friends as you have been to me. Rather die!

I should be sorry also if that letter had misscarried for the two letters enclosed in it, one to my good Dr. Osgood, and one to Mrs Beecher Stowe[2] that I entreated you to forward. And my dear Rebecca, pray, let me know so soon as you have got this if the letters are not come right. Then these dear excellant people must not think a moment that I can neglect them, and if my letters to them have misscarried I must write new ones directly.

"Married!" Yes indeed Rebecca, I am married for life, but only to the idea that God has given me to cherish and forward and work for, in life and death, and that inspires me at this moment more than ever; and of that you know something, and you will know more when you come here. Shall I indeed see you here, in my own land my own home Rebecca and Marcus, my dear precious friends?! Marcus makes me hope it, and I shall anxiously wait for the confirmation of that hope to settle my plans for this summer. If you will come I shall wait for you and go with you through a part of Sweden and return to work my work in my own dear country as I think it is the will of God. Yesterday I had a good kind letter from Marcus. Thank God that he is so much better, and thank God also, that he has got for travelling companion in Italy a young Swede, Mr Ehrenheim, who will also be to him a true friend. Young E. is a young nobleman of good family and fortune, and what is better, of an uncommonly good heart and head, a most excellant and amiable young man respected by every body at home. I cannot tell you how glad I am that he is with Marcus. I enjoy greatly all you say about Marcus, my dear Rebecca. I know it all to be but right. I always looked upon Markus as one of the most pure and noble works of God. I do not think I have seen a mind so pure and good as his. May God bless him, and let you two unite in happiness, in Europe and America. A[bou]t your new noble plans with the Rarita[n A]ssociation I have written to you, in that[3] behind-hand letter, and of my joy in it, and faith in the Eagles prophetic return. Beautiful prophecy! And about your gift the picture of the Hudson in its beautiful guilded [gilded] surrounding that now adorns our parlour in Stockholm, and many things I have written. To day I must write but few lines, then I have a quantity of letters to write, but still I must say thank[s] and God bless you, my dear dear Rebecca! These dear children I wish I could kiss them, dear little Marcus Herbert above all. Eddy must certainly become an artist; I think he is born to that. Oh my dear Rebecca, may I see you once more and Marcus, and be allowed to make you happy in my dear Swedish home. It is the innermost heart wish of your

Fredrika.

Of myself I have not much to say. I am well, and work at my soon finished work about America and live in quiete and comfort, though not without cares. My poor Mother had for some weeks since an attack of Apoplexy that has left her without the use of her limbs and [the] future looks for her heavy ennough. But thank God she is cheerful and patient — I have hopes and plans, and God permitting my life will still be a more useful one than it has been.

----

1. MS, HL. Address: Perth Amboy, N. J.
2. Harriet Beecher Stowe, 1811-1896, American writer.
3. One word missing.

47.   To Anne Howland.[1]

Stockholm 7 April 1853

Dearest Anne, my kind friend and hostess in the sunny south! I write to you in the midst of a fierce snowstorm belonging to the accustomed delights of our swedish spring in April. And you, my dear Anne, I see now amidst roses and honey suckle, humming birds

and fig-trees in the garden about your house! Ah would I could
see you in reality and speak with you, and hear you speak!! You
have certainly wondered why you have not heard from me for a
long time. My dearest Anne, I have been writing and hoping to hear
from you, and anxiously too, as it was long since I had any news.
But recently I have got the intelligence that I have a letter from
you on the way to me, and that you and yours are well. Thank God
for that, and that my dear home in Charleston had so far been
exempted from sorrows. May it be so even now, and the new spring
see new hopes and happiness grow there. — I have not much to tell
you about me, my dear Anne; my life, since I came home, has been
a very quiet one, uniform, and thank God not without calm growth
inwardly nor without blessings in outward measure, though many a
cloud still dims my day. My poor mother has had this winter an
attack of apoplexy from which she hardly will wholly recover and
though clear in mind and will in the upper part of the body, she
is perfectly unnable to walk or stand and has to be carried between her bed and a sopha. This is a melancholy state and may
last long. Thank God she is cheerful and calm, and grace to Him
that every care and comfort can be bestowed on her who never
spared care or any thing to alleviate the sickbeds of those who
were dear to her! Her situation, of course, confines me more
than before, and the merry voices of friends in the evenings are
no more heard in our house, as she cannot bear much company. Nor
do I repine at the solitude; I always loved that; and this winter
I have taken a young girl in the house who reads aloud to me in
the evening to spare my eyes who are not good. She is poor so it
is good for her, she is young and strong so it is good for me, and
her fine character and lively soul adds a new charm to my life as
it gives a new love to my heart. My chief occupation, life and
delight this long time has been to live over again the days I have
lived in America with my dear friends there, in the North, in the
South, in the West; and writing over again the letters I from
their homes wrote to my home in Sweden. You know my dearest
Anne that I have been employed since last spring with that work;
but little did I at its beginning anticipate its magnitude to me, and
also — to the reader to be, then it will be a big work in size and
perhaps too big for many an impatient reader. During all this
time I have been as magnetized by the western world, and obeying
the will of its spirit in what I have said and written. I think that
in no work of mine I have been so divested of self-will as in this,
and only following the dictates of the genius of the land and people
whose realms have been opened to me. My work is now approaching
i[t]s close; in the course of this summer I think it will come to you.
Recently I have there lived over with you the last time in Charleston and our Florida trip, the pleasant days in your home and our

night on Sullivans island! I know that you will look on these pages with pleasure and recall those days, and feel in your kind and noble heart some joy in having given me so much; and the letter to the Queen of Danmark finished in your home will show you that I claim you as a Scandinavian and will not allow you to be American wholly. Indeed I think you have much of the scandinavian mind and temperament, and belongs to us by a right divine.

Of my prospects I shall tell nothing, as I for the time to come, have none beyond the care of my poor Mother. I shall, during that period, try to make me inwardly fit for whatever work my great Master will point out to me. This summer I shall perhaps have the joy to welcome to my land some of my dearest friends in America the *Springs* and the *Osgoods*.[2] May I be able to do so according to the wishes of my heart!

And now my dearest Anne I long so much to hear from you, that I must ask you to write again to me by some good opportunity or with the post. (But then you must take some very thin paper; the post is very high still between America and Sweden and is unreasonable ennough to tax 5 to 6 Swedish Dollars a letter from one of my dear friends.) But write to me my dear Anne of you of the dear girls and dear little Willie, and of all yours, and of our common friends in Charleston. Distance seems only to have endeared them to me, and made your home seem more beautiful. And Justina, my good and noble Justina must write to me a little letter and tell me about "Mother" and her home. I know Justina will do it, and I shall write and ask her.

In Sweden we are very quiet and try to better our affairs, which is well needed. Our good King[3] has been long and dangerously ill; he is now well again and his illness has made the love of the people for him both in Sweden and Norway come forth in a truly striking and touching way. On his recovery there have been every where feasts and illuminations and beautiful contributions to the poor and suffering in the name of King Oscar. We are truly a Monarchical people and deserve good Kings. In the dayly papers I always look for news from America, and always follow affairs there with the greatest interest. The *New President*[4] and *Uncle Tom* have been to Europe the chief Lyons [lions] of this time in the new world and the Caloric Machine of the Swede *Erikson*[5] in New-York; thank God for that noble invention and that the genius of Sweden through it has for ever closed a bond with that of America. It will make the dreadful incidents on your r[ive]rs and railways ceace and save millions of lives and sorrows. Alas! it could not save the best of my friends the noble and gifted Andrew Downing. It came to[o] late. His loss has been and is a severe pang to my heart. God bless my dearest Anne and all she loves, Husband, sisters, brother, children my dear young friends *Justina Illione Sarah Willie Laura!* Remember

me in kindness to them all. Tell Mrs Hollbrook that she is as present
to me as ever and that she still will know in what way. Remember
me to common friends and those that were kind to me in Charleston.
They have not been so to an ungrateful mind! And above all, my
dear kind Anne, remember me as yours in grateful love and sisterly
affection

Fredrika Bremer.

P.S.

Pray, my dear Anne, let the enclosed little letter to Mrs Le Vert
be sent to its ad[d]ress so soon as possible! — Old dear Mr Gilman
and his lady — young good Mr Richard — dont forget to give my
special remembrances!

------

1. MS, FBF. Parts of this letter were printed in New York *World,* March
28, 1878, p. 2.
2. The Osgoods visited Sweden in 1853, the Springs in 1854.
3. King Oscar I, 1799-1859.
4. Franklin Pierce, 1804-1869, fourteenth president of the United States.
5. John Ericsson, 1803-1889, Swedish-American inventor.

48.   To Maria Lowell.[1]

Götheborg 13 Aug. 1853

My dear kind Maria! On the eve of parting with my dear friends
Dr and Mrs Osgood from Boston, who have visited me in Sweden,
I write in haste a few words just to thank you, my dearest friend,
for your letter, and its life so dear and warm and genial though
written in the sick bed![2] I saw you again all yourself, but alas — that
you should have so much to suffer! It seemed to me that the Angel
in you had no need of these difficulties to disingage its wings. What
shall I say my dear Maria, but that I wish that I had wings that
could make me fly to you, and then I should sit by you, serve you,
listen to you, look on you and also talk to you and try to make weary
hours pass more swiftly and bring better days more near. It seems
to me that we have so much, so very much to talk about, things
that have passed, things that are coming, and those things that
never pass, eternal and cheerfull things, the minds repose and delight. Indeed, dear Maria, I feel that we will never have done talking with one annother; and that my com[m]union with you must
endure for ever; so even with James though you are personally
nearer to me, he most so in his song, his noble and charming poetry.
How I long to hear him again! When you are well again, dear Maria,
pray write to me, tell me about yourself and James and all things
about you; and may I again see the sun shining in your home; then
so long as I see you suffering I can see no sun there. I have not
been able yet to ascertain the things that your good father wishes
to know and about which he wrote to me; but I shall, if possible, find

it out this fall. I suppose that the old church he speaks of is the church of *Solna*, and I shall make an excursion to that as soon as I am again in Stockholm. I am now in Gothenburg, on the west coast of Sweden, in company with my dear friends the Osgoods with whom I want to be as long as they are in my country. About myself I have not much to tell you dear Maria. I am well, and thankful for many things, only flagging now and then in feelings (spirits) though not in faith. Troubles in my family, make me sad at times; but things have not become worser of late and may become better. Reality is not rich about me in my home; but fiction (that is a higher reality) will, I hope, help me well on through the fall and winter. God bless you my sweet dear Maria, and make you happy again! Kindest love to your father and husband, kind remembrance to Rebecca etc. Kiss to dear little Mabel! I shall soon again speak with you, and be with you in spirit; as always your loving friend

Fredrika Bremer

----

1. MS, HCL.
2. Maria Lowell died October 27, 1853.

49.   To [Charles Kingsley].[1]

Stockholm 8 Sept. 1853.

My dear Sir, and — let me say — friend!

If you were not a genius I should feel as if I ought to excuse myself for not having long, long since thanked you for the good and cordial letter, that you were kind ennough to write to me, for — more than a year since; but I have a strong confidence in the clairvoyence of such minds as yours, and feel sure that you have, through the night of silence, seen and read the unspoken thoughts of a heart that has not ceased to beat in warm sympathy with yours since the moment when it was thrilled by those warmblooded words of yours that came to me on the Atlantic as from a kindred spirit, burning with thoughts that long since had possessed my soul. And so you must have known that if you not have heard from me it was that my soul and time were taken up in a way that would not allow me to turn to you with full and undivided attention; and that I otherwise would not ad[d]ress you. But always you have been present to my mind and I believe that there have not been many days when I have not felt your attraction, felt as if *you should not* live so far away from me, as if that was not the will of God, then I had much to say to you, much to hear from you, and above all wanted the refreshing influence from a mind fresh and glowing as yours. Then — I was once so, but now — I am growing old, and feel the snows of life settling even on my heart, and — this I would not. I have long looked for a quiet time when I could com[m]une with

you after the wish of my heart, at least with pen and ink. But now
it is come I feel that time and space are bad impediments, and that
the necessity to write a letter when you wish to speak with a friend
is a heavy drawback to conversation. Still I must write now, then
I must speak with you, must tell you in words my heartfelt sympathy
and interest in you and in your work. Little of your life and doings
of late have transpired to my northern home, but I know that you
are living, and then I know that you are loving, working, battling
for universal good, for the saving truths of this age. Then yours is
a Universal mind and God has ap[p]ointed you a leader in his
Militant church until that has conquered political society, and
christianized the politics as it has done the morals of the civilized
world. May He bless you with patiance and perseverance as he has
done it with courage and genius — patience with the dullness, the
stupidity in fellow workers and friends, or those that should be
such, perseverance to overcome these worst trials to a warm and
daring mind. And with a partner such as that sweet and noble wife
of yours, and friend such as that true Christian sage Mr Maurice,[2]
you cannot but feel that God has given you Angels on your way.

But, seems to me, that lately He is fighting himself in your
cause helping it on. He has opened the gates of this world (our
planet) and given such outlets to the toiling and working people
shut up in old Europe that they have become and are becoming
quite scarce there, and so will be able to dictate where they were
formerly forced to obey. Their time for good is come. Oh! that you
could infuse in them that noble and christian spirit who will not
stoop to retaliation, who will not think only of self, but rising up to
the full dignity of man will from out of the God-heart (or head)
set a new example, dictate new laws to the world.

Is there any hope of such a growth among the working classes
in England? Or will they only rise to crush others, and glory in
tyranny over those that were tyrants once — will they only repeat
the old story of the french revolution? Oh you, who has power and
talent, and the ear of those classes for whom you have felt and
worked in sympathy, speak to them, inspire them with great and
noble thoughts so that they may give the world a new and dignified
spectacle, and win grace before God and men, let Alton Locke rise
again a new man in a new time and set to his co[u]ntrymen the example of forgiv[e]ness, moderation, Generosity, true Christian
grandeur — or better still let a woman stand forth. —

A young friend of mine in England Mr Joseph Kay[3] has written me that you have recently published a book with the name of
Hypathia. (We have it not here, but I hope we shall soon.) What is
Hypathia? Is it *the woman,* her that I look for? In almost all your
works (known to me) I have observed a yearning or a hopeful look
to Woman as to the redeeming Angel for the woes and wrongs of

society. Even I look to the advent of the true Woman in her fully rounded sphere of life as to the true advent of Gods kingdom in social life. But miserably narrowed by the crushing institutions and trainings of thousands of centuries she has hitherto lacked power to come forward in her true worth and dignity. She gropes still in the dark, seeking her true self, her true position; winning it sometimes by chance, or by the Grace of God, and then gracing life and society in the place where her place has individually been marked out; — oftener skulking away from the battle to forget her nobler aspirations in the loves of private life and its enjoyments, or in stern (or sour or mean) resignation to sit down and be nothing, or feed on the crumbs of the table spread for the lords of earth; som[e]times fighting blindly away in bold self assertion, without nobleness in aim, without dignity in action, wanting seemingly only to rule, to be something uncommon. Alas! for the many, many minds lost to their high mission from want of understanding it, from want of consciousness of their true relationship to God and to society!

Marg[a]ret Fuller Ossoly [Ossoli] (whose life I have not read but whom I know a good deal of through her friends and even her writings) was, as I think, one of these. Man and [wo]man were in her in juxtaposition. Her metamorphosis was incomplete. She was and wanted to be more than a commonplace woman, but looked for that to the intellect more than to the growth of the heart from out of the selfish one in the Universal. Intellect should in woman enlarge in great sympathies else it will never be truly great in her. (Mrs B. Stowe has written romance with true womanly intelligence and of course power.) Marg[a]ret F. is a figure strongly characteristic of the ambiguity in womans position and consciousness in this age of transition. But who am I to speak, to judge of others? What have I done or written that can show that I am more than the rest? Alas! — Still could you know that heart of mine, its aspiration, its history, you would in the social position of woman, combined with the natural tenderness and piety of her heart find the clue to the question why she, as yet, is so far from her Ideal, why she is generally so far below her own best aspirations. And you might also see that I have not done yet, and may with the grace of God yet do a better work than hitherto.

In your portraits of women two things have struck me, nam[ely] the power with which you want to invest women over the hearts of men, and — the want of initiative in these same women. Even the noble Ellinor (in Alton Locke) is in her social working inspired by her husband, and Elisabeth of Hungary (in that most touching but heartrending tragedy!) is — so it would seem more driven by the awe and fear of her Confessor than by the love of Jesus and the working of his spirit in her. /And I own to you that I think you there are a little wrong. Such a mind as hers has more initiative and more consolation from within. Otherwise it would be to[o] *terrible.* Conrad is a most admirable and finished character most masterly drawn./ Alas! that want is but to[o] true wherever womans affection or heart is not interested. And if woman has hitherto lacked in power to work in larger scale for fellow beings it is that she from childhood is forbidden to look beyond home, or beyond the church where she has been thought [taught] — generally very narrow ideas of the great Universal Father.

Interest her heart, her mind, her best feelings in the cause of humanity from the time of her childhood; make her feel that she can work for it with every pulsation of her heart and you will have enlisted the most powerful worker in the redemption of society. Then the new Woman will breed the New Man! —

I speak so freely with you then I cannot but think that both you and your Fanny are in sympathy with me on the subject. And this is a subject I have *at heart;* then I have much suffered, and seen much suffering, and wil[l] too, from the injustice done by society to woman. I have many a time ap[p]roached the subject in my writings but never so fully as in my latest book "the homes of America!" I have ordered a copy of the book to be sent to you from the part of the Author. Pray dont be frightened, if you can help it, at its dimensions and do not read it through (but this I need hardly recommend) but just look at matters in the Index (I suppose there is such a thing in the English publication) and read what you like. Some things may be of interest to you. I have written at large in this work. Now I shall concentrate both thoughts and writing, and God willing, say, in a better or more taking way, what God has given me to say.

The work of life and death is going on in my land with a good deal of activity at this time. The Cholera visits almost all our cities and takes off good many people especially among the poorer classes. And in Stockholm there is just at this time much of sickness and mortality. But in the whole land (and even in Stockholm) there is a moral resurrection going on, and a great raising of voices for putting a stop to the deluge of *"Burning vine"*4 (Whiskey) which has since several years half drowned our population and made it sick both morally and materially. Voices also rise for material improvements, industrial and sanitary reforms, and Association is at work among the working classes to spread knowledge and taste for reading, art and refinement. Indeed, the necessity to associate in order to be strong and to do strong things is felt among all classes and leads to cor[r]esponding action. We look a good deal to England in our industrial and com[m]ercial enterprizes, but try at the same time to keep our national ground and see what befits us as Swedes.

Leading minds, minds with large, generous ideas and courageous spirit, genial, sun-like minds, alas, I see *none;* and sometimes I am ready to weep over it, sometime to feel — no good feeling. But I see that Gods work is going on, I see many good and wellmeaning persons driven on by a spirit more strong than they; and I try to be patiant. I shall feel better when I have taken myself a more active part in the work of elevation than I have done hitherto. Before next spring I may be able to tell you somewhat about it. And now adieu. God bless you and your doings. I do not ask you to tell me about them, about yourself, your beloved ones, your views and works; I know that you will do it if — you are very good, if you will do me good, and if you see in this letter something akin to the workings of your own heart. Ever and ever shall you be dear to me, and the day passed in your home a bright and genial spot in my life. I am not a Swedenborgian, but faith in spiritual cor[r]espondence and in the union of related spirits belongs to the Scandinave and has always been mine, and so I am sure that you cannot always live far from me; you and your sweet wife must one day be of my family circle.

My love to her, and to your children — beautiful little beings! God bless you in all your loves!

Most truly and affectionately
Yours
Fredrika Bremer.

My kind and respectful remembrance to Mr Maurice! *If* you write to me, tell me of him! Such men are not many in this world.

------

1. MS, owned by S. Rooth. Charles Kingsley, 1819-1875, English clergyman, author of *Alton Locke* (1850) and *Hypatia* (1853). (F. Bremer received a copy of *Alton Locke* from Professor E. Scherb as a parting gift and read it en route to England, 1851.)
2. Frederick Denison Maurice, 1805-1872, English theologian.
3. Joseph Kay, 1821-1878, English economist and author of books on social welfare.
4. Swedish *brännvin.*

50.   To Marcus and Rebecca Spring.[1]

Stockholm 28 Nov. 1853.

Best beloved, kindest of Friends, Marcus and Rebecca, now I must have a moments Chat with you, though I snatch it from many a pressing care and buissness. But I cannot bear longer not to have a regular speak out with you, at least of a few minutes, o! my dear friends. First, thanks and blessings to you Rebecca for your dear and beauteful letter of the 23 Sept. from Hampstead! It made me happy to see you well again and ever happy in the harmony of your soul and your love, happy to know Marcus so well and strong again! Thank God for it! I was glad to see you go south; but still have some missgivings about your finding yourself well in France. English comforts and cleanliness you will not find there, at least not in French hotels or houses. But then you may easely find an English one in Paris. And then I will hope the best. Certainly the air and sun of Paris are bright and invigorating; and there the Parisian life, the promenades etc. is picturesque and amusing and places of public resort full of beauty and interesst are many. How happy Eddy and Jenny will be in Jardin des Plantes! You will write to me my dear friends and tell me how you are settled in Paris, and lett me know of your comforts and pleasures and walks and talk, — will you not?! —

And then, when the hot sun of the latter end of May rises over Paris; then perhaps you will think of the cool woods and seas of Sweden, and — afford me the delight of once more seeing your dear faces, and of clasping you to my fond and ever grateful heart. With Midsummer generally beautiful summer comes to Sweden — short, it is true, hardly of more duration than three months, but still rich and luxuriant in soft beauty. Ah! that it may be permetted to me to pass some Swedish summer days with you, to offer you some of my fruits and flowers, and make you feel at home in my dear land! — it seems to me as if I should after that feel my heart more at ease in this world. My beloved friends — may "the Inner light, the inner voice" guide you to me, and may I be able to be to you what my heart requires. In one instance I could not. I could not now more, as I once so fondly anticipated, receive you in my country home, and make you partake of the peculiar comforts of a Swedish country life. My noble Årsta is gone, sold and gone the whole great landed property of my family. But were it not for that I cannot more there call you my guests I must rejoice at the affair. Then it has taken us out of great troubles and anxiety for the future, and at once assured me and mine of a situation, not rich or wealthy, but still above the necessaries of life, and that may still improve. You will be glad to hear of that, I know, my dear friends. And though I cannot open to you the great halls of Årsta and dress them with flowers for you; still I may be able to open to you a home as comfortable and pleasant, — may be able to go with you and show you somewhat of what is best and loveliest in my land. Much had I longed to see you here the past summer; then Årsta was mine, as yet. But I see that it was for the best that you came not. The Cholera came and I must fear to see here the friends dear to me. The Cholera being nearly over in Stockholm, a society of ladies[2] have united for the purpose of taking care of all the orphan Children and suffering families through the pestilence in the Capital who amount to several hundreds. And as I am at the head of the society I have much to do and to think of, much to write and to speak both in

private and in public. But I earnestly hope that this union will work
a great deal of good in society both present and coming; and thank
God for the success that hitherto has met our endeavors. I have
organized our society in a manner after the pattern of the Constitution of the United States. We have eight separate Com[m]unities
(one in each of the eight parishes of the Capital) and a federative
government, where two members from each parish-com[m]une
preside as representatives. The machinery works well; the society
is growing and rising in power. Still there is much to do to give it
stability and to bring a right understanding to the minds of the
members. These cares now take up the greater part of my time and
will take it up till Christmas. Meantime it is a great happiness to
be able to redeem many a poor child from the arms of famine, vice
and missery ready to crush it; and to make the light of love and
hope come in many a dark and desolate home. And then, with this
comes many a thing that will make even Sweden by and by sing a
new Song unto the Lord, and the women of the land take their
part in it in union with the men. Our society begins this Christmas
to start a Swedish litterature for small children, most especially for
the children of the poor; a thing which hitherto has been totally
wanting in Sweden.

    It was sweet and precious to me, my dear Rebecca, to hear
you speak of my American letters. Indeed, I could not believe that
I should be at varience with you and Marcus on any capital or vital
questions, nor yet in the spirit of the work. I have earnestly and
piously sought for the truth and for nothing but the truth; and my
heart has been warm with the love inspired me by Americas grand
ideas and its best men and women. I cannot have been much in
the wrong. And whatever foibles my work may have, I feel that the
pure light of the sun, the clear air, the forest stillness — my best
conscience and my best friends do not blame or find much fault
with me. /If this is boasting or false I hope they will tell me so!/
In Sweden the book has been received as seldom a book in Sweden
and the names of my dearest American friends come to me from
the lips of My country men and women in a manner and with a
feeling most delightful to my heart. "We had no idea they say that
the people there were such." It is hardly credible how prejudiced
against America and Americans a great part of European society
yet is. But — when you come to Sweden, o, my dear friends you
will find many friends there beside your Swedish sister.

    I cannot write more to day then I must attend meetings and
Com[m]it[t]ees. But I feel quite happy to have had a little Chat
with you. Have you got a letter that I wrote to you in Sept. and
that Mrs Howitt was to forward to you to Paris, in case you already had left London? Mary Howitt *is* a generous and kind creature by nature. But Mr Howitt and circumstances do not always let

her remain right. Still, God bless her. Her heart is pure and right. Her translation of my late work has made me suffer and makes me suffer a good deal of anxiety, then she evidently knows to[o] little of the Swedish language to have undertaken the work. (This, entre nous.) Her own stile is excellant and her language also, — if only she knew the Swedish as well! It is almost wonderful that she has succeeded so well on the whole. But there are some serious blunders and misstakes. One that I just now have seen and am truly sorry for is about Mrs Child. I Vol. page [15] it is said that Mrs Child seems to me to[o] *angular* to be happy! The Swedish word is to[o] "*känslig*" which means *sensitive* or delicate in feeling. Mrs Child *Angular!* What an expression. I must write to Mrs Child and correct at least that misstake. But there are many more. In the latter part of the work the translation seems much better and in the last volume often good and even excellant. Mrs H. evidently has entered in the spirit of the language and become more accustomed to its life and turns. Still I have seen mistakes even there. But such must come. Such a translation is a difficult work. I know that Mary Howitt has done her very best and most [conscientiously?] worked.

Forgive dearest that I speak so much of this. I have not long since received the work from England. In Sweden the whole work is not yet out.

My Mother is lame still, but else well and cheerful. My life and home have love and comfort. But — *my friends*, the best, the nearest dearest are gone all, all dead or away. There are two of them now in Paris. May they write to me *soon, soon,* and my heart will feel less lonely. The head and Mind have plenty to fill their cravings. /This winter we have Diet (the Congress of Sweden) in Stockholm; and I have many relations from the country now in the City./ But the poor heart! —

Love to the dear Children. God bless them. My dear Rosecolored friends of dear Rose Cottage let me soon hear from you! You don't know how dear you have become to many Swedish hearts, nor how dear you are to that of your

Fredrika

———

1. MS, HL.
* 2. *Stockholms fruntimmersförening för barnavård.*

51. To Anna Maria Hall.[1]

Stockholm 9 Januar[y] 1854.

Dear Mrs Hall! Did ever a word or a thing come from you that were not inspired by the spirit of kindness and that did not give pleasure? I believe not. It is the privilege of your beautiful nature to do so. Thank you most kindly for the letter of Dec. which gave me a great pleasure, both for its good news and its good will. Indeed many letters from England confirm to me these good news (about my work the Homes etc) in a manner far exceeding my hopes. But from America some letters have caused me great both pain and surprise; you will have seen the effects of them in a Card inserted in the Times.[2] I wish Mrs Howitt would show you the letter from me which did accompany the card to her. If she will, you will better than by the Card understand my position to her, and the measure I have taken for the sake of American friends as well as in justice to myself. But the pain and anguish the mistakes of Mrs Howitt have made me suffer, have carried me to[o] far in some matters as in wishing a t[h]orough revision of the english translation, though I allow of its faithfulness in general and its excellance in many parts. And I shall take the first opportunity to say a word of peace and full ap[p]reciation in this matter, that, I hope, will fully satisfy Mrs Howitt and her friends, and also *you* who must look with pain on a dissention between us. This opportunity will soon come as a letter from Mrs Howitt tells me that she has answered my card in the Times, and, to judge by the letter, the answer[3] will be a violent, and hardly a good one. But this I did not expect. She has been deeply wounded and cannot understand my feelings or motives in this matter. Nevertheless nothing will, I hope, tempt me to utter in reply any thing that will not tend to bring matters right again and make good both her faults and mine. It would be to[o] bad if a beeing by nature loving and grateful, dreading to give pain as much as she dreads hell, should be doomed to inflict pain or displeasure lastingly where she wanted only to thank and bless. I hope to God that it will not be so. Such things make me very unhappy. It was a great missfortune to my work that Mr Howitt went off to Australia and left it alone to Mrs Howitt. He was, as I understand, by far the best swedish scholar of the two. With Mrs Howitts imperfect knowledge of the Swedish language it is wonderful how she has been able to succeed so far. Then indeed, I like to repeat it, her work is on the whole good; and in many parts most excellant, could not be better. Native genius and good will have been her helpers.

Excuse, dearest Maria that I occupy your attention so much with this, but this has now so much occupied me. Thanks for the delightful little relations in your letter; and how glad I am to see you well and happy and every thing prosperous about you! Indeed sunshine must attend every where such persons as yourself and Mr Hall.

For me, I have many reasons to be thankful for my part in life. Things that looked gloomy a year since have cleared up and settled themselves better, much better than I dared to hope. Thank God I can now look forth to a life sheltered from outward care in economical point of view, and I can devote myself in peace to those studies that become dearer and dearer to me. Then I feel it, with the summer of my life the spirit of romance is past. I shall hardly write love stories as before. Still I shall write of love, but in annother way.

This whole season I have had, and still have much to do with our great ladies-association for the relief of families and children suffering after the ravages of the Cholera in our Capital; and this has taken up my time so that I have not been able to think of writing or hardly talking about other things. And I now feel almost starving of hunger for the realms of poetry, or the occupation with these. I have begun to give out several small stories and songs for the children of the poor and so given a start to an original swedish litterature for children. Several friends have joyned with me therein, and it will be a good and useful thing. My dear Mother is always confined to her room, but sits in her sopha patient and cheerful. All my moments of leasure and my evenings I pass with her. A young girl reads in the evenings aloud to us both. Many relations and friends living in Stockholm this winter enliven our home, and many a great interest and hope makes my heart warm. It seems to me that my great Father more and more clearly shows me the work I have in future to accomplish, and this feeling is to me a great comfort and joy. My best wishes as well as my best thanks are with you and Mr Hall /and England alway[s] the land of promise to me for the humanisation and happiness of the earth!/ dear Maria! God bless you and make you happy now and always! Most truly and affectionately

Yours
Fredrika Bremer

10 Januar[y]. I have now Mrs Howitts reply to my Card and — thank God that was so that I could say in reply all that I wished and wanted to say to make her as easy as I could. I send you the broullion[4] dear Maria of my last word [in] the matter and hope that you will be glad of it. It will be in the Times about the same time that you will receive this.[5]

------

1. MS, HSP. Anna Maria Hall, 1800-1881, was the wife of Samuel Carter Hall, 1800-1889, English author and editor.
2. London *Times*, December 23, 1853.
3. London *Times*, December 26, 1853.
4. *Brouillon*: French for "rough draft."
5. F. Bremer's "Reply to Mrs. Howitt" was printed in the London *Times*, January 24, 1854.

52. To James Hamilton.[1]

Stockholm the 16 Januar[y] 1854.

Mr James Hamilton.

To you, who once offered yourself to me as a Father, to you whose kind and benevolent heart and look methink I still can see through the mist that misconceptions and bitter words (but not from me) have conjured up between us, to you for whom I always have felt and still do feel respect and affection, to you I must write and *try*, at least, to dispel the cloud that darkens my soul to you, and yours to me. Friend of my dearest and nearest friend in America[2] listen to me for a moment!

Probably you have by this time seen my Card to the reading public in America, printed in the National Intelligencer;[3] and it may already have explained to you some things in my letters on America that must have seemed to you and your daughters almost inexplicable. But by the reproaches that have been directed to me by two members of your family — one of them says with *your* authorization! — and which have grieved but still more astonished me, I clearly see that my Card will hardly offer explanation ennough about things that seem to have offended you and your family. To you, who once were so good to me, and to whom I feel bound by gratitude for that goodness, I will say all I can say for myself in this matter.

When the strange mistakes and misconceptions of the translator in the pages relating my visit to your family are cleared away it is to me impossible to think that any thing there can possibly give offence to sound and unprejudiced minds. I know that I have written it with feelings of love and ap[p]reciation that should not have allowed me to say any thing unpleasant to the family whose hospitality I enjoyed. "A picture of beautiful family life" that picture has been called by persons of high refinement both in Sweden and out of Sweden; nor could I have painted otherwise what I deeply felt as beautiful and lovely. But if, when the picture will be restored to its original character, you still should find it "shocking," well, then I must say, that the fault lies in the difference of our characters, of our moral eye, and that we *cannot* understand one annother. But I still hope it may be otherwise. And permit me to say what makes me think so, except the feeling of affection that I have intertained for you personally.

Mr Downing, whose delicacy and refinement you know as well as I, was fully aware of the character of my private letters, as the deep intimacy of mind and heart that grew up between us as a beautiful flower of my life in the new world made me write to him with the abandon and frankness with which I wrote to my dear sister at home; and when I consulted him about the fitness of publishing letters such as these, or *these letters* to my home *he ap-*

[p]rooved of it as he thought "they would give the most true and lifelike image of the inner life of a people but little known and commonly misrepresented in Europe." He even suggested that I should insert in these letters the small sketshes and portraits of persons that I made every where during my visits. "Then," I said "you must lead the way, my friend!" He smiled assentingly. This idea I gave up later, fearing that my portraits would not look well in the book, and not be very agre[e]able to their originals. But it could never enter in my mind that pictures of beautiful family-life even in its minute details could be disagre[e]able to the families concerned. And if persons of the refinement of Mr Downing did not think it; if even now persons of the highly refined and fastidious Aristocracy of England after having read my "Homes of the new world" write to invite me to their homes asking me to come and stay there long time (though knowing well the danger they may incur from so dangerous a guest) and if every week brings to me fresh express[i]ons from near and afar of delight in American homes and in the people of these homes, certainly you will allow that there are different manners of looking on these things and that I may be allowed to question w[h]ether the judgment that here should pronounce: "guilty," is directed by a law accepted by society in general, but rather belongs to a certain society or certain individuals, and that I therefore must be excused if I have transgressed what I was not aware of, what I could not know.

Howsoever that may be, let me ask, let me intreat you, and those of your family who want to look this subject fairly and fully en face, to look upon it in this way:

Have my descriptions of the homes and the home life in America thrown any shadow or blame or ridicule over these, or have they aided to make them ap[p]ear more beautiful, noble and holy than ever was supposed in Europe? Have they not revealed the sunside of the hearts and he[a]rths of its people? Will they not make the people of the United States more universally understood, esteemed and beloved, its future destinies ap[p]ear more morally great, hope giving and glorious?

If this is the case — and who will, who can deny it? — Oh! might I not be excused to say to some of my friends in America: "why do you reproach me? Why do you look black upon me for divuldging that reality and beauty in you that makes you ap[p]ear as a link of beautiful humanity among all peoples of the earth? Why should you frown at touches that make you look not as mere abstractions, but as real human beings with life and blood, lovely to look upon. Come out my friends, come out of your exclusiveness; in the broad, full light of Gods universal sun, vouch[s]afe to ap[p]ear as simple, beautiful human beings, in the brotherhood of humanity who will be glad to know that in your secluded homes there are hearts and minds such as yours!"

Yes my dear Sir, my kind American father that was, my lady friends, dear, kind noble minded Mrs Skyler, Mary, Angelica, who at least now, in this clear and pure moment, look to me as sisters, think of this and perhaps you will absolve me from any intention any *deed* in these matters that should not be absolved by a Jury of Angels. And to such a one I have thought that some of you did belong.

"But" you will perhaps say "*there are* remarks in your book that may be disagreeable to persons that have befriended you?" Are there? May be there are; may be that even when the errors of the translation will be done away with, things will remain that may shock delicate feelings of nicety. I think it very possible that it is so; then I am but little touchy in such matters as to myself, and always intent upon *the true* and *the real* I may sometimes overlook the delicate, especially where that is mostly conventional. But if I have erred unintentionally in this way, in two or three cases, is that indeed *so grave,* so *great* a thing? And are there in my work, as a whole, no remunerating things, no largeminded love, no views, no ap[p]reciation, no great good will that can make these smaller faults unseemly, make them forgotten by large and noble minds? And, oh my dear Sir! Ladies that I believed my friends, if you were displeased with me, was there no other, more kind, more generous, more both you and me befitting way to ap[p]rize me of it than that which has been choosen? Indeed, Indeed, I must still doubt that you, *you* can have given your sanction to it, that you have known of it but distantly, imperfectly! — Should it be otherwise, then — but be that as it may, and whatever may still come to me from your house my once kind friend giving me pain, no return will be made by me but words of love, of blessings for you, your wife, your daughters.

Fredrika Bremer.

1. MS, NYPL. James Alexander Hamilton, 1788-1878, American lawyer and politician; third son of Alexander and Elizabeth Schuyler Hamilton.

2. Andrew J. Downing.

3. Washington *Daily National Intelligencer,* January 10, 1854.

53.   To Marcus and Rebecca Spring.[1]

Stockholm 18 Januar[y] 1854.

My dear, best beloved friends, Marcus and Rebecca I can hardly tell you how happy your dear, delightful letters have made me! It was so long, so very long since I had heard from you, it made me quite sad and depressed; and now at once to have these dear

letters so full of life and light, so full of yourself! Oh it was delightful. And now I am full of plans and projects for you, so full that it
must come out and at once take a run from Stockholm to the Pyr-
enees. But what ails my dear Rebecca?! Marcus I was prepared to
find not well or strong for a time to come; but Rebecca! Why it
must be sheer sympathy for Marcus that makes her so delicate, and
now you must take care of one annother. But my dear friends, it is
clear to me that you must not think of returning to the Climate of
America and the work at Eaglewood before you have grown a
little more Eagles yourself. And that your wings may grow fast
and strong I am sure you must keep travelling and going about
changing air and changing place, then such change makes sleep
come on and ap[p]etite grow and a new fluid of life and spirit pervade the whole constitution. Mrs Osgood, who with her husband, my
good physician visited me last summer and who was so feeble
when she left Boston that she hardly could walk, became every day
of her voyage, especially in Sweden, more and more strong, and
she writes me now from America that her health is quite restored.
Now let me sketsh my plans for your excursions this summer and
fall to come, just as I see them in my head and heart, and then, dear
friends think on them and let the inner light shine on them and
direct you. First: when merry May lights her torch high in the sky
and pours its life and light over the fields of the earth you must be
up and out. I see you in Tyrol and in Switzerland breathing the
invigorating air and enjoying the grand scenery of its mountains in
June and July. Towards August you must turn your thoughts and
steps to Sweden. August and half September, so sultry in France
and Germany is commonly the best part of summer in Sweden. You
must arrange to be in Sweden by the first of August, and there on
the shore, if she is living and well, you will be met by your Swedish
sister. Now we are in Stockholm and there we will run about on
the waters in the large boats managed by stout Dalkullas, picturesque and refreshing to look upon in their national costumes; we will
go and dine on the lovely green islands clustering every where about
Stockholm, the Venice of the North; and after having seen the finest
places and old historical palaces in and about Stockholm we will
take a trip to old Upsala, there see The Cathedral and Professor
Bergfalk, and drink Meth [mead] on the hills of Thor and Odin.
And when you have grown strong of that, then we must make a still
farther trip. There is namely in the Baltic a beautiful Swedish island
called *the eye of the baltic,* seat of our oldest history and still of our
most beautiful ruins, the Island of *Gothland* w[h]ere I have not yet
been, but have always thought to go one day, and how happy I
should be to go there with you! A sea voyage of twelfe hours would
carry us thither, and there we should walk and talk and live as comfortably, I hope, as at Con[e]y Island, and among the high, though

now crumbling arches of old palaces and churches we should speak of days to come, of Eaglewood and the great and beautiful ideas connected with your Union. Having given some days to Gottland and perhaps also to Oland we should return home to Stockholm, and from there take the Canal way through Sweden from the Baltic to the Atlantic. This is a voyage of great interest and variation, and on the way we must give a couple of days to the falls of Trollhätta, its Giant kettles in the rocks, and picturesque scenery. Then I would say to you: let us take a trip to Norway, during a week or two we will be ennabled to see in very comfortable manner some of its most beautiful scenery, its deep valleys, high mountains and strong rivers! or — if you wish to have a quiet and yet healthy time — I would take you to — a rock in the midst of the salt sea, with delightful baths and an air which has given that place the name of the Madeira of Sweden. There amidst the gray, rugged rocks the chevrefeuille (honeysuckle?) grows wild and the epheu,[2] and the white lilys grow in great abundance and higher than any where else in Sweden. There you would rest yourself and take the soft salt seabaths, or inhale the soft and yet bracing air till — you must go, if indeed you *must* go, and leave me your cicerone, friend and sister! But what a good time we could have together, and what a good talk we might enjoy. And then, may be that once I could come and visit you at Eaglewood. Ah! if there is a place where I could live and work heartely and earnestly except in Sweden it would be there and for the noble ideas who live there. As long as my dear Mother lives I will not now leave Sweden except for very short time; and I have just now and for one or two years to come a great deal to do in Sweden of which I shall speak more when I shall be with you. But then. —

Dear friends, I have now told you my plans and wishes and my — hopes. I shall not say a word more as invitation or compulsion, fearing that after all I could not make you here so happy or comfortable as I would, but still I must hope that it will be so, and oh! how happy that would make me. Think of this my dear friends. Meantime this hope will be my summer child and I shall nurse it fondly.

Thank you for all you wrote about your doings and the Children. I saw it and enjoyed it all as if I was with you in reality. And thank you dear Marcus for what you wrote about the Mormons. It came yet in good time as the third Vol. of my letters on America is not yet published here, and as the Mormons are beginning to make converts both in Norway and in Sweden, I am glad to know more of the later history of that sect, and to rectify the too favorable notice I have given about them. All information I could gain when in America was rather in favor of these people than otherwise. But it was easy to see that their doctrine could easely degenerate. As to my work, my dear friends, you speak of it *just so* as I could have hoped and wished you to speak. And I cannot say how dear and delightful it is to me to find you about it in so full a sympathy with myself. This work has in Sweden a success which has astonished me; and letters and papers from England every week now tell me of its full success even there. The sale in England has been so rapid, that in two months after its publication the book had wholly repaid its outlay. From America voices speak differently some warmly and praisingly, some angrily and upbraidingly. Alas! I do not wonder at this and I expected a good deal of that. My own faults and Mrs Howitts also deserve a deal. But I hope that by and by the noble and large minded of the people will, as you have done, forgive or forget the little things, and the failings of the work for — its better part. I have never done any thing under a stronger feeling of compulsion by a higher will than mine, than this work. And though some people grumble at the many small things I am not sure that they do not help to gulp down the big ones without these sticking in the throat. Some people say even so, and that the book could not and should not be otherwise. But I think with you that a good deal could be retrenched. And it will be so in the next edition. /My treatment of the Slavery question seems to rise in favor both in America and in England, and you know, my dear friends, it was my secret little boast with you that I would take up that theme in a new and more effective manner than had been done. If it will work as I have hoped and now have reason to think it will, and if this will be the chief work of my work, then indeed I must look upon my coming to your land and what met me there as Gods special will. Then certainly I had not myself plans or any intentions to work in that directions./

We have deep, heavy dark snowy winter in Sweden, and have not seen the sun for a long time. Within doors all is quiet and comfortable. My dear Mother sits in her sopha always lame but always cheerful and kind. I see company when I want it, but I do not want or wish much of it. Prospects in the family look calm and rather sunny since the sale of our estates has ennabled us to clear our debts and to settle our affairs for the future. I have not much, but I have all I need, and a little more. A great deal have I had and have yet to do, with the children of the poor in Stockholm orphans by the Cholera, and the families suffering from its ravages. An association of ladies has formed itself to take care of these all over the Capital and as I am at the head of it I have a great responsibility, and, a little more to do than is pleasant to me. Then it takes all my thoughts and time. /. . .³/ But something good has come and will come out of these things. When things will be fully in order in these affairs I shall write a story. I long to be a little tête à tête with imagination. Reality — and often very dreary reality has had all my life for more than three months. By the papers I have seen about the dreadfull fire in New York and the Misfortune of the Harpers.[4] These fires in the Cities of the United States are peculiar as I think to American cities, and are a strange phenomenon. Even they seem to speak of the too hot pressure of life in your country.

I am so glad dear Marcus, that you ap[p]roove of my note to the American public; And indeed I could not but write it. But the pain it has given Mrs Howitt (I wrote to her about it, and in great kindness) has given me great pain. To her answer in the Times, I have in consequence written a reply, that I hope will satisfy her and put things right. If you have the Times Newspaper in Pau you must dear Marcus look through its numbers in December last, and in Januar[y] 54 and you will find the answer and the reply. If not — it matters not much; I would not fatigue your dear, "blessed" head with reading unnecessarily. Ah! how well I remember the fatigue I experienced by reading when in America, especially Manuscript, as even you. It was a strange thing that I had never experienced before. But as you still read *books*, as I suppose, I wish you and dear Rebecca would read "Nouvelles Etudes Evangeliques" par A. Vinet[5] (a Swizz divine) then I read now these here, or rather my rosy cheeked little lectrice reads them to me at evenings, and I am perfectly delighted with the beauty and grandeur of its views and its language in the sfere of religious truth and life. I would so relish to read these things with you. And perhaps we may this summer. Not so satisfactory is Vinet in speaking about intelligence and philosophy.

Now my dear, kind friends, you must not more write to me any *long* letter; delightful as your letters are to me I must fear in reading them that you have in writing them done to[o] much for me, and that should not make me happy. But by the opening of spring I shall expect a few words about our summer plans and prospects. Love to the dear Children! May they and you be well and happy, and Oh! may you once in Sweden, my own dear land, tell that you are so to your ever loving and grateful Swedish sister and friend

Fredrika

----

1. MS, HL.
2. *Epheu — Efeu*: German for "ivy."
3. See p. 136 for omitted passage.
4. Harper & Brothers' New York printing establishment was destroyed by fire December 10, 1853.
5. Alexandre R. Vinet, 1797-1847, Swiss theologian and author.

54.   To Marcus and Rebecca Spring.[1]

Stockholm 7. July 1854.

Just received your dear letter from Paris my best and dearest friends Marcus and Rebecca! You are coming to Stockholm. Thats brave and good of you, and may God bless resolution. To me it has been a great relief, and howsoever things may stand at home I shall welcome you as a boon of providence. Last week I wrote to you on Paris (care of Greene et Co) to tell you how things looked for me and for you here. I trust you have the letter now. You will see there that though I must conclude that I could not be your cicerone through my country as I had wished and hoped, still I could be it in Stockholm and its environs and — finally that I could not let you go back over the ocean without once more seeing you, without having had you for my guests; and still that I could not take it upon me to *invite* you to come, but etc, quite a gordian knot of pro et contra! You have cut it through at once and made me feel happy and comfortable, and I have nothing to say but welcome, a thousand times welcome! And now dearest, you must immediately write to me about the time of your coming; and the day you will take the Steamer from Lübeck or from Stettin, so that I may meet you on the Swedish shore, and prepare things here for you so comfortably as possibly. I am already planning for our excursions in Stockholm and its environs. You will find many a thing worth seeing. And then, if my Mothers state continues very much the same I may venture to make with you the trip through the Canal of Götha and repose with you by the falls of Trollhätta. If we can we will go from Gothenburg to Christiania in Norway from where we may, in an easy way, see some of its finest Mountain scenery; from Christiania we should take the Steamer to Kopenhagen, and there see the Museum of Thorwaldsen,[2] and the fine Beechparks for which the environs of Kopenhagen are with justice reknowned. Then, dear friend, you should have seen the three Capitals of the Scandinavian North and at the same time the character of the natural scenery of the three countries, who are united by language, history, political and geografical position and interests; at this moment united more than ever. From Kopenhagen you will easely and safely come over to Germany again. If I am free I shall certainly go with you to Copenhagen where I have many friends, if not still I think you should make that tour through Scandinavia, as it is easy and affords much to see of what is most characteristic in our countries. But we will have time to speak about all that, in my quiet home. I shall then truly see you here, at my table, as my guests! I can hardly believe it. And yet I thank God for the hope of it. We will talk of many things. Earnest things are going on both in east and west; and the position and part of my country and people is one of great interest and great danger at once. And America!! No, I cannot fear for freedom in America. And the Nebraska Congress bill,[3] will meet the free men of Massachusett[s] on the spot in question. The decissions of Congress must become rectified by the still larger Congress of the people.

All in my home is the same; the long and painful struggle of my poor mother between life and death makes it sad and silant. Still there is the light of love and good will to light it up, and now for me the light of hope to see you soon. Thank you my dear American brother and sister! Yours in love

Fredrika.

Thank you dear Marcus for the little flower from the Pyrénées!

————

1. MS, HL.

2. Albert B. Thorwaldsen, 1770-1844, Danish sculptor.

3. The Kansas-Nebraska Bill was signed by President Franklin Pierce on May 30, 1854.

55.   To Marcus and Rebecca Spring.[1]

Stockholm 12 Nov. 1854.

My dear, kind Friends, Marcus and Rebecca! I have both your precious, most welcome letters of September and October. God bless you for them, and all their cheering and to me so delightful expressions about our Scandinavian "Summerchild." Indeed the Memory of this baby will ever be a peace and joy bringer to my spirit, rather apt to be dissatisfied and morbid (chiefly with myself) in looking back upon past days and events. But your kind words will exorcise that demon from my soul when it comes near this Summers-child. Dear Rebecca, the morning I left Copenhagen, just before my setting off from the hotel I popped my head through the door in your room listening if you were awake. I longed to kiss your cheek, and breathe a blessing upon your brow before parting; but all was so still in your rooms; I feared to waken you, and so I kissed and blessed you in spirit and went off with Marcus. How I enjoyed to see in your letter how pleasantly you lived with the friends in Copenhagen after my departure. I was sure it would be so. The Jerichaus[2] were old a[c]quaintences to me; I had been to see them in the morning of the day previous to that of my departure and planned with the Örsteds[3] your a[c]quaintence with them. They are a noble and genial couple and I had spoken of them to you.

How glad I was also to see you united again with your children and all well and happy. Alas for the sad news that came to you soon after. But oh! how very, very beautiful is the life, the words, the spirit, and the parting of that excellant woman and sister whose grave now consecrates the young settlement of Eaglewood; and how much do I thank you dear brother Marcus for having written to me so much about her and of her last letter. Indeed I cannot think of a parting more beautiful than hers and methink I hear again and see the old Simon: "Lord! Now may thy servant depart in peace; then I have seen thy glory, which thou hast prepared for all peoples." The fact that she relates of the Union having formed

itself and declared itself a *Religious Union* is intimately connected
with this joyful anticipation of a glory and happiness to come, then
with this your Union has at once taken the highest position possible
on the social scale and will attract all deep and earnest minds, and
be sheltered from the influence of the spirit of this world and its
adepts, children of selfishness and of Mammon. Your good and
pious, and most noble sister having partaken of this most important
act (the very ground stone of the whole establishment) and in
great part, perhaps, influenced it could indeed close her eyes in
peace over the earthly scene; its heavenly mission was decided and
begun, and she could now influence and bless it from the spirit
world in which her pure spirit had entered. And as I now through
your letters have learned to love her as I did not so before (then I
did not know her so well, though I always liked her extremely and
thought her most noble in soul and ladylike in manners) so I
never felt such a confidence in the advancement and prosperity of
your Union as now. The religious basis is of so high an importance;
Next to that comes the natural beauty and advantages of the position, the school and its excellent direktor. Could you get a good
teacher or Master of Gymnastics and also of swimming for the
young folks, would not that be capital?

How I shall enjoy once to come and look upon this young community *the community* par excellance. But it will not be in 1856; or
with Channings. I shall not be ready then nor would the colony yet
present a somewhat settled aspect so that one could judge with
certainty of its futurity. And then you know I must first write my
big novel,[4] then I want to come to the Union also as a fund-holder,
at least of a thousand Swedish dollars, as a token of my faith and
love for its idea. I shall tell you when I think I shall come. I have
a strong presentiment that after three or four years from hence
Marcus will feel a little overwearied with the work of the Colonny,
and will need some capital movement to recreate his forces; and
then our dear Rebecca which we, with the good Queen of Danemark,
think both very good and intelligent, will say: "Marcus! take our
Eddy with you and go with him to the north of bracing Europe (this
will be in spring time) go and see those mountains and valleys of
Norway that we had not time to see on our last tour, and let Eddy
see and enjoy with you these great scenes; then go to Sweden to our
Swedish sister; and let her show you those beauties of Sweden and
Stockholm which she now is sorry not to have been able to show
you at our first visit; and let Eddy with you see those noble statues
of Birger Jarl[5] and Charles Jo[h]an[6] who have been errected since
our departure, and see the old Scandinavian Gods that we did see.
Fredrika, I know, has much in store for you yet in her land and
home. And then Marcus when summer is over in Sweden, and the
Indian Summer spreads its golden veil over our woods then come

again and take Fredrika with you; then she will then be ready with her big book, and just be ready to take a run over the Atlantic and joyn our union for one year at least personally, as for ever in spirit. And then we will all joyn in a trip to Texas and see Considerants[7] Utopia and compare it with our own."

Now I think this the most sensible and rational speech that dear Rebecca ever could make, and I think we will follow it up to the point. Indeed I cannot help to feel as if this plan should realize itself; and I look upon such a meeting and life with you my dear friends as a thing as possible and probable as any thing in this world. And gladly should I cross the great oc[e]an once more with Marcus.

The statues of which Rebecca speaks are two noble works of art (by the Swedish sculptor Fågelberg[8] whom I think you saw one evening at my home) that now adorns my good Capital, since only two weeks. The statue equestre of the late good king is especially splendid and errected in a most beautiful situation between the baltic and the Mälar sea. We have had great festivities on the occasion, and every thing has gone on beautifully and successfully. We are now here only thinking of feasts and toasts while by the black sea bloody battles ar[e] fought and the feats of war are preparing to spread wider and wider in Europe.[9] It is a general belief in Sweden that next year (or summer) we must joyn the campaign against Russia. I am sorry for it. I do not like our being forced in a war against a people that have done us no wrong, and which war cannot bring us any true good, but certainly many sorrows. Still if, as seems more and more clear, this war is no private affair, but a war for truth and freedom against the false life and civilization of the east now represented by Russia and its Czar, then we will joyn and fight with a good heart then it is the cause of God. It is repeatedly said in our papers that the government of the United States secretly allies itself to the Russian power. I will not believe it.

Thanks my dear brother Marcus for your pleasant news about my American work! It seems as if your ever kind soul saw with clairvoyant eyes my morbid dispos[i]tion to torment myself about my past failings and errors, and as if you had wanted to sooth[e] the stings. God bless you for that kindness. True: I cannot but think my work good in the main; but more and more sharply do I feel partial blemishes, some of which I cannot conceive how I can have left them there, and must attribute it to the deep weariness and heaviness of body and soul that I suffered after my return partly through the great difficulties of my position and its dayly annoyences, now, thank God, in great part over. But now those faults, and partial unkindnesses will rise and sting me often, in the depth of the night, by the dawn of the morning and in the bustle of the day, and magnify themselves and make me unhappy. Sometimes I shake them off as raindrops from the Lions mane, sometimes (and oftener) I take them to my heart and ask them to humble and to purify it. And so I hope they will, my dear brother, and your kindness will help so too. Truly cheering is to me to see by letters of other friends that yours and Rebeccas loving ap[p]reciations of my work seems now to spread in Amerika as the opinion of the earnest and good in the land. You said my dear brother it should be so, and it seems you will be right.

In France the work seems almost more successful than any where else, as I have seen in several reviews now also of the frensch translation. Dear Marcus I think it may please you to make the a[c]-quaintance of my frensch translatress Mlle *du Puchet*[10] and I know yours and Rebeccas will be *most welcome* to her. I therefore write her ad[d]ress on the enclosed paper. I do not think her a person of much talant or geniality. But she is conscientious and faithful as translator; and has long worked at translating my books. I therefore thought it just (right) to give her the right of translation and publication of this work, instead of giving it to annother person (a bookseller in Paris) whose offer had been to me advantageous in a pecuniary point. Of the other persons whose names I have given I will say some words. Mme *Holtenmann* is an old lady extremely amiable. Married to a Swede of great fortune (Mr Holtenmann, now dead) she had, when we were in Paris, (1822) a beautiful home and manner of living. We and her daughters had great amusement in playing Charades in action together every week at her house. Now all these daughters are dead, and she has an only grandson, her great pet of course and continues as I am told to be amiable and be as hospitable and kind as possible to the Swedes and to her former friends and then she must be so also to their friends.

Mr *Bordier*[11] I do not know personally, but he was married in a Swedish family of my friends the *de Rongs* and to a charming young lady that I saw a good deal as a child. He is a widower now; and I have heard him spoken of as equally distinguished as a litterary and as a good and amiable man. I do not doubt that you will enjoy him and he you. I thought to ad[d]ress you to his father in law, old Mr de Rong, but I have lately heard that he is dying of an attack of apoplexy.

The fourth name Mr Aimé Martin is that of a very distinguished litterary man and Professeur de l'Academie. I do neither [k]now him personally, but as he has had the amiable attention to send me a book of his with D^o [ditto] words (for which gift I hope he has received my thanks) I think he will find a pleasure in receiving so dear friends to me, and he will in several things sympathize with and interest you. He has written a book on woman with many gloriously poetic pages and beautiful thoughts; but the work lacks in depth and strong principle. It will do the Author good to learn from republican minds such as yours. His ad[d]ress I do not know but it will be easy to learn it in Paris. /I should also be glad if you could make the a[c]qua[i]ntance of Mr Laboulaye, the litterary man whose noble and graceful Article about my Homes you showed me in Journal des Debats.[12] I think that he must be a good and agre[e]able man./ This is the very scanty list of my a[c]quaintences in Paris, which I think may interest you.

While you are in Paris, should you not dear Marcus, make a trial with the Swedish *sick Gymnastic* called Kinepathie, which is much en vog[u]e both in London and Paris. The science is of Swedish invention, and wonderfully powerful for strengthening the body giving sleep and vigor to the whole frame. Quantities of middle aged and even old gentlemen in Sweden regularly go through a course of gymnastics in the winter, to renew and invigorate themselves. My brother in law does so and with wonderful success. My dear Marcus try the thing; it can do no harm, and can do much good, and you may make such an establishment at Eaglewood hereafter. If I mistake not a young very able and skilful man, a Swede by the name of *George* is now in Paris practising as a Master of this kind of Gymnastics. I shall try to ascertain this.

Thanks my dear Rebecca for your writing to Mr Hedlund[13] about his brother in law! He thanks you very much for it and had just received a letter from Mr Rudensköld stating that he was going to Illinois with some countrymen of his. It seems that their persuasions and no dissatisfaction with Eaglewood prompted his departure. Of Eaglewood he says nothing ex[c]ept that Mrs Arnold was *extremely good* (innerligt god) to him. God bless her! I think his disposition was somewhat wayward and restless. Still now he writes from Illinois near Chicago /his ad[d]ress is there Care of Rev. Gustave *Uneonius*.[14]/ in good spirits and courage. So my dear friends be easy about him.

All your friends here send love, and are glad to hear from you. /Ehrenheim has got a big boy, his wife is well and he so happy and busy about her as possible./ Mrs Due said that when she saw you it was all she could do to refrain from hugging you in her arms. I have received complaints from Christiania (in Norway) for our not coming there and from Fryxdalen (the Valley of Fryxen) in Wermland where quantities of young laidies were expecting us with bouquets of flowers. Pity we could not go! /and to day a letter from Geijers widow and daughter (the gifted young Countess Hamilton at Kinekulle,) grumbling and complaining that when you were so near them at Kinekulle you did not visit them. I am sorry for it too, then you would have enjoyed them as they you. But we could not stay to visit every body on our way./

In my home all is peaceful, but my Mother continues lame on her bed, and — oh! it is certainly dreadful to lose by one hasty blow those that are dear to us, but it is more dreadful still to see them die, soul and body by inches, and be forced to wish for the last sleep, the last wandering of the weary half idiot mind! — May my poor mother and those about her be spared a too long struggle! Thank God that she is free from pain. Sister and brother in law are pretty well and charmed with little Jenny happy and chir[r]up-ing as a bird on its branch. Fabian Wrede is on a special Mission of the government, now in Austria, and greatly taken with the young Emperor. I have much to do with my children and other com[m]unal-affairs, also with editing some little books for our children, one with Scripture passages and one with Swedish prov-erbs. The cold is come, and we prepare for winter. The fires blaze in the kamins (*Kakelungnar*[15]). The twilight hour is pleasant with these. At this time of the day from 1/2 past four or 5 to near 7 oclock, you may see me, my dear friends wandering or sitting by the light of the kamin fires in the two rooms between my Mothers and my rooms. I am then all alone and enjoy the quiet of the hour and of the house, and rarely light up light to write or do any thing else during this time. At 7 oclock Mathilda comes down (she has now a room up stairs in my house and home) and lights the lamp (a simple but pretty little lamp shedding a soft, clear light) and reads to me first the paper of the day then books (now mostly of Vinèt and his spiritual followers). With reading, then, and visits to and scraps of friendly intercourse with Mamma, 10 oclock comes on, and we retire to bed, I, always thankful to be permitted now to live in so retired and quiet a way, and to have with me my good and bright girl Mathilda for a lectrice. She goes famously on with her engraving and she and three other young girls give me pleasure by their progress in self reliance and different kind of good and beautiful work. In the morning from 8 to 10 I receive visitors of all kind; and try after that to be alone in my room till about 1 oclock. Then I go out on visits or errands till three, when I dine. At 4 oclock I again receive those that wish to speak with me, so till about 5. And there's my day! Sundays I generally see some friends at dinner and at tea, and we often discuss things tending to the amelioration of the situation and character of women in my land. The *poor* women are in Sweden very badly off. Laws opinion and customs have done every thing to keep them down morally and mentally.

Give my kind remembrance to the good Elisabeth Pibody [Pea-body]; if she will write to me I shall be very glad of it, and write again and tell her all I know. I always liked her, and now, since I have heard the tale of her life from Rebecca, I sincerely admire and love her.

I am glad to know H. W. Channing drawing nearer to me. You must sometime tell him of a strange mistake made by Mrs Howitt: a place in my letters relating him: Pag. 108, 1 Vol. line 14 it is said: "with a polemical creed which never wounded the divine law."[16] This passage without the slightest meaning is in Swedis[h] thus: "with a polemic never wounding the law of goodness (or kindness)." Wonderful that the same persons who can translate so well can also at times translate so ill!—

I must now end this long thing. Love to the Children! Oh how I should like to take little Herbert in my arms and kiss him. Love also to our good and noble friend Channing. Happy shall I be to see and hear him again. /Mrs Osgood writes most warmly about a beautiful antislavery speech of his. You must sometimes. . .[17] him to know Mrs Osgood. She is a most lovely woman, sweet and ladylike in temper and Manner and with no common mind. De [The] Doctor is a good conscientious man and excellant physician./ Blessings on you both dear American brother and sister! Ever yours

Fredrika

––––––

1. MS, HL.

2. Jens Adolf Jerichau, 1816-1883, Danish sculptor, and his wife, Elisabeth Baumann-Jerichau, 1819-1891, painter and author.

3. Hans Christian Örsted, 1777-1851, Danish physicist.

4. *Hertha* (1856).

5. Birger Jarl, d. 1266, Swedish regent.

6. Karl XIV Johan, 1763-1844, French-born king of Sweden.

7. Victor Considérant, 1808-1893, French socialist, who founded "La Réunion" community in Texas.

8. Bengt E. Fogelberg, 1786-1854, Swedish sculptor.

9. Crimean War.

10. Rosalie du Puget.

11. Henri Bordier, an archeologist, had been married to Hélène De Ron.

12. *Journal des Débats,* May 10, 1854.

13. Rebecca Spring's letter of October 8, 1854, to Sven Adolf Hedlund, from Bonn on the Rhine, is at FBF.

14. Gustaf E. Unonius, 1810-1902, Swedish pioneer.

15. *Kakelugnar*: Swedish for "tile stoves."

16. In the 1854 edition of *HNW*, I, the quotation is on p. 105.

17. One word illegible after the word *sometimes*.

56.   To Octavia Le Vert.[1]

Stockholm, 5th Dec. 1854

Thank you a thousand times my sweet Octavia for your letter. Perfumed with the sweet breath and flowers of Alabama, it reached me amidst the snows and darkness of my own land, but brought to my heart all the summer, light and life of yours. God bless you — and He will, for that warm and gentle heart of yours, that spreads its atmosphere of happiness on all around.

Stern cares and duties, dear Octavia, have filled the thoughts and hours of the last two years from the terrible malady of mind and body that afflicted my poor dear mother; but after six months struggle with death, life has prevailed; and though palsied, she is, thank God, free from pain. So peace is again in my heart, and I can think of pleasant scenes, of happy lands, and much loved friends. — And you, my rose of Alabama, are ever the sunniest of my Southern memories.

When you were near me, the dread cholera forbade me to wish your presence. It left in Stockholm alone, more than five hundred destitute orphan children, and the formation of a society of ladies to take charge of these poor babes has given me, with great labor, much interest and enlivening life. I have also entered into several similar enterprises not only for poor children, but for old and destitute women. We are also forming a fund and asylum for aged governesses — much needed in my land I know, and fear it is so in most.

. . . But the quiet evenings at home are gracious to me. At twilight, which comes now about three o'clock, the fires are lit up in the camins, the parlors and drawing room, and I walk from each to each, or silently sit and enjoy their warming and illumining flames. At seven comes my little Gertrude — the lamp is lighted — and the good and sensible girl reads to me until ten. One day in the week another comes for the same purpose and reads general history to me and Mathilda; and thus time passes on, bringing me many a pleasure in the interest I take in the advancement of some good girl. The world, my dear Octavia, is rich and full of treasures, only we cannot or will not see them.

The war, the great, growing terrible war[2] — so near my country — is matter of earnest interest; and it seems a universal opinion here that we shall be in it before the next summer. I am sorry for it — but maybe the result will be a blessing to the cause of humanity, indeed I believe it, and will not repine, but trust love and good will bloom the more richly, and hasten on the day of grace.[3]

Meanwhile, our Sweden has enjoyed a peaceful time — the Diet has formed good and useful laws — and erected bronze statues of our old heroes and Kings. Christmas too, is coming! Christmas, the great festival of the year throughout all Sweden, when earnest joy and charity light up every heart. God has fixed it in the midst of dreary winter that benevolence may feel the strongest stimulus to deeds of mercy.

God bless you, my sweet rose of Florida! my dear, good and lovely Octavia; ever associated in my heart and memory with all that charmed me most in the sunny south of America.

Fredrika Bremer

––––––

1. Copy owned by Miss Mabel Greene, Kansas City; received through the courtesy of Caldwell Delaney, Mobile, Ala.

2. Crimean War.

3. This paragraph was quoted in the Chicago *Daily Democratic Press,* January 30, 1855, p. 1. Part of the third paragraph was also paraphrased, with the remark: "The benevolent authoress was engaged in forming and organizing a society of ladies to take care of 'these poor babes,' and also in raising a fund and building an asylum for old and destitute women and superannuated governesses."

57. To George Putnam.[1]

Stockholm, April, 1855.

To Mr G. Putnam.

Many changes among my friends in America have happened since I was there, some of these to[o] painful to me to speak of. One there is which give[s] me both pain and pleasure and that is the removal of Mrs W. Howland and her family from their home in Charleston to Ashton Hill Seminary, near New York. I grieve that a change of fortune should meet a family using the gifts of fortune in so noble a way, and should induce it to leave a beautiful home, (as hospitable as beautiful) where I myself have, during weeks, been a happy inmate. But I must rejoyce when I think of the enlarged influence which their new position and scheme of life will give this most excellent family; I rejoyce that many young minds will a[c]quire in their establishment what is infinitely more precious than pearls and jewels, *a good Education* in the highest sense of the word. Had I a daughter I should be happy to place her there then I know that high moral feeling, strong Christian principle, good sense, good manners and every thing which, from the very roots of things, the heart and mind make woman good and lovely will be imparted to her, from the excellant Mrs Howland *whose whole life was so good* and her daughters. I know that my child in this family and their home should find in its mistress the most kind and careful Mother and in her daughters, not only able and talented teachers but also loving sisters. All this makes me look upon this event as a boon of Providence rather than any thing else. And I trust that the members of this truly good and Christian family will one day, feeling their sfere of action widened, look upon it in the same light, then *they loved to do good!*

Fredrika Bremer

––––––

1. MS, FBF.

58. To Anne Howland.[1]

Island of Gotland, 20th July, 1855.

. . . It was, I think, about the same time that I received your letter that my good, dear mother had a new, slight paralytic stroke which was followed by a fever which brought on the last heavy grief. ... And now, my dear friend, I feel myself quite alone in the world and will need a little time of solitude and refreshment to collect my spirits and reflect on my life to come. Thus for the first time in my life I am the sole mistress of my life and actions, and have none on earth to account to for what I may choose. Still duty marks out my path, bound as I am to my country. I have a little fortune, enough to make me live in perfect independence and allow me to live for pursuits dear to my heart and mind. I have taken a new lodging in Stockholm, where I suppose that I shall continue to live, though I may now and then make an excursion in or out of my country. I am now on a great plateau or antediluvian monument, all made up of animal petrificates[2] in the midst of the Baltic, for the purpose of recruiting strength and spirits by sea bathing, sea air and freedom from care and business during the summer. Every morning soon after six o'clock, I dip myself in the ocean and then again at noon; this is delightful. I also read and write a little. I have here read the much spoken of American books the "Lamplighter"[3] and the "Wide, Wide World."[4] The latter book I have just begun. It seems to me its name should rather be: the small, small world! The former is good and the end interesting, but these books are small things compared with "Uncle Tom's Cabin." This book is a great thing, not only as to the subject, but in an artistic point of view. But every book which speaks to me of America, of its South, of its North, interests me beyond any, showing me scenes still engraved in my memory, full of the memory of dear friends with whom I have seen them.

. . . .

---

1. Published in New York *World,* March 28, 1878, p. 2.
2. Cf. Sw. *petrifikat* — fossil.
3. *The Lamplighter* (Boston, 1854), by Maria S. Cummins.
4. *The Wide, Wide World* (New York, 1852), by Susan Warner.

59.   To Marcus Spring.[1]

Brüxelles 24 Sept. 1856.

My dear brother Marcus! in the house of Mr Ducpetiaux[2] of Brüxelles, where you and Rebecca also have been, and where you are well remembered, I write to you a few lines only to tell you, what you may know already, that I love you, that no day of my busy wandering life is spent without a wandering of my thoughts to you and yours, often with an anxious question how yo[u] all are and especially you, dear Marcus, on whom so much of public and private care devolves and who, I must fear, cannot economize well his bodily or mental forces, but spends more of them than he can well afford. May I be wrong; may you be well, and dear Rebecca and the Children, and comfortably established at Eaglewood or somewhere else! Perhaps that some dear letter from you, for me, is travelling now to Lausanne and Geneva to tell me about all this and that I will know it all when I come there, in a forthnight or so. Meantime I will have a little chat with you all by myself. I have been travelling in Swizzerland the whole summer and have seen much of the grandeurs and splendors of Nature. In the first week of September I went down the Rhin[e] to come to Brüxelles by the time the "Congrès de Bienfaisance" was to open. Mr Ducpetiaux had sent me an invitatio[n] for it and charmed by the very idea of such a Congress, which seemed to me just what was wanted, and indeed something new under the sun, I resolved to come and hear and learn in this midst of good will, benevolence and science. I was on my arrival made a Member of the Congress, whose proceedings you, dear Marcus, probably may see in your papers by extracts from the "Moniteur Belge." You will then, also, perhaps, see my ad[d]ress to the Congress in behalf of the women of the poorer Classes in Europe; and I know that I will have your ap[p]roval and sympathy. Much have I enjoyed during these sessions to hear and to feel the general, generous and liberal movement of the minds of its members (about 200) towards all good reforms, and to see also many an able man bring his special study and art to bear upon the wellfare and comfort of the working classes in general and in all lands. *The great measure* or *result* of the Congress, however, is to have brought about that special Com[m]it[t]ees in different lands have been created who will cor[r]espond with the Central Com[m]it[t]ee in Belgium about the reforms in question and adopted by the Congress, work for them in their own lands, and joyn in the yearly General Meetings or Congresses "de Bienfaisance" which will hereafter be held in the several Cities of Europe. By these means a certain uniformity of action and measures may be obtained, and all countrie[s] may profit by the experience or Genius of one and of each. It was to me a Matter of astonishment and disap[p]ointment that no American partook of the Congress as representative of the United States, who yet take so eminent a part in the Matters which it had to discuss. You must send us one, dear Marcus, for the Congress next year, in Sept. (which is to be in Frankfurth,) or better still, *come yourself.* How delightful if I could see you there! What should greatly interest you here is the "éxposition industrielle et domestique" arranged by Mr Ducpetiaux /a rare man for [hi]s [a]ctive benevolence, comprehension, and ability!/ tending to make known all kind of articles in which goodness of quality is combined with great cheapness. It is wonderful to see what here is to be had at very low prices, and how in cloths and pott[e]rie (especially) elegance is to be had at the same time with the strength and cheapness of the articles. Of the Charitable institutions which hitherto have most interested me in the Catholic countries that I have visited is the "petites soeurs des pauvres" in Brüxelles[3] who adopt all the miserable old people who come to them, beg for them in the houses and Markets, feed and clothe them, take care of them and he[lp] them by their tenderness and pious care to become better and to *end well*. I saw there more than 100 of these poor old creatures of both sexes, made comfortable and happy by those charming "petites soeurs" of which several were young and pretty, several of the good families of Bruxelles. With my good host and hostess I shall soon start on a tour to see several sc[h]ools of reform which I think you visited when here, and the Béguinages of Gand etc. After that I shall go to Paris for a little time mostly to see two of my dear young Swedish girls and the[n] go on to Genève where I shall spend the greater part of the winter.

Mr Clarke at presant your Charge d'affaires in Bruxelles has kindly offere[d] to send some letters for me to the United States and I have seized the opportunity to speak some words to my dearest Manly friend there. God bless my dear American brother, my sister Rebecca and their dear Children!

Ever yours
Fredrika Bremer

I am well and strong in health de[a]r Marcus and my prayer of every day is that I may be able to employ my health and experiences to the service of my heavenly father or of his poor children!

A letter from Miss Howland (Justin[a], a noble girl who in the lap of slavery ha[d?] to abhor it and who refused an advantageou[s] Match and where her heart was interested only because her wooer was a proslavery man and a slaveholder) which letter speaks of the "melancholy death of Captain Wulff" and of your taking care of his poor sister in New York to help her to reembark for her home. How is that? I have not heard of this sad case. Poor unhappy Henriette Wulff who must loose a brother so wholly devoted to her! She will not survive him long.

Tell me if you have received your Norwegian engravings! Mr G. Vickers promised to send them for you to New York.

Mr and Mme Ducpetiaux ask me to present to you their kindest remembrances! When you write tell me about Elisabeth Hoar and how it is with her. I long [for] that nobleminded woman happy in her way.

———————

1. MS, HL.

2. Édouard Ducpétiaux, Belgian director-general of prisons and benevolent institutions.

3. Cf. F. Bremer's *Life in the Old World*, I, pp. 221-226.

60.   To Marcus Spring; to Rebecca Spring.[1]

Lausanne 23 Dec. 1856.

My dear Marcus! I have just received Rebeccas letter with
your post scriptum and must speak of that first, because it is now
uppermost in my head. Dear Marcus, I am quite stupefied and mortified at the affair with the Norwegian prints, and do not understand
it a bit. Before leaving home I had received, for you, from Mr Gum-
pert in Gothenbourg, a series of Norwegian views finely executed
and all in good order, not one duplicate. For these I had paid of
the money that you left me for that purpose 10 D Bco (15 Riksdol-
lars) and had received the a[c]quittal ac[c]ordingly. /I have still
in my pocketbook your little note on that subject./ They were before my departure left by me to Mr Naylor Vickers in Stockholm,
who promised me to send them to you at New York by a Ship which
was freighted for his house and would sail for New York in the
course of June last summer. (I left Stockholm at the end of may.).
The other Norwegian prints which you ordered at Mr Bonniers in
Gothenbourg (I think that they were prints of Tiedemans[2] pictures
of Norwegian life,) did not come to Stockholm though I asked for
them several times. At length I signifyed to Mr Bonnier in Gothenbourg that I would not wait for them any longer from his hands, but
would bye them directly at Stockholm, in order to send them to you
with the same opportunity as the other prints. It was then said to
me that the edition of the prints of Tiedemann was nearly gone out,
and that the editor wanted the price doubled for the few copies
which still remained. I said: "If this is so I must take it as it is, then
I must have a copy. Send it me directly." But it did not come while
I was in Stockholm and so I gave directions to my bookseller Mr
E. T. Bergegren in Stockholm to receive it when it came and to
put the payment on my account. The parcel was to be forwarded to
Mr Naylor Vickers who was to send it to you with the other, which
he promised me earnestly, both with mouth and hand, carefully to
do. Now, what has been done? I cannot understand it. Which of
the prints or the parcel of prints is it of which you have received
duplicates, and for which you should pay to Mr Nutt? What, in
all the world, has Mr Nutt to do with this affair. Mr Naylor Vickers
promised to send them free with his ship. And why should you pay
any thing to Mr Nutt for them or to any body? You know, dear
Marcus that you left me at your departure 32 D Rgd. to pay for all
these prints when they should arrive; and though through the negli-
gence of Mr Bonnier the price for the Tiedemann prints became
higher, it was not you who should pay for that, but your friend in
whose hands the affair was laid. In fine, dear Marcus, in this egyp-
tian darkness I do not see what to do ex[c]ept that I shall write to
Mr Naylor Vickers in Stockholm, ask from him what has been done
and what signifyes this bill of Mr Nutts? At all events you shall

not pay it. You have paid to me the cost of the prints and it is my affair to see that they shall be paid. I suppose, that by some Miss-conception my bookseller Mr Bergegren has sent to Mr Vickers the bill that I should have paid for the prints not yet arrived. But I shall write to him and try to clear the affair. But pray, do not pay any thing before having heard from me farther. I cannot suppose that this charge of Mr Nutt can be for the transport of the prints to America? Indeed I am most heartely annoyed at the turn of this affair and cannot understand it.

This naughty story has taken up my paper and time so that I have hardly time to say how dear and precious it was to me to know you, dear Marcus, and yours well, and going on well with your enterprize. The letter that you wrote to me to Stockholm was sent to me in Paris; but your letter which in early summer was directed to me in Lausanne I am still in search of. I am living here earnestly and studiously trying to prepare myself for the earnest task which is before me; Religious and social questions are my dayly bread, and my dayly prayer: "give me thy spirit!" Friends as you and Rebecca were and are to me I have not found here nor anywhere; but still good and true friends worthy of respect and affection. Brother! It is to me a precious thing to know and to love thee. And so I shall here and hereafter

Thy sisterly friend
Fredrika!

My dear Rebecca! Thank you a thousend times for your kind letter. I would, oh! indeed I would come to you and joyn in your work and injoy your dooings but — but I have not yet quite done with Europe. I must still have a year or two with her to get her last word, as far as I am able to take it. And then, oh! then I should so like to come and spend a year with you at Eaglewood in cheerful life and work.

I was so glad to see the little print of your new establishment, the little house where you and Marcus and your children have your peaceful home, and where I too, one day, may rest my weary head. It looks pretty and pleasant. Thank God that you are all well and going on well. Only Marcus' "too busy" makes me anxious. Remember, dear Rebecca, to send him to me when you see that he is near beeing over done, and then I shall take care of him take him to Norway, and follow him to Eaglewood. Next year I shall, please God, again be in my quiet Swedish home. For this Winter I am settled in Lausanne and Geneve where I shall go in Februar[y] and stay March and April. When summer comes and for next winter I may take a peep at Italy. In Paris I did see my friends that have become yours and all asked to know about you and wanted to be remembered to you. I have had a good and rich time during my European ramble; only too much for thought and mind to take well in, and so it is still. But thank God my health is good and the mind can do its work every day. I ask God earnestly, every day, to give me his spirit, and I try to give myself wholly to its direktion, as to what I have to do and how. But I know and feel well that it is no easy matter to divest the mind of its selflove so that it may hear the love and learnings of the heavenly Father. After all, prayer is the great affair of life, and he that can pray well must walk and work well, then the divine fire (or spirit) will come and dwell in him and direct him.

I am living here in a Free Church, t. i. a church or community which has separated itself from the state and rules itself by its own elect members. It is a Church of prayer, and rich in much that is true and good but wanting in larg[e]ness of mind and depth of thought, as well as in that poetical intuition which sees in nature a symbolical language glorifying the Creator and all his Mysteries, and which incorporates that in the life of the Church its temples and ceremonies. "L'Eglise libre" of Canton de Vaud is still the cold, rational church of Calvin, and my mind cannot there find its home or its heaven. The Lutheran creed comes nearer fullness and will perhaps yet be the mediating link between the Catholic and the protestant Church when that will, by a new inspiration of Christ, have become truly evangelical. Social life here has much which reminds me of life in American society, but has less of vigour and newness or freshness, (youth) of life. Unions such as yours attempting to realize the true Christian or divine society I find here none.

How is Channing? how is Emerson? Elisabeth Hoar? Tell me something of them when you write next, dear Rebecca! And the Womens rights conventions — do they still go on? And how?

How much would I not ask and how much have to tell; but hard time wont allow of more to day. At this moment peaceful Swizzerland is all in agitation about the threatening war with the King of Prussia and no one can tell how things will turn. Central Europe is full of inflam[m]able materials and may be that soon a European war will follow the oriental one. You in America will, I know it also be at war for freedom or slavery and the c[h]aracter of your new President,[3] as I have been told of it, will make the strife more fierce than hitherto. But it must come to that. How good to know my dearest friends busy in a work of peace which, without entering in the great strife, must tend to promote the great cause of freedom and good will.

Good bye for to day, dear American sister, blessings to your young ones and love from your Swedish sister and friend

Fredrika

----

1. MS, HL.
2. Adolf Tidemand, 1814-1876, Norwegian painter.
3. James Buchanan, 1791-1868, president-elect.

61.   To Dr. and Mrs. David Osgood.[1]

Rome, 26 Januar[y] 1858.

My dear Doctor, my dear Mary Anne, best and kindest of
friends! let me now tell you that I am in Rome and that in old Rome
I think of you, and bear you in my heart, where ever I go, on the
Capitol, or in the Vatican, in San Pietro or San Paulo, which you
will easely understand! And tell you I must also how much I long to
hear from you and know how you are in health and in every thing
else. But, alas, it is far, very far from Rome to Boston, though just
now, and since a week such a hard, severe cold has set in here,
that I fancy you and I, must breath[e] about the same air, and feel
the same cold, and make the same protestations about such a head-
strong freezing and sneezing-making temperature. Now, if it only
made freese and sneeze, but — what says my dear Doctors Neuralgia
and Mary Annes chest or head? I am almost afraid of an answer,
then if cold is so illnatured in Italy and in Rome, how must it work
in the Pilgrim state of America and in that stony Boston, which
would have killed me had it not been for its kind hearts, which
made me warm and well indeed! But now I just will hope the best
for you both, and tell you a little about my doings since last I wrote
to you from Geneva, (I believe). From thence I took three young
ladies under my wings and climbed (*flew* would be a little to[o]
strong a metaphor) up the *Monte-Rosa* and saw the valleys and
giants of everlasting snow, of never melting, secular ice. The rays
of the sun pearcing through the clouds, caressed the immense snow-
rose /*Monte Rosa,* 12 000 feet high, in the midst of a plain of ice
surrounded with giiant Alps, is so called from its form which is
exactly that of a centifolian rose, wery unlike other alps which generally rise in pyramidical forms./ lovingly, and cleared up the
depths of its Calice,[2] and all the snowy giiants arround seemed to
look on this courtship between the sun and the snowy Alprose, and
sometimes a lavine thundered down in applause while the rival
of the rose, the fierce Mount *Matterhorn* (a stony lady 15 000 feet
high, wrapt up in a snow mantle and with an immense Crenoline)
grew in a rage of jealousy, drew round her brow a diadem of black
clouds and sent forth a storm which spoiled every thing. But we had
seen ennough of the wonderful scene never to forget it. This excursion, through the lovely Valley of Zermatt, up to the Riffelberg,
from where you enter in the snowy realm of the Monte Rosa Alps,
which I made all on foot, with these dear young girls, botanizing
with them, dining with them under de [the] green [trellises] of the
Valley, by its clear fountains, and drinking out of them, while
our Mulets grazed and our guides reposed a little farther off, this
excursion was my last and certainly my most charming in Swizzerland. From thence I went alone over the Simplon, among clouds
and snows, and down to Italy in the midst of thunderstorms and

showers of rain which made me think of the deluge. This was not very agre[e]able, but it was grand, and I enjoyed it, especially as it alternated with days of elysian beauty and calm; during such I lived on the shores of Lago Maggiore, and visited its famed Islands *Isola Bella* and *Isola Madre* the first of whom is a magnificent childs toy, on a great scale, and the latter one a true little paradise of flowers and rare trees and shrubs, which I wonder that some eccentric American or English Gentleman has not fixed upon for his bridal tour and as a spot made exactly for his honey month.[3] From there I went to the Valleys of Piemont, the valleys of the Waldenses, the homes of the little flock who from the third century of the christian church protested against the pretentions and worldliness of Romanism, and kept faithful to the simplicity of the primeval church. Its faithful testimony, long suffering, terrible trials, and final wonderful strife and triumph had made it to me of the highest interest, and made me resolve to pay to it my first visit upon my coming to Italy. And so I did. And I lived among this people a month, wandering through their wonderfully lovely and fertile Walleys, conversing with the "Barbes" (or ancients) of the people, liustening to their tales, and strong religious convictions, visiting the huts on the high mountains, eating the Waldensian Polenta,[4] and looking with joy on the efforts made by the good and and [the] wise to carry forward in wisdom and virtue this now triumphant Evangelical church, the only one as yet on Italias soil. This was a delightful time full of pleasant things and thoughts. This was in September last. Then I went to Turin, had there a conversation with Mr de Cavour[5] (the Ministre-king /the real King does nothing but hunt the deer and care for his pleasures letting his prime Minister govern the state. He is a "bon vivant" but still a brave and an honest man./ of Piemont at present) which made me happy by convincing me of the conscient principles upon which this rarely gifted Statesman leads his state onward on the road of constitu[tio]nal liberty, and makes it go ahead with the most liberal nations of Europe. From Turin and its beautiful circle of snowclad Alps I went to Genua, saw its glorious sea prospects, its marble palaces and Laurel and orange groves, its stirring and picturesque people, went from there to Pisa, was nearly taken down or overcome by its troops of beggars, following you by half a dozen or more, every where, promising you their interest with "la Madonna" and all the pleasures of paradise if you will only give them a "Quat[t]rino." I escaped to Florence, where beggary was great also, but where beauty and gladness of life were still greater, and where the beggars themselves were easely coaxed into laughing and to fall out of their lamentable role. Still this beggary is a dreadful plague in Italy and makes you often ask yourself if you have a right to enjoy life while so many thousands are asking for bread. But you should, in a day, become a beggar

yourself, if you should give to all those who ask. And then, many —
(it is well known) ask without great need, or any at all. I give two
or three bajocs[6] a day, only to sooth[e] a little my conscien[ce.]
From Florence I went to Sienna and from thence to R[ome] at the
end of November. And there, dear friends, now see m[e] in a comfortable little home, by the great and noisy *Corso*, quietly established with a young swedish friend, bearing the beloved name of
Jenny Lind,[7] but without a single musical note in her throat. A good
and beautiful girl she is, and charms my evenings by her soft voice
reading good things. But we are seldom alone, then the Scandinavians in Rome often come and sit down by our tea table, and then
we sometimes go to "conversationes." To me, Rome offers matters
of high interest, giving me strong incitement to compare ancient
and modern civilisation, Pagan and Christian religion, Roman Catholic and Evangelical church. I try in every matter and thing to ascertain its best and its worst comparing them with the ideal, and
then to build on, or to see how to ap[p]roach this Ideal — wonderful
attractive perfection, which draws soul and society onward and
upward to their primeval and final home by God. My days are taken
up with these questions, and with visits to galleries, churches, places
etc, and so time passes on, alas, always to[o] swiftly for what I
would accomplish, and sometimes the thought of it almost makes
me sick. But I must take patiance, and I take it, and thank God every
day for life and health, praying him to permit me to use them in
his service. People here are now preparing for the Carnival and its
childish fun of which my young friend will be a partaker, and I a
quiet looker on. At spring-time she will return to Sweden and probably soon marry; and I will go to Neaples and Sicily and from
thence to Greece. God permitting I shall pass next winter in Athens,
and the following spring or summer return to my native home,
never to quit it more, it should then be that I could run over the
ocean to visit you! But my running about years will soon be over,
and old age command to be quiet and prepare all things for the
last remooval. I am well, my dear Doctor, nose and all, and much
stronger than when I saw you last. I am now, as it were, settled on
the Autumnal side of life. Its Indian summer is over; the weather is
cool but steady and clear. Now my dear friends let me know soon
from you and all about you, and ad[d]ress the letter to *"the Care of
Mr G. Bravo Consul of Sweden and Danemark in Rome."* It will
find me here until the end of April. The dreadful Com[m]ercial
earthquake[8] which, beginning in Amerika, has shaken the whole
northern part of Europe and made hundreds of houses totter and
fall has made great disaster also in Sweden, but it has not touched
me or mine ex[c]ept by sympathy. May my dear friends in America
also have been untouched by it, to their fortunes! Once by your
bright evening fire, in your quiet home you will, perhaps, read

what the old classic world has told your swedish sister friend. May
you go with her over those old spots gladly as you did over the
beautiful meadows of the new world!

Ever yours
Fredrika Bremer.

I enclose a little note to Doctor Lowell, recom[m]ending it
to your kind care.

------

1. MS, HCL. Address: 37 Chauncey Street, Boston, Mass. (Picture of
"Basilica di S. Pietro In Vaticano" at top of p. 1.)

2. Calyx.

3. Cf. Sw. *smekmånad* — honeymoon.

4. *Polenta*: a thick porridge (Italian).

5. Camillo Benso, Count of Cavour, 1810-1861, Italian statesman.

6. *Bajocco*: Italian word for a Roman copper coin worth about half a cent.

7. Johanna Charlotta Lind, born 1832, married Captain L. O. Stjernstedt
in 1859.

8. The financial panic of 1857.

62.   To Anna Maria Hall.[1]

Rome, — April, 1858
Casa Tarpia, by the Capitol.

Dearest Maria!

It is now nearly a year since I last wrote to you from Swizzerland, a year that I have been waiting for an answer. And now I begin to be very confident that you either have not got my letter or
that your answer on it has been lost. And indeed the post in Swizzerland was so little orderly and I have lost so many letters there
that I should not wonder if this should be the case. Now, dear
Maria, you wrote to me in April (I think or March) a year since,
that you and Mr Hall intended to make a tour to the United States,
and you expressed a wish for some letters of introduction to my
friends there. I instantly wrote back telling you how happy I should
be to write these and asking for some details about your intended
tour and the parts and cities which you would visit. On this letter
no answer. When I left Swizzerland I asked that letters which may
come to Genève after my [departure] should be sent to me at Turin,
but none came there from you, nor from other friends in England
(Mrs Howitt and Mrs J. Key) to whom I wrote about the same
time that I wrote to you.

In Rome, where I arrived last Autumn I met a pleasant lady a
Mrs Daubeny who knew and loved you, and she said that you and
Mr Hall had postponed your grand tour over the ocean, till — she
knew not when. Now I make this attempt to come to you dear
Maria with a young lady Miss Rivaz who goes from here to London,

and who will put this letter in your own hands. And then I am
sure that you will tell me what I long to know, how you are, which
of our letters has gone astray, or if both, and what you intend about
your transatlantic tour. I need not say how happy I should be to
introduce you to some of my dear friends in America. Mrs Daubeny
told me you were writing a new story. I am glad of it, and hope to
hear more of it by and by. But in Rome few English books, ex[c]ept
by roman Catholics, are to be had. Government is afraid of the
spirit of freedom in them. I also have been writing a story this
winter or rather this spring, and I do not think I have ever written
one with more true pleasure or more perfect adhesion of my head
and heart. Its theme is filial love as the most perfect love in life, its
title: "Father and daughter." It wants to make clear how "love com-
pels and freedom binds much stronger than any law." I have proposed the book to Mr Arthur Hall, G. Virtue et Co and asked Mrs
Howitt for its translator.

Why do not Mr Hall and you come to Rome? Here would be
a life for you as artists and thinkers; indeed it is a rich and wonderful life though more of relics and memories than of actual real
life. Still there is a rich beauty and charm. How much have I not
lived and do still live here too much indeed to speak of in a letter.
From Swizzerland, from the h[e]ights of Monte Rosa and of the
Simplon I went to Lago Maggiore and to its paradis[ia]cal Islands,
then to the Valleys of the Waldenses, wandered through them and
lived with their people more than 5 weeks, delightful weeks they
were (a Mrs Fierz, a sister of your great man Mr Cobden,[2] and
living in the Valley of Lucerna, gave me great pleasure through
her kindness and company) visited the people, learned their songs
and their wonderful story, ate of their Polenta, lived in their homes,
attended their Churches. Then I went to Turin, saw and conversed
with Cavour — a fine, noble and genial man! then to Genua, Pisa,
Florence and so to Rome. Here I have been interested by art, but
still more by Catholicism and the confessional differances between
the Roman Catholic and the Protestant Church. Just now I have
come out of a Convent where I have allowed myself to be shut up
for a week, (at the instigation af [of] some zealous Catholic friends)
in order to examine more closely the doctrines in question. I have
come out of this "retiro" (as it is called) even more Evangelical (in
doctrine) than before, but with a clearer view of some precious
doctrin[e]s of the Catholic Church for which I shall ever be thankful, though I *never, never* shall become a Roman Catholic. In a few
days I shall go to Neapel, and from there to Sorrent[o] where I shall
pass the hottest part of summer. In the Autumn I shall proceed to
Greece, stay in Athen[s] next winter, and, *perhaps* go on to Jerusalem, but this last, will depend on means and company. The voyage
may be more costly than I can afford, and I would not go alone nor

in company too large or not in sympathy with me. Well, this may be or not be, ever shall I thank God for this my journey and its harvest! Next year, before summer sets in, I hope to be again in Sweden, never to quit it more. The Autumn of life is come, and winter is near at hand. It is time to prepare winter quarters. And then I have plenty to do in my native land. Things are going forward there, thank God. The victory won for the lawful liberty and life of women, at the present diet is a good and important thing. Now more care will be taken of their education and abilities. You could not like my Hert[h]a, I know it. She was the child of bitterness and protest; but my "Father and daughter" you will like, I feel sure of it. They are the children of gratitude and of free love.

The Pope[3] I have seen and conversed with, seriously ennough. He is a good soul but not very clever or spiritual, and now so cased up in his Popery, that he believes it all right that he should be advered [revered] and obeyed by all nations. And those who do it not, are he says their own gods or idols. "Si la reine Victoria ne veut pas du Pape c'est qu'elle veut, elle même, être papesse!"

Deeply have I sympathised with the severe trials which England has suffered in India this last year and, perhaps, suffers still! But her Queenly nature will make her come out of it more grand and noble than ever.

Dear Maria! Let me know about you, your doings and your plans! I do not think a letter from you now will go astray if directed to the care of *Count Wachtmeister Ministre plen. of Sweden and Norway in Neapel.*

Give my best and grateful remembrance to Mr Hall, and my love to your daughter Jeanie who now must be quite a young lady; and remember me, dear, kind Maria as your affectionate and ever grateful friend

Fredrika Bremer

————

1. MS, owned by S. Rooth.
2. Richard Cobden, 1805-1865, English economist and statesman.
3. Pope Pius IX, 1792-1878.

63.   To Mrs. Anna Hazard Barker Ward.[1]

Monte Tarpeo, Rome 3 Maj. 1858

My dear Mrs Ward! How very sorry I was that you went away without your two books! I thought that I had said to you that my present dwelling was at the Capital and that you said that "you would come and see me there or send for the books." So was my impression; and therefore I waited, and not seeing you before Saturday the   [of] April, I concluded that your departure had once more been delayed. But I learned soon that you were gone, and had asked for your

books at my former home, by the Corso. Greatly annoyed I went
to your banker Mr. Hooker, to ask how the thing was to be helped,
and your books come to you again? He said they could easily be
sent to you in London, with some occasion, (which now come
often) and that he would take care of them, as he had your ad-
[d]ress, and also would send you this letter to Edinbourg. And so,
to day, I will put these things in his hands, and hope they will reach
you safely. But excuse me, I pray, most humbly, for the mistake or
slove[n]liness which has so long deprived you of the books — your
dear companions! — Meantime they have afforded me a good deal
of interest, and a good deal to think of. Then Mr. Hecker[2] is a true
American, and goes to the questions in quite a new world spirit,
openly and bravely, and this is fresh and good. He has also put
some capital questions and in a capital way. He has also bravely and
most justly attacked some of the weak points of the reformation,
and of the protestant confession, and vindicated as well, some of
the strong points of the roman Catholic one, and in this he has done
well. But, has he understood the central point and life of the reform-
atory movement? Has he done justice to the vital christendom
and meaning and mission of the Evangelical Church? Has he understood and justly appreciated the wants and errors of the *roman*
Cat[h]olic Church, and its wants of true cat[h]olicity and truth?
To both these questions, I must answer, from my deepest conviction,
no. He has not.

And it seems to me strange that he should so total[l]y depre-
cate protestantism as a folly and a monstrum, when he is so often
quoting as proofs for the truth and beauty of Christianity a preacher
of this same Church, nam. the good and noble Dr. Channing! It
seems that there must be some power and vital Divine truth in a
Church which can bring forth such men! . .

Dear Mrs Ward! you who have turned to roman catholicism
with a heart so entire and from motives all pure, and who[m] God
has given a mind full of benevolence, you will never be unjust as
Hecker and indeed most roman Catholics are to their brethren in
Christ! And bringing out what your chosen Church has most grand
and deep of Christian truths and harmonies, and making them known
in a spirit of love, you will help to lessen bitterness and misunderstandings on the other side, perhaps on both sides, — and make
protestants aware of these truths and beauties in the Catholic
church which they reject without knowing them. This I conceive
to be the good effect, for others, of your conversion, this your mission
to them. Mine is the other way. I want to make Roman-Catholics
see and feel the real meaning, high worth and great mission of the
reformation-movement, and (if I can), make it better understood
by the protestants themselves. For this purpose my stay in Rome
with the retreat at "la Trinita," and the books I have read (the

controversial ones) and the discussions I have had (at the Trinita they were serious ennough, especially with the Carmelite monk[3]) has been to me of great help and great worth.

I must leave you now, and I do it with regret, then you have become more dear to me than it seems that two or three interviews could make a person to annother. But so it is; the earnestness of your mind and the sweetness of your disposition, your frankness, your personal charms, all make me desire that I could see you more and be more with you. But — this shall not, probably never be on earth. May God bless you, and give you all your heart desires, is the wish and prayer of one who begs to be remembered by you as one of your affectionate and most true well wishers and friends

Fredrika Bremer

----

1. MS, HCL. Mrs. Ward was the wife of Samuel Gray Ward, a friend of Emerson. See *Journals of Ralph Waldo Emerson*, V, pp. 278-280.

2. Isaac Thomas Hecker, 1819-1888, American Roman Catholic clergyman.

3. Père Marie Louis.

64.   To Rev. J. H. Hill.[1]

[Athens] Thursday 11th Aug. 1859

My dear Sir and kind friend! Your most tempting and charming proposition makes me regret that it comes just *one hour* to[o] late for me to say: "yes with all my heart!" Then I have said yes to annother proposal for promenade! But you will I know, remember in kindness at some other occasion, your thankful friend

Fredrika

----

1. MS, *s.l.*, ASHM. The Reverend Hill had been sent to Greece by the American Missionary Society.

65.   To Marcus Spring.[1]

Athens, 10de Oct. 1860.

Thank you Marcus, dearest brother, for the greeting from your hand and heart, which came to me the other day, in the Christian Inquirer (No 47). I cannot say how delightful it was to me there to breath[e] anew that good, strong spirit of the new (young) world which, when I was there, gave me the feeling of growing young again of a new, more vigorous and universal life, how delightful to see minds still at work which I had known there, and still at work for the same great ends. Some have gone away, it is true, and left for higher callings, or larger sferes of activity: Horace *Mann*, the genial Schoolmaster of young America, and Parker the brave and the good defensor of the op[p]ressed race. But their work will

not pass away, and is carried on by other minds true and faithful
as theirs to the cause of humanity. The first sermon I heard in New
York was preached by Bellows, and well do I remember how I, as
well as my friend Bergfalk, was struck with its lofty and all embracing christian character, so far from any thing narrow or sektarian,
so true, to what should be the Evangelical mission of the great new
World. It seemed to me that I saw the *spiritual Cathedral* wide and
high as heaven, arching itself over aspiring and praying multitudes
of all nations united in the same love in the same good will. In the
"letter on the religious prospects of the West," whi[c]h you have
marked in the paper, I find the same lofty charackter, the same mind
the same man. And this I would venture to say; by my knowledge
of minds such as his, and those tendencies which I find uppermost
in the civilizing work of your republic, that however many different
Churches that great western walley may have, and certainly will
have, they will all subordinate to one great and central aim — to
make the Kingdom of God reign upon earth, and in this the[y] will
unite and for that they will work together as brothers. It is the
glory of Unitarism as a sekt to have brought forward that great Idea
and aim for which Christ lived and died, while other sekts or
churches absorbed Christian life, (or made it consist) chiefly in
certain dogmatical professions. And though I am not a Unitaria[n]
in dogmatical faith, /because it does not give me the light and
comfort I need for the past, presant and future destinies of Mankind, nor explain as I think annother faith does the heart and will,
the *personal character* of *the Father/* I must say that I have found
no separate church which I think stands on a more *universal* christian ground and to which I, in this point feel myself more united. And
as to that point, and its result — *the work to do* — all separate
Churches must become Unitarians; and they *will*, when it will become more and more clear to men that the realisation of the Kingdom of God on Earth (or in the world) is the chief work for every
man, every church and every state and every people which will deserve the name of Christian — divine humanity. But where is the
land which has Unitarians such as W. E. Channing,[2] and some
others I could name, ex[c]ept America, and where is the land which
as America (and chiefly its great western walley) unites different
peoples and churches? America must effect the great Union, which
of many members will make one family, and make many heads and
hands work as with one heart. Many churches joyn in teaching the
same way to heaven.

The Notice on Antioch-college and several other things gave
me great pleasure in your paper — all speak to me of a large and
liberal mind working resolutely and fearlessly on in many ways
to realize its object — the true human or Christian (then poor humanity has two faces, the one of a God the other of a wolf) state.

Much should I wish to see one day, in that good paper, a full statement of your colony, dear Marcus, of its end, means and working.
But that will come by and by. I fancy that your noble baby must
yet have time to grow and develop its character before it can be
fully characterized.

16 Oct. I have your letters of late August and Sept. dear, dear
friends! What good, rich letters; and how much I thank you both,
Marcus and Rebecca, to write so to me and to let me once more so
feel as if I was with you. Ah me! Shall I ever be so again? Shall I
live with you in your work, take my part in it, in what I can, enjoy
your society, your home and public life, see your dear children,
and again those of your friends which I have learn[ed] to love?
Ah! Age is growing upon me, and night is coming on! But this I
know, that should any thing induce me to leave once more my
father-land, it would be the desire to live and to die on that green
spot where your Eagles nestle, and to give my last tribute of love
and hope for Earth to that little realm where the spirit of true Freedom and love tries to realize on a small scale, but in a universal
spirit those aspirations which belong to the best of this our world. If
I, on my death bed, could see yours and Channings faces smiling
on me, methought I should die happy in the vision of a better world,
still to come on earth.

Good and brave Channing! How I like to hear him speak so,
to see him feel "more son of his country" as its strife and danger
grows, and long to be there and battle for the right until the last
breath. /We are now reading, during the evenings, a recent but
very remarkable German work on *Naturrecht auf dem Grund[e] der
Ethik,* which I should wish translated in your language. There is
a most capital chapter about and against slavery (Negro-slavery
included). Nobody can, after having read that strong reasoning
book speak of slavery as something right or good or useful to —
any body. The Author, a Mr Trendelenburg[3] is professor of law in
Berlin and as distinguished in his character as in his science./ How
much do I enjoy to see your affairs going well on, and Marcus
building and planning; but more than all do I enjoy to see him
eating and sleeping capitally, then this is the one thing needful
after all, in order to be able to go on with better things. It will be a
capital thing to have good and able preachers of different churches
to lecture in your new church, men able as Channing, Beecher and
Bellows to point strongly out the one thing needful in Christian
church and life. Your whole little colony should testify to that, but
it is good to have it spoken out by christian speakers of different
denominations.

Yes, how wonderfully things go in Italy. Who would have
thought two or three years since, that such a revolution was near.
So it may come also with the reform of America in *the great ques-*

tion. In my notes over Italy you will see how I there felt a better state of things preparing, by the spreading influence and writings of some noble minds such as Gioberty,[4] Balbo,[5] Lambruschini[6] etc, and the political preponderance of constitutional Piemont. The state of the Pope and Popery, at this moment, is one of intense interest. You will see a good deal about these things in my work, and I have not been a spectator out of doors in them. I have had my personal grapple with both persons and ideas. Cavour has dissap[p]ointed my faith in him as a truly great Statesman. Then no statesman is great in the highest style who stoops down to ignoble means and lies, nor does he serve his country in a great style. I am truly glad that honest Garribaldi,[7] the man of the sword, has bravely risen up in this thing and spoken out against the man of the pen and the Cabinet. This thunder will a little cleanse the air and make honesty rise in the political scale.

In Sweden all things go on well at presant; freedom and railways are growing through the land. Thank you, dear Marcus, for sympathizing with these dooings though having so many other on your hands.

Great things are now preparing in the Orient; but though it seems to me very clear that a better state of things for humanity and civilization will come out of the Catastrofe which is preparing, it is to be feared that a great tragedy (and bloody) will be enacted before it is completed, and a strong warrior people will consent to relinquish its rich prey and go away in the desert. The affairs of Turkey are in a desperate state, a state of complete bancruptcy. A revolution is expected every moment; but the Massacres in Syria have recently shown how great is the danger of the christian population admidst the fanatic and desperate Mussulmans. Happely Frensh troops are already at hand there, and Russia is not far, and Russia has now a noble minded man, and a liberator of the serfs for its head.[8] I have begun to love Russia and to hope much of its influence for a better state of things in Asia. *Greece* — alas! Greece is not all what its friends would desire and hope. It knows little as yet the true worth and nobility of liberty. It thinks political freedom to be every thing. Its moral conscience is at sleep — in great part the fault of its religion! — a form without a soul in it. /But several good m[e]n and women too begin to be fully aware of these faults. National virtues among the modern Greeks are family love or piety (patriarc[h]al virtues) purity of morals (in regard to sexual connections) hospitality, love of their country, and love of their religion though this love has more a political than a Christian spirit./ Still riches and culture are growing, and European influences are growing with them, the chaff comes with the wheat. Great changes must take place ere modern Greece will take its place among the peoples who carry humanity onward towards its glorious goal. Yet I tarry in Greece, and will be there through this winter. The home which God has given me in Athens, and the intercourse which I enyoy there with some very clever and in the affairs of the day well initiated men are my chief inducements. It is good for me to be here while writing out for the press my note[s] on Palestine and Turkey.[9] Next spring I shall go home.

This summer has passed to me very delightfully in making a sailing tour /The King of Greece put to my disposal, for that, his own excellent little Jacht its Captain and Crew, during two months, which gave me much freedom and pleasure. My good hostess here Mrs Hansen, and a young clever German Archeolog[ist] accompanied me.[10]/ to several of the Greek Islands and in passing several weeks at Naxos, a splendid Island and the most beautiful by far of the Islands of the Aegean sea. Its people is amiable and kind, indeed so that you may fancy yourself among the shepherds of the golden age; and the fruitful Valleys between the lofty crags, — with monte Zeuz and Monte Coronos rising high in the blue aether, — the clear rivulets which run through them bordered with oleander and white Sabinas, magnificent Platanes and fig trees, give you a kind of distant view of paradise. I say distant, because on coming near you see many things which are not of paradise at least not of that one where all was good. Some spots in the new world have seemed to me much nearer unto that. After this tour to the Islands of Greece I have been to T[h]essaly (Turkish Greece) in order to know somewhat of the land of the Olymp, of the Ossa and Pelion, and of its presant population (chiefly Greek) a very interesting tour in many respects. This oldest home of the Hellenes will, with its sister-state Epirus, not long more remain under turkish dominion. Their freedom loving population grows every day in numbers and wealth, and has no stronger aspirations than to a union with free Greece.

Next week I intend to make a pilgrimage to Delphi and the Parnassus, after which I have done with my travels in Greece and will sit quietly down in Athens until the Swallows go northward and then — I shall go with them to the "old holy North."

The results of my travels in the East will come to you, my dear friends as, I trust by the time you receive this letter, my diary, [S]wiz. and Italy[11] has done. I have as yet [rec]eived no answer from *Ticknor et Field* but I trust they have, through you, received my letter, and that they are good and honorable men. So I alway[s] heard, and have therefore been glad to come in connexion with them.

I enclose here two small but good photographies of the King and Queen of Greece.[12] /in their national dres[s — the king] always dresse[s] so, but the queen more often in European [clothing?] which fits her better. Her two young Maids of honor are[13] girls, always in the old rich Greek dress and would make [a] furore in the new world. One of these, Aspasie, is as good as pretty, and my personal little friend. I hope a good deal of the spirit which is beginning to grow in some of the young Athenian ladies. There is perhaps not a more nobleminded girl in the world than the young Princess Lily Cantacouzenos, who[m] I love as a young sister and who will, I hope, be the means of much good, then she is rich and independent, and ready for every good work./ Though taken some years hence [ago] they are still good likenesses. Both King and Queen are persons of high moral character, he the most good she the most clever and bright of the two, both most happy and exemplary as a married pair, though he is a roman Catholic and she a protestant; and certainly they are, through the purity of thei[r] life and their good will to their people a blessing to the land as well as in many things an example. But their being strangers and not of the religion of the land keeps down their influence.

And now good bye, dear America[n] brother and Sister; thank you[14] more for the sunny image [of] Eaglewood and its life which y[our] letters have made me see. I feel happy when I think of you and no cloud casts its shadow over the bright sight. I shall always be with you in mind and aspiration, now and — ever. Love to the children kind remembrances to common friends from Your own
Fredrika Bremer.

---

1. MS, HL.

2. William Ellery Channing, 1780-1842, American Unitarian clergyman and writer.

3. Friedrich Adolf Trendelenburg, 1802-1872, German philosopher.

4. Vincenzo Gioberti, 1801-1852, Italian philosopher and politician.

5. Cesare Balbo, 1789-1853, Italian statesman and author.

6. Luigi Lambruschini, 1776-1854, Italian cardinal.

7. Giuseppe Garibaldi, 1807-1882, Italian patriot and general.

8. Alexander II, emperor of Russia from 1855 to 1881.

9. *Travels in the Holy Land* (London, 1861).

10. F. Bremer described this trip on the "Leon" in *Greece and the Greeks* (London, 1863); the archeologist was Mr. Michaelis.

11. *Life in the Old World: or, Two Years in Switzerland and Italy.*

12. King Otto and Queen Amalia.

13. One word missing.

14. One word missing, probably "once."

66. To Anna Maria Hall.[1]

Stockholm 18 Nov. 1861.

If the St. James Magazine is your *pet*, dear Maria, you must take up in it *my pet* t. i. the little girl described upon the here enclosed 2 sheets, provided, of course, that you do not think her misplaced there!

I have looked out some time longingly for news from you, for your long silence made me fear that you were not well. /or that my missive from Athen[s] had some misshap/ And now when you have cheered me with a letter, I am truly pained to see by it, that you are not well indeed, but suffer from a very painful complaint which, generally, affects the soul as well as the body. Happily it is one for which there is pretty certain to find a cure in a German bath. But why should you not go to *the bath* for sufferings of the liver — *Carlsbad?* It is well known that no bath in the world is equal to that in healing power. My brother in law, Judge Quiding, was at about 40 years of age so badly suffering from the liver, that it was not believed he could live. He was as a skeleton, and the right side terribly swollen. Two seasons at Carlsbad restored him completely, so completely that he now, at 64 years, is more green and well than he ever was since his young days; and God be thanked for that, for he is the best man and brother in the world.

Dear Maria, try Carlsbad! Only do not go to[o] early in summer, not before July. The place is beautiful but cold and rainy before that time.

I am at home since 4 months, and *so happy* to be at home, after my long pilgrimage, so charmed with my home my friends my country! /I have had *no* domestic afflictions since the death of my Mother in 55 the year before I started on my great tour./ I cannot describe how I felt it upon coming home i[n] the high summer of Sweden when life seems doubled in intensity and beauty, — the light of the nights the life of the days, the incessant feast of men and nature — it was intoxicating! And I was as intoxicated by it; I felt it as a new love, o! it was delightful! — And then all was so good, friends, prospects, near and far. Sweden had advanced wonderfully and is progressing in every way mentally and materially; I had never seen my country so prosperous and so promising. Indeed, I do not believe any country in Europe is now, on a better way and in a better state than just my good land. Only my good land is a little too cold just now.

Some recent institutions here interest me specially, nam. the great schools opened for womens learning and industrial development. The seminary for teachers[2] endowed by the state is a noble thing. It has been to me a pleasure to adorn its beginning library with several of yours and Mr Halls beautiful works,[3] and it should give you pleasure to see with what ap[p]reciation and sageness they have been received.

As to my little work for the St. James Magazine, I have no objection to be remunerated or paid for it as the money does not go from your purse. I shall welcome it gladly what it may be, if Mr. Maxwell (or you dear Maria) will let it come to me by b[u]ying a draft at the *Union bank of London* 2. *Princes Str. Mansion House* or on some of our Bankers in Stockholm Mr *Bendix* or Mr *Arwidson* and send it me in a letter. And if you and Mr Maxwell should wish it I shall next send you a letter about present life in Sweden under our new young somewhat excentric but honest and wonderfully openhearted King.

But alas! you will see more blunders in my English now than in my letter from Athen[s]. That one was corrected by a friend; here I have no English one near at hand. I write english easely, almost as easely as my own language but I am not conversant with its grammar and have no rules to preserve me against mistakes in the turning of phrases or right application of words.

Your Jeanie has my best wishes for her change of condition, but I know that she will find no better friends nor sweeter home than those she now has. I send you my Photograph as you wish it, but I do not think it good. It was made in Wienna. I shall ask Mr Blackett to send you a present copy of my late work over Palestine and Turkey which I beg you will accept. This winter I shall be bysy with Greece. Perhaps that next summer I may, from Germany where I shall go (please God) take a trip over to London to see your new great Exhibition. The Misses Beaufort have kindly invited me, and I should be happy to see you and Mr Hall once more (thanks for your kind words which open your heart and home to me.) Methink I should enjoy to take a last great look at the world and its doings before I go home — to rest for ever on this earth. I feel old and weary.

I do not know if Newspapers can be sent by the letter-post nor how the Magazine can come to Stockholm at this time of the year but I shall inquire and write about it.

With best wishes and grateful love

ever yours

Fredrika Bremer

––––––

1. MS, NYPL.

2. Stockholm Teachers College for Women.

3. Among these were: *Marian* (1850) by Mrs. S. C. Hall and inscribed: "To Miss Bremer with the author's affectionate regards, 1851"; and the *Art Journal* (1851), ed. by S. C. Hall and inscribed "Miss Fredrika Bremer with the homage and respectful regards of the editor."

67.

Stockholm 30th March, 1862.

To my American friends.[1]

Returned to my home in Sweden after a journey of more than five years in southern and Eastern countries, I did find that home enriched by gifts of American friends sent to me during my absence. Most of these gifts consist in books, good and beautiful products of

American litterature. Some of these are endeared to me by letters from their givers, others by kind words on the title page but signed only with initials — several have no mark at all of the friendly hand whose gift they are. These spirit-signs have come to me from different parts of the United States in the North, in the West and the South. They have made me most joyfully alive to my ties of everlasting sympathy with the great western world, its life and aspirations; but they have also left me op[p]ressed with — gratitude. For how shall I be able to acknowledge those fresh tokens of good will from a people which, perhaps, more than any other delights in giving, in the noble hospitalities of the soul? Alas! Most of these kind messages are two or three years old; many of these letters speak of changes to come in the lifes or residances of the writers; if I now should write to them where could I find them? And where and how reach brilliant meteors who as Bayard Taylor[2] pass over the countries of this earth and vanish from our sight leaving only after them a bright sign or memory (which happily will not pass as they)? How [reach] those unknown friends whose very names have been concealed from me though they have made evident their good will. Yet how can I but long to make know[n] to these known and unknown friends how much they have enriched not only my bookstore[3] but still more my heart? Such expressions of my feelings could not hurt them, and would make me more easy, by letting me feel a little less in debt. But how shall I reach them?

Thanks to God, and next — to Guttenberg, if I cannot come to them by the written word I can do so by the printed one, and make that hundred-tong[u]ed bird *the press* bear to them the expressions of my gratitude, wherever the[y] may be in the great pilgrim land; for the American press has too liberal a spirit not to lend its far-reaching voice to one who requires its agency.

May, therefore, those friends in Amerika who have written to me during my absence and have received no answers in return, here read my everlasting sense of their continued kindness, my heartfelt wishes for their wellfare! May those unknown friendly givers also here learn to know that their kind intentions have been attained, that they have made me richer in mind and heart. Among the anonym[o]us givers I suspect two publishers who, while I was in America and afterwards have given me in beautiful and valuable works repeated tokens of their generosity and good will. Let me for many such here thank Mr *G.* [*P.*] *Putnam* and Messrs *Ticknor and Field* of New York!

And now, after having relieved my heart on that matter, let me speak two words more to my friends in Amerika on annother matter not alone of private interest.

It is especially with my friends in *the homes* of the United States, those good and blessed homes in the north, the south and the west, in the free states and in the slave states, where I have been a happy guest that I wish to speak, to com[m]une as I did when I was with them as a sister with brothers and sisters.

You know it well, my friends, without my saying it, what a deep interest I have taken in your present civil strife. But you cannot know how bitterly I have felt to see a bloody, fratricide war pollute a country gifted beyond all others with all the blessings of this earth, a country of which men such as *Horace Mann* and *A. J. Downing* (each in his way) have worked to make (as God seems to have intended it to be) a paradisi[a]cal home for Mankind, a land whose richness of life and beauty recently made a young frensh traveller /Maurice Sand, son of the celebrated frensh Authoresse George Sand (Mme Dudevant)/ exclaim: "How can people go on killing in a land so full of beauty? This is a country for poets and lovers of nature!"

From the beginning of the war I have thirsted and hungered to see started some measure for pacification by which the purity of the principle of individual and civil freedom — the very life-principle of your great republic, — should be made to coincide with justice, equity and *possibility* on all points. I have hoped of the Genius of America that it could bring out such a wonderful thing.

Praise be God and that good Genius, such a thing has now come indeed!

The recent Message of President Lincoln and his proposition of a compensation, or pecuniary remuneration by the Government of the United States to those slave-states who[4] would be willing to give up the institution of slavery and reenter the Union as free states, this proposition made in terms as wise as its tone is manly and resolute seems one of those measures of *high politic*[s] which alon[e] can rule over lower ones[,] conciliate the interests at war and make the United States government rise to the dignity of a high moral principle. It is just, it is practical. It is also simple — as the egg of Columbus; (you will know the anekdote to which I allude).[5] It seems *the thing* to be done.

Such inspirations come from God to good and upright minds. It makes them natural Presidents of the peoples. In this case it seems clear that the chief Magistrate of the United States, by this measure, has associated to himself all honest, unselfish hearts in your great land for one great work for right and freedom and peace, for the good of all. Clear it seems to me that the father and mother will talk about it in their home with their children and servants; that the brother will confer about it with his sisters and brothers; that every body will come forward to give his mite of work and good will; the widow her penny, the child its darling toy; that there will henceforth be, both in the south and the north, a third party which may be named *Christs party,* a party for brotherly love, for sacrifice for peace and good will, and that every christian man and woman will enlist under its banner. The stars of that banner will never fall off, but they may shed a new lustre over those[6] of the United States, and bring a harmony and prosperity to the homes of Amerika which they have not known before. Difficulties may come, must come in the carrying out of the proposed measure, and its consequences, new sacrifices may be required on all sides, but no difficulties will proove to[o] intricate, no sacrifices to[o] great for a great people determined to go forward in the cause of justice and equity to every one. And then angels in heaven once again may sing as they once did in prophetical vision: "Glory to God on high, peace on earth, and good will unto men!"

You can hasten that day, my friends, the day of release, of peace and joy to you, your country and millions of hearts interested in her glory! Permit me among these to name also myself; for never more than in this hour did I feel myself so truly and entirely Yours

Fr. Bremer

––––––––

1. MS, HL. This letter was published in a normalized version in New York *Daily Tribune,* May 1, 1862, p. 3. (Also in Johanson and Kleman, *op. cit.,* IV, pp. 196-198.) This is her complete original letter.

2. Bayard Taylor, 1825-1878, American poet and traveler.

3. F. Bremer's original word — *bookstore* — was corrected to *bookshelves* by another hand.

4. F. Bremer's original word — *who* — was corrected to *which* by another hand.

5. Anecdote refers to Columbus's simple solution of how to stand an egg on end: by slightly cracking the eggshell.

6. In the *Tribune, those* was changed to *the people,* spoiling F. Bremer's image.

68.   To Marcus and Rebecca Spring.[1]

Stockholm 1 April, 1862.

Oh, this indeed, my dearest friends, is a com[m]union of souls! The very evening of the day on which I last wrote to you about the Message of your President (which I had read in the Swedish papers,) there was a thundering knocking at my door. Though it was late and nearly my bed time (10 hour) I knew it was the postman and opened. And what came in? *the Tribune,* from my dear brother Marcus, with *the Message* from the President encircled in a glory[2] (no matter if of ink,) which told me how you looked upon it; and that this was just so as I had done. This was charming! And the Message in its own tongue and simple, earnest, clever words looked still more admirable, and, [in] its way, a perfect thing, than it had looked in the ab[b]reviated translation of it in Swedish (though

that was good and expressive). And now, dearest friends what will
you say to the letter or ad[d]ress I have enclose[d] for a purpose
which you will easely understand? The first part of it was written
soon after my coming home, in the fall; but was left unfinished because I wanted to say something about the present war and — I did
not find any thing good to say; I felt dispirited and — but you my
friends know how I have felt, for I have laid my heart open to you.
After President Lincolns Message however I did feel such a strong
desire to chime in with the feelings that it must call forth in all
rightminded citizens, and to swell the general voice with one voice
more (you know that the little bells must joyn with the great ones
if the chorus shall be complete) and also to give my tribute of love
and sympathy for Americas great cause — one with that of humanity
— that I wrote at once what I send here. To you, my dearest friends,
I leave to do with it what you think fit. If you think that it could
hurt the National pride in America to see a stranger taking this kind
of part in its affairs, and propose, as it were, a kind of association
which had better be proposed from an American man or woman;
then, my friends, sup[p]ress my letter and my name, and try to
make the proposition come out in some other way or manner. For I
think it should be made. If you think that this effusion of sympathy
from a person which is known as a warm friend to Americas best
aspirations and life, and who has been every where in your land
treated with the most kind and generous hospitality, if, I say, you
think that its publishing could do some good and no harm, then —
make it public, if it so pleases you. I su[b]scribe blindly to whatever
you do in this case. I cannot but repeat to you how happy this turn
in your moral warfare, especially in this moment when the material
war on every point turns in the favor of freedoms cause, has made
me. This is the moment for generous sacrifice on the part of the
north, and Magnanimous acting returning the good for the bad.
This may be the greatest moment in Americas history and in that
of any free people. It may show that a nation *can* rise to the full
dignity of a Christian Man. Now farewell, dearest and best!

Bergfalk has just been to see me; he sympathizes with me and
you in every thing. He is delighted with me at the goodness, manli-
ness and also *cleverness* in your Presidents Message. Nothing better!
We look impatiantly to see how this message will be received by
the American people at large. We know already that it has been
ap[p]rooved by both your houses. Thank God! Ever Yours

Fredr. Bremer

---

1. MS, HL. Part of letter was published in a normalized version in New
York *Daily Tribune*, May 1, 1862, p. 3. (Also in Johanson and Kleman, *op. cit.*,
IV, pp. 195-196.) This is her complete original letter.

2. Cf. Sw. *gloria* — halo.

69.   To Marcus and Rebecca Spring.[1]

Stockholm 10th Jan. 1863.

Dearest friends Marcus and Rebecca!

Yesterday night I read by my evening lamp in our papers a report from New York of the terrible battle at Fred[e]ri[c]ksburg, near Richmond and the dreadful defeat and slaughter of the Union-army.[2] It made my night restless, but now as the morning of a dim and dark winter day dawns over me and tears dim my eyes while writing to you I feel something bright and great in my heart a swelling as of pride and joy. Why so? Dear friends, there is something in war greater than victory and success, it is the unflinching, heroic sacrifice of life for the cause of right and duty it is the brave resolute death on the battle field. The bloody affair of Fred[e]ri[c]ksburg is to my eyes one of the noblest deeds of your Armies, and as I believe certainly one which will more than many victories win the admiration of Europe to your spirit and its sympat[h]ies to your cause. I would to its commemoration have in your cities a "Te Deum" not a "Miserere" sung. "The blood of Martyrs is seed of eternal life" says an old proverb. The brave martyrs of that bloody day will not have offered themselves in vain. Their blood will let "flaming seed" grow out of your soil.

And now as there probably will be a pause in the civil war during the winter weeks or months, and probably also there will be endeavors meantime to settle matters in a peaceful way between North and south, tell me dear Marcus, where is the chief difficulty, from northern point of view, in allowing a separation between North and South, allowing the south to form, as it requires, a separate republic? — Is it, as some people think here, the Missis[s]ip[p]i and its outlet which then would be in the power of the south? (But could not easely a compromise way be made about that point, and Northern "Monitors" have their station by New Orleans?) Is it the slavery question? Hardly; for slavery would yet be doomed in principle and practise by having a wholly free and to slavery opposed country so near the slave states. Is it ambition within your government, pride within your people wanting not to give up to the rebellious and treacherous south? Verely, however *just* the feelings of the North may be on this subject I cannot believe that any other power but that of freedom can settle matters in the conflict. The south must have freedom to organize its government according to its interests. Nor can these in the long run be injurious to those of the north; I think the reverse. And I feel perfectly sure that a Union which is more than a sham-Union can nevermore be effectuated between the two bel[l]igerent powers, any more than between a married couple who once has divorced and whose contrahents have tried to murther [murder] each other /or to speak more ac[c]urately where one party has attempted to murther the other and thereby provoked it to desperate fight/ can again joyn in holy matrimony.

Dear friends (and I speak to Channing here also!) *it will never do!* You must give up the past Union and only think of doing it with best grace and on the best terms for your cause and for those whose rights you are connected with it. Now, excuse my speaking so and giving *you* advice, and if I am wrong, teach me better.

So far had I written when the postman brought me an American paper with Marcus' dear handwriting on it. It was the Christian examiner and it gave me joy to see by it how Unitarians in England begin to feel for your cause, and also to see how generously in the midst of the heavy taxes for war you at the same time are doing for the unfortunate operatives in England thrown out of work by this war! Even the Northern Iron working provinces of my land are suffering from it. My faith is firm in its final issue, yet I cannot but joyn in the chorus which prays to God that for the benefit of humanity that issue may soon come, and rather by a rational divorce than by a Union internally untrue and unsafe.

In mine own good land all things go on in prosperity and peace. Somewhat too high living and a good deal to[o] much frivolity in the male sex in its relations to the other sex, in which our else good and brave young King[3] gives a most detestable example, is the fault of the Sweedes as it ever was. My good brother in law with wife and little girl (little Jenny) are this winter at Nizza and enjoying extremely its climate, life and the healthful feelings and ap[p]etite etc. which it gives them, especially to my good brother in law, who was in miserable health when he left Sweden. I am *well* dear friends, and have a widening circle of activity mostly for young persons with aspiring minds of many kind, which gives me a good deal to do, but also a good deal of interest to my life and heart. Thank God for the peaceful and not fruitless Autumn which he has prepared for me and prepared me for! May he strengthen me for his work!

Mr Blackett, my publisher in England sends me word that he has sent to you (as I had ordered) as well as to my good Doctor Osgood in Boston my recent Work about Greece and its Islands. You cannot have time or leisure to read it now. When you can have it, I hope that work will give you pleasure. As translation it seems to me the very best one of Mrs Howitts works as faithful as faultless.

Womans cause is quietly but surely progressing here. A most noble speech is lately made at our Diet by a *peasant* asking for a law resolving that woman may be admitted to every office in the state which her knowledge and position makes her able to fill. I have asked the brave man to sup with me next Freyday in order that I may know him and thank him. Oh! that you my friends and *our* Channing could be with me here also! How I should like to make you acquainted with some fine, noble-minded young women here, "my girls"; and some good men also! Well, that time may yet come! — When you write again tell me news of our common friends, and remember me to them as a friend to their cause, and as your own Swedish sister

Fredrika.

Tell me also about your children. Eddy (professor Bergfalk asks me often news of him) Jeanie and dear little Herbert.

––––––––

1. MS, HL.
2. Battle of Fredericksburg, December 11-15, 1862; Lee defeated Burnside.
3. Charles XV, king of Sweden and Norway from 1859 to 1872.

70.   To Marcus and Rebecca Spring.[1]

[Sweden, August, 1863]

. . . .
At the old Castle of *Widtsköfle*[2] now belonging to General Stjernhjelm, an old place with towers, walls and gloomy cellars and corridors, and plenty of ghost-stories, if not of ghosts, I had the great pleasure of meeting in the governess of the young ladies an old a[c]quaintence of yours, a Mlle Simmerding (?) who was with *your Children* at Bonn while you were on your visit in Sweden. She spoke in love of you and your children especially of little Herbert, and was very astonished to hear that Jeanie was already a wife, and would soon become a mother. She is a pleasing, sensible woman, very much beloved in the family where she had now lived many years, but now, by the failing of her eyesight almost disabled to fulfill her place as a governess. Much did we speak of you to whom I promised to give her best compliments. I have had a very interesting and rich time this summer, going from friends to friends and often meeting Grandfathers and Grandmothers in those very individuals which I had known as young boys and girls. Often I have thought: "O! that I could have Marcus and Rebecca see these places or know these people!" Baroness Barnekow (the friend at whose home I am now staying and with whom I have visited many a home this summer) is a dear, poetical creature full of wit and good nature, and of natural nobility at the same time an excellant sample of *good* aristocracy, whom you would much enjoy. I cannot give up the hope of seeing you once more in Sweden. And in two, or, at the highest, three years, the great railway-lines which will be accomplished will give the travellers occasion to see much of what is most original and beautiful in this land, and in such a pleasing manner! Indeed I think that the arrangements, especially for ladies, on the Swedish railways are superiour to any I have known either in the

old or in the new world. *Skåne*, the province most south of sweden is wonderful for its fertility in Corn, its beautiful old dominions and Castles (from the time of the Middle ages,) and its magnificent beach forests. Many fruits of the south also: grapes Apricots and Peaches ripen in quantities in the Gardens. The peasentry is rich but terribly aristoc[r]atic, much more so than the old counts and Barons in their Castles. The peasants daughter who would marry a labourer having no farm of his own, would be disowned by her whole family. Alas for poor humanity! The Aristocracy belonging to name and title is swiftly melting away in its exclusivety, but the aristocracy of wealth is rising in its place. Still that will not long be ruling where true cultivation (that is a christian one,) will take in the land. That it will so and pervade all the ranks of society here, is what our progressive statesmen now are working for in union with the best writers of the land. Let me among the first of these statesmen name to you *Baron Louis De Geer*[3] author of the new *system of representation,* a most excellant man (and brother to that baroness Wrede whose good and pure face Rebecca liked so much). But now I must end this letter. Remember me to Channing to your Children and to common friends! Ever yours

Fredrika.

To Morrow I shall be on the sea, on a somewhat stormy passage, I fear, over the Kattegatt on my way to Got[h]enburg from where I go by the railway to Stockholm, and there take up my quarters for this Winter. From Stockholm, please God, I shall write to you again!

––––––––

1. MS, *s.l. et a.* (incomplete), HL.
2. Vittskövle.
3. Louis Gerard De Geer, 1818-1896, Swedish statesman and author.

71.   To Marcus and Rebecca Spring.[1]

Stockholm 26 Nov. 1863.

Most dear Friends, My brother Marcus, my sister Rebecca! I am heartely ashamed and also angry at myself for having suffered weeks, nay, nearly two months to pass, before my telling you what a great joy you have bestowed upon me by your letters, likenesses and other gifts which awaited me in my home on my return, the last day of September! Thank you a thousand times dear, kind friends for these precious signs of you and your life. The photografs were certainly but *shadowy lik[e]nesses,* still the[y] are like and tell me that my dear rose-colored family has not faded a bit though years and many a care and saddening thought has weighed on them, but, thank kind Providence, and their faith in him[,] without weighing them down. And the Military Academy is a splendid thing, and a capital undertaking, which cannot fail to bring good results both moral and material! One thing made me very sorry, nam. not having been able to meet and in some way to serve the Gentleman, Mr Gilmore your friend who brought those things to me. I never knew of his visit before it was much to[o] late and he long since away. He should have had only two words to our friend Professor Bergfalk, who would most gladly have helped him, and *freely*, to any thing that he wanted to know or to do in his law-suit. Bergfalk was in Stockholm throughout the summer; I was not. I went in June on a kind of nomad-excursion to the south of Sweden and continued there going from mansion to mansion /I wrote to you in August from an old Castle where I met, as governess in the family a German lady, a Miss Simnerding[2] (or something such) who knew and loved you and your youngest children./ from friends to friends untill the end of September when I came home. My letters were kept for me at home until my return, and I met quite a society of these from persons at home and abroad on the table of my drawing room, and many a friendly photografic face from friends in Switzerland, Italy, Germany, etc came out of these and looked at me, — as yours did, dearest of friends, — it was quite a Christmas evening to me that evening of my return home, and among letters and books and other precious souvenirs stood a magnificent giant Jericho rose fresh from Jerusalem. This was the sunny side of the coming home; another brought me many cares and anxious occupations not of a deep nature, but swallo[w]ing time and thought. A poor old servant wholly depending on my care, though for several years not in my home, got incurably ill, and after several weeks died, and I had much to do before and after her death in her behalf. Then — but why enumerate the cares of the hour and day which have kept me from writing and thanking you as I wanted to do every day ever since my return. Now, though I am far from at leasure I will and must let a few words from my heart and pen run over to America. . . . [3] If you have the "revue des deux Mondes" in New York, you should read a most noble article there about: "la Guerre civile en Amerique," which will give you pleasure.[4] Emerson is quoted there, in one place, and I think he has never said more truer and beautiful things. This able "revue" treats always the American war with high attention, and I need not say that its sympathies are all on the side of the Antislavery cause. Some parts of that article and of Marcus' letter I shall soon make use of in a preface which I have promised to write to the new swedish edition of my letters from America.[5] This will be a cheap edition in which the old, somewhat diffuse work, is shortened and made to suit the popular libraries who are now beginning to be established in all provinces and parts of Sweden. The good and able lady[6] who has undertaken the work will have the profits of it, but I shall have the moral enjoyment of teaching the

Mass of my people better than it now does to understand the great things which are working at the bottom of your awful civil war, better to understand the ideal, the true America, the land and people which *I* have understood, and which still will become a reality. But shall we live to see the end and issue of the present crisis?! — What we already see is the changed position of the slave population and the ap[p]ro[a]ching end of slavery, with the end also of cotton monopoly in the southern states. Is it not remarkable how by this time Afrika comes out of its millenial night, and landscape after landscape, sources, seas, mountains, tribes stand forth in the new morning light, the high lands of Senegal, the sources of the Nile, the seas and peoples of the interiour, the Montes Lunae and other high Mountains who feed with waters from high the great rivers of the land — the

[End of MS]

My sister and brother in law are this winter still in Nizza but I expect them back in spring.[7]

––––––––

1. MS (incomplete), HL. (Two pictures of Stockholm — *Slottet* and *Norrbro* — at top of p. 1.)

2. Perhaps Zimmerding.

3. See p. 141 for omitted passage.

4. Auguste Laugel, "La Guerre Civile aux Etats-Unis," *Revue des deux mondes,* XLVII (1863), pp. 872-897.

5. F. Bremer added an appendix to *Hemmen i nya verlden* (Stockholm, 1866), Part II, pp. 377-425.

6. Octavia Carlén.

7. Marginal note.

72.   To Justina Howland.[1]

[Sweden, ca. 1865]

.   .   .   .

It grieves me to see in this grand and rising *New World* the same troubles and difficulties of life troubling many of its noblest souls that we find in the kingdoms of the Old World. I always thought and hoped that *Ammerika* would have for its inhabitants more work, more hope, more general and true happiness than Europe, at least that no conscientious and earnest worker would there be without full remuneration — morally and materially — in the long run. But, alas I fear it never will come to this as long as poor humanity remains poor humanity; 'tis for war on this our planet, though society certainly *can* and *does in fact grow* towards this ideal of just retribution. That there should be for everybody a time of probation, of hard work with seemingly small or no profit (morally), is, I believe it, by my own experience, good, and more truly educating and developing than we in that period understand, but it should not last too long!

My life has been a restless one, not outwardly but inwardly, and from inward causes. These have driven me out in the world, over seas and lands, among foreign jungles, amid many dangers and savages, but through all these I have essayed and prayed and tried at least to do my best, or sought for the better, even if it should condemn myself and my work, and God has helped me — not to be what I wanted to be, but to get storms from my mind and peace of mind, and from my earthly life — the two needful things for our Martha and Mary nature. . . .

––––––––

1. Published in New York *World*, March 28, 1878, p. 2. Justina Howland, 1828-1902, oldest of the seven children of William and Anne Howland.

73.   To Marcus and Rebecca Spring.[1]

Stockholm 20th March, 1865.

Thanks dearest friends, a thousand thanks for your papers just arrived with the great, great news of Shermans[2] victories! We — your friends here — expected them since several weeks, but a winter uncommonly severe, frozen seas and snowstorms have for a time almost isolated the scandinavian north from the rest of the world, and we would not sing victory before we were quite sure of it. Now we are and we sing Te Deum with you. Yes, *I do,* though my heart bleeds for that city of Charlestown, which I last saw as a city of Roses and where I enjoyed so sweet hospitality, as well as for other places, now ravaged, in the south; but so does yours, I am sure, so does that of Sherman, — brave and *good* man I deem from his letter to Mrs Gilman — and yet we must rejoyce, for only through such victories can a new and better state of things be attained, can peace be won. This is now but too clear. What a wonderful course is that of General Sherman, that which he has accomplished and still pursues! What a strange and tragic scene — a doom of God it almost seems — to see B[e[auregard[3] retreating (flying) northward before Sherman; the southern chief pushed out of the south, as it were, by the Northern General! There is something fated and deeply symbolical in this. It seems to me quite a wonder that the cecessionists still can persevere, that they do not in time try to come to terms with the superiour power, before they must surrender without conditions. Certainly the war cannot now last much longer; the south is pierced through and through. A battle won, or even two, could not help the rebel-cause any more, if even they should retard the close of the conflict. Theoretically, principally it is closed; the practical ratification cannot be far off. And then, o my friends! and all you who have from the beginning unflinchingly and uncompromisingly stood up for right and christian liberty, how happy, how elated you must feel, how thankful and hopeful for the great work and the great prospects which from this moment opens to your people and country. One of the greatest and most important problems which your people from now will be expected to solve, not only for itself but theoretically for the whole world, is how to turn the Negro-population into a free and industrious people, capable of self government. The greatest difficulties will meet in the hitherto enslaved negroes of the south at once emancipated, without any preparation. In small states, as in Maryland, and in the Danish Islands[4] (where the freed slaves remain under a state of tutorship) this may be done easely ennough, but great dangers and difficulties will attend this sudden transformation on the large plantations of the far south. Of course, difficu[l]ties *must* come, but when the best part of the south unites with the best North in order to meet them they *must be overcome* in a Manner to make England and whole Europe applaud. The work of peace after this terrible war will not be less arduous than that of destruction, but how different in means and effects! Here we will see realized the profecy of Christ: "blessed are the peaceful for they shall pos[s]ess the earth!"

About these questions I take great pleasure in having now and then a conversation with your new Minister in Stockholm Mr Campbell[5] (a stout Lincolnian and Antislavery man) and especially with his amiable and very intellectual lady. As for Bergfalk, he and I are in constant cor[r]espondence (when we do not personally meet) about your affairs telegrafing to one annother (we have about half an hours way between us) the news or sending the papers from America which we receive. I feel it a true blessing to have among my best frie[n]ds so warm and clearminded a combination in this interest.

25th March!

Your letters of the 22d Febr! Again, most cordial and joyful thanks, dearest friends, for these communications of your great birth-day-revival and your Hymns of praise. An excellant idea this to make your Washingtons birth day serve as the herald of the new birth which your people is achieving. Ah! The labours and woes of it are not yet over, but that the child is safe and the mother also we already see; and hitherto very blind eyes — as are many in old Europe — begin now to open wide to it, and their owners to deliberate if they must not clap hands to the victorious fact.

"Victory (or suc[c]ess)" says Göthe in Tasso, "is a King attended with a magnificent train."

Not less gratifying to my heart, dear friends, than the success of your cause is to hear (and see) how well and youthful you are growing body and soul. I do not by any means wonder at this wonder in present circumstances, but I thank God that my dear rose colored family of rose cottage has been allowed to live and prosper to prepare and now so fully to partake in this Jubilee of humanity effected by their own people. . . .[6] Pity there are no spirit rapping telegrams to be had!! —

N. America is at this time the only truly interesting scene on the globe.

In Sweden the greatest event of this winter has been its uncommon severity. It has been for many weeks intensely cold in Stockholm, from 25 to 31 degrees, Celcius, in Norrland above 40, (degree when the quicksilver freezes). But the hearts of my people are never of a cold temperature, and so much fuel has been dispensed by the well off to the poor that it is probable that they have never had so warm and comfortable homes as just this Siberian winter, which still lasts, and gives no sign of resigning, though April is at hand. I have lived in my old way, but been taken up by affairs not my own in a way which takes me all too much from my own thoughts and pursuits. But I have been suc[c]essful and have been able to do a little good, principally through my pen; and for this I am thankful. One of these affairs originated by Queen Louisa[7] (wife of our King) has brought me in close contact with her, and has given me pleasure by the a[c]quaintance of her noble and sweet but extreemly timid personality. I struggle my way pleasantly ennough between many engagements, /My sister and brother in law are very well, little Jenny also who is grown and well promising. They have fine and sunny rooms in town and look out to planting and gardening in spring at their little summer home which you may remember. They seem quite fixed for the rest of life./ but it is *a struggle* and I look with longing to my retirement in the country, at Årsta, where I hope to be in June. This spring my American letters will appear in a new edition and reduced volume. They will be supplied with a Map and a fine portrait of president Lincoln who is a favourite of mine.[8] God bless you a thousand times, dearest friends, in all your interests. Next to my own country none is dearer to me than yours! Remember me to your Children and our common friends! Ever Yours

Fr. Bremer.

---

1. MS, HL.

2. William Tecumseh Sherman, 1820-1891, Union general.

3. Pierre G. T. de Beauregard, 1818-1893, Confederate general.

4. Three of the Virgin Islands.

5. James H. Campbell, born 1820; American diplomat, appointed minister resident to Sweden by President Lincoln, 1864.

6. See p. 144 for omitted passage.

7. Queen Lovisa, 1828-1871, wife of Charles XV, King of Sweden and Norway.

8. An engraving of Lincoln by E. Skill was the frontispiece of the 1866 edition of *Hemmen i nya verlden,* but a map was not included.

74. To Marcus and Rebecca Spring.[1]

Årsta 8 Sept. 1865.

Now for You, Friends of my heart and mind, my best relations with the great New World, in whom I breath[e] and live what it has best, truest and most universal life, dear Marcus, dear Rebecca, Good Morning, and "Guds Frid!" (Gods peace!). /a morning and evening greeting used among the peasantry in several provinces of Sweden./ Here, in my old country home again, I have given some weeks to entire repose of Mind and body, then some to a new absorbing study, and now I come to you, full of the t[h]oughts inspired by your dear, cheering letters of the 4 July (which have been with me since a couple of Weeks) Marcus letter dated: "Year of National Independance 89; Year of National Liberty 1." How I enjoy to see you both so cheerful and happy in your home and beautiful realm of peaceful moral work, surrounded by young people, old trees, good and pleasant friends and prospects. May long this lot be yours, you dear springlike couple, that you may spread your influence and make spring come out again and again near and far in the world! Yes, dear Friends, you are right, God has in this great cause, in a wonderful and evident way turned Evil to Good, and through this bloody war brought out a work of freedom and peace, not only for Amerika but for the whole Earth, which work otherwise would have taken centuries to accomplish. I see and I own it, blushingly, when I remember my fears and shrinking in view of the Misery and Moral horrors which always are the companions of Civil War. Honor and thanks to the brave American patriots, who have shrunk from nothing ex[c]ept yealding to wrong. They, next God, have saved the New-World for new and better generations. W. H. Channing and those who may have heard of my doubts and fears know this confession of sin. For it is sinful to compromise with wrong, especially in a great human cause. Let it be my excuse that I have known many a kind slave-holder and seen happy slaves in the south, and known many a hard hearted free man (and woman too) in the North and — — As to the *right* and the *principle* in question I never doubted that, and its final victory; my doubts related only to *the Manner.* But God knew better, and made the rebel-cause fall on the sword it had drawn. May the blood, the misery it has cost be, as you, dear Marcus, always anticipated, a purifying baptism for a nobler, truer life for the whole people of N. America!

Justina Howland (a noble woman now teacher in the school at Murray Hill, N. York, who refused the hand of a rich landowner in S. Carolina, when she found out that he was a decided proslavery man) shows, in a letter I recently have from her, strong fears of the democratic and southern sympat[h]ies of pres. Johnson,[2] because, says she "he appoints Southern men as Governors in the recently rebel states." But *if* only these men are good and loyal Union men, they will as southerners do more and better for the transformation of these States from slave to free labour, than Northern men who should want the good will and confidence of the white inhabitan[t]s. Great difficulties will certainly occur, in every way, for this transformation with *the presant* generation of black labourers.

Whatever the results of Lincolns murder may be for the cause of freedom in Amerika (I am very apt to think of it, as you, dear Marcus) it had a marvellous effect on public opinion in Europe. It was as if eyes at once opened to the serpant-nature of the rebel cause and War; and in the general shock and shudder electrically felt from this serpent sting, a pedestal rose under the feet of the Victim raising him and the cause for which he died higher and higher above all towers and walls and mountains of Earth, so that he became visible to all nations as ascending towards heaven in the glory of divine light and sanctification. It was, indeed, a wonderfully dramatic effect. From this time almost all sympathies have been turned from the south and to the North and its cause.

And now, Americas best minds both female and masculine have a great and noble educational task to fill, in accomplishing the work of freedom whose corner stone was laid by Lincolns hand in the Act of Emancipation.

And now, dear friends, your Military Academy must change its name! Is it not so? Perhaps it will transform itself in a *Naval Academy* and help to make Christian civilisation at home on the Ocean and its sailing or steaming locomotives. I am sure that such schools are greatly wanted in all countries with extended naval communications. — The eagles of Eaglewood will soar as well over sea as land, in the glorious sunlight of the New World.

If you should once more visit Sweden (oh, how I wish you would!) you should find there a great and good change as to outward things. Comfortable railway-trains are now running in all directions of the land, uniting great and small parts and social centres, province to province, and, soon also Norway to Sweden, so that you could from here take a run in them, without encountering the dangers of a stormy sea passage. This of course makes a great addition to running and commercial life in the land; nor do I think that intellectual and spiritual interests stand back for that. On the contrary I think there is a rising also in these departments, an awakening from slumber to more thought and aspiration.

Religious and Church-matters are discussed with earnestness in the periodical press, and the late interesting and wonderful discoveries of natural science become, also by that, the common property of the public mind. How grand and inspiring is not the recent discovered fact, that not only the Mathematical and optical laws but also *chemical matter* are the same in the whole Universe in the farthest suns and planets as well as on our little Earth, that the architectonic material is the same for the whole universe! In these last days I have also been delightfully taken up by studying Mr Petermans[3] Map (in his Geografis[c]he Mittheilungen) of the ocean-currents in connection with his project of a Northpolar expedition direct from Nord Cap and Spitzbergen. It delights me there to see the waters of Your rivers in Missis[s]ippi come out in the Mexican gulf, and through the warm Gulf-strom bring warmth and life to the shores of Sweden and Norway and driftwood to warm even the icy coast of Spitsberg; it delights me there to see even the woods of cold Sibery compelled to give their lark[4] trees and timber to the ocean streams which carry them, (in connection with those of North american Canada), to the frozen tree-less shores of Grönland [Greenland] and other northern Islands. This is a new face of the life on Earth, which shows a providential care in its system of circulation by water, and in those ocean-currents which unite and benefit so distant lands and parts of Earth I cannot but read cor[r]espondences and prophecies of spiritual things.

And now, my dear, kind friends of rose-cottage, if you will take a peep at your Swedish sister friend you will find her sitting in a very large and high room, full of light from four high window-cases, and with several tables covered with books, maps, photographes etc. etc. and she at a small table writing to you. Near that room is, separated by a drapery, her bedroom, from which she sees, on the western horizon rise the spire of the parish church pointing upwards, and to her also telling of the place of repose where her body will in no long time be laid down with those of her parents, sisters and brothers. /The views from the windows are very vast and now showing fields covered with golden crops, under a most beautiful September sky. The summer has been, after three weeks tropical heat, disagre[e]ably rainy and cold; but we have *now* a perfect summer-time, which is very rare here in September. Oh, the *Indian summer* in America! It is almost *too* beautiful, almost intoxicating! — —/ As to the situation of my mind I could almost word for word copy what you Marcus in your last letter write about yourself:

"I am trying — spite of the great disparity between my plans and my doings, which sometime make[s] me impatient with myself — 'to get into the quiet' — as the Quakers say — of a Childish faith that I am not required to hurry and struggle and work myself to death in order to do and to learn all that I see ought to be done and a[c]quired. I have found etc etc, and so I have learnt to *live and work more quietly* and sleep better — perhaps not to work much less steadily but more joyfully and hopefully *and with less care to see immediate results."*

Dear brother! There is great wisdom in these words, but it is a wisdom which hardly ever will, nor perhaps *should* be the wisdom of people in the high day of life. Those need the spur of impatience to make lifes work go ahead. But, — thank God that there is, for us, a season of calm and of calmer activity of patience with the world and with ourselves! And how thankful I feel to be permitted to enjoy that season free from earthly cares and troubles! In the home of my childhood I now enjoy a comfort and freedom greater than when it was that of my family. Nor am I with out family life there, and its good and pleasent bonds and pleasures.

You speak, dear Marcus, half contemptuously of the spiritual phenomenas of our days. And yet there may be more in these than it seems, judging by *one* kind of these; and I have been recently, for the first time, *really* and highly interested by (in) these things, through Mrs A. M. Watts (Mrs Howitts married daughter) and through Mrs de Morgans able and clever book ("from Matter to Spirit"[5]) about the Natural laws in the both lower and higher manifestations of spiritualism. If you can have it, read it, dear friends, especially the chapters on *"the home of the Spirit,"* and "the spiritual body." There is deep truth at the bottom of these things, /Not that I think that the light or wisdom given by the clair-voyants Mediums as yet come up to the views and anticipations of the Christian philosopher or simply of the *thinking* Christian; but in many cases doubts may be solved, hopes, dear to our hearts, con-firmed by these spiritual sights and witnesses./ and the spirit with which they are treated is of a high order. But I must end this letter. May God bless you and yours dearest friends as he has done hitherto, included Your loving and grateful swedish sister

Fredr. Bremer

Bergfalk (The Professor) has recently paid me a visit here. He is well (but now quite whitehaired) and always a delightful companion to me in American interests. My sister and her husband and your other friends here are well. How much I should wish to know a little more about our American friends, about Channing, Bellow[s], /I had about a year ago a touching little letter from Mrs Bellow[s] which showed me a depth of kind feeling in her, which I little thoug[h]t of./ Lowell, and Emerson (the sfinx of Con-cord) and that good and noble Elisabeth Hoar!

_____

1. MS, HL.

2. Andrew Johnson, 1808-1875, seventeenth president of the United States.

3. August Petermann, 1822-1878, German geographer and map maker.

4. Larch — Swedish *lärkträd* (*Larix sibirica*).

5. The complete title is *From Matter to Spirit: The Result of Ten Years' Experience in Spirit Manifestations. Intended as a Guide to Enquirers* (London, 1863), by Sophia E. de Morgan.

75. To Justina Howland.[1]

[Årsta, Sweden, September, 1865]

And now, dear friend, you see me again in the home of my childhood, at that A[r]sta that old estate of my father, of which you have heard me sometimes speak in Ammerika. I have come here to thank God and collect my thoughts undisturbed before I die. I have come here to try to do a last good work before I leave this scene of our existence. For this I need quiet of mind and body, solitude and collectedness, and that I can never have in Stockholm, where social evenings of many kinds always encumber my time and attention. But God has graciously so ordained that my old paternal estate and home, though it has passed into other hands, is open again to me, and that I could live there even with more comfort and independence than when it was in my family. And so I have taken up my abode here — to live my remaining years, and — here to die. From my bedroom, and from my very bed, I can see rising at the western horizon the church belonging to this parish. It points out my way to me, and reminds me also of the resting place of my nearest and among these are some of my dearest ones, and where I also have mine marked out. This house of A[r]sta is large, the rooms uncommonly spacious and high. Mine are in the upper story; there I live solitary and like to walk by myself, to think and read and write. How I thank God for this calm retreat for my old age. In my former days I looked upon A[r]sta as a kind of convent and could not bear its solitude, now I look upon it as a blessed harbor given me by the grace of God after a long and stormy voyage. The views from the windows are very extended over large and well-cultivated fields, bordered at the horizon by a garland of mountainous land dotted with dark fir woods. The sky expands as a vast cupola about and over the scene. I look over it, and my thoughts take wings and expand all the better for these fine prospects. [How] Often do they not carry me over the ocean and to your great New World, your glorious New World — so I must call it, though shadows dim its sunny light. . . .

––––––––

1. Published in New York *World*, March 28, 1878, p. 2.

Bibliography

I. *FREDRIKA BREMER MANUSCRIPTS AND DRAWINGS*
    IN THE UNITED STATES AND SWEDEN

United States

American Swedish Historical Museum, Philadelphia. F. Bremer Room.

Letters to:

1. Charles de Révérony de St. Cyr, Årsta, Sweden, March 3, 1847.
2. Unknown man, Årsta, Sweden, August 24, 1847. (Published by Marshall W. S. Swan, "Fredrika Bremer, Symbol and Self," *A Quarter Century of Progress.* Philadelphia: American Swedish Historical Foundation [1951], pp. 39-40.)
3. Lydia H. Sigourney, Newburgh, N. Y., October 18, 1849.
4. Marianne Silsbee, Boston, Mass., January 25, 1850.
5. Unknown man, Richmond, Va., June 18, 1851.
6. Miss McIntosh, Newburgh, N. Y., September 7, 1851.
7. Eliza Acton, Stockholm, May 11, 1852.
8. Henri Frédéric Amiel, Stockholm, March 28, 1864.
9. Mrs. Duncan, *s.l. et a.* (without place and year).
10. Marianne Silsbee, Stockholm, *s.a.* [1853?].
11. Fru Freder. Abrahams, *s.l. et a.*
12. Hans Christian Andersen, *s.l. et a.* [Copenhagen], April 23.

Notes to:

1. Rev. J. H. Hill, *s.l.* [Athens], August 11, 1859.
2. S. Arnold, *s.l. et a.* [Sweden].

Autographed sentiments:

1. *s.l. et a.*
2. *s.l. et a.*
3. Stockholm, February 18, 1864. (Published by Johanson and Kleman, *Fredrika Bremers Brev,* IV, p. 637, note to letter 1344.)

Boston Public Library.

Letters to:

1. [John S. Hart], New Orleans, La., December 30, 1850.
2. Joseph M. Field, Mobile, Ala., January 8, 1851.

One signature in autograph.

Harvard College Library.

Letters to:

1. [Vice-Consul Benzon], Cambridge, Mass., December 24, 1849. (Published by Johanson and Kleman, *op. cit.,* III, p. 191.)

2. Maria Lowell, *s.a.*, Boston, Mass., [January, 1850?].
3. Maria Lowell, *s.l. et a.*, [Boston, Mass., February, 1850?].
4. Maria Lowell, Boston, Mass., February 9, 1850.
5. James Freeman Clarke, *s.l.*, February 12, 1850.
6. Rebecca Spring, *s.l. et a.*, February 25 [1850?].
7. Maria Lowell, White House on the Pee Dee, S. C., April 21, 1850.
8. Maria Lowell, Washington, D. C., July 3, 1850 (incomplete).
9. James R. and Maria Lowell, Philadelphia, Pa., July 26, 1850 (incomplete).
10. Maria Lowell, Cincinnati, Ohio, December 12, 1850.
11. Maria Lowell, Gothenburg, Sweden, August 13, 1853.
12. Dr. and Mrs. David Osgood, Rome, January 26, 1858.
13. Mrs. Anna Hazard Barker Ward, Rome, April 7, 1858.
14. Mrs. Anna Hazard Barker Ward, Rome, May 3, 1858.

Notes to:

1. Mrs. Anna Clarke, *s.l. et a.*, [February, 1850?].
2. [Hurst & Blackett, publishers], *s.l. et a.*

One signature in autograph.

Historical Society of Pennsylvania.

Letters to:

1. [Lucas Siegmund] von Arnim, *s.l.* [Sweden], April 12, 1845.
2. I. K. Tefft, Niagara, N. Y., September 9, 1850.
3. Elizabeth Peabody, *s.l. et a.* [1851].
4. Anna Maria Hall, Stockholm, January 1, 1852.
5. Anna Maria Hall, Stockholm, February 14, 1853 (incomplete).
6. Anna Maria Hall, Stockholm, January 9, 1854.
7. Anna Maria Hall, Gotland, August 1, 1855 (incomplete).

Autographed sentiments:

1. Cincinnati, Ohio, December 4, 1850.
2. *S.l. et a.*

One signature in autograph.

Huntington Library.

Letters to Marcus and/or Rebecca Spring:

1. *S.l. et a.* [U. S. A., November, 1849?].
2. Boston, Mass., December 9, 1849.
3. Cambridge, Mass., December 21, 1849.
4. Concord, Mass., January 19, 1850.
5. Charleston, S. C., March 28, 1850.
6. White House on the Pee Dee, S. C., April 22, 1850.
7. Philadelphia, Pa., June 22, 1850.
8. Washington, D. C., July 13, 1850.
9. Niagara, N. Y., September 8, 1850.
10. Chicago, Ill., September 22, 1850.
11. Galena, Ill., October 28, 1850.

12. Crystal Springs near St. Louis, Mo., November 10, 1850.
13. Matanzas, Cuba, February 20, 1851.
14. Cafetal "La Industria," near Cárdenas, Cuba, April 9, 1851 (incomplete).
15. Charleston, S. C., June 5, 1851.
16. Philadelphia, Pa., July 16, 1851.
17. Salem, Mass., August 5, 1851.
18. Lenox, Mass., August 24, 1851.
19. Stockholm, March 20, 1852.
20. Stockholm, June 12, 1852.
21. Stockholm, January 12, 1853.
22. Stockholm, March 11, 1853.
23. Stockholm, November 28, 1853.
24. Stockholm, January 18, 1854.
25. Stockholm, July 7, 1854.
26. Stockholm, November 12, 1854.
27. Brussels, September 24, 1856.
28. Lausanne, December 23, 1856.
29. Athens, October 10, 1860.
30. Stockholm, April 1, 1862. (Published in New York *Daily Tribune,* May 1, 1862; also in Johanson and Kleman, *op. cit.,* IV, pp. 195-196.)
31. Stockholm, January 10, 1863.
32. *S.l. et a.* [Sweden, August, 1863] (incomplete).
33. Stockholm, November 26, 1863 (incomplete).
34. Stockholm, March 20, 1865.
35. Årsta, Sweden, September 8, 1865.

Letter "To my American friends," Stockholm, March 30, 1862. (Published in the New York *Daily Tribune,* May 1, 1862; also in Johanson and Kleman, *op. cit.,* IV, pp. 196-198.)

Iowa State Department of History and Archives, Des Moines.

Letter to N. C. Monroe, Charleston, S. C., June 10, 1851. (Presented by the wife of Captain J. McIntosh Kell, Chief Executive Officer of the Confederate War Steamship *Alabama.* Published by Johanson and Kleman, *op. cit.,* IV, pp. 545-546.)

Library of Congress.

Letter to Elizabeth Peabody, Washington, D. C., July 8, 1850. (Published by Johanson and Kleman, *op. cit.,* IV, pp. 542-543.)

Longfellow House, Cambridge, Mass.

Letters to Henry Wadsworth Longfellow:

1. Cambridge, Mass., December 24, 1849.
2. Boston, Mass., February 26, 1850. (Published in *Final Memorials of Henry W. Longfellow,* Boston, 1887, pp. 31-32.)
3. Niagara, N. Y., September 9, 1850.
4. Stockholm, May 15, 1856. (These four letters were quoted by H. W. L. Dana and M. Hawthorne in "The Maiden Aunt of the

Whole Human Race," *American-Scandinavian Review*, XXXVII, 1949, pp. 217-229.)

Massachusetts Historical Society.

One autographed sentiment.

One signature in autograph.

Minnesota Historical Society.

Letters to:

1. [Andrew Jackson Downing], Årsta, Sweden, October 28, 1846.
2. Miss Parsons, Cambridge, Mass., December 19, 1849.

New York Public Library.

Letters to:

1. I. K. Tefft, Savannah, Ga., May 17, 1850.
2. George Putnam, Stockholm, January, 1852.
3. James Hamilton, Stockholm, January 16, 1854.
4. Anna Maria Hall, Stockholm, November 18, 1861.

Note to Fröken Henriette Wulff, *s.l. et a.* (The note, in which the author expresses doubt as to being able to accept an invitation, may have been written in America because F. Bremer met H. Wulff in Boston, according to a letter by F. Bremer to H. C. Andersen, Johanson and Kleman, *op. cit.*, III, p. 232.)

Yale University Library.

Fifty letters to Andrew J. and/or Caroline Downing, dated from September 24, 1848 to February 8, 1856. (This collection has been edited and published by Adolph B. Benson, and therefore it is not included in the Appendix. See "Fredrika Bremer's Unpublished Letters to the Downings," *SSN*, XI, 1930-1931.)

Letter to Charles Kingsley, London, October 14, 1851.

Note to G. Virtue, Stockholm, March 8, 1859.

Poem to the singing ladies on board the *Canada*, in memory of the night of the 1 October, 1849.

One signature in autograph.

In possession of Signe A. Rooth.

Letters to:

1. Charlotte Cushman, New York, N. Y., October 31, 1849.
2. Lydia H. Sigourney, Cambridge, Mass., December 26, 1849.
3. Lewis R. Gibbes, Charleston, S. C., June 12, 1851.
4. Marianne Silsbee, *s.a.*, Nahant, Mass., [1851].
5. Charles Kingsley, London, November 1, 1851. (Published in *The Works of Charles Kingsley*, Philadelphia, 1899, VII, pp. 301-302; also in Johanson and Kleman, *op. cit.*, III, p. 213.)
6. [Charles Kingsley], Stockholm, September 8, 1853.
7. Madame Alexandre Vinet, Jargonnant (near Geneva), Switzerland, August 31, 1857.
8. Anna Maria Hall, Rome, April, 1858.

Three autographed sentiments.

Sweden

Fredrika-Bremer-Förbundet, Stockholm.

Fourteen letters to Anne and Justina Howland, dated from May 2, 1850 to September 23, 1856. (The collection was presented by Miss Frances M. Howland of Duxbury, Mass., granddaughter of Anne Howland. Excerpts from these letters were translated into Swedish and published by Ellen Kleman: "Fredrika Bremers Charlestonvänner," *Hertha,* Vol. 24, 1937.)

Letter to George Putnam, Stockholm, April, 1855.

Sketchbook containing 61 pages of Bremer drawings from Denmark and America.

The Royal Library, Stockholm.

Notebooks and manuscripts: Ehnemark Collection, *Utkast, excerpter, anteckningar,* Vf 55, Vf 56; Täckhammar Collection, 15 letters from F. Bremer to Per Böklin (1833-1846) and 103 letters or fragments from Böklin to F. Bremer (1832-1865), Ep. B 13a.

University of Uppsala, Carolina Rediviva Library.

Sketchbook containing 42 pages of Bremer drawings from America and Cuba.

II.   BOOKS BY AND ON FREDRIKA BREMER

Adlersparre, S. L—d, and Leijonhufvud, Sigrid. *Fredrika Bremer: Biografisk Studie.* 2 vols. Stockholm [1896].

Aho, Juhani. *En idéernas man: Biografi öfver August Fredrik Soldan.* Helsingfors, 1901. Pp. 230-232.

Axberger, Gunnar. *Jaget och skuggorna: Fredrika Bremer-studier.* Stockholm [1951].

Benson, Adolph B. (ed.). *America of the Fifties: Letters of Fredrika Bremer.* New York, 1924.

Botta, Anne Charlotte Lynch. *Hand-book of Universal Literature.* Boston, 1875. Pp. 402-403.

——————. *Memoirs of Anne C. L. Botta.* New York, 1894. Pp. 7-8, 176-177, 323-328.

[Botta], Anne Charlotte Lynch. *Poems.* New York, 1849. Pp. 54-55.

Bremer, Charlotte (ed.). *Life, Letters, and Posthumous Works of Fredrika Bremer.* Translated by Fredr. Milow. New York, 1868.

Bremer, Fredrika. *The Bondmaid.* Translated from the Swedish by M. L. Putnam. Boston, 1844.

——————. *Brothers and Sisters: A Tale of Domestic Life.* Translated by Mary Howitt. New York, 1848.

——————. *England om hösten år 1851.* Edited by Klara Johanson. Stockholm [1922].

——————. *Hemmen i den nya verlden.* 3 vols. Stockholm, 1853-1854.

——————. *Hemmen i nya verlden.* Stockholm, 1866.

——————. *Hertha.* Translated by Mary Howitt. London, 1856.

————. *The H— Family; Trälinnan; Axel and Anna.* Translated by Mary Howitt. New York, 1844.

————. *The Home.* Translated by Mary Howitt. New York, 1843.

————. *Homes of the New World: Impressions of America.* 2 vols. Translated by Mary Howitt. New York, 1854.

————. *Morning Watches: a Few Words on Strauss and the Gospels.* From the Swedish. Boston, 1843.

————. *The Neighbors.* Translated by Mary Howitt. New York, 1850.

————. *New Sketches of Every-day Life: A Diary; Strife and Peace.* Translated by Mary Howitt. New York, 1844.

————. *The President's Daughters.* Translated by Mary Howitt. New York, 1843.

Böök, Fredrik, and Sylwan, Otto. *Svenska litteraturens historia.* Vol. II. Stockholm, 1919. Pp. 458-466.

Carlson, Alfred Martin. "Fredrika Bremer as the Originator of the Swedish Novel." Unpublished Master's thesis, University of Minnesota, 1927. 71 pages.

Cederblad, Carin. *Fredrika Bremer.* [Stockholm, 1945.]

Child, Lydia Maria. *Letters of Lydia Maria Child.* A Biographical Introduction by John G. Whittier. Boston, 1883. Pp. 65-67.

Cortambert, Richard. *Les Illustres Voyageuses.* Paris, 1866. Pp. 127-161.

Cross, John W. *George Eliot's Life.* Vol. I. New York and London, 1903. Pp. 186-191 *passim.*

Downing, Andrew J. *Rural Essays.* Edited, with a Memoir of the Author, by George W. Curtis; and A Letter to His Friends, by Frederika Bremer. New York, 1853.

Duyckinck, Evert A. *Portrait Gallery of Eminent Men and Women.* Vol. II. New York, 1873. Pp. 145-149.

Ehnmark, Elof. *Fredrika Bremer.* Stockholm [1955].

Ek, Sverker. *Fredrika Bremer.* "Studentföreningen Verdandis småskrifter," No. 188. Stockholm, 1912.

————. *Svenskt Biografiskt Lexikon.* Vol. VI. Stockholm, 1926. Pp. 182-196.

Elovson, Harald. *Amerika i svensk litteratur 1750-1820.* Lund, 1930.

Emerson, Ralph Waldo. *The Letters of Ralph Waldo Emerson.* Edited by Ralph L. Rusk. Vols. III and IV. New York: Columbia University Press, 1939. Vol. III, pp. 147, 195, 341; Vol. IV, pp. 176-177, 184.

Emerson, Sarah Hopper (ed.). *Life of Abby Hopper Gibbons.* New York, 1897. Vol. I, pp. 198, 230-232; Vol. II, p. 334.

Fiske, Willard. *Memorials of Willard Fiske.* Collected by Horatio S. White. Vol. II. Boston [1920]. Pp. 81-82.

Flodman, Anders. *Kritiska studier.* Stockholm, 1872. Pp. 39-73.

Fredén, Gustaf. *Arvet från Fredrika Bremer: En bild av Fredrika Bremer sammanställd ur hennes skrifter.* Lund [1951].

Fredrika-Bremer-Förbundet. *I Fredrika Bremers spår, 1884-1944.* [Stockholm, 1944.]

Garnett, Richard. *Life of Ralph Waldo Emerson.* "Great Writers Series"; London, 1888. Pp. 160-161.

Gilchrist, Herbert H. (ed.). *Anne Gilchrist: Her Life and Writings.* London, 1887. Pp. 233-234.

Grimberg, Carl. *Svenska folkets underbara öden.* Stockholm [1925]. Vol. IX, pp. 55-89.

Hale, Edward E., Jr. *Life and Letters of Edward Everett Hale.* Boston, 1917. Vol. I, p. 218.

Hale, Sarah J. *Woman's Record; or, Sketches of all Distinguished Women.* New York, 1870. Pp. 586-592.

Hall, S. C. *A Book of Memories of Great Men and Women of the Age, from Personal Acquaintance.* London, 1871. Pp. 411-415.

Hamilton, Catherine J. *Women Writers: Their Works and Ways.* 2d series. London, 1893. Pp. 44-71.

Hawthorne, Nathaniel. *Passages from the French and Italian Note-Books of Nathaniel Hawthorne.* Boston, 1883. Pp. 171-172; 212-216.

Hierta-Retzius, Anna (ed.). *Tvenne efterlämnade skrifter jämte några bref af Fredrika Bremer.* Stockholm [1902].

Hilen, Andrew. *Longfellow and Scandinavia: A Study of the Poet's Relationship with the Northern Languages and Literature.* New Haven: Yale University Press, 1947.

Hokanson, Nels. *Swedish Immigrants in Lincoln's Time.* New York and London [1942]. Pp. 7, 9, 12, 55.

Holmgren, Ann Margret. *Om kvinnosakspionjären Fredrika Bremer.* "Studentföreningen Verdandis småskrifter," No. 260. Stockholm [1922].

Howitt, Margaret (ed.). *Mary Howitt: An Autobiography.* 2 vols. London, 1889.

Howitt, Margaret. *Twelve Months with Fredrika Bremer in Sweden.* 2 vols. London, 1866.

Hunt, Harriot K. *Glances and Glimpses.* Boston, 1856.

Johanson, Klara (ed.). *Det unga Amerika: Skildringar av Fredrika Bremer sammanställda och kommenterade av Klara Johanson.* Stockholm [1927].

Johanson, Klara, and Kleman, Ellen (eds.). *Fredrika Bremers Brev.* 4 vols. Stockholm [1915-1920].

Kastman, Carl. *Fredrika Bremer: Hennes lefnad berättad för svenska folket.* Stockholm [1908].

Kjellén, Alf. *Sociala idéer och motiv hos svenska författare.* Vol. I. Stockholm, 1937. Pp. 133-170.

Kleman, Ellen. *Fredrika Bremer.* "Svenska Kvinnor III"; Uppsala [1925].

Kleman, Ellen (ed.). *Fredrika Bremer i brev: ett urval redigerat av Ellen Kleman.* "Fredrika-Bremer-Förbundets skriftserie," No. 9. Stockholm [1944].

Lagerlöf, Selma. "Mamsell Fredrika," *Osynliga länkar: berättelser.* Stockholm, 1925. Pp. 187-200.

Lee, Amice. *Laurels and Rosemary: The Life of William and Mary Howitt.* London, 1955. Pp. 136, 144, 154-155, 196.

Le Vert, Octavia W. *Souvenirs of Travel.* 2 vols. New York, 1857. Vol. I, pp. viii, 69; Vol. II, pp. 276, 336-337, 344.

Longfellow, Samuel (ed.). *Final Memorials of Henry Wadsworth Longfellow.* Boston, 1887. Pp. 31-32.

————. *Life of Henry Wadsworth Longfellow.* Vol. II. Boston, 1886. Pp. 10-11, 152-153, 160-161, 199.

Lowell, James Russell. *Letters of James Russell Lowell.* Edited by Charles Eliot Norton. Vol. I. New York, 1894. Pp. 168, 174.

Marshall, Helen E. *Dorothea Dix, Forgotten Samaritan.* Chapel Hill: University of N. Carolina Press, 1937. Pp. 142-146.

Nordström-Bonnier, Tora. *Resa kring en resa: I Fredrika Bremers fotspår.* Stockholm, 1950.

Oterdahl, Jeanna. *Hon älskade människorna — Fredrika Bremer.* Stockholm [1950].

Oterdahl, Jeanna (ed.). *Levande Låga: Ur Fredrika Bremers brev och skrifter.* Uppsala [1951].

Putnam, George Haven. *George Palmer Putnam: A Memoir.* New York and London, 1912. Pp. 112, 144 ff., 400 f., 407 f.

Sanborn, Franklin B., and Harris, William T. *A. Bronson Alcott: His Life and Philosophy.* Vol. II. Boston, 1893.

Schück, Henrik, and Warburg, Karl. *Illustrerad Svensk Litteraturhistoria.* Vol. VI. Stockholm [1930]. Pp. 165-215.

Sedgwick, Catharine M. *Clarence: or, A Tale of Our Own Times.* Preface to the New Edition. New York, 1849.

————. *Life and Letters of Catharine M. Sedgwick.* Edited by Mary E. Dewey. New York, 1872. Pp. 315-318.

Smith, G. Barnett. *Women of Renown.* London, 1893. Pp. 1-41.

Stevens, John H. *Personal Recollections of Minnesota and Its People.* Minneapolis, 1890. Pp. 31, 90.

Thomas, William Widgery, Jr. *Sweden and the Swedes.* Chicago and New York, 1892. Pp. 359-365.

Tiffany, Francis. *Life of Dorothea Lynde Dix.* Boston and New York, 1890. Pp. 161-165.

Tigerstedt, E. N. *Svensk litteraturhistoria.* Stockholm, 1948. Pp. 336-337, 546.

Unonius, Gustaf. *A Pioneer in Northwest America, 1841-1858: The Memoirs of Gustaf Unonius.* Translated from the Swedish by Jonas O. Backlund, Edited by Nils W. Olsson. Vol. I. Minneapolis: University of Minnesota Press [1950]. Pp. 311-313.

Wade, Mason (ed.). *The Writings of Margaret Fuller.* New York, 1941. Pp. 587, 590.

Wahlström, Lydia. *Svenskar från förra seklet: Biografiska studier.* Vol. II. Stockholm, 1915. Pp. 53-174.

Whittier, John G. *The Chapel of the Hermits, and Other Poems.* Boston, 1853. Pp. 73-74, 117-118.

Willis, Nathaniel Parker. *Hurry-Graphs; or, Sketches of Scenery, Celebrities and Society, Taken from Life.* New Orleans, 1854. P. 223.

Wägner, Elin. *Fredrika Bremer.* "Svenska Akademiens Minnesteckningar." [Stockholm, 1949.]

III. *PERIODICALS, PAMPHLETS, AND ESSAYS*

American Phrenological Journal (New York). "Frederika Bremer," XLIII (March, 1866), p. 78.

American-Scandinavian Review (New York). "A Meeting in Havana" by Adolph B. Benson, V (November-December, 1917), pp. 351-356.

————. "The Maiden Aunt of the Whole Human Race" by Henry Wadsworth Longfellow Dana and Manning Hawthorne, XXXVII (September, 1949), pp. 217-229.

American Swedish Monthly (New York). "Fredrika Bremer Here a Hundred Years Ago" by Signe A. Rooth, XLIV (September, 1950), pp. 13, 25, 29.

A Quarter Century of Progress, 1926-1951. "Fredrika Bremer, Symbol and Self" by Marshall W. S. Swan, pp. 31-40. Philadelphia: American Swedish Historical Foundation.

Athenaeum (London). "Review of *The Homes of the New World,*" No. 1353 (October 1, 1853), pp. 1153-1154, 1557-1558.

Autograph Collectors' Journal (New York). "Fredrika Bremer" by Signe A. Rooth, V (Spring, 1953), pp. 54-55.

Blätter für literarische Unterhaltung (Leipzig). *Die Heimat in der Neuen Welt,* No. 10 (March, 1854), pp. 182-183; No. 30 (July, 1855), pp. 552-553.

Bulletin of the American Swedish Institute (Minneapolis). "Mamsell Fredrika" by Selma Lagerlöf, V (March, 1950), pp. 3-9; "Letters from Fredrika Bremer" by Ernestine King, pp. 10-12; "Fredrika Bremer — Trail Blazer" by Hanna Rydh, pp. 13-18, 32.

————. "Fredrika Bremer's Dalecarlia" by William Mulder, X (Summer, 1955), pp. 13-17.

Charleston One Hundred Years Ago; Being Extracts from the Letters of Fredrika Bremer. Charleston, 1951. 21 pages.

Christian Examiner (Boston). "Novels of Frederika Bremer" by [Mrs.] L. J. H[all], XXXIV (July, 1843), pp. 381-394.

————. "Frederika Bremer's Theology" by S. O[sgood], XXXVI (January, 1844), pp. 98-103.

————. "Miss Bremer's Novels" by H. J. B[urton], XXXVIII (March, 1845), pp. 169-178.

————. "Notices of Recent Publications: *The Homes of the New World*" [by G. E. Ellis], LV (November, 1853), p. 479.

Christian Remembrancer (London). "Miss Bremer's Novels," XVII (January, 1849), pp. 18-62.

Dial: A Magazine for Literature, Philosophy, and Religion (Boston). "Record of the Months," III (April, 1843), p. 532; IV (July, 1843), p. 135.

Edda: Nordisk Tidsskrift for Litteraturforskning (Oslo). "Fredrika Bremer as a Critic of American Literature" by Lawrence Thompson, XLI (1941), pp. 166-176.

Every Saturday (Boston). "Hawthorne and Fredrika Bremer," III (September 30, 1871), p. 323.

Fleissner, E. M. "The Swedish Angle on America." Unpublished six-page essay submitted in Swedish American Line Essay Contest, 1948.

Fortnightly Review (New York). "Mamsell Fredrika" by Angela Thirkell (new series), CXXVI (August, 1929), pp. 217-229.

Fredrika Bremer and America. [By Ellen Kleman.] Stockholm, 1938. 16 pages.

Gleason's Pictorial Drawing-Room Companion (Boston). Picture of "Frederika Bremer, the Swedish Authoress," II (January 24, 1852), p. 53.

Godey's Lady's Book (Philadelphia). "Fredrika Bremer" by Mary Howitt, XXXIX (October, 1849), pp. 289-290.

————. "Miss Bremer's Visit to Cooper's Landing" by "One Who Was There," XL (February, 1850), pp. 125-130.

Graham's Magazine (Philadelphia). "Review of *The Neighbors*," XXII (June, 1843), p. 367.

————. "Review of New Books: *The Homes of the New World*," XLIII (December, 1853), pp. 645-647.

Hakstad, Sigrid T. "Bibliographical History of Fredrika Bremer's *America of the Fifties*." Unpublished paper compiled at the Chicago Public Library, 1934. 16 pages. (Uncatalogued.)

Harper's New Monthly Magazine (New York). "Jenny Lind" by F. Bremer, I (October, 1850), pp. 657-658.

————. "Impressions of England in 1851. From the Letters and Memoranda of F. Bremer," IV (April, 1852), pp. 616-620.

————. "Literary Notices: *Homes of the New World*," VII (November, 1853), pp. 857, 860.

————. "Editor's Easy Chair," VIII (December, 1853), pp. 130-131.

————. "A Reminiscence of a Foreign Celebrity's Reception Morning" [by C. M. Sedgwick], XIV (April, 1857), pp. 655-658.

————. "Our Foreign Bureau," XXII (February, 1861), p. 419.

Harper's Weekly (New York). "Fredrika Bremer," X (March 10, 1866), p. 156.

Hertha (Stockholm)."Fredrika Bremers Charlestonvänner" by Ellen Kleman, Vol. 24 (January, 1937), pp. 2, 5-8; (February, 1937), pp. 33-36; (March, 1937), pp. 61-64.

————. "En glimt av Fredrika Bremer i U. S. A." by Hanna Rydh, Vol. 26 (May, 1939), pp. 135-137.

————. "I Fredrika Bremers spår genom Amerika" by Gunhild Tegen: I "I Philadelphia och Washington," Vol. 28 (June-July, 1941), pp. 137-138; II "I Södern" (October, 1941), pp. 196-197; III "Bland Nya Englands poeter," pp. 222-223.

————. "Fredrika Bremer's 'Campaign' in America" by Signe Henschen, Vol. 37 (1950), pp. 18-19, 31.

Hours at Home (New York). "A Visit to and a Visit from Fredrika Bremer" by M. S. De Vere, VI (December, 1867), pp. 148-154.

House & Garden (Greenwich, Conn.). "In the Days of Downing" by Richard H. Pratt, LII (December, 1927), pp. 102-103, 134, 136. (Picture of F. Bremer, p. 134.)

Journal of English and Germanic Philology (Urbana, Ill.). "English Influences in Fredrika Bremer" by Alrik T. Gustafson, XXX (April, 1931), pp. 223-235; XXXI (January, 1932), pp. 92-123; XXXII (July, 1933), pp. 373-391.

————. "Walt Whitman's Interest in Swedish Writers" by Adolph B. Benson, XXXI (July, 1932), pp. 332-345.

Literary World (New York). "Miss Bremer's *Homes of the New World*," XIII (October 22, 1853), pp. 196-197; "Miss Bremer's *Homes of the New World*. Second Notice," XIII (October 29, 1853), pp. 211-212.

Littell's Living Age (Boston). "Miss Frederika Bremer" by G. W. Lay, III (November 2, 1844), pp. 52-55.

————. "Miss Bremer's Novels," XX (March 24, 1849), pp. 529-550.

————. "Fredrika Bremer" by Mary Howitt, XXIII (October 20, 1849), pp. 129-130.

————. "Review of F. Bremer's *Summer Journey*," XXIII (December 8, 1849), pp. 472-475.

————. "Whittier's Poem 'To Frederika Bremer,'" XXIII (December 15, 1849), p. 518.

————. "Miss Bremer's *Homes of the New World*," XXXIX (October 22, 1853), pp. 217-223.

————. "Fredrika Bremer," XXXII (March 24, 1866), p. 864.

————. "Fredrika Bremer and Her Swedish Sisters," II (August 4, 1866), pp. 259-270.

Michigan History (Lansing). "Fredrika Bremer's Visit to Michigan" by Adrian Jaffe, XXXVII (June, 1953), pp. 152-154.

Minnesota Historical Society. Collections (St. Paul, 1915). "A Sheaf of Remembrances" by Rebecca M. Cathcart, XV (1909-1914), pp. 515-552.

Minnesota History (St. Paul). "Fredrika Bremer: Traveler and Prophet" by John T. Flanagan, XX (June, 1939), pp. 129-139.

————. "Governor Ramsey and Frontier Minnesota: Impressions from His Diary and Letters" by Marion Ramsey Furness, XXVIII (December, 1947), pp. 309-328.

————. "Fredrika Bremer's New Scandinavia: Minnesota in 1850," XXXI (September, 1950), pp. 148-157.

————. "In Fredrika Bremer's Footsteps" translated by Elsa R. Nordin, XXXII (June, 1951), pp. 106-108.

Monthly Religious Magazine (Boston). "Fredrika Bremer" by Crito, XXXV (March, 1866), pp. 187-194.

Nordisk Tidskrift för Bok- och Biblioteksväsen (Uppsala and Stockholm). "Nya Fredrika Bremer-papper i Kungl. Biblioteket" by O. H. Wieselgren, Vol. 4 (1917), pp. 12-18.

Nordisk Tidskrift för Vetenskap, Konst och Industri (Stockholm). "Fredrika Bremer i sina bref" by O. H. Wieselgren, VIII (1916), pp. 465-480.

North American Review (Boston). "Critical Notices: *The Neighbours; a Story of Every-day Life*" [by G. S. Hillard], LVI (April, 1843), pp. 497-503.

————. "Miss Bremer's Novels" [by W. B. O. Peabody], LVII (July, 1843), pp. 128-149.

————. "New Translations of the Writings of Miss Bremer" [by J. R. Lowell], LVIII (April, 1844), pp. 480-508.

Norton's Literary Gazette and Publishers' Circular (New York). "Miss Bremer's New Work," III (October 15, 1853), p. 176.

Ord och Bild (Stockholm). "Några Fredrika Bremer-skisser från Amerika" by Gunnar Svanfeldt, Vol. 52 (1943), pp. 161-170.

Panoramas de Antaño: San Antonio de los Baños en el siglo XIX (Havana). "Fredrika Bremers," by Drs. Julián Vivanco, Francisco Pérez de la Riva, Rodolfo Tro Pérez, and Rosario de Cárdenas de Pérez de la Riva (1951), pp. 38-45.

Philadelphia Forum Magazine. "An Historical School and an Historical Occasion" by Harvey M. Watts, XVIII (October, 1938), pp. 15-16, 24.

Pioneer (Boston). "Literary Notices: *The Neighbors*," I (March, 1843), pp. 141-142.

Prärieblomman (Rock Island, Ill.). "Fredrika Bremer och Jenny Lind i Förenta Staterna" by Gust. N. Swan, IV (1904), pp. 165-198.

Publications of the Modern Language Association of America (Menasha, Wis.). "The Essays on Fredrika Bremer in the *North American Review*" by Adolph B. Benson, XLI (September, 1926), pp. 747-755.

Putnam's Monthly Magazine (New York). "Editorial Notes: Frederika Bremer's *Homes of the New World*," II (November, 1853), p. 567; "Miss Bremer's *Homes of the New World*" (December, 1853), pp. 668-672.

Revista de la Biblioteca Nacional (Havana). "El Centenario de la Visita de Fredrika Bremer a Cuba" by Signe A. Rooth, II (April-June, 1951), pp. 35-70.

Revue des deux mondes (Paris). "Revue Littéraire Américaine" by Émile Montégut (second series), IV (October, 1853), pp. 399-403.

Samlaren (Uppsala). "Fredrika Bremers *Syskonlif*" by Alf Kjellén, Vol. 27 (1946), pp. 31-51.

Sartain's Union Magazine of Literature and Art (Philadelphia). "Christmas Eve and Christmas Matins" by F. Bremer, translated from the Original Manuscript by Mary Howitt, IV (February, 1849), pp. 143-147.

————. "The She-Eagle" by F. Bremer, translated from the Original Manuscript by Mary Howitt, IV (March, 1849), p. 166.

————. "Leaves from the Banks of the Rhine; or, Marienberg and Kaisersworth" by F. Bremer, translated by Clara Hardinge, IV (May, 1849), pp. 289-294; V (July, 1849), pp. 1-4; V (November, 1849), pp. 261-267.

————. "To Frederika Bremer" by Sarah H. Browne, V (December, 1849), pp. 325-326; Editorial, p. 386.

————. "Life in the North" by F. Bremer, translated by Mary Howitt, VI (February, 1850), pp. 157-164; (May, 1850), pp. 329-336. Book Notices: *The Neighbours*, p. 175. "A Card from Miss Bremer," p. 176.

————. "Jenny Lind" by F. Bremer, VI (June, 1850), pp. 409-410.

————. "The Man and the Rose," poem by F. Bremer, VII (July, 1850), p. 27.

————. "Fredrika Bremer" by Anne C. Lynch, VII (September, 1850), pp. 169-173.

————. "A Tribute to the Memory of General Taylor" by F. Bremer, VII (September, 1850), p. 184.

————. "Northern Loves and Legends" by F. Bremer, VIII (January, 1851), pp. 49-51; (February), pp. 89-92; (March), pp. 165-167; (April), pp. 241-244.

————. "Greeting to America," poem by F. Bremer, VIII (February, 1851), p. 117.

————. "A California for Women; Better Than Silver and Gold" by F. Bremer, IX (October, 1851), pp. 309-310.

————. "Editorial: Miss Bremer," IX (December, 1851), pp. 496-497.

Scandinavian Studies and Notes (Menasha, Wis.). "American Ideals among Women Writers of Sweden" by Adolph B. Benson, V (February, 1919), pp. 157-168.

————. "American Appreciation of Fredrika Bremer" by Adolph B. Benson, VIII (February, 1924), pp. 14-33.

————. "Fredrika Bremer's Unpublished Letters to the Downings" by Adolph B. Benson, XI (February, 1930), pp. 1-10; (May, 1930), pp. 39-53; (August, 1930), pp. 71-78; (November, 1930), pp. 109-124; (February, 1931), pp. 149-172; (May, 1931), pp. 187-205; (August, 1931), pp. 215-228; (November, 1931), pp. 264-274.

————. "Another Unpublished Bremer Letter to the Downings" by Adolph B. Benson, XII (May, 1933), pp. 40-42.

Spirit of the Age (New York). "Miss Fredrika Bremer," I (October 13, 1849), p. 239; "Miss Frederika Bremer," I (November 10, 1849), pp. 294-295; I (November 24, 1849), p. 334.

Svenska Kulturförbundets Kvartalsskrift (Chicago). "En svenska på besök i Mellanvästern för 100 år sedan" by Gösta Franzen, Vol. 3 (Spring, 1948), pp. 5-6.

Swedish-American Historical Bulletin (St. Peter, Minn.). "Fredrika Bremer's Predecessors" by Roy W. Swanson, I (March, 1928), pp. 53-62.

Swedish Pioneer Historical Quarterly (Rock Island, Ill.). "Unpublished Fredrika Bremer Manuscripts in Stockholm" by Signe A. Rooth, I (October, 1950), pp. 9-12.

——————. "Fredrika Bremer's Impressions of America" by Signe A. Rooth, I (Spring, 1951), pp. 5-16.

——————. "Fredrika Bremer and Ralph Waldo Emerson" by Karl A. Olsson, II (Autumn, 1951), pp. 39-52.

——————. "Something About My Writings" by F. Bremer, translated by Paul Elmen, VI (July, 1955), pp. 71-76.

UNESCO World Review. "Women's Rights in Scandinavia — The Story of Frederika Bremer" (December 8, 1951), pp. 9-11.

Ungdomsvännen (Rock Island, Ill.). "Små hågkomster af Fredrika Bremer" by Mosa [Mrs. Louise Johnson], XX (February, 1915), pp. 48-49.

Universalist Quarterly and General Review (Boston). "Frederica Bremer" by L. M. B., II, Article XV (April, 1845), pp. 168-175.

Victoria Magazine (London). "Frederika Bremer in the United States and Cuba" by P. F. Andre, VII (May, 1866), pp. 1-11; VII (June, 1866), pp. 97-116.

Wisconsin Magazine of History (Menasha, Wis.). "The Swedish Settlement on Pine Lake" by Mabel V. Hansen, VIII (September, 1924), pp. 38-51.

——————. "The Origins of Milwaukee College" by Louise Phelps Kellogg, IX (July, 1926), pp. 386-408.

Yale Review (New Haven, Conn.). "Four Scandinavian Feminists" by Hanna Astrup Larsen, V (January, 1916), pp. 347-362.

IV. NEWSPAPERS

Albany *Daily State Register.* September 3, 1850.

Albany *Evening Atlas.* September 5, 1850.

Albany *Evening Journal.* September 3, 7, 17, 1850.

Augusta (Ga.) *Daily Chronicle & Sentinel.* May 21, 1850.

Baltimore *Sun.* June 27, July 4, 8, 26, 29, 1850.

Boston *Daily Bee.* October 6, 8, November 6, 9, 27, December 1, 4, 7, 13, 21, 31, 1849; January 9, 22, 25, 28, February 1, 11, 12, 13, 18, 20, March 6, 13, 18, 1850.

Boston *Daily Evening Transcript.* October 5, 8, 16, 19, November 27, December 3, 4, 11, 1849; January 3, 24, February 9, 16, March 22, 1850.

Boston *Daily Evening Traveller.* October 15, 1849.

Boston *Liberator.* March 1, September 6, October 18, 1850.

Brooklyn *Daily Eagle.* April 9, August 17, 18, 29, September 8, 1846.

Brooklyn *Evening Star.* October 5, 8, December 14, 1849.

Burritt's Christian Citizen (Worcester, Mass.). December 1, 8, 1849.

Cambridge *Chronicle.* October 11, December 27, 1849.

Charleston *Courier.* June 11, 1850; May 12, 1851.

Chicago *Daily Democrat.* September 24, 1850.

Chicago *Daily Democratic Press.* January 30, 1855.

Chicago *Daily Journal.* September 9, 16, 17, 23, 25, 26, October 5, 1850.

Chicago *Weekly Journal.* July 29, 1850.

Chicago *Western Citizen.* August 27, October 22, 1850.

Cleveland *Daily True Democrat.* April 4, 1849; May 22, August 29, 1850; June 18, 1851.

Cleveland *Herald.* May 19, July 1, July 13, August 24, 1843; December 31, 1845.

Columbia *Tri-Weekly South Carolinian.* May 28, 1850.

Cummings' Evening Telegraphic Bulletin (Philadelphia). June 18, 19, August 5, 1851.

Daily Cincinnati Gazette. November 20, 21, 26, December 2, 11, 16, 1850.

Davenport (Iowa) *Gazette.* September 25, October 10, 17, November 7, 21, 1850.

Galena (Ill.) *Weekly North-Western Gazette.* October 1, 8, 15, November 5, 12, 1850.

Hartford *Connecticut Courant.* February 23, September 14, 1850.

Hartford *Daily Courant.* September 17, 1851.

Jacksonville *Florida Republican.* May 22, 29, 1851.

Madison *Wisconsin Argus.* October 1, 8, 22, 1850.

Madison *Wisconsin Democrat.* October 5, 12, 1850.

Madison *Wisconsin Express.* October 3, 1850.

Madison *Wisconsin Statesman.* September 12, October 1, 8, 22, 1850.

Middlesex Standard (Lowell, Mass.). August 1, 1844.

Milwaukee *Daily Free Democrat.* September 18, 20, 26, 27, October 12, 17, 1850.

Milwaukee *Daily Sentinel and Gazette.* September 26, 28, 1850.

Minneapolis *Tribune.* August 20, 1945.

Mobile *Daily Advertiser.* January 8, 1851.

Newark *Daily Advertiser.* August 26, 1846; October 5, 6, 9, 13, 31, November 19, 26, 28, December 4, 12, 22, 1849.

Newburgh *Highland Courier.* October 6, December 1, 1849.

New Orleans *Daily Picayune.* December 25, 26, 1850; January 9, 16, 1851.

New Orleans *Weekly Delta.* January 6, 20, 27, 1851.

New York *Albion.* October 6, December 1, 1849; September 13, 1851.

New York *Brother Jonathan.* July 4, 1851.

New York *Commercial Advertiser.* October 1, 1844; September 13, 1851.

New York *Daily Tribune.* October 21, 1853; May 1, 1862; January 26, February 5, 1866.

New York *Herald.* October 5, 7, 18, December 4, 6, 1849; September 12, 1851.

New York *Morning Express.* September 13, 15, 1851.

New York *Observer.* October 13, December 1, 22, 1849.

New York *Semi-Weekly Express.* October 9, November 6, 30, 1849.

New York *Times Book Review.* November 23, 1924.

New York *Weekly Evening Post.* October 4, 11, December 6, 1849.

New York *Weekly Tribune.* October 13, November 24, 1849.

New York *World.* March 28, 1878.

North American and U. S. Gazette (Philadelphia). July 19, 1850.

Oneida Morning Herald (Utica, N. Y.). September 11, 1850.
Philadelphia *Public Ledger and Daily Transcript.* June 19, 20, 1850.
Providence *Republican Herald.* October 10, 1849.
Richmond *Enquirer.* June 17, 1851.
Rochester *Daily American.* September 7, 9, 14, 1850.
St. Louis *Daily Missouri Republican.* November 6, 1850.
St. Louis *Intelligencer.* November 6, 1850.
St. Paul *Minnesota Chronicle and Register.* October 21, 28, November 4, 1850.
St. Paul *Minnesota Pioneer.* October 17, 24, 1850.
Savannah *Daily Republican.* May 1, 11, 15, 1850; May 12, 1851.
Springfield (Mass.) *Daily Republican.* September 15, 1851.
The Times (London). December 23, 26, 1853; January 24, August 28, 1854;
　　　January 10, 1866.
Washington *Daily National Intelligencer.* July 4, 16, 1850; October 26, 1853;
　　　January 10, 1854.
Washington *National Era.* November 15, 1849; September 26, 1850.
Washington *Republic.* July 1, 1850.
Washington *Southern Press.* June 29, 1850.
Worcester *Massachusetts Spy.* October 24, November 7, December 5, 12, 1849.

Notes

Preface

1. By Adolph B. Benson, Henry Wadsworth Longfellow Dana, John T. Flanagan, Gösta Franzen, Karl A. Olsson, Gust. N. Swan, Marshall W. S. Swan, Roy W. Swanson, and Lawrence Thompson, among others; see bibliography of periodicals. In 1938, in connection with the Delaware Tercentenary, a pamphlet entitled *Fredrika Bremer and America* by Ellen Kleman was published in Sweden.

2. Among them, Adlersparre and Leijonhufvud, *Fredrika Bremer,* II, pp. 108-150; Carin Cederblad, *Fredrika Bremer,* pp. 115-127; Ann Margret Holmgren, *Om kvinnosakspionjären Fredrika Bremer,* pp. 72-83; Ellen Kleman, *Fredrika Bremer,* pp. 186-209. A condensation, with notes, of *Hemmen i den nya verlden* was made by Klara Johanson: *Det unga Amerika* (1927).

3. Adolph B. Benson published YUL's collection of letters by F. Bremer to the Downings in *SSN,* XI (1930-31).

Chapter I

1. F. Bremer letter to Downing, Årsta, October 28, 1846; in Minnesota Historical Society.

2. Klara Johanson and Ellen Kleman (eds.), *Fredrika Bremers Brev* (Stockholm [1915-1920]), II, p. 364.

3. *Ibid.,* II, p. 371.

4. Samuel Longfellow (ed.), *Life of Henry Wadsworth Longfellow* (Boston, 1886), II, pp. 10-11.

5. F. Bremer, *New Sketches of Every-day Life: A Diary* (New York, 1844), p. viii.

6. Cleveland *Herald,* December 31, 1845, p. 3.

7. Anna Hierta-Retzius (ed). *Tvenne efterlämnade skrifter jämte några bref af Fredrika Bremer* (Stockholm [1902]), p. 32.

8. Johanson and Kleman, *op. cit.,* II, p. 478.

9. *Memoirs of Anne C. L. Botta* (New York, 1894), p. 324.

10. This book is now in *Högre lärarinneseminariet* (Teachers College for Women), Stockholm.

11. F. Bremer note (place and date not given), to S. Arnold; in ASHM. The original is in Swedish; it is accompanied by this translation, also a note dated Stockholm, June 13, 1847, by S. G. Arnold.

12. F. Bremer letter to Downing, Stockholm, September 24, 1848; in YUL. This letter has been ed. (and normalized) by Adolph B. Benson, "Fredrika Bremer's Unpublished Letters to the Downings," SSN, XI (1930), pp. 5-6.

13. Charlotte Bremer (ed.), Life, Letters, and Posthumous Works of Fredrika Bremer (New York, 1868), p. 76.

14. Johanson and Kleman, op. cit., III, p. 183.

15. Margaret Howitt (ed.), Mary Howitt: An Autobiography (London, 1889), II, p. 85.

16. F. Bremer, HNW (New York, 1854), I, p. 1.

17. F. Bremer letter to Anne Howland, Richmond, Va., June 16, 1851; at FBF.

18. Johanson and Kleman, op. cit., I, p. 199.

19. Jaget och skuggorna (Stockholm [1951]), pp. 193-234. A collection of correspondence between F. Bremer and Böklin, as yet unpublished, was presented to the Stockholm Royal Library in 1950. The Täckhammar Collection (Ep. B 13a) consists in part of 15 letters from F. Bremer to Böklin (1833-1846), and 103 letters or fragments from Böklin to F. Bremer (1832-1865).

20. The Royal Library, Stockholm, Ehnemark Collection, Vf 56.

21. Johanson and Kleman, op. cit., III, p. 147.

22. C. Bremer, op. cit., pp. 361-367.

23. Ibid., p. 364.

24. G. Barnett Smith, Women of Renown: Nineteenth Century Studies (London, 1893), pp. 40-41.

25. [Ellen Kleman], Fredrika Bremer and America (Stockholm, 1938), p. 2.

26. Frank L. Mott, Golden Multitudes: The Story of Best Sellers in the United States (New York, 1947), p. 319.

27. Margaret Howitt, op. cit., II, p. 23.

28. "Literary Notices: The Neighbors," The Pioneer, I (1843), p. 141.

29. "Record of the Months," The Dial, III (1843), p. 532.

30. Letters of Ralph Waldo Emerson (New York: Columbia University Press, 1939), III, p. 147. (Names of publishers have not been included in footnotes and bibliography except for books printed by university presses.)

31. George W. Cooke, in An Historical and Biographical Introduction to Accompany The Dial, II (Cleveland, 1902), p. 207, suggests "R. W. Emerson (?)" as author of the notice on Bremer's Neighbors.

32. In July, 1843, this notice of The H. Family and The President's Daughters appeared in The Dial (p. 135): "The Swedish authoress has filled all sitting-rooms with her fame. One of our best friends writes us of the President's Daughters, that it is a good piece, much better than the H. Family, not so well as the Neighbours. Miss Bremer is a vivacious, right-minded woman, from whom a good novel may yet be expected."

33. Benson discussed these and other reviews of F. Bremer's works: "American Appreciation of Fredrika Bremer," SSN, VIII (1924), pp. 14-33.

34. "Miss Bremer's Novels," *North American Review*, LVII (1843), p. 149.

35. L. J. H[all], "Novels of Frederika Bremer," *Christian Examiner*, XXXIV (1843), p. 385.

36. *Ibid.*, XXXIV, p. 389.

37. S. O[sgood], "Frederika Bremer's Theology," *Christian Examiner*, XXXVI (1844), p. 98.

38. Benson, "The Essays on Fredrika Bremer in the *North American Review*," *Publications of the Modern Language Association of America*, XLI (1926), pp. 747-755. The same conclusion had been reached earlier by J. Thomas; in the *Universal Pronouncing Dictionary of Biography* (Philadelphia, 1871), p. 431, he named Lowell as the author of the 1844 *North American Review* article on F. Bremer. William Cushing, in his *Index to the North American Review. Volumes I.—CXXV.* (Cambridge, 1878), p. 13, also gave J. R. Lowell as the author.

39. The editorial is listed in Thomas Franklin Currier, *A Bibliography of John Greenleaf Whittier* (Cambridge, Mass.: Harvard University Press, 1937), p. 471.

40. F. Bremer, *New Sketches of Every-day Life: Strife and Peace* (New York, 1844), p. 133.

41. *Middlesex Standard* (Lowell, Mass.), August 1, 1844. (This editorial was called to my attention by Henry J. Cadbury, Chairman of the Historical Research Committee, Friends Historical Association, Cambridge, Mass.)

42. New York *Commercial Advertiser*, October 1, 1844, p. 1.

43. L. M. B., "Frederica Bremer," *Universalist Quarterly*, XI (1845), p. 169.

44. Benson discussed Whitman's writings on F. Bremer in "Walt Whitman's Interest in Swedish Writers," *Journal of English and Germanic Philology*, XXXI (1932), pp. 332-345.

45. The editorial is included in Emory Holloway's *The Uncollected Poetry and Prose of Walt Whitman*, I (New York, 1932), pp. 113-114.

46. Brooklyn *Eagle*, April 9, 1846, p. 2.

47. Brooklyn *Daily Eagle*, August 18, 1846, p. 2.

48. *Ibid.*, August 29, 1846, p. 2.

49. Johanson and Kleman, *op. cit.*, III, p. 187.

50. F. Bremer, *HNW*, I, p. 331.

51. F. Bremer letter to A. Howland, Stockholm, April 7, 1853; at FBF.

Chapter II

1. F. Bremer, *HNW*, I, pp. 12-13.

2. "Miss Bremer's *Homes of the New World*," *Putnam's Monthly Magazine*, II (1853), p. 669.

3. F. Bremer, *HNW*, I, p. 18.

4. New York *Herald*, October 7, 1849, p. 1. Several spellings of the author's name appeared in the American press: Frederika, Fredericka, and Frederica, in addition to Fredrika, which she herself used.

5. New York *Semi-Weekly Express*, October 9, 1849, p. 1.

6. New York *Weekly Tribune*, October 13, 1849, p. 3.

7. New York *Herald*, October 18, 1849, p. 1.

8. Boston *Daily Evening Transcript*, October 16, 1849, p. 2.

9. Sarah H. Browne, "To Frederika Bremer," *SUM*, V (1849), p. 325.

10. Articles, poems, and letters by Fredrika Bremer published in America, 1849-1851:

Sartain's Union Magazine:

"Christmas Eve and Christmas Matins," February, 1849, pp. 143-147.

"The She-Eagle," March, 1849, p. 166.

"Leaves from the Banks of the Rhine," May, 1849, pp. 289-294; July, 1849, pp. 1-4; November, 1849, pp. 261-267.

Author's Preface dated October, 1849, to the American edition of *The Neighbors* (New York, 1850), pp. vii-x.

Boston *Daily Evening Transcript*: "A Card from Miss Bremer," December 11, 1849, p. 1.

Sartain's Union Magazine:
"Life in the North," February, 1850, pp. 157-164; May, 1850, pp. 329-336.

"Jenny Lind," June, 1850, pp. 409-410.

"The Man and the Rose," July, 1850, p. 27.

"A Tribute to the Memory of General Taylor," September, 1850, p. 184.

Albany *Evening Journal*:
"To James R. Lowell, with a Gold Pen," September 17, 1850, p. 2.

Daily Cincinnati Gazette:
Letter to Mr. David Christy, December 16, 1850, p. 2.

Sartain's Union Magazine:
"Northern Loves and Legends," No. I, January, 1851, pp. 49-51; No. II, "My Friend's Love Story," February, 1851, pp. 89-92; No. III, "Fireside-Talk," March, 1851, pp. 165-167; No. IV, "Fireside-Talk," April, 1851, pp. 241-244.

"Greeting to America," February, 1851, p. 117.

"A California for Women," October, 1851, pp. 309-310.

Letter to Professor John S. Hart, December, 1851, pp. 496-497.

11. F. Bremer, *HNW*, I, p. 32.

12. Catharine Sedgwick, *Clarence* (New York, 1849), p. ix.

13. *Life and Letters of Catharine M. Sedgwick* (New York, 1872), pp. 315-316.

14. *Ibid.*, pp. 317-318.

15. *Second Catalogue*, Peabody Institute Library (Baltimore, 1896), Part I, p. 502, lists C. M. Sedgwick as the author.

16. "A Reminiscence of a Foreign Celebrity's Reception Morning," *Harper's New Monthly Magazine*, XIV (1857), p. 656.

17. *Ibid.*

18. F. Bremer, *HNW*, I, p. 29.

19. *Ibid.*, I, p. 30.

20. Johanson and Kleman, *op. cit.*, IV, p. 533. (Letter written in November, 1849.)

21. F. Bremer, *HNW*, I, p. 22.

22. *Ibid.*, I, p. 60.

23. *Memorials of Willard Fiske*, II (Boston [1920]), p. 81.

24. F. Bremer, *HNW*, I, p. 65.

25. A copy of the preface, formerly owned by G. P. Putnam — dated Newburgh, October, 1849, in Downing's hand — is in NYPL.

26. F. Bremer, *The Neighbors* (New York, 1850), pp. vii-viii.

27. George Haven Putnam, *George Palmer Putnam: A Memoir* (New York and London, 1912), p. 144.

28. Cf. Johanson and Kleman, *op. cit.*, III, pp. 575 f., note to letter 903.

29. F. Bremer, *HNW*, I, p. 107.

30. See p. 158.

31. New York *Weekly Tribune*, November 24, 1849, p. 1.

32. New York *Herald*, December 6, 1849, p. 2.

33. Mason Wade (ed.), *The Writings of Margaret Fuller* (New York, 1941), p. 590.

34. *Letters of Lydia Maria Child* (Boston, 1883), pp. 65-67. (Dr. Johann K. Spurzheim, the German physician, died in Boston in 1832. The 56-year-old doctor had started out on a tour of America, lecturing on phrenology, but he came to an untimely end.)

35.

TO FREDRIKA BREMER

Welcome from thy dusky Norland,
   Daughter of the Vikings bold!
Welcome to the sunny Vineland
   Which they sought and found of old!

Soft as lapse of Silga's waters
   When the moon of summer shines,
Strong as winter from his mountains
   Roaring through the Northern pines,

Swan of Abo! we have listened
   To thy saga and thy song,
Till a household joy and gladness
   We have known and loved thee long.

By the mansion's marble mantel,
   By the log-walled cabin's hearth,
Thy sweet thoughts and Northern fancies
   Meet and mingle with our mirth;

And o'er weary spirits keeping
   Sorrow's night watch, long and chill,
Shine they like the sun of summer
   Over midnight vale and hill.

Sweet eyes smile for us in Norland,
   Household forms we love are there;
In their bitter grief of parting
   And their bridal joy we share.

We alone are strangers to thee,
   Thou our friend and teacher art;
Come and know us as we know thee,
   Let us meet thee heart to heart!

To our household homes and altars,
   We, in turn, thy steps would lead,
As thy loving hand has led us
   O'er the threshold of the Swede.

                 J. G. W.

Amesbury, 11th month, 1849.
       — Washington *National Era,* November 15, 1849, p. 2.

36. John G. Whittier, *The Chapel of the Hermits, and Other Poems* (Boston, 1853), pp. 73-74.

37. *Ibid.,* pp. 117-118.

38. F. Bremer letter to the Down-ings, Boston, February 3, 1850; in YUL. Published by Benson, *SSN,* XI (1930), p. 114.

39. Anne C. Lynch, *Poems* (New York, 1849), pp. 54-55.

40.　　　　TO ANNE CHARLOTTE LYNCH.

A bird of paradise I wished to see;
One of those beings more than others free,
Who soar o'er earth with colors bright and gay,
But never lower down to touch its clay;
Who, frail and delicate, yet need not cling
For rest or help but to their soaring wing.

My wish was heard; a being bright and gay
I saw; who was on earth as was not earth its stay;
Who, in this crowded world looked all alone,
With eyes that melancholy, yet serenely shone;
A being young in years, but wonderfully wise —
It is Anne Lynch, my bird of paradise.

— Memoirs of Anne C. L. Botta, pp. 176-177.

41. F. Bremer, *HNW,* I, p. 70.

42. High Bridge: aqueduct across Harlem River in New York City, com-pleted 1848.

43. *Spirit of the Age,* I (November 24, 1849), p. 334.

44. Edward E. Hale, Jr., *Life and Letters of Edward Everett Hale,* I (Boston, 1917), p. 218. (Letter dated February 3, 1850.)

45. F. Bremer, *HNW,* I, p. 110.

46. *Ibid.,* I, p. 129.

47. Karl A. Olsson made a study of "Fredrika Bremer and Ralph Waldo Emerson," *Swedish Pioneer Historical Quarterly,* II (1951), pp. 39-52.

48. *Letters of Ralph Waldo Emer-son,* IV, p. 176.

49. *Ibid.,* IV, p. 177.

50. F. Bremer, *HNW,* I, pp. 175-176.

51. Lawrence Thompson, "Fredrika Bremer as a Critic of American Liter-ature," *Edda,* XLI (1941), p. 170. (This article was drawn to my atten-tion by Boel Smedmark in Stockholm.)

52. F. Bremer letter to the Down-ings, Boston, January 23, 1850; in YUL. Published by Benson, *SSN,* XI (1930), p. 112.

53. Newark *Daily Advertiser,* De-cember 22, 1849, p. 2.

54. Herbert H. Gilchrist, *Anne Gil-christ: Her Life and Writings* (Lon-don, 1887), p. 234.

55. J. W. Cross, *George Eliot's Life* (New York and London, 1903), I, p. 190. (Letter dated October 19, 1851.)

56. *Ibid.,* I, p. 191.

57. F. Bremer, *HNW,* I, p. 224.

58. F. Bremer letter to Downing, New York, March 15, 1850; in YUL. Published by Benson, *SSN,* XI (1930), pp. 118-119.

59. F. Bremer letter to the Down-ings, Brooklyn, Monday, March, 1850;

in YUL. Published by Benson, *SSN*, XI (1930), p. 120.

60. Henry Ward Beecher, 1813-1887, American preacher and orator.

61. F. Bremer letter to the Springs, Charleston, March 28, 1850; in HL.

62. Lawrence Thompson, *op. cit.*, p. 171.

63. F. Bremer, *HNW*, I, p. 43. (F. Bremer's copy of Emerson's *Poems* — Boston, 1850 — is in the Stockholm Teachers College for Women.)

64. Johanson and Kleman, *op. cit.*, III, p. 541, note to letter 778.

65. This copy of *The Bondmaid* is in the Antiquarian Society, Concord, Mass.

66. F. Bremer, *HNW*, I, p. 123.

67. S. L—d Adlersparre and Sigrid Leijonhufvud, *Fredrika Bremer* (Stockholm [1896]), II, p. 117, note 1.

68. *Letters of James Russell Lowell*, I, p. 174.

69. F. Bremer, *HNW*, I, p. 131.

70. *Ibid.*, I, p. 151.

71. F. Bremer letter (undated) to Maria Lowell, Boston [January or February, 1850?]; in HCL.

72. Cambridge *Chronicle*, December 27, 1849, p. 2.

73. F. Bremer's contacts with Longfellow and Hawthorne are described in "The Maiden Aunt of the Whole Human Race" by Henry Wadsworth Longfellow Dana and Manning Hawthorne, *American-Scandinavian Review*, XXXVII (1949), pp. 217-229.

74. Longfellow's copies of F. Bremer's novels are at Longfellow House, Cambridge, Mass. (For a list of them, see Hilen, *Longfellow and Scandinavia*, p. 170.) Seven of F. Bremer's works in English, formerly in the possession of the Longfellow family in Portland, Me., are in ASHM.

75. Dana and Hawthorne, *op. cit.*, p. 220.

76. Hilen, *op. cit.*, p. 41.

77. Dana and Hawthorne, *op. cit.*, p. 220.

78. *Ibid.*

79. *Ibid.*, p. 221.

80. F. Bremer letter to Longfellow, Cambridge, December 24, 1849; at Longfellow House. (I am grateful to Thomas H. de Valcourt, curator of Longfellow House, for his cooperation.)

81. This is Mary Howitt's translation of the poem:

AXEL TO ANNA.
With a Rose.

Take the Rose! In it so fair
   Is thy charming visage beaming;
   In the rose's crimson gleaming
Shines love's image also there.

Yet I would not see displayed,
   Type of our love in it either;
   Roses fade away and wither,
But our love will never fade.

From the days of Adam even,
Were they different from each other;
Earth is but the rose's mother,
Love, it is the child of heaven.

— F. Bremer, *The H— Family; Trälinnan;*
Axel and Anna (New York, 1844), p. 89.

82. This book is at Longfellow House.

83. Longfellow's journal, 1849-1850; at Longfellow House.

84. Dana and Hawthorne, *op. cit.,* p. 223.

85. Longfellow's journal, 1849-1850; at Longfellow House.

86. F. Bremer letter to Longfellow, Boston, February 26, 1850; at Longfellow House. Published in Johanson and Kleman, *op. cit.,* III, p. 193.

87. Boston *Daily Evening Transcript,* December 11, 1849, p. 1.

88. Brooklyn *Evening Star,* December 14, 1849, p. 2.

89. F. Bremer, *HNW,* I, p. 173.

90. F. Bremer letter to the Downings, Boston, January 23, 1850; in YUL. Published by Benson, *SSN,* XI (1930), p. 114.

91. Louisa M. Alcott, *Little Women* (Boston, 1868), p. 62.

92. For example, *The Liberator,* ed. in Boston by William L. Garrison, on March 1, 1850 (p. 35), reprinted this item from the Cincinnati *Gazette:* "*Frederika Bremer.* — This distinguished writer, the editor of the *Nonpareil* is informed, by an acquaintance of hers, will visit Cincinnati in the course of a few weeks. She has many countrymen and countrywomen here, who will give her a warm welcome — but by none a warmer one than she will meet here, among the admirers of her writings, of a native growth. — Cincinnati *Gazette.*"

93. Boston *Daily Evening Transcript,* January 3, 1850, p. 2.

94. *Ibid.,* January 24, 1850, p. 2.

95. *Ibid.,* February 2, 1850, p. 1.

96. *Ibid.,* February 9, 1850, p. 2. This itinerary was reversed. After visiting the South she went to Niagara Falls, then proceeded to St. Paul, sailed down the Mississippi River, and from New Orleans went to Cuba.

97. *Ibid.,* February 16, 1850, p. 2. (Cf. F. Bremer's own account in *HNW,* I, p. 224.)

98. Boston *Daily Bee,* February 12, 1850, p. 2.

99. In 1850 Lowell had 33,000 inhabitants.

100. Boston *Daily Bee,* February 20, 1850, p. 2. (Reprinted from the Lowell *Courier.*)

101. *Godey's Lady's Book,* XL (1850), pp. 129-130.

102. This book is now in the Stockholm Teachers College for Women.

Chapter III

1. F. Bremer, *HNW,* I, p. 254.

2. F. Bremer letter to the Springs, Charleston, March 28, 1850; in HL.

3. Ellen Kleman wrote about "Fredrika Bremers Charlestonvänner" and translated into Swedish some of F. Bremer's letters to Anne Howland; *Hertha,* Vol. 24 (1937).

4. New York *World,* March 28, 1878, p. 1.

5. F. Bremer letter to the Springs, White House on the Pee Dee, April 22, 1850; in HL.

6. F. Bremer, *HNW,* I, p. 276.

7. John C. Calhoun, 1782-1850, American statesman.

8. Joel R. Poinsett letter to G. Kemble, White house [South Carolina], April 26, 1850; in HSP.

9. F. Bremer letter to Anne Howland, Montpelier, May 2, 1850; at FBF.

10. Columbia *Tri-Weekly South Carolinian,* May 28, 1850, p. 1.

11. Charleston *Courier,* June 11, 1850.

12. *Cummings' Evening Telegraphic Bulletin* (Philadelphia), June 18, 1850, p. 2.

13. *North American and U. S. Gazette* (Philadelphia), June 19, 1850, p. 2.

14. *Cummings' Evening Telegraphic Bulletin,* June 19, 1850, p. 2.

15. F. Bremer, *HNW,* I, p. 409.

16. Baltimore *Sun,* June 27, 1850, p. 1.

17. F. Bremer letter to R. Spring, Philadelphia, June 22, 1850; in HL.

18. F. Bremer, "The Man and the Rose," *SUM,* VII (1850), p. 27.

19. Baltimore *Sun,* July 4, 1850, p. 2.

20. *Ibid.,* July 8, 1850, p. 2.

21. Washington *Daily National Intelligencer,* July 4, 1850, p. 4.

22. F. Bremer letter to Maria Lowell, Washington, D. C., July 3, 1850; in HCL.

23. F. Bremer, *HNW,* I, p. 441.

24. *Ibid.,* I, p. 444.

25. Nels Hokanson, *Swedish Immigrants in Lincoln's Time* (New York [1942]), p. 55.

26. F. Bremer, *HNW,* I, p. 443.

27. *Ibid.,* I, p. 451.

28. The letter dated July 8, 1850, is in the Library of Congress; the text is published in Johanson and Kleman, *op. cit.,* IV, pp. 542-543.

29. F. Bremer letter to the Springs, Washington, July 13, 1850; in HL.

30. Anne C. Lynch, "Fredrika Bremer," *SUM,* VII (1850), p. 169.

31. Washington *Daily National Intelligencer,* July 16, 1850, p. 4.

32. F. Bremer letter to Anna Maria Hall, Gotland, August 1, 1855; in HSP.

33. Johanson and Kleman, *op. cit.,* III, p. 197.

34. Juhani Aho, *En idéernas man: Biografi öfver August Fredrik Soldan* (Helsingfors, 1901), p. 232.

35. F. Bremer letter to the Lowells, Philadelphia, July 26, 1850; in HCL.

36. F. Bremer letter to C. Downing, Cape May, August 15, 1850; in YUL. Published by Benson, *SSN,* XI (1931), p. 170.

37. Albany *Evening Journal,* September 3, 1850, p. 2.

38. F. Bremer letter to the Springs, Niagara, September 8, 1850; in HL.

39. F. Bremer, *HNW,* I, p. 587.

40. F. Bremer letter to the Springs, Niagara, September 8, 1850; in HL.

41. Rochester *Daily American,* September 7, 1850, p. 2.

42. Albany *Evening Journal,* September 17, 1850, p. 2.

43. F. Bremer letter to M. Lowell, Cincinnati, December 12, 1850; in HCL.

44. F. Bremer, "Jenny Lind," *SUM,* VI (1850), p. 410.

45. F. Bremer letter to the Springs, Chicago, September 22, 1850; in HL.

46. F. Bremer, "Greeting to America," *SUM,* VIII (1851), p. 117.

47. Gösta Franzen wrote an article entitled "En svenska på besök i Mellanvästern för 100 år sedan" in *Svenska Kulturförbundets Kvartalsskrift,* Vol. 3 (1948), pp. 5-6.

48. Chicago *Daily Journal,* September 17, 1850, p. 2.

49. Mrs. Kinzie later sent a copy of her book, *Wau-Bun, the "Early Day" in the Northwest* to F. Bremer inscribed "With the affectionate regards of the Author." It is now in the Stockholm Teachers College for Women.

50. F. Bremer letter to the Springs, Chicago, September 22, 1850; in HL.

51. Chicago *Daily Journal*, September 25, 1850, p. 3.

52. F. Bremer letter to the Springs, Chicago, September 22, 1850; in HL.

53. Milwaukee *Daily Sentinel and Gazette*, September 26, 1850, p. 2.

54. Milwaukee *Daily Free Democrat*, September 27, 1850, p. 2.

55. Milwaukee *Daily Sentinel and Gazette*, September 28, 1850, p. 2.

56. Louise Phelps Kellogg, "The Origins of Milwaukee College," *Wisconsin Magazine of History*, IX (1926), p. 400.

57. Milwaukee *Daily Free Democrat*, October 17, 1850, p. 2.

58. F. Bremer, *HNW*, I, p. 626.

59. Madison *Wisconsin Argus*, October 1, 1850, p. 3.

60. Madison *Wisconsin Statesman*, October 8, 1850, p. 3.

61. Madison *Wisconsin Argus*, October 8, 1850, p. 2.

62. Galena *Weekly North-Western Gazette*, October 15, 1850, p. 2.

63. F. Bremer letter to M. Lowell, Cincinnati, December 12, 1850; in HCL.

64. F. Bremer's Minnesota visit has been described by John T. Flanagan — "Fredrika Bremer: Traveler and Prophet," *Minnesota History*, XX (1939), pp. 129-139.

65. St. Paul *Minnesota Chronicle and Register*, October 21, 1850, p. 2.

66. Marion Ramsey Furness, "Governor Ramsey and Frontier Minnesota: Impressions from His Diary and Letters," *Minnesota History*, XXVIII (1947), pp. 317-318.

67. Ann Loomis North letter to George and Mary Ann Loomis, St. Anthony Falls, October 20, 1850; in HL.

68. F. Bremer, *HNW*, II, p. 55.

69. John H. Stevens, *Personal Recollections of Minnesota and Its People* (Minneapolis, 1890), p. 90.

70. St. Paul *Minnesota Pioneer*, October 24, 1850, p. 2.

71. St. Paul *Minnesota Chronicle and Register*, October 28, 1850, p. 2.

72. See Theo. J. Anderson, *History of Bishop Hill, 1846-1946* (Chicago [1946]).

73. Davenport *Gazette*, November 7, 1850, p. 2.

74. St. Louis *Intelligencer*, November 6, 1850, p. 2.

75. F. Bremer letter to M. Spring, Crystal Springs near St. Louis, November 10, 1850; in HL.

76. *Daily Cincinnati Gazette*, November 20, 1850, p. 2.

77. *Ibid.*, November 26, 1850, p. 2.

78. *Ibid.*, December 16, 1850, p. 2.

79. A de luxe edition of *Uncle Tom's Cabin* in two volumes is in the collection of books F. Bremer gave to the Stockholm Teachers College for Women.

80. F. Bremer, *HNW*, II, p. 108.

81. Autographed sentiment dated December 4, 1850; in HSP. The quotation is a free translation of the Scandinavian: *"Lyssna till den granens susning vid vars rot ditt bo är fästat."* On the title page of *Kalevala* (Helsingfors, 1841) it is called a Finnish proverb.

82. Autographed sentiment in Massachusetts Historical Society.

83. Autographed sentiment owned by S. Rooth.

84. Autographed sentiment; ASHM.

85. Autographed sentiment dated Forest Hill, November 17, 1849; owned by S. Rooth. (Quotation from Linnaeus.)

86. Autographed sentiment in HSP.

87. *Jotunheim*: in Norse mythology, the home of the giants.

88. F. Bremer letter to M. Lowell, Cincinnati, December 12, 1850; in HCL.

89. She took with her a copy of the book, *American Education, Its Principles and Elements,* by Edward Mansfield, with the following inscription: "Miss Fredrika Bremer, with the respects of the author, / Cincinnati 1850." This copy is in the Stockholm Teachers College for Women.

90. F. Bremer, *HNW,* II, p. 185.

91. New Orleans *Weekly Delta,* January 6, 1851, p. 4.

92. F. Bremer, "Northern Loves and Legends No. III: Fireside-Talk," *SUM,* VIII (1851), pp. 165-166.

93. F. Bremer, *HNW,* II, p. 209.

94. New Orleans *Weekly Delta,* January 6, 1851, p. 3.

95. F. Bremer, *HNW,* II, p. 217.

96. New York *World,* March 28, 1878, p. 2.

97. F. Bremer, *HNW,* I, p. 338.

98. *Ibid.,* II, p. 205.

99. September 1, 1844, entry from the diary of Octavia Le Vert; in a private collection in Augusta, Ga. (I am indebted to Caldwell Delaney of Mobile, Ala., for this and other material by Mrs. Le Vert, as well as the anecdote of F. Bremer's visit to the Choctaw camp.)

100. January 31, 1851, entry from the journal of Octavia Le Vert; in Alabama State Department of Archives and History, Montgomery, Ala.

101. F. Bremer went to the Lyceum Library, of which Mr. Monaghan was a board member in 1851. No record of her autograph is at the New Orleans Public Library, an outgrowth of the Lyceum Library.

102. New Orleans *Weekly Delta,* January 27, 1851, p. 1.

Chapter IV

1. Cf. Benson, "A Meeting in Havana," *American-Scandinavian Review,* V (1917), pp. 351-356.

2. F. Bremer letter to the Springs, Cafetal "La Industria," near Cárdenas, Cuba, April 9, 1851; in HL.

3. In a letter by Jenny Lind dated London, October 2, 1882, the singer said she had left Sweden in order to protect two beloved people from themselves. See "Ett unikt brev" by Holger Nyblom, *Ord och Bild,* Vol. 61 (1952), pp. 199-203.

4. Johanson and Kleman, *op. cit.,* II, p. 436.

5. Henry S. Holland and W. S. Rockstro, *Memoir of Madame Jenny Lind-Goldschmidt,* II (London, 1891), p. 422. (Letter dated March 1, 1851.)

6. F. Bremer letter to Longfellow, Niagara, September 9, 1850; at Longfellow House.

7. Minutes (1845-1860) of *Svenska Societeten,* New York; through the courtesy of the president, Carl G. Nelson, Brooklyn, N. Y.

8. Johanson and Kleman, *op. cit.,* III, pp. 230-231.

9. Karl Müller, Arranger, "The Dream" (Baltimore: F. D. Benteen).

10. F. Bremer, *HNW,* I, p. 256.

11. Seven pages of *HNW* about San Antonio de los Baños were translated by Dr. Rodolfo Tro Pérez in *Panoramas de Antaño: San Antonio de los Baños en el siglo XIX* (Havana, 1951), pp. 38-45.

12. Francis Tiffany, *Life of Dorothea Lynde Dix* (Boston and New York, 1890), p. 164.

13. Dana and Hawthorne, *op. cit.*, p. 226.

14. F. Bremer, *HNW*, II, p. 442.

15. An amusing contemporary footnote to F. Bremer's interest in Cuban dancing was provided in 1949 and 1950, when a "Samba till Fredrika Bremer" became popular in Sweden. The ditty by Ulf Peder Olrog jokingly credits her with having introduced the samba to Sweden as a result of her Cuban visit and tells of her fascination for the native dancing. (*Rosenbloms Visor*, Del V [Stockholm, 1949]).

16. F. Bremer letter to Anna Maria Hall, Stockholm, February 14, 1853; in HSP.

17. Savannah *Daily Republican*, May 12, 1851, p. 2.

18. F. Bremer, *HNW*, II, p. 460.

19. Jacksonville *Florida Republican*, May 22, 1851, p. 2.

20. Cleveland *Daily True Democrat*, June 18, 1851, p. 2.

21. New York *World*, March 28, 1878, p. 1.

22. Richmond *Enquirer*, June 17, 1851, p. 1.

23. F. Bremer letter to Anne Howland, Richmond, Va., June 16 and 17, 1851; at FBF.

24. M. S. De Vere, "A Visit to and a Visit from Fredrika Bremer," *Hours at Home*, VI (1867), pp. 151-152.

25. *Ibid.*, VI, p. 154.

26. The passages in *HNW* about the still flourishing Philadelphia School of Design for Women were included in a history of that school: *An Experiment in Training* (1922) by Theodore C. Knauff.

27. F. Bremer letter to M. Spring, Salem, August 5, 1851; in HL.

28. Dana and Hawthorne, *op. cit.*, p. 228. (Letter dated February 20, 1854.)

29. F. Bremer, *HNW*, II, p. 597.

30. F. Bremer letter to the Springs, Cafetal "La Industria," near Cárdenas, Cuba, April 9, 1851; in HL.

31. New York *World*, March 28, 1878, p. 2.

32. New York *Herald*, September 12, 1851, p. 1.

33. Willis had written the following paragraph for the *Home Journal* in 1849 and it was later reprinted in *Hurry-Graphs*:

FREDERIKA BREMER.

MISS BREMER left New York, in the glow of a second impression which had entirely superseded the first. By the dangerous experiment of displacing a glowing ideal by an unprepossessing reality — substituting the flesh and blood for the imaginary image — she seemed at first to be a sufferer. The slowness with which she spoke, and the pertinacity with which she insisted on understanding the most trifling remark made to her, a little dashed the enthusiasm of those who newly made her acquaintance. Farther intercourse, however, brought out a quaint and quiet self-possession, a shrewd vein of playfulness, a quick observation, and a truly charming simplicity, which re-won all the admiration she had lost, and added, we fancy, even to the ideal of expectation. Those who have seen her most intimately pronounce her to be all goodness, truth and nature, and she is, (as far as our own observation goes,) a walking lesson of *manners of another school*, of which our own may well profit in the study.

— N. Parker Willis, *Hurry-Graphs; or, Sketches of Scenery, Celebrities and Society, Taken from Life* (New Orleans, 1854), p. 223. (This item was called to my attention by Miss Lisa Cappelin, former librarian at ASHM.)

34. New York *Morning Express,* September 13, 1851, p. 2.

35. F. Bremer, "To Professor John S. Hart," *SUM,* IX (1851), p. 497.

36. *Ibid.,* IX, pp. 496-497.

37. F. Bremer, "A California for Women," *SUM,* IX (1851), p. 310.

38. Hartford *Daily Courant,* September 17, 1851, p. 2.

39. F. Bremer, *HNW,* I, p. 123.

40. Mrs. Lillie Buffum Chace Wyman, niece of Rebecca Spring, informed Klara Johanson and Ellen Kleman on September 6, 1916:

"I wonder if it is known in Sweden that the opponents of slavery, known as Abolitionists when Miss Bremer was in this country, were very much disappointed in Miss Bremer's attitude towards slavery. Mrs. Spring tried to prevent Miss Bremer from palliating the wrong of slavery, but did not succeed to her own satisfaction. She regretted Miss Bremer's course, but loved her and tried (I think) to feel that it was not strange that when she went South she saw things as the slaveholders *wanted* her to. Wendell Phillips expressed his regret in a public oration, saying that he hoped that Miss Bremer had not quite understood what she was doing when she wrote complimentary sentences about the Slaveholders. My mother wrote to Mrs. Spring that she did not care to meet Miss Bremer saying in evident reference to the opinion she had formed of her, because of her failure to condemn slavery *absolutely,* 'less sentiment and more principle' were what she preferred in a person."

— Johanson and Kleman, *op. cit.,* III, p. 557, note to letter 854.

41. Wendell Phillips, *Speeches, Lectures, and Letters* (Boston, 1884), p. 57.

42. F. Bremer letter to R. Spring, Stockholm, June 12, 1852; in HL.

43. F. Bremer, *HNW,* II, p. 542.

44. Elsa Ewerlöf [president of *Fredrika-Bremer-Förbundet*], "Welcome Mrs. Roosevelt!", *Hertha,* Vol. 37 (1950), p. 16.

45. Cf. Hanna Astrup Larsen, "Four Scandinavian Feminists," *Yale Review,* V (1916), pp. 347-362, and Benson, "American Ideals among Women Writers of Sweden," *SSN,* V (1919), pp. 157-161.

46. New York *World,* March 28, 1878, p. 2.

47. Dana and Hawthorne, *op. cit.,* p. 224.

48. Crito, "Fredrika Bremer," *Monthly Religious Magazine,* XXXV (1866), pp. 189-190.

49. F. Bremer, *HNW,* II, pp. 650-651.

50. *Ibid.,* I, p. 176.

51. *Ibid.,* II, p. 151.

52. New Orleans *Weekly Delta,* January 20, 1851, p. 6.

Chapter V

1. F. Bremer letter to James Hamilton, Stockholm, January 16, 1854; in NYPL.

2. Johanson and Kleman, *op. cit.,* IV, p. 554.

3. A. J. Downing, *Rural Essays* (New York, 1853), p. lxii.

4. *Ibid.,* p. iv.

5. Benson, *America of the Fifties,* p. vii.

Index

(In alphabetizing, the diacritical marks of the Swedish letters å, ä, and ö have been disregarded.)

N

Nachbarn, Die, see *Neighbors*
Nahant, Mass., 107, 113
Narrative of the Life of Frederick Douglass, an American Slave, 72
Natchez, Miss., 93
Natchez *Courier,* 93
National Council of Swedish Women, 148
Naturrecht auf dem Grunde der Ethik, see Trendelenburg
Nebraska, 92, 147
Neighbors, The, 3, 11, 13, 14, 19, 24, 32, 38, 46, 79, 83, 86, 128, 145
Newark *Daily Advertiser* 20
Newburgh on the Hudson, 24, 30, 155, 200, 201
New England, 1, 39, 44, 55, 113, 120
New Hampshire, 119
New Home — Who'll Follow?, A, see Kirkland, C. M.
New Jersey, 117
New Lebanon, N. Y., 71, 114
New Mexico, 66
New Orleans, La., 52, 92-101, 187
New Orleans *Daily Picayune,* 93, 99
New Orleans *Weekly Delta,* 93-96, 99, 124
New Sweden, 62
New York, 1, 4, 6, 11, 13; visit to, 22-39; 41, 42, 52, 55, 56, 71, 73, 77, 103, 112, 116, 117, 120, 126, 155
New York *Commercial Advertiser,* 18
New York *Daily Tribune,* 141, 145, 146
New York *Herald,* 24, 25, 34, 117
New York *Morning Express,* 38, 117
New York *Observer,* 25
New York Public Library, 153
New York *Semi-Weekly Express,* 24
New York *Weekly Tribune,* 25, 33
New World, The (newspaper), 3, 13
Niagara Falls, N. Y., 53, 68, 71, 73, 75, 76, 95, 177, 179, 180
Nicander, Karl August, 47
Nightingale, Florence, 138

Niles, Mich., 75
Nina, 11, 19, 78, 79, 83, 86, 145
Nord, Mrs. Walter G., 149
Norrland, 13
North, Mr. and Mrs. John W., 84
North American and U. S. Gazette (Philadelphia), 62
North American Phalanx, 33-34, 40, 117
North American Review, 15, 16
North Carolina, 110
"Northern Loves and Legends," 95, 184
North Star (newspaper), 72
Norton's Literary Gazette and Publishers' Circular, 127
Norway, 10, 11, 12
Norwegian settlements, 81, 184
Nouvelles Etudes Evangéliques, 232
"Novel and the Novels, The," 12
Nylander, Mrs. Lennart, 149

O

Oehlenschläger, Adam, 5
Ogden, William Butler, 181
Ohio, 89
Ohio River, 52, 89
Old Swedes' Church, Philadelphia, 62, 63
Oneida, N. Y., 72
Örsted, Hans Christian, 5, 166, 240
Oscar I, King of Sweden, 65, 214
Osceola, Indian chief, 169; sketch, 170
Osgood, Dr. David, 46, 49, 135, 161, 198, 199, 211, 214-216, 229, 240, 269; letter to, 249-252
Osgood, Frances, 119
Osgood, Mary Anne (Mrs. David), 135, 214-216, 229, 240; letter to, 249-252
Osgood, S., 16
Ossoli, Marchioness Sarah Margaret Fuller, 15, 34, 41, 70, 113, 138, 177, 218; *Woman in the Nineteenth Century,* 138
Otto, King of Greece, 260-261

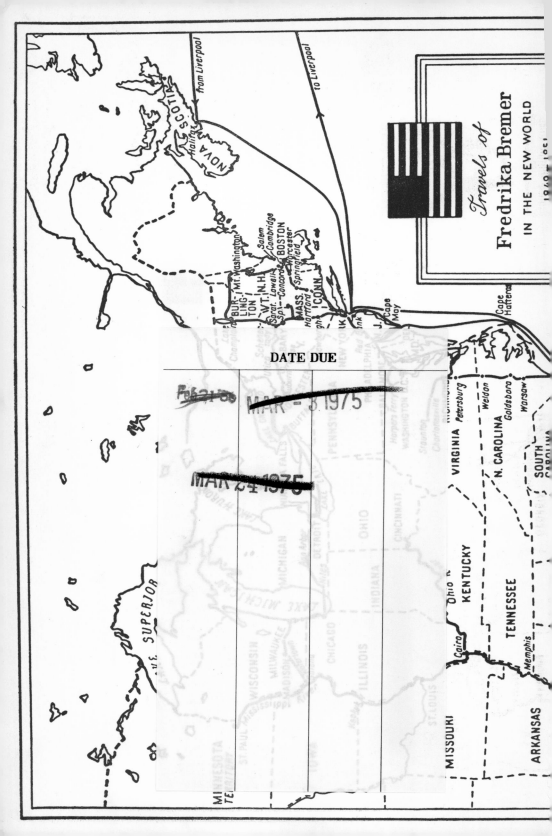

Travels of
Fredrika Bremer
IN THE NEW WORLD
1849—1851